THE CHURCHES OF CHRIST

Recent Titles in
Denominations in America

The Unitarians and the Universalists
David Robinson

The Baptists
William Henry Brackney

The Quakers
Hugh Barbour and J. William Frost

The Congregationalists
J. William T. Youngs

The Presbyterians
Randall Balmer and John R. Fitzmier

The Roman Catholics
Patrick W. Carey

The Orthodox Church
Thomas E. FitzGerald

The Methodists
James E. Kirby, Russell E. Richey, and Kenneth E. Rowe

The Lutherans
L. DeAne Lagerquist

THE CHURCHES OF CHRIST

RICHARD T. HUGHES
AND R. L. ROBERTS

Denominations in America, Number 10
Henry Warner Bowden, *Series Editor*

Greenwood Press
Westport, Connecticut • London

Library of Congress Cataloging-in-Publication Data

Hughes, Richard T. (Richard Thomas), 1943–
The churches of Christ / Richard T. Hughes and R.L. Roberts.
p. cm.—(Denominations in America, ISSN 0193–6883 ; no. 10)
Includes bibliographical references and index.
ISBN 0–313–23312–8 (alk. paper)
1. Churches of Christ—History. I. Roberts, R. L., d. 1998. II. Title. III. Series.
BX7075.H83 2001
286.6'3—dc21 00–033128

British Library Cataloging in Publication Data is available.

A student edition of *The Churches of Christ* is available in paperback from
Praeger Publishers, an imprint of Greenwood Publishing Group, Inc.
(ISBN 0–275–97074–4).

Library of Congress Catalog Card Number: 00–033128
ISBN: 0–313–23312–8
ISSN: 0193–6883

First published in 2001

Greenwood Press, 88 Post Road West, Westport, CT 06881
An imprint of Greenwood Publishing Group, Inc.
www.greenwood.com

Printed in the United States of America

The paper used in this book complies with the
Permanent Paper Standard issued by the National
Information Standards Organization (Z39.48–1984).

10 9 8 7 6 5 4 3 2 1

Copyright Acknowledgment

The authors and publisher gratefully acknowledge permission to quote from the letters of E. W. McMillan by permission of the family of E. W. McMillan.

This book is lovingly dedicated

to Thomas H. Olbricht (1929–)

and to the memory of J W Roberts (1918–1973), brother of R. L. Roberts

—gifted Christian scholars whose work in biblical and theological studies

continues to inspire countless scholars, preachers, and teachers

in Churches of Christ

CONTENTS

Series Foreword ix

Preface xi

Abbreviations for Standard Sources xvii

Part One The Churches of Christ: A History
by Richard T. Hughes

1 Understanding Churches of Christ 3

2 Alexander Campbell and His *Christian Baptist* 15

3 The Legacy of Alexander Campbell 41

4 The Rise and Fall of the Apocalyptic Tradition among Churches of Christ 61

5 The Fight over Progress and Modernization 99

6 The Challenges of the 1960s 121

7 Renewal 151

Part Two A Biographical Dictionary of Leaders in Churches of Christ
by R. L. Roberts

Biographical Entries 163

Chronology 325

Bibliographic Essay 329

Index 339

SERIES FOREWORD

The Greenwood Press series of denominational studies follows a distinguished precedent. These current volumes improve on earlier works by including more churches than before and by looking at all of them in a wider cultural context. The prototype of this series appeared a century ago. Between 1893 and 1897, twenty-four scholars collaborated in publishing thirteen volumes known popularly as the American Church History Series. These scholars found twenty religious groups to be worthy of separate treatment, either as major sections of a volume or as whole books in themselves. Scholars in this current series have found that outline to be unrealistic, with regional subgroups no longer warranting separate status and others having declined to marginality. Twenty organizations in the earlier series survive as nine in this collection, and two churches and an interdenominational bureau have been omitted. The old series also excluded some important churches of that time; others have gained great strength since then. So today, a new list of denominations, rectifying imbalance and recognizing modern significance, features many groups not included a century ago. The solid core of the old series remains in this new one, and in the present case a wider range of topics makes the study of denominational life in America more inclusive.

Some recent denominational histories have improved with greater attention to primary sources and more rigorous scholarly standards. But they have too frequently pursued themes for internal consumption alone. Volumes in the Greenwood Press series strive to surmount such parochialism while remaining grounded in the specific materials of concrete ecclesiastical traditions. They avoid placing a single denomination above others in its distinctive truth claims, ethical norms, and liturgical patterns. Instead, they set the history of each church in the larger religious and social context that shaped the emergence of notable denominational features. In this way the authors in this series help us understand the interaction that has occurred between different churches and the broader aspects of American culture.

Each of the historical studies in this current series has a strong biographical focus, using the real-life experiences of men and women in church life to highlight significant elements of an unfolding sequence. The first part(s) of every volume singles out important watershed issues that affected a denomination's outlook and discusses the roles of those who influenced the flow of events. The last part consists of biographical sketches, featuring those persons and many others who contributed to the vitality of their religious heritage. This format enables authors to emphasize the distinctive features of their chosen subject and at the same time to recognize the sharp particularities of individual attributes in the cumulative richness that their denomination possesses.

Richard Hughes, the author of this volume, is currently a professor in the Religion Division of Pepperdine University. Almost all of his professional career has been associated with this and other academic institutions supported by the religious tradition that forms his subject. Thus he brings a lifetime of close personal acquaintance, first-hand observation, and thoughtful analysis to the topics that form the content of this book. Of those topics, perhaps the most distinctive is a deeply-felt impulse to reform Christianity by recapturing its earliest expressions. This revisionist tendency, generally referred to as "restorationism," has emerged at many times in Christianity in several different cultures. But it has been particularly outspoken and vigorous in the United States. While other churches, especially Protestant ones, have tried to improve themselves by returning to the original, none was more pronounced in these efforts than the Stoneites, Campbellites, and Disciples of Christ. Author Hughes gives full attention to these predecessors and then moves to bring his most intensive focus on the latest and strongest of these revisionist movements: the Churches of Christ. He places origin in context, explains reasons behind new developments, and covers important events down to contemporary times. Readers of other volumes in this series are fortunate to have this as the latest installment in the panoply of American denominationalism. And they will readily understand how this one is uniquely attuned to our national culture as it has unfolded over the past two centuries.

HENRY WARNER BOWDEN

PREFACE

This book has been a very long time in the making—nineteen years, to be exact. In 1995 I completed the first version of this book, a volume that William B. Eerdmans Publishing Company released in 1996 under the title *Reviving the Ancient Faith: The Story of Churches of Christ in America*. While the historical narrative section of the present volume is roughly one-half the length of the narrative that makes up *Reviving the Ancient Faith*, I have sought to make the present narrative more streamlined without sacrificing significant detail. Readers who might hope to gain a quick overview of Churches of Christ will, therefore, find the present volume especially appealing.

The other significant feature of this book is its expansive section of biographical sketches that explore the life and work of significant leaders among Churches of Christ from the earliest years of the Stone-Campbell tradition down to the present day. In the mid-1980s I enlisted R. L. Roberts, archivist in the Center for Restoration Studies at Abilene Christian University (ACU), to write these sketches. Before he could complete the sketches, however, R. L. passed away on September 12, 1998. He was seventy-three years old.

His passing represents not only a great loss for this particular project; it also represents a significant loss for me personally, for insofar as I have been able to accomplish anything in my work on the history of Churches of Christ, he was my mentor. He was also my friend. I shall never forget the day I first met R. L. It was the fall of 1982, and I had just arrived at ACU to begin my research on this book. I was on leave that year from Southwest Missouri State University, and I seriously thought I would research and write this book in that twelve-month period. When I expressed this ambitious agenda to R. L., he replied with three well-chosen words: "Not so fast." He knew, as I did not, the depth and breadth of the primary literature that this tradition has generated, and he knew it would take me many years to read that literature and bring this project to completion.

By the time my year's leave from Southwest Missouri State University had expired, Abilene Christian had asked me to join the faculty there. As a result, my one year at ACU turned into six, and R. L. and I worked closely together on a daily basis for each of those years. He routinely guided me into a variety of primary sources, many of them obscure and little known, and made suggestions regarding ways I might best interpret the story that was unfolding as I worked through that literature. Not only did he and I enjoy a comradeship generated by common scholarship during those years; we also became the closest of friends. I miss him greatly.

Yet, the loss of R. L. Roberts transcends my own personal loss, for R. L. freely shared his knowledge with the hundreds of students and professional scholars who studied this tradition. The truth is, R. L. probably knew more about the history of Churches of Christ than any other human being. Though his knowledge of this tradition was both wide and deep, he specialized in the history of the "Christians in the West"—that frontier Christian movement led by Barton W. Stone. He pored over the primary sources related to this tradition, and over the course of a long career, he identified well over one hundred preachers who worked with Stone, most of whom are little known today. Then, through painstaking research, he pieced together their individual biographies, the ways in which their lives intersected, and the ways in which, together, they formed a powerful movement dedicated to the restoration of the ancient Christian faith and the union of all Christians.

R. L. seldom wrote and published the things that he had learned, however. Instead, he was content to serve the hundreds of scholars, students, and ordinary people who looked to him for assistance with their research. This is precisely why the biographical sketches that make up the second half of this book—and especially the sketches of Barton Stone's associates—are so valuable. These sketches are the fruit of a rich career, dedicated to painstaking inquiry into the history of that tradition. Indeed, one can learn from no other source what one can learn from the biographies in this book that chronicle the lives of the preachers who worked alongside Barton W. Stone on the southern frontier in the early years of the nineteenth century.

R. L. passed away before he completed all the sketches intended for this book. The sketches on Stone's associates were, for the most part, complete. Many others were not. It fell to me, therefore, to do considerable editing and rewriting and, in some instances, to write particular sketches from scratch. Occasionally, I asked other scholars to prepare biographies that would appear in this text. Loretta Long of Abilene Christian University wrote the entry on Selina Bakewell Campbell; Robert M. Randolph of M.I.T. wrote the entry on E. W. McMillan; Calvin Bowers of Pepperdine University wrote the entry on R. N. Hogan; and Jerry Rushford, also of Pepperdine University, wrote the entry on John Allen Gano. Helen Young supplied extensive information on M. Norvel Young, Fountain Livingston Young, and Irene Young Mattox, and Thomas H. Olbricht helped provide information on Nathan Mitchell and James Walter Nichols.

There is no way I can adequately express my appreciation to two of my graduate students without whose dedicated labor I could not have brought to completion as quickly as I did the section of biographical sketches. Krystin Higgins spent scores of hours entering into the master text alterations in those sketches that I had made by hand. At the same time, John Richter researched countless pieces of data—publication dates, birth dates, death dates, bibliographic information, and so on—that were missing from the biographical sketches when I first received them on disk following R. L.'s death.

I also want to thank Professors Michael Casey of Pepperdine University and Douglas Foster of Abilene Christian University, who read the manuscript for the narrative section of this book and who made a variety of helpful suggestions. I am also indebted to Professor Jerry Rushford, who, even though he was teaching in Pepperdine's London program at the time, graciously checked the biographical sketches for any mistakes that may have crept in along the course of their production. Still, as the final author-editor of this volume, I must take full responsibility for any mistakes or shortcomings that may appear in the narrative section of the text or in the collection of biographical sketches.

Beyond these acknowledgments that pertain to this, the Greenwood Press version of this book, the acknowledgments that appeared in the preface to *Reviving the Ancient Faith* pertain to this text just as well. After all, the narrative section of this book is, for the most part, a condensation of *Reviving the Ancient Faith.* The people who contributed to that text, therefore, also contributed to this one.

A number of benefactors helped provide the financial support that enabled me to take a year's leave of absence from Southwest Missouri State University in the 1982–83 academic year and launch this book: Mr. and Mrs. Bill H. Branch of Roanoke, Virginia; Dr. and Mrs. Quinton Dickerson and Mr. and Mrs. J. C. Redd of Jackson, Mississippi; Mr. and Mrs. Dwain Evans, Mr. and Mrs. Robert Fitts, Mr. and Mrs. Joe Foy, Dr. and Mrs. Norman Garner, Mr. and Mrs. David S. Holland, Dr. and Mrs. Terry Koonce, Dr. and Mrs. Bill Love, and Mr. and Mrs. Robert Norris, all of Houston, Texas; Dr. and Mrs. Claude Hocott of Austin, Texas; Mr. and Mrs. Ray McGlothlin of Abilene, Texas; and the Church of Christ of Chapel Hill, North Carolina. Terry and Beverly Koonce have provided financial assistance to support my work each and every year since 1982, and to them I am especially grateful.

Neither this book nor its predecessor, *Reviving the Ancient Faith*, could have been completed had it not been for the faith that Dr. William J. Teague, at that time the president of Abilene Christian University, placed in me when he named me Scholar-in-Residence at Abilene Christian University for the 1982–83 academic year. That appointment made me eligible for support services at ACU along with an office in the Herman and Margaret Brown Library at that institution. Dr. Teague renewed that appointment on a half-time basis for the 1983–84 and 1986–88 academic years, thereby providing me with a reduction in teaching load that helped me to move this project ahead even further.

I continue to be grateful to four Pepperdine University students who assisted me with this project in a variety of ways between 1988 and 1996: Chad Huddleston, Ron Cox, Margaret Smith, and Carl Flynn. I am also grateful to Pepperdine University for a grant that allowed me to work full time on this project during the summer of 1990, and to the Pew Charitable Trusts for another grant that freed me from teaching responsibilities for one semester of that same year, allowing me to make additional progress on this project.

Words cannot express my gratitude to the staffs of two libraries: the Herman and Margaret Brown Library at Abilene Christian University, where I did so much of the research for this project, and the library of the Harding Graduate School of Religion in Memphis, Tennessee, where I did virtually all the research for the material dealing with race relations in Churches of Christ.

Many people graciously consented to read all or parts of this text at various stages along the way, and most of those people made extraordinarily helpful suggestions from a variety of perspectives. Those readers include Leonard Allen, Dan Anders, Judy Anders, Molefe Kete Asante, David Baird, Calvin Bowers, Walter Burch, Fran Carver, Michael Casey, John Allen Chalk, Dan Danner, Dwain Evans, Harry Robert Fox, Anne Frashier, Loyd Frashier, Edward Fudge, Leroy Garrett, Fred Gray, Andrew Hairston, David Edwin Harrell, Jr., Don Haymes, Samuel S. Hill, Jr., Bill Jenkins, David Jones, Eugene Lawton, Steven Lemley, Hubert G. Locke, Bill Love, William Martin, Martin Marty, Lester McAllister, Rob McRay, Lynn Mitchell, Tom Olbricht, Roy Osborne, Kathy Pulley, Robert M. Randolph, R. L. Roberts, Jerry Rushford, J. Harold Thomas, Grant Wacker, and Dewayne Winrow.

I especially want to thank the general editor of the Greenwood Press "Denominations in America" series, Professor Henry Bowden of Rutgers University, who has exhibited extraordinary patience as I have taken nineteen long years to bring this project to completion. More than that, Professor Bowden has provided encouragement at every step of the way, and for that, I am profoundly grateful.

I am grateful in ways that words cannot express to the two most important people of my life—my wife, Jan, and my son, Andy—since this project has virtually defined all of our lives for the better part of two decades. As I wrote in the preface to *Reviving the Ancient Faith*, this project "has meant upheaval in the form of two moves, taking us halfway across the United States, and it has meant certain summer months away from home and long hours in the office." Through it all, however, they have offered nothing but support for my work on this project. In fact, each has taken an active interest in this project, frequently offering insights that have proven helpful as I have sought to interpret in meaningful ways the story of Churches of Christ in America.

Finally, two paragraphs from the preface to *Reviving the Ancient Faith* are as pertinent here as they were there. With reference to the nature of this text, I wrote then,

I never set out to write a history of Churches of Christ the centerpiece of which would be an abundance of facts—names, dates, and places. Instead, from the beginning I sought to produce a book that would explain the character of Churches of Christ—who they are and why, and how they have changed over the years from one stage to another.

And with reference to my own emotional and spiritual involvement in the production of this book, I wrote the following:

Writing this book has not been an easy task. I am a lifelong member of Churches of Christ but also an historian of American religion. Those two commitments have pulled at one another in a variety of ways over the years that this book has been in production. One's allegiance to one's own tradition always prompts one to tell only the good, to negate the bad, and to make the story look better than perhaps it really is. As an historian, however, I had to resist that temptation. I have tried in this book to tell the truth as I see it. The book is not without interpretations, though I have sought to inform those interpretations by seriously engaging the extensive literature produced by Churches of Christ for almost two hundred years.

ABBREVIATIONS FOR STANDARD SOURCES

DAB	*Dictionary of American Biography*, ed. Allen Johnson and Dumas Malone, 20 vols. (New York, 1928–37)
POT	*Preachers of Today*, ed. Batsell Barrett Baxter and M. Norvel Young, 4 vols. (Nashville, 1952–70)

The following periodical abbreviations are also used:

ACR	*American Christian Review*
AC	*Apostolic Church*
AT	*Apostolic Times*
AW	*Apostolic Way*
BB	*Bible Banner*
Chr	*Christian*
CA	*Christian Age*
CB	*Christian Baptist*
CC	*Christian Chronicle*
CE	*Christian Echo*
C-E	*Christian-Evangelist*
CFL	*Christian Family Library*
CH	*Christian Herald*
CJ	*Christian Journal*
CL	*Christian Leader*
CMag	*Christian Magazine*
CM	*Christian Messenger*

CPal	*Christian Palladium*
CP	*Christian Pioneer*
CPr	*Christian Preacher*
CRe	*Christian Record*
CR	*Christian Reformer*
CRep	*Christian Repository*
CRev	*Christian Review*
CS	*Christian Standard*
CWom	*Christian Woman*
CW	*Christian Worker*
CG	*Civil Government*
Disc	*Discipliana*
En	*Encounter*
Ev	*Evangelist*
FF	*Firm Foundation*
GA	*Gospel Advocate*
GG	*Gospel Guardian*
GL	*Gospel Luminary*
GT	*Guardian of Truth*
HGL	*Herald of Gospel Liberty*
HD	*Heretic Detector*
JAAR	*Journal of the American Academy of Religion*
JMH	*Journal of Mormon History*
LQ	*Lard's Quarterly*
LM	*Living Message*
MH	*Millennial Harbinger*
MM	*Mission Messenger*
OR	*Octographic Review*
OP	*Orthodox Preacher*
RQ	*Restoration Quarterly*
RR	*Restoration Review*
SHQ	*Southwestern Historical Quarterly*
SS	*Spiritual Sword*
TCM	*Texas Christian Monthly*
20thCC	*20th Century Christian*
WW	*Word and Work*

Part One
THE CHURCHES OF CHRIST: A HISTORY

By Richard T. Hughes

1
UNDERSTANDING CHURCHES OF CHRIST

With its twentieth-century heartland in a geographic swath that runs from Middle Tennessee on the east to Texas on the west, Churches of Christ began as a promising frontier movement that burst with great vitality onto the American religious scene in the early nineteenth century. Led especially by Alexander Campbell and Barton W. Stone, this strapping new movement went by several names throughout its early years: Churches of Christ, Disciples of Christ, and Christian Churches. By 1860 it had become the fourth largest Christian denomination in the United States, thriving from the Midwest to the Upper South and trailing in membership only the Baptists, Methodists, and Presbyterians.[1]

Before the Civil War, however, a disastrous division inspired by theological, cultural, and economic factors began to rend the ranks of this movement. When the dust had settled by the turn of the century, the conservative Churches of Christ emerged as a distinct religious tradition centered especially in the Upper South, whereas the more liberal and ecumenically minded Disciples of Christ emerged as a distinct religious tradition especially in the Midwest. In 1907 David Lipscomb, the most influential leader among Churches of Christ from the Civil War through the first decade of the twentieth century, urged S.N.D. North, director of the Federal Census of 1906, to list "Churches of Christ" and "Disciples of Christ" as two entirely separate religious entities.[2]

The division took an enormous toll on Churches of Christ in terms of both numbers of members and financial resources, since the majority of urban congregations went with the Disciples of Christ. While thriving still in rural areas, Churches of Christ were left virtually to begin all over again in many urban centers from Tennessee to Texas. Their comeback was, nonetheless, remarkable. Building on a radically sectarian message that proclaimed themselves the one true church, Churches of Christ won hundreds and thousands of converts in the 1920s, 1930s, and 1940s, then capitalized on the post–World War II religious revival to enhance their numerical base even further.

Though this communion suffered a variety of internal divisions throughout the twentieth century, it did enjoy relatively steady growth for virtually all of the twentieth century. No completely reliable membership figures exist for Churches of Christ nationwide, since congregations are independent of one another and reliable national statistics are difficult to assemble. The U.S. religious census of 1926 pegged the membership of Churches of Christ at 433,714. Building on that base, the best estimates suggest the church had perhaps 558,000 in 1936, 682,000 in 1946, 835,000 in 1965, and 1,250,000 by 1994.[3] Congregations of Churches of Christ were especially concentrated in a belt running from Nashville, Tennessee, on the east, to Abilene, Texas, on the west, but they were also scattered virtually throughout the United States and abroad.

KEY THEMES IN THE HISTORY OF CHURCHES OF CHRIST

If one wishes to understand Churches of Christ, one must first understand several themes that have been central to the identity of this tradition. First, Churches of Christ have been dedicated since their inception to the restoration of primitive Christianity, that is, to a replication of the beliefs and practices of the church of the apostolic age. To designate this commitment, I will use the terms *restoration* and *primitivism* interchangeably throughout this book.

Second, so long as they maintained their commitment to the restoration ideal, they took on all the characteristics of a sect, that is, a Christian tradition that stands in judgment both on the culture in which it lives and on competing Christian traditions. After all, a commitment to restore ancient Christianity suggests that authentic Christianity is in short supply and that those who seek to restore the ancient church believe that they and they alone represent the only bona fide expression of Christianity in a given society. This is precisely the posture that characterized Churches of Christ throughout the nineteenth century and well into the twentieth.

Third, during the 1920s Churches of Christ began their slow evolution from sect to denomination. The word *denomination* signifies a Christian tradition that has made its peace with important strands of the culture in which it exists and that recognizes many other Christian traditions—to some degree at least—as authentic expressions of the Christian faith. The fact that Churches of Christ embarked on such a course in the 1920s suggests that the restoration vision no longer held for them its original power and meaning. Indeed, the power of the restoration vision has continued to erode as Churches of Christ have moved further and further down the road to denominational status. At the same time, it must be said that by the waning years of the twentieth century, the transition of Churches of Christ from sect to denomination was still incomplete.

Fourth, though Churches of Christ had experienced the evolution from nineteenth-century sect to twentieth-century denomination, they always argued that neither of these terms described them in the least. Instead, they claimed that by virtue of their commitment to restore the ancient church, they were nothing more or less than a replication of the church of the apostolic age. For this reason, they argued, they transcended the categories sect and denomination altogether. The terms *sect* and *denomination* might well apply to other Christian traditions, they argued, but not to them. They therefore routinely described themselves as nondenominational.

Accordingly, we must be clear regarding what Churches of Christ meant when they used the adjective *nondenominational* to describe themselves. When at their best, Churches of Christ used the term to point to a biblical ideal toward which they aspired but which they had not necessarily achieved. According to this understanding, the Bible knows only one church and warns against the fragmentation of the body of Christ, implying—as Churches of Christ understood the New Testament—that the denominational arrangement is inherently sinful. When Churches of Christ sought to be nondenominational, therefore, they sometimes simply articulated their desire to conform to the nondenominational ideal of the Bible.

Far more often, however, Churches of Christ identified *themselves* with the nondenominational ideal, claiming that they were neither sect nor denomination, but simply the one true church that Jesus built in the first age of the Christian faith. This means that Churches of Christ comprised a denomination that erected its most fundamental self-understanding on claims that it was not a denomination. This seductive kind of self-understanding would build irony upon irony into the long, two-century history of this tradition.

A SHORT HISTORY OF CHURCHES OF CHRIST

If one wishes to view the history of this tradition in a nutshell, one might well begin by exploring the various factors that help explain the division between Churches of Christ and Disciples of Christ. First, in the early nineteenth century, long before the formal division got underway, the thriving religious movement led by Barton W. Stone and Alexander Campbell proclaimed a simple agenda that held great appeal for Christians on the American frontier: the restoration of primitive Christianity would provide a solid foundation for the unification of Christians not only in America but throughout the world.

This vision made sense to many Americans at that time for two reasons. First, Christianity on the American frontier was badly fractured, composed as it was of Christians from national and dissenting churches from all over Europe. And second, the appeal to the first Christian age seemed an obvious way to overcome divisions inspired over the years by the particularities of time and place.

Yet, when it became apparent that well-meaning Christians understood primitive Christianity in very different ways, it became obvious that primitive Christianity would not provide an adequate basis for the unity of all Christians. Slowly, therefore, the movement began to divide precisely along the lines of its most fundamental commitment: restoration of primitive Christianity as a means to the unity of all Christians. Those especially committed to the unity of all Christians gradually sloughed off the restoration vision and took their stand on an explicitly ecumenical agenda. As the nineteenth century wore on, partisans of the ecumenical vision increasingly designated their churches as Disciples of Christ and/or Christian Churches and less and less as Churches of Christ. At the same time, those chiefly committed to the restoration of primitive Christianity slowly left behind the designation Disciples of Christ and increasingly claimed exclusive use of the name Churches of Christ.

Second, the division between Churches of Christ and Disciples of Christ had a great deal to do with fundamental differences between Alexander Campbell and Barton W. Stone, especially regarding the question of human potential in relation to the sovereignty of God. Affirming human potential and the possibility of human progress, Campbell and many of his followers argued that the union of Christians, predicated on the ancient Christian faith, would inaugurate a millennial age of peace, truth, and righteousness. More than this, Campbell conformed to a model that we might designate as *postmillennial*. In other words, Campbell believed that human beings themselves, through the power of religion, science, and education, could transform the world and inaugurate the millennial dawn. The second coming of Jesus was not crucial to the birth of the millennial age and therefore would occur only *after* the millennial age had run its course. Jesus' second coming would therefore be *post*millennial or following the millennium.

In contrast, Stone and many of his followers subscribed to what we might designate as an *apocalyptic worldview*—a perspective radically different from Campbell's postmillennialism. According to this outlook, Stone and his followers believed that human beings were far too flawed to usher in a millennial age. If human society was to be renovated and renewed, that kind of transformation could be accomplished only by the power of God. In the meantime, however, the Stoneites eagerly anticipated the time when God would establish His kingdom and rule throughout the earth, and they sought to live their lives *as if* the kingdom of God were fully present in the here and now. That commitment played itself out mainly in ethical terms, for the Stoneites typically refused to participate in civil government, believing that human governments subverted the sovereign rule of God; embraced pacifism as the Christian alternative to militarism and violence of all sorts; and rejected many of the values and standards of the surrounding culture, especially greed, materialism, and slavery.

One would make a serious mistake if one identified Stone's apocalyptic worldview with *premillennial* perspectives—the notion that Christ Himself would return to earth, set up his throne, and rule for a literal or figurative thousand years, thereby inaugurating the millennial age Himself. The truth is, Stone *did* subscribe to premillennial perspectives, as did many of his followers, but premillennialism is not the same as an apocalyptic perspective. If premillennialism signifies a particular understanding of how the millennial age would finally come, an apocalyptic outlook—as I use the term in this book—signifies a commitment to lead one's life *as if* the final rule of the Kingdom of God were fully present in the here and now. Stone's apocalyptic perspective had therefore less to do with theories about the millennium than it did with a countercultural lifestyle, and it was that countercultural dimension that placed Stone and many of his followers on the opposite side of the table from Alexander Campbell in so many ways.

Campbell's progressivism and Stone's suspicion of schemes devised by human initiative helped determine how each of these men embraced—or failed to embrace—the theme of restoration of primitive Christianity. In the first place, Campbell focused the restorationist lens not so much on ethical concerns as on the forms and structures of the ancient church. And though he always proclaimed his interest in the restoration of primitive Christianity, his progressivism finally outweighed his primitivism. The authentic followers of Campbell, therefore, eventually shifted their commitments from the restoration of the ancient church to the unity of all Christians, separate and apart from any concern with primitive Christianity.

To be sure, Barton Stone also looked to the ancient church as a model for the church in his own age. At the same time, deeply suspicious of human potential but awed by the power and authority of a sovereign God, Stone also looked to the ancient church as a model for the kind of kingdom God would establish in the final age and therefore for the kind of lives Christians should live in this fallen world. In this way, Stone's apocalyptic orientation infused his restoration vision with strongly ethical dimensions, rendering it vibrant and dynamic. In the final analysis, therefore, Stone's apocalyptic worldview sustained his primitivism in ways that Campbell's postmillennial eschatology did not and could not. In later years, when the apocalyptic orientation lost its power among Churches of Christ, the restoration vision shriveled into a hard and legal shell, a parody of its former self.

During the very earliest years of the nineteenth century, the Stone and Campbell movements worked in complete isolation from each other, and each was virtually ignorant of the other's existence. In the aftermath of the great Kentucky revival of 1801, Stone led a movement dedicated to the restoration of primitive Christianity, the unity of Christians, and allegiance to the kingdom of God. For the most part, he concentrated his work in Kentucky, Tennessee, and surrounding regions. Campbell, in contrast, immigrated to the United States from Ireland in 1809 and settled in southwestern Pennsylvania. There, along with his father Thomas Campbell, he proclaimed the restoration of primitive Christianity as a means to Christian union. Farther south, most of the followers of Barton W. Stone had never even heard of Alexander Campbell until Campbell arrived in Kentucky in 1823 for a much-heralded debate with W. L. McCalla. Once the two movements discovered each other's existence, they naturally began to explore common ground.

In spite of their differences, the similarities between the Stone and Campbell traditions—especially their common commitments to the restoration of primitive

Christianity and to the unity of all Christians—were sufficient to prompt many in these two movements to unite with one another in 1832. Many greeted that union with considerable fanfare, believing it held great promise for the future success of the combined Stone and Campbell movements in later years. Few saw that beneath their agreements on restoration and unity, Stone and Campbell disagreed over a far more fundamental issue: the issue of human potential and its relation to the sovereignty of God.

This fundamental difference between Campbell and Stone contributed not only to the division between Churches of Christ and Disciples of Christ but also to the sectional alignments of these two traditions. Not surprisingly, those who most seriously embraced the optimistic, progressive, and ecumenical vision typically lived in the old Campbellian heartland of the Middle West, especially western Pennsylvania, Ohio, and Indiana, though the Campbell message also made significant inroads in Kentucky. These were precisely the regions where the Disciples of Christ would especially thrive in later years. In contrast, those who most rigorously embraced the restoration vision typically hailed from the old Stoneite heartland of the border states and the Mid-South, especially southern Kentucky, Middle Tennessee, and northern Alabama. These were the regions that would finally comprise the heartland of the restorationist tradition known as Churches of Christ.

The Civil War provided yet a third factor that contributed to the final division between Churches of Christ and Disciples of Christ. As Prof. David Edwin Harrell has pointed out, the war seriously alienated the southern-based Churches of Christ from their brothers and sisters farther north.[4] In 1863, for example, the American Christian Missionary Society—a mission agency that since its founding in 1849 had served virtually all the churches in the Stone-Campbell heritage—passed a resolution of loyalty to the Union. Tolbert Fanning and David Lipscomb, clearly the most important leaders of the southern churches at that time, responded bitterly. "Those brethren who believe that political resolutions are the Gospel can do so; and those who desire to contribute to such an object can do so; *we cannot do it*." In addition, when Lipscomb and Fanning resurrected in 1866 the *Gospel Advocate*, a paper that served the southern churches and had suspended publication during the war, Lipscomb explained its rebirth in sectional terms. "The fact that we had not a single paper known to us that Southern people could read without having their feelings wounded by political insinuations and slurs, had more to do with calling the *Advocate* into existence than all other circumstances combined." Fanning even called for "a consultation meeting" for southern Christians only.[5]

One should, however, be careful not to ascribe to these southern Christians too strong a political bias in favor of the South and against the North. To be sure, they were southerners and no doubt resented the high-handed tactics of their northern brethren who passed the resolution of loyalty to the Union. At the same time, as Christians who stood in the lineage of Barton W. Stone, their commitment was to the kingdom of God, not to any human government or political entity. Virtually all their protests against the political activities of their northern counterparts can be understood in these terms. Even the consultation meeting that Fanning called for southern Christians only can be understood as a meeting of those whose loyalty was to the kingdom of God rather than to a political faction, whether North or South.

In the twentieth century Churches of Christ underwent radical and far-reaching changes, most of them related to the demise of the apocalyptic world-view that had nourished and sustained the restoration vision for Barton Stone, Tolbert Fanning, David Lipscomb, and thousands of ordinary members of the southern-based Churches of Christ for much of the nineteenth century. By 1875 the apocalyptic orientation was in serious trouble, and by the mid-twentieth century it was virtually dead. That development effectively severed the restoration vision from its much needed nutrients and allowed the restoration vision to shrivel into a shell of its former self. Accordingly, Churches of Christ grew far more concerned with legalistic considerations regarding the forms and structures of the primitive church than with the ethical mandates of the kingdom of God. At the same time, they increasingly accommodated themselves to the values and norms of the culture in which they lived. In a word, Churches of Christ were slowly leaving behind their sectarian status of the nineteenth century and embracing a denominational standing that would increasingly characterize them in the twentieth. Several factors facilitated these transitions.

In the first place, Alexander Campbell exercised an increasingly significant influence on the old Stoneite Christians in Kentucky and Tennessee, once the Stoneites first learned of Campbell in 1823. Mainly, this was because the Stoneites, though interested in primitive Christianity, had developed no systematic understandings regarding the forms and structures of the ancient church. Nor had they developed a theology that might alleviate their Calvinist anxieties regarding their eternal salvation. Campbell spoke effectively to both these concerns. He lined out in substantial detail the outlines of the primitive church that ought to be restored,[6] and he argued that one gains salvation just as soon as one believes in Jesus Christ, confesses the lordship of Christ, and is baptized—a rite Campbell defined as immersion of adult believers. With that kind of certainty and precision, Campbell won the allegiance of many of the old Stoneite Christians. Accordingly, his optimism and progressivism slowly displaced the old apocalyptic orientation that had characterized so many in the Stoneite communities of Kentucky and Tennessee. As the nineteenth century wore on, Campbell's influence grew more and more dominant, and the influence of Barton Stone slowly receded into the background.

Second, following their separation from Disciples of Christ in the late nineteenth and early twentieth centuries, Churches of Christ found themselves few in number, especially in urban centers, and lacking in both wealth and social prestige. This sort of remnant status was unacceptable to a people who for so long had been part of one of the largest and most promising religious movements in America. Their remnant status was all the more unacceptable now that Churches of Christ were slowly giving up their apocalyptic orientation.

Then, into this situation came World War I. Once committed to involvement, the U.S. government demanded complete and absolute loyalty to the war effort on the part of every American citizen. With a membership composed of many pacifists, however, Churches of Christ were in no position to comply with these demands. But since Churches of Christ so desperately wanted to regain a measure of the status that had characterized the Stone-Campbell movement in its glory days, could they really afford to refuse support for this war? It was quite clear to many church leaders that Churches of Christ would continue as a small and marginal remnant on the American religious scene if they persisted in their pacifism and in the apocalyptic orientation that sustained it. Not surprisingly, therefore, key church leaders quickly launched an all-out campaign to rid Churches of Christ of what remained of its historic, countercultural commitments.

R. H. Boll, a twentieth-century heir to the apocalyptic orientation of the nineteenth century, provided the occasion for this campaign. In 1915, as the front page editor for the Nashville-based *Gospel Advocate*—since 1866 the most influential journal among Churches of Christ—Boll wrote a series of articles in which he argued for an explicitly premillennial perspective. Although Barton Stone and many of his heirs in the nineteenth century had embraced a premillennial outlook, that perspective had all but disappeared under the influence of Campbell's postmillennial progressivism. If church leaders were prepared to scuttle what remained of the apocalyptic orientation, they were certainly in no mood to tolerate a blatantly premillennial eschatology on the front page of the church's leading journal. They therefore promptly dismissed Boll from the *Advocate* staff.

Boll soon became editor of *Word and Work*, a premillennially oriented journal based in his home town of Louisville, Kentucky. Through this journal Boll proclaimed apocalypticism, premillennialism, and pacifism for the next forty years and became the acknowledged leader not only for premillennialists in Churches of Christ but also for many who remained committed to the countercultural apocalyptic perspective of the past. For most of those forty years, mainline Churches of Christ engaged in a concentrated campaign to discredit Boll and to drive premillennial sentiments—along with those who embraced them—from their ranks. The real issue, of course, was not premillennialism but, rather, the apocalyptic worldview and the countercultural ethic it sustained—commitments of which premillennialism was more a symbol than anything else. By the mid-1940s, premillennialists in Churches of Christ had dwindled to a tiny band of believers concentrated in and around New Orleans, Louisiana, and Louisville, Kentucky. Even more important, the apocalyptic sentiment was essentially dead, pacifism was virtually forgotten, and Churches of Christ had made their peace with many of the values of the surrounding culture. Clearly in transition from sectarian to denominational status, Churches of Christ would soon take their place as one of the dominant religious traditions from Texas to Tennessee.

The fight over premillennialism had barely ended when yet another battle engulfed Churches of Christ and moved the broad mainstream of this tradition even further into the mainstream of American religion. Erupting in the aftermath of World War II, this battle ostensibly focused on the question of whether institutions over and above the local congregation were biblical. In reality, however, this question symbolized two other issues. To the liberals in this dispute, this question had everything to do with the need for modernization and bureaucratization in a world come of age. To the conservatives, this dispute stood at the very heart of the identity of Churches of Christ: the preservation of a radically democratic polity that Churches of Christ had always identified with the model of the primitive church.

The battle over institution building surfaced in several ways. First, in the wake of World War II, Churches of Christ grew interested in European missions. But how could a radically democratic tradition like Churches of Christ—a tradition with no central headquarters and with no organizational structure over and above the local congregation—possibly hope to evangelize the European continent? It soon became apparent to key progressive leaders that they would have to erect some kind of organizational structure that would permit the consolidation and efficient distribution of funds. As a result, several of the larger congregations—most notably the Broadway Church of Christ in Lubbock, Texas—announced that they would serve as clearinghouses for funds earmarked for European missions.

Second, following World War II, Churches of Christ determined to employ both radio and television on a national scale as a medium for domestic missions. Like European missions, however, nationally broadcast radio and television evangelism—and especially television evangelism—required a level of funding that no single congregation could supply. As a result, the Highland Church of Christ in Abilene, Texas, announced that it would sponsor a radio and television ministry called the "Herald of Truth" and urged individuals and congregations throughout the fellowship of Churches of Christ to provide financial support for this project.

Third, by the close of World War II, five small, struggling colleges already stood in relation to Churches of Christ, though typically they were supported by individuals, not by congregations. Indeed, Churches of Christ typically were reluctant to support colleges out of the congregational treasury for two reasons. First, the sponsoring congregation would gain a measure of prestige and control not available to smaller congregations that were unable to sustain these colleges, thereby upsetting the democratic, egalitarian ethos Churches of Christ identified with the primitive church. And second, Churches of Christ generally feared that large, strong colleges might gain power and control over the congregations themselves.

When the war was over, however, thousands of G.I.s returned home to begin or to complete their college education, thereby filling to overflowing almost every institution of higher learning in the United States. Suddenly, a serious question faced Churches of Christ: How could the five small colleges related to this tradition accommodate this enormous influx of students without the massive development of new facilities on existing campuses, or perhaps even the creation of new colleges as well? But how could this kind of massive development be achieved unless the colleges were supported by congregations, not simply by isolated individuals? This question was all the more acute in the context of the religious revival that swept the United States in the postwar era. In that context, many progressive leaders of Churches of Christ saw the colleges as a strategic means of capitalizing on the postwar revival and enhancing the cause of Churches of Christ nationwide.

These and similar issues drew the proverbial line in the sand between progressives, on the one hand, who sought to render Churches of Christ more efficient through the creation of parachurch institutions and supercongregations that functioned as parachurch institutions; and conservatives, on the other hand, who remained committed to the radically democratic structures that Churches of Christ had always identified with the ancient, apostolic order. The battle over these issues raged from the close of World War II through the mid-1950s when B. C. Goodpasture, editor of the *Gospel Advocate*, used the power of this still highly influential paper virtually to read the anti-institutional movement out of the mainstream of the Churches of Christ.

The consequences of this dispute were momentous. On the one hand, it isolated the conservatives who in many ways remained loyal to the nineteenth-century agenda of Churches of Christ. On the other hand, it effectively divorced the mainstream Churches of Christ from their nineteenth-century heritage, propelled them even farther into the mainstream of American religion, and helped to establish Churches of Christ as a full-fledged denomination, a part of the religious establishment in those regions of the United States where they were strong.

If, by the close of the 1950s, Churches of Christ had already fought two major battles that moved them farther down the road from sect to denomination, they faced in the 1960s perhaps the greatest challenge of all. Having long since scuttled their apocalyptic, countercultural orientation, Churches of Christ were hardly prepared for the countercultural values so many of their own children promoted in the 1960s.

Over the years mainstream Churches of Christ had slowly embraced the values of conservative Protestantism in the United States. Accordingly, for all practical purposes they were Protestant and resisted Catholicism; they were characteristically white and typically resisted racial integration; male-dominated, they often found it difficult to come to terms with equal opportunities for women; and since they had long since abandoned any commitment to pacifism and nonviolence, they generally formed a united front in support of America's military effort in Vietnam. Yet, these were precisely the values that so many of their own children rejected.

Further, many of their children found the traditional restoration rhetoric of Churches of Christ either irrelevant to their concerns or hollow, or both. When Churches of Christ used the language of restoration to suggest that they and they alone comprised the one true church of the apostolic age, the youth of the countercultural generation found such claims both offensive and irrelevant to the pressing social issues of that period. At the same time, since the restorationist agenda of Churches of Christ no longer embraced a strongly ethical, countercultural dimension, many in the younger generation rejected the very notion of restoration as a hollow shell. Accordingly, a great host of bright young people abandoned Churches of Christ in the 1960s for other Christian traditions that seemed to address in more significant ways the concerns of that period.

The decade of the 1960s was a critical period for Churches of Christ in other ways as well. In the first place, they suffered in that period a major polarization between conservatives and mainstream progressives. The conservatives recommitted themselves to the traditionally exclusivist claims of Churches of Christ. Although many mainstream progressives sought to move their tradition toward a posture of grace and tolerance, they were unprepared to embrace the more radical criticisms emanating from the countercultural generation.

In addition, Churches of Christ underwent considerable racial turmoil in the 1960s. For most of their history, Churches of Christ established a decidedly lackluster record regarding racial integration and civil rights. The decade of the 1960s, however, witnessed numerous efforts to bridge racial divides, though few of those efforts have left a lasting legacy.

Following the 1960s, Churches of Christ began to exhibit numerous changes. Perhaps most important, a theology of grace began to displace the radical exclusivism that generally characterized Churches of Christ for the hundred years from 1850 to 1950. At the same time, many congregations underwent renewal at a variety of levels. Some congregations sought to incorporate women into the public life of the church in ways that are both biblical and meaningful. Other congregations—though admittedly few and far between—committed themselves to thorough-going racial integration. Still other congregations committed themselves to social and urban ministries. And many congregations, especially in urban centers, sought to revitalize their worship through vibrant new forms of music ministries.

In outline form, these are the major themes that have characterized Churches of Christ for almost two centuries. We turn now to explore these developments in greater detail.

NOTES

1. Edwin S. Gaustad, *Historical Atlas of Religion in America* (New York: Harper & Row, 1962), p. 52, fig. 40.

2. David Lipscomb, "The 'Church of Christ' and the 'Disciples of Christ,' " *GA* 49 (18 July 1907): 457.

3. The best summary of growth patterns among Churches of Christ is Michael Casey, "Church Growth: New Information," *Image* 3 (1 May 1987): 14–15, and "Church Growth: New Information," *Image* 3 (15 May 1987): 20–21. See also Flavil R. Yeakley, Jr., *Why Churches Grow* (Broken Arrow, OK: Christian Communications, 1979). For the 1994 figures, see Mac Lynn, comp., *Churches of Christ in the United States* (Brentwood, TN: Morrison and Phillips Associates, 1994), p. 15.

4. See David Edwin Harrell, Jr., "The Sectional Origins of the Churches of Christ," *Journal of Southern History* 30 (August 1964): 261–77; *Quest for a Christian America: The Disciples of Christ and American Society to 1866* (Nashville: Disciples of Christ Historical Society, 1966), pp. 91–174; and *The Social Sources of Division in the Disciples of Christ, 1865–1900* (Atlanta: Publishing Systems, 1973), pp. 243–46.

5. Tolbert Fanning and David Lipscomb, "A Reply to the Call of W. C. Rogers, Corresponding Secretary of the A.C.M. Society for All to Disseminate the Gospel," *GA* 8 (27 March 1866): 109; Lipscomb, "The Advocate and Sectionalism," *GA* 8 (1 May 1866): 273; and Fanning, "A General Consultation Meeting Suggested," *GA* 8 (16 April 1866): 241–42.

6. Alexander Campbell did this especially in a series of articles he entitled "A Restoration of the Ancient Order of Things," which ran in thirty separate installments from February 1825 to September 1829 in the *Christian Baptist*, the journal he edited from 1823 to 1830.

2
ALEXANDER CAMPBELL AND HIS *CHRISTIAN BAPTIST*

It is difficult to understand Alexander Campbell's contributions to American religion at large or to Churches of Christ in particular, apart from the heady, utopian climate that prevailed in the United States in the early nineteenth century. Inspired by the reality of freedom and the promise of democratic government, many Americans of that era believed that their nation had given birth to a golden age that would soon bless all the peoples of the world. The Great Seal of the United States graphically symbolized that expectation. Depicting human history prior to 1776 as a barren wasteland, the Seal portrayed the United States as an unfinished pyramid that would presumably be complete once the nation's ideals prevailed throughout the earth. God himself looked down upon this enterprise while a Latin phrase proclaimed his response: "He has smiled on our beginnings" (*annuit coeptis*). Beneath it all, another Latin phrase heralded the notion that the United States was not just another nation in the long, slow progression of human history. Instead, this nation was "a new order of the ages" (*novus ordo seclorum*), a social and political order never witnessed before in the history of the world.

This radically utopian climate helped give birth to a number of new religious movements on the American frontier, each of which celebrated in its own way the promise of perfection that the new nation had announced. Chief among these new movements were the Shakers, the Mormons, and a group led by Alexander Campbell, alternately called Churches of Christ, Disciples of Christ, or Christian Churches.

Although wildly diverse at first glance, these three religious movements nonetheless shared a common commitment to restore the ancient Christian faith and, on that basis, to bring about a millennium of peace, justice, and righteousness on this earth. The Shakers sought to achieve that objective by banishing sexual relations from their various communal societies, scattered from New England to Kentucky. The Mormons blended their utopian commitments with one of the major intellectual currents of the early nineteenth century: romanticism. Accordingly, they sought to restore what they thought to be the essence of primitive Christianity, namely, direct communication between God and humankind. On the basis of that restoration, they argued, a full-blown millennial age would soon emerge. Yet, to the extent that early Churches of Christ were led by Alexander Campbell, they blended their utopian commitments with another major intellectual current of the nineteenth century: the Enlightenment. They therefore committed themselves to a rational reconstruction of the ancient Christian faith and argued that once that faith had been fully revived, the millennium would commence.[1]

ALEXANDER CAMPBELL'S *CHRISTIAN BAPTIST*

If one wishes to understand how Alexander Campbell pursued the rational reconstruction of the Christian faith in the early years of his ministry, nothing sheds more light on that agenda than the journal he edited from 1823 to 1830, the *Christian Baptist*. Similarly, nothing compared with the role the *Christian Baptist* played in shaping the long-term character of Churches of Christ. Even though he launched a new journal—the *Millennial Harbinger*—in 1830, the spirit of the *Christian Baptist* dominated even that journal, at least through 1836. It is proper, therefore, to speak of the *Christian Baptist* as more than a journal. Rather, it was a mindset, a way of conceiving the Christian faith that governed the thinking of the young Alexander Campbell and that Campbell bequeathed in turn to Churches of Christ.

Campbell left no doubt in the *Christian Baptist* regarding the message he sought to communicate: the restoration of primitive Christianity would bring about the unity of Christians that would in turn usher in the long-awaited millennial age. Simple enough at face value, that message nonetheless concealed profound ambiguities that Campbell himself failed to recognize at the time. To fully grasp the complexities of Campbell, we must explore those ambiguities and how they were finally resolved in the movement that he led.

Restoration as a Means to Christian Unity

In the first place, Campbell apparently failed to understand—at least through 1830—that the restoration and unity motifs, as he defined them, not only failed to complement but stood in substantial opposition to each other. This was true, since Campbell often embraced the task of restoration in sectarian terms that hardly nurtured the goal of Christian unity.

It is possible to track the sectarian dimensions of Campbell's restoration vision during the *Christian Baptist* period in several ways. First, Campbell believed that authentic Christianity, defined in thoroughly biblical and apostolic terms, had simply disappeared from the earth. For him, it was a foregone conclusion that Catholicism was apostate, but he also argued that the Protestant reformers had really not moved much beyond the heresies of Rome. "The christian religion has been for ages interred in the rubbish of human invention and tradition," he characteristically argued in 1832.[2]

Second, Campbell claimed that his movement was the first in the entire history of the Christian faith that sought to "unite and build upon the Bible alone." Even in his own age, he argued, "there is not one voice heard in all the world outside of the boundaries of the present reformation, calling upon the people to return to the original gospel and order of things."[3]

Third, Campbell not only believed that his movement was the first in the history of the Christian church to seek to build on the Bible alone; he also believed, at least in the early years of his reform, that the movement he led had fully restored the truths and essential practices of the ancient Christian faith. Although Christianity had "been buried under the rubbish of human traditions," he wrote in 1835, it "has never been, till recently, disinterred." He acknowledged that "various efforts have been made" and that "considerable progress attended them." Nonetheless, "since the Grand Apostasy was completed, till the present generation, the gospel of Jesus Christ has not been laid open to mankind in its original plainness, simplicity, and majesty." Accordingly,

> we flatter ourselves that the principles . . . on which the church of Christ—all believers in Jesus as the Messiah—can be united . . . ; on which the gospel and its ordinances can be restored in all their primitive simplicity, excellency, and power . . . :—I say, the principles by which these things can be done are now developed, as well as the principles themselves, which together constitute the original gospel and order of things established by the Apostles.[4]

No wonder Campbell believed that "no seven years of the last ten centuries" had contributed more to the dawn of millennial bliss than had "the last seven" when he had produced the *Christian Baptist.*[5]

Fourth, Campbell provided his *Christian Baptist* readers with precise descriptions of the ancient church and of the form the restored church should take. The immersion of adult believers for the forgiveness of their sins took center stage in Campbell's reenactment of the ancient faith. Other pivotal ordinances included the Lord's supper, celebrated every first day of the week as a simple memorial feast, and four other acts of worship: preaching, praying, singing, and contributing of one's means to the work of the church. In addition, Campbell argued that each congregation of the Church of Christ should be strictly independent, governed by qualified elders. Beyond that, evangelists would preach, and deacons would tend to the day-to-day affairs of the church, especially benevolence.[6]

Fifth, Campbell employed a hard, combative style to defend his restoration, and he regularly launched withering assaults on his opponents. John Rogers, one of Campbell's most ardent followers and a long-time preacher for the

Church of Christ in Carlisle, Kentucky, provided a lucid description of this dimension of Campbell's work during the *Christian Baptist* period.

> All religious parties were more or less agitated by his powerful, argumentative, scriptural, & sometimes terribly sarcastic pen. He was regarded as a sort of religious Ishmaelite—his hand against every Sect, & the hand of every Sect against him. He raised against himself a fearful storm, by his scathing onslaught upon the "Kingdom of the Clergy." They were about his ears as thick as wasps or hornets, whose nests had been rudely disturbed.

One of Campbell's strongest Baptist critics, Jeremiah Jeter, concurred. "The publication of the *Christian Baptist*," Jeter wrote, "was an open, formal declaration of war against all the religious sects and parties in the country."[7]

Sixth, Campbell yoked his sectarian theology with his combative style to forge a vibrant debating tradition. After vanquishing his opponents in a number of significant debates, Campbell declared in 1843 that "a week's debating is worth a year's preaching . . . for the purpose of disseminating truth and putting error out of countenance."[8]

In addition to all this, Campbell fostered a legalistic approach to the Christian faith, even though—ironically—he also prized God's sovereign grace. However, he understood God's grace in ways substantially different from the classic Reformation or Catholic formulations. He described the doctrine of justification by faith alone—a doctrine central to both Luther and Calvin—as "unscriptural" and "unreasonable," "absurd in theory, and false in fact. It is an unwholesome doctrine and very full of misery. It is a doctrine of darkness and doubts!"[9]

Instead, Campbell argued that God made his grace evident through his commands. "To present the gospel in the form of a command is an act of favor," he wrote, "because it engages the will and affections of men, and puts it in their power to have an assurance of their salvation from which they would be necessarily excluded if no such act of obedience were enjoyed." In part, Campbell developed this understanding of the gospel out of his disillusionment with Calvinism. For years he had witnessed Calvinists who fretted over the question of their own predestination and who therefore never felt confident of their own salvation. This is why he described the doctrine of justification by grace through faith as one of "darkness and doubts." If one obeyed God's commands, however, one might enjoy the "assurance of . . . salvation" that might otherwise be denied.[10]

After reviewing these seven dimensions of the sectarian side of Alexander Campbell, two questions are in order. First, if Campbell embodied such a sectarian spirit, how could we possibly construe him as an ecumenist, passionately concerned with the unity of all Christians?[11] The answer to that question is not difficult to find. Campbell sought to unite all Christian people, but he did not seek to unite all Christian denominations. Instead, he believed that the various denominations had no right to exist, and he therefore sought to destroy them. In this way the authentic Christians who were scattered throughout the denominational world would be liberated from apostasy and freed to join one another on a single common foundation: the primitive church of the apostolic age.

Second, how did the sectarian side of Campbell help to create and shape the Christian tradition we know today as the Churches of Christ? The answer to that question is also not difficult to discover. Many of Campbell's followers found especially compelling his emphasis on Christian unity. In time many of these people became disillusioned with the restoration agenda as a means to ecumenical progress and formed the modern denomination we know today as Disciples of Christ—a development discussed in the previous chapter. At the same time an entirely different group of Campbell's followers—located chiefly in the Upper South though not confined to that region—failed to discern the ecumenical side of Campbell's thought but instead found especially attractive his exclusivist, sectarian rhetoric. In other words, these people mistook the means for the ends, and during Campbell's own lifetime they formed the nucleus of what would finally emerge as a distinct denomination known as the Churches of Christ.

Moreover, Campbell bequeathed to Churches of Christ the hard, combative style that he both employed and advocated during the *Christian Baptist* period. He regularly encouraged his followers to take on their denominational competitors, characteristically writing in 1830 that "no man ever achieved any great good to mankind who did not wrest it with violence through ranks of opponents."[12] Those who formed the nucleus of the emerging Churches of Christ took this advice at face value, so much so that until recent years, verbal fighting and debating became a stock-in-trade in this tradition.

Finally, those among Campbell's followers most infatuated with the sectarian side of his theology were also impressed with the legal dimensions of his thought. In this way Churches of Christ embraced from an early date a strongly legalistic orientation as an important part of their heritage. This dimension will be considered in substantially more detail in chapter 5.

In line with this legal dimension, Campbell seldom if ever described the New Testament as a theological document. Instead, he saw it as "the constitution and law of the primitive church," which in turn would serve as "the constitution and law of the restored church."[13]

Restoration as a Means to the Millennial Age

If Campbell promoted the restoration of the ancient church as a means to Christian unity, he also promoted restoration of the ancient church as a fundamental way to hasten the millennial age. In 1825, for example, he argued that "just in so far as the ancient order of things, or the religion of the New Testament, is restored, just so far has the Millennium commenced." Four years later, when he debated the socialist Robert Owen, he affirmed that "a restoration of ancient christianity, and a cordial reception of it" would "fill the world with all the happiness, physical, intellectual, and moral, which beings like us in this state of trial could endure."[14]

If Campbell failed to see the tension between restoration and unity, he also failed to see the tension between the restoration ideal and his postmillennial expectations. That tension grew from the fact that primitivism and postmillennialism pointed in fundamentally opposite directions. Primitivism pointed to the values of the past, not to the values of the future, and stood fundamentally opposed to eighteenth- and nineteenth-century notions of human progress.

In contrast, Campbell's postmillennialism was a modern construct, pointing not to an ancient past but to a gloriously progressive future characterized not only by religion but also by science, technology, education, and republican institutions. Indeed, Campbell routinely lauded modern scientific discoveries as means that would, along with the restoration of the ancient Christian faith, hasten the millennial dawn.

None of Campbell's confrontations illumined this point any more clearly than his 1833–34 dispute with Samuel M. McCorkle, a preacher in the Stone-Campbell movement from Rockville, Indiana. Disillusioned with modern progress, McCorkle challenged head-on Campbell's notion that a restoration of the primitive church would hasten the millennial age. "The present cannot be renovated," he objected. "No means on earth can bring or restore the administration back to primitive rectitude; it grows worse yearly in despite [*sic*] of all the efforts that can be made to heal."[15]

Campbell was shocked that McCorkle could possibly make such assertions and, tellingly, Campbell grounded his response to McCorkle precisely in his Enlightenment-informed faith in human progress. He pointed McCorkle to Bacon, Locke, and Newton, and to the progress they had inspired in both politics and modern science. He spoke glowingly of "the invention of gunpowder, the mariner's compass, the printing press, the discovery of America, [and] the American Revolution." In the same breath, he pointed McCorkle to his own religious movement, this "restoration" that would "bless the world in ten thousand ways." Campbell concluded, "This is, of all ages and of all generations, the most unpropitious for the assertion of the dogma that moral and intellectual means can benefit society in no very valuable nor permanent way. Almost every common newspaper presents insuperable difficulties to such a preposterous opinion."[16]

A quarter of a century later, in 1858, Campbell made precisely the same point when a group of eastern clergy suggested that the revival of that year might well mark the dawn of the millennial age. Campbell could not understand how anyone could make such preposterous claims, especially when "it was but yesterday that the mariner's compass was discovered, that printing was shown to be practicable, that steam power was laughed at as an absurdity, and the electric telegraph ridiculed as the hobby of a vagarian's brain. . . . We have too much faith in human progress . . . to subscribe to the doctrines of these theological gentlemen who hint the last days are at hand."[17]

CAMPBELL'S SCIENTIFIC UNDERSTANDING OF THE BIBLICAL TEXT

Since Campbell sought to blend emphasis on the ancient Christian faith with boundless faith in human progress, it is worth asking how he managed to reconcile these two themes, which pointed in such fundamentally opposite directions.

The answer to that question is found in his commitment to an immensely popular eighteenth- and nineteenth-century school of thought known as Scottish Common Sense Realism, popularly designated "Baconianism." This outlook simultaneously emphasized both the primitive and the modern and thereby served Campbell well.

To understand the nature of Baconianism and the appeal of this school of thought to Campbell and his contemporaries, one need only recall that several eighteenth-century philosophers—most notably Immanuel Kant and David Hume—had cast radical doubt on the ability of human beings to know anything at all with absolute certainty. The Scottish proponents of Baconianism rose up to challenge such skepticism. One can know a very great deal with complete certainty, they argued, but only if one abandons the "deductive" method of reasoning and employs the "inductive" method of reasoning instead. Deduction was a method of inquiry whereby one sought to find the facts that would support a preconceived conclusion—a method widely used for centuries prior to the eighteenth-century Enlightenment. In contrast, the inductive method demanded that one first locate all the evidence that might possibly bear on a given question, then form one's conclusions solely on the basis of those facts. Any modern person would quickly recognize induction as the heart of the scientific method. In honor of Francis Bacon, who had articulated the principles of the scientific method in the seventeenth century, the school of Scottish Common Sense Realism rapidly acquired the designation "Baconianism."

Baconianism held enormous appeal for Alexander Campbell for several reasons. First, as an advocate of Christian unity predicated on a universally common understanding of the biblical text, Campbell needed some way to virtually guarantee that all people might understand the biblical text alike. Baconianism seemed to offer such an assurance. After all, if Christians were to lay aside their presuppositions and form their conclusions only after a thorough investigation of the biblical text, Campbell thought, perhaps they would come to common conclusions regarding the heart of the Christian faith. Second, Campbell was about the business of reconstructing the ancient Christian faith. One could do that, he believed, only if one put aside one's biases and honestly inquired into the biblical evidence regarding the fundamental structures of the ancient Christian church. Because Baconianism promoted an outlook seemingly free from artificial contrivance, bias, or presupposition, it seemed especially well suited to Campbell's effort to restore primitive Christianity, a commitment supposedly free from preconceived creedal and confessional judgments. Accordingly, Campbell argued that the "inductive style of inquiring and reasoning, is to be as rigidly carried out in reading and teaching the Bible facts and documents, as in the analysis and synthesis of physical nature."[18]

By now we can see how Campbell's commitment to Baconianism helped him bridge the gulf between the primitive Christian faith, on the one hand and the modern world, on the other. Baconianism was a modern philosophical method closely allied with the principles of modern science. At the same time, when employed by Alexander Campbell and people who shared his outlook, it promised to open up the truths of the ancient Christian faith.

All this suggests that Campbell in many ways viewed the Bible as a scientific text, filled not so much with theological motifs as with facts that could be understood with scientific precision. "The Bible is a book of facts," he argued, "not of opinions, theories, abstract generalities, nor of verbal definitions. . . . The meaning of the Bible facts is the true biblical doctrine." He therefore argued that when Christians speak of biblical ideas, they should confine their speech to the very language of the Bible, lest they drift from "Bible facts" and fall victim to "abstract generalities . . . and verbal definitions." For this reason he berated "religious philosophers of the Bible"—especially Calvin, Arminius, and Wesley—for developing speculative notions that in Campbell's judgment had more to do with human theories about the Bible than they did with "Bible facts."[19]

In all these ways Campbell sought to employ a modern, scientific worldview as a tool for the restoration of the ancient Christian faith. When we understand that point, we can appreciate how Campbell could imagine that a restoration of primitive Christianity would combine with scientific and educational progress to usher in the millennial age.

Campbell's effort to marry Christian primitivism to postmillennial eschatology, however, was no more successful than his effort to join a sectarian restoration vision to his ecumenical ideals. In due time these combinations fell apart. The restoration vision—defined, to be sure, in scientific terms—increasingly became the exclusive property of those who formed the early vanguard of Churches of Christ, whearas postmillennial hopes and ecumenical expectations more and more characterized those who heralded the birth of a separate denomination known as Disciples of Christ.

CAMPBELL'S REORIENTATION

The slow disengagement of these ideals from one another first took place in the thinking and actions of Alexander Campbell himself. This occurred for two reasons. First, by the mid-1830s Campbell's fears of a Catholic takeover of the United States prompted him to cast his lot with American Protestantism, something that would have been unthinkable in earlier years when he often defined the task of restoration in sectarian terms. Second, also about the mid-1830s, it became increasingly apparent to Campbell that many of his followers had misread his agenda. Fascinated with his efforts to restore the ancient faith and to destroy the various denominational structures of Christendom, these disciples of Campbell lost sight of his ecumenical ideals altogether. When this development became more and more apparent to Campbell, he quickly shifted his emphasis to a more forthright ecumenical strategy, downplaying along the way the sectarian strategies of the past. In order to understand Campbell's change, we will consider these two developments in turn.

Campbell as Defender of American Protestantism

In many ways it is shocking that Campbell would even consider defending American Protestantism. Throughout the days of the *Christian Baptist*, he routinely castigated Protestantism as a corrupted form of the Christian faith that had since the Reformation relied on the power of the state to ensure conformity to its unbiblical traditions. Although the First Amendment to the Constitution had placed all these denominations on an equal footing before the federal law, the various states had been slow to embrace the principle of separation of church and state. Further, Campbell feared that power-hungry Protestant churches would seek to reassert their control by forming various interdenominational agencies and societies. Accordingly, throughout the 1820s, he launched scathing attacks on missionary societies, Bible societies, tract societies, Sunday school societies, and virtually every ecclesiastical organization that even remotely threatened to supplant the local congregation.

Under the withering assault of Campbell's pen, the Protestant clergy fared no better than the denominations they represented. In Campbell's view, they were wolves in sheep's clothing who sought wealth and power and who exploited ordinary Christians to achieve their ends.

By the mid-1830s, however, Campbell was growing less and less fearful of Protestantism and more and more fearful of the Pope in Rome. There are several reasons why this was true. In the first place, Massachusetts became in 1833 the last state in the Union to disestablish and to embrace in law the separation of church and state. Campbell's knowledge that every state had now accepted this principle must have alleviated his anxieties over Protestantism, at least to some degree.

Second, Campbell observed in the early and mid-1830s a vast Catholic immigration into the great valley of the Mississippi. He concluded that there was, "on the part of the Roman See, a settled determination, accompanied with a lively expectation of success—a fixed purpose, from which 'His Holiness' is never to depart, to bring these United States into the bosom of the Catholic Church, and to add all America, North and South, to the territory of its dominions."[20]

Finally, in 1836, the citizens of Cincinnati, Ohio, requested Campbell to defend the interests of American Protestantism against the claims of Rome. Since that development was crucial to Campbell's change, it deserves to be narrated here in some detail.[21] The story began at the fifth annual convention of the Western Literary Institute and College of Professional Teachers, meeting in Cincinnati in October 1836. That organization was not a college or a school at all, but a group of civic-minded citizens committed to promoting public education in the West. Along with Campbell, a number of well-known public figures participated in this group, including William Holmes McGuffey of *McGuffey Reader* fame, Lyman Beecher, Calvin Stowe (husband of Harriett Beecher Stowe), and the Roman Catholic bishop of Cincinnati, John Baptist Purcell.[22]

On October 3, 1836, Campbell addressed the members of the College and, in his speech, attributed to the spirit of Protestantism the high value English-speaking peoples placed on the proposition that every person should "think for himself."[23] Not surprisingly, Bishop Purcell objected to this assertion, and the two men agreed to meet for public discussion the following week.

Before that discussion had run its course, fifty-seven of Cincinnati's leading Protestant citizens submitted to Campbell a request that he engage Purcell in full-blown debate and thereby defend the interests of "Protestantism in the West."[24] Significantly, Campbell accepted that invitation. The debate took place in Cincinnati from January 13 through January 21, 1837.

Don Haymes has argued that this debate marked a crucial watershed in Campbell's religious development. From then on he presented himself more and more as a mainstream Protestant and less and less as a simple, primitive Christian.[25] In the years to come, he identified himself with what he called "a common Christianity"—what we today might call a civil religion—inspired by the Protestant faith. And, in a telling reorientation, he attributed to that common faith certain benefits that he had, during the *Christian Baptist* years, attributed exclusively to a restoration of ancient Christianity. Most notably, he now argued that this common civic faith had unified American Christians as nothing had before. Accordingly, he claimed in 1841,

> notwithstanding all our sectarian differences, we yet have something called a common Christianity;—that there are certain great fundamental matters—indeed, every thing elementary in what is properly called piety and morality—in which all good men of all denominations are agreed; and that these great common principles and views form a common ground on which all Christian people can unite, harmonize and co-operate in one great system of moral and Christian education.[26]

If this common Christianity had unified American Christians, might one legitimately expect that it would usher in the millennial dawn as well? That is precisely the position Campbell took in 1849 when he claimed that God would soon extend the influence of Protestant, Anglo-Saxon peoples around the globe, from north to south, "as they have already from east to west." When this development had run its course, Campbell exulted, "then will 'they hang their trumpets in the hall, and study war no more.' Peace and universal amity will reign triumphant. For over all the earth there will be but one Lord, one faith, one hope and one language."[27]

In light of these sentiments, one should not be surprised to discover that as early as 1837, Campbell began to behave as a mainstream Protestant as well. In that year, only months after his debate with Bishop Purcell, Campbell responded to a woman in Lunenburg, Virginia, who had been "very much surprised . . . , while reading in the Harbinger, to see that you . . . say, you 'find in all Protestant parties Christians.' " Taking her stand squarely on Campbell's earlier *Christian Baptist* position, the woman challenged Campbell to explain why he failed to confine the label "Christian" to "those who believe the gospel, repent, and are buried by baptism into the death of Christ."

Campbell's response to this woman provides a telling indication of the extent of his shift toward mainstream Protestant values. "Should I find," he wrote, "a Pedobaptist more intelligent in the Christian Scriptures, more spiritually-minded and more devoted to the Lord than a Baptist, or one immersed on a profession of the ancient faith, I would not hesitate a moment in giving the preference of my heart to him that loveth most." In line with the spirit of perfectionism that still dominated his understanding of Christianity, he conceded that he could not be "a perfect Christian without a right understanding and a cordial reception of immersion in its true and scriptural meaning and design." Nonetheless, he stoutly maintained his conviction that "he that thence infers that none are Christians but the immersed, as greatly errs as he who affirms that none are alive but those of clear and full vision."[28]

Three years later, in 1840, Campbell founded Bethany College. There one finds further evidence that Campbell was rapidly turning his back on the sectarian values that had characterized the *Christian Baptist*, embracing instead the values of the common Christianity he now so much admired. Campbell made no requirement that trustee membership be confined to sectarian primitivists. Instead, trustees represented a wide variety of Protestant persuasions. Further, Campbell invited "respectable ministers of various denominations" to preside over Sunday worship at the college church.[29]

By 1849 Campbell's transition was complete. The man who had once denounced missionary societies, Bible societies, tract societies, and every organization that threatened the autonomy of the local congregation—this same man allowed himself to be elected that year to the presidency of the American Christian Missionary Society, an organization that served especially the progressives in the Disciples of Christ and Church of Christ movement that Campbell led. In all these ways Alexander Campbell was spearheading the classic transition from sect to denomination, but Churches of Christ would not experience that same transition for many years to come.

The Sectarians in Campbell's Ranks

It is likely, however, that none of these changes would have occurred had it not been for the vast numbers of people in Campbell's movement who misread his intentions and imagined that the sectarian side of Campbell's thought and behavior, so evident on the pages of the *Christian Baptist*, was an end in itself. Campbell knew from an early date that these people were distorting his ecumenical intentions, and he registered a resounding protest in 1826.

> This plan of making our own nest, and fluttering over our own brood; of building our own tent, and of confining all goodness and grace to our noble selves and the "elect few" who are like us, is the quintessence of sublimated pharisaism. . . . To lock ourselves up in the bandbox of our own little circle; to associate with a few units, tens, or hundreds, as the pure church, as the elect, is real Protestant monkery, it is evangelical nunnery.[30]

It will be helpful here to identify some of the most important figures who provided leadership for the sectarian side of Campbell's movement. Needless to say, these same people also provided leadership for the embryonic Churches of Christ.

Walter Scott

Walter Scott (1796–1861), a Scottish Presbyterian who settled in America in 1818 and in Pittsburgh the following year, contributed substantially to the emerging Churches of Christ, especially in his claim that he was the first to fully restore the "ancient gospel" of Jesus Christ.[31]

Scott and Campbell became acquainted in 1821 and soon became fast friends. Over the years, Campbell turned to Scott for advice on a host of significant issues, and Scott viewed his relationship with Campbell as similar to Philip Melanchthon's relationship with Martin Luther. Accordingly, Scott wrote regularly for the *Christian Baptist* with articles appearing over the pen name "Philip." When Scott died in 1861, Campbell lamented, "I knew him well. I knew him long. I loved him much."[32]

Several factors helped shape Scott's theological outlook. First, shortly after arriving in America, Scott encountered in Pittsburgh a small church enamored with the restorationist teachings of the Scottish separatists Robert Sandeman and James and Robert Haldane.[33] Insisting on baptism by immersion, foot washing, and the "holy kiss," this congregation also exercised discipline within the church and carefully nurtured a wall of separation between themselves and other Christians. Soon Scott abandoned his Presbyterian heritage, submitted to immersion, and became a member of this primitive "Church of Christ."

The spirit of the Enlightenment also shaped Scott's thinking in extraordinary ways. Two dimensions of the Enlightenment deserve notice here. First, Scott was especially enamored with "Baconian" Common Sense Realism. If one of the purposes of that perspective was to uncover the natural order of things—that is, the way things were meant to be from the beginning—Scott saw in Baconianism the potential to reveal the glories of the uncorrupted, ancient Christian faith. And if the Baconian method helped scientists and philosophers to organize the natural world into manageable data, Scott trained the Baconian lens on the New Testament in an effort to discover the essential "facts" of authentic Christianity. Nothing makes this dimension of Scott's work more apparent than a book he published in 1836: *The Gospel Restored: A Discourse of the True Gospel of Jesus Christ, in Which the Facts, Principles, Duties, and Privileges of Christianity Are Arranged, Defined, and Discussed.* In 1836 Scott helped establish the first college associated with the Campbell movement, appropriately named Bacon College "in honor of Lord Francis Bacon, father of the inductive method of reasoning and the new science." When inaugurated as the school's first president, Scott used that occasion to praise the virtues of Bacon's scientific method and especially his classic treatise, *Novum Organum.*[34]

The second aspect of the Enlightenment that held sway over Scott's imagination was John Locke's book *The Reasonableness of Christianity*. There Locke taught that the substance of the Christian faith was the simple proposition "Jesus is the Messiah," proved by miracles and fulfilled prophecies. From his Baconian perspective, Scott found in that proposition the central "fact" of the Christian religion.

Scott's dependence on the spirit of the Enlightenment became especially evident when he described the process of conversion in strictly rational terms. He portrayed the gospel as "a rational advocacy . . . [that] pleads the faith in its saving proposition from evidence." He claimed that "the Christian faith . . . belongs to the science of inference—reason—logic, and depends for its reception in society on proof." He argued that the task of the Holy Spirit in conversion is not to "enter the soul of the sinner" but to convince "us as we convince one another—by truth and argument."[35]

For our purposes here, Scott's chief significance lay in his development of a "plan" or "plan of salvation," a notion he also described as the "ancient gospel." He announced in 1823 that he had discovered the "one uniform and universal plan of teaching the [Christian] religion."[36] Actually, Scott's plan at that time was nothing more than John Locke's claim that the heart of the Christian faith involved the proposition that Jesus is the Messiah.

Soon, however, he expanded the plan into a six-point covenantal arrangement between God and sinners. The duties of the sinner were three: to believe that Jesus was the Messiah, to repent of one's sins, and to be immersed for the forgiveness of sins. God responded with the forgiveness of sins, the gift of the Holy Spirit, and eternal life. By 1827, when Scott was preaching with great success on the Western Reserve, he collapsed the last two points of the plan into one: the gift of the Holy Spirit. He marketed his revivals by teaching this five-point plan of salvation to children returning home from school, placing one point on each finger of a child's hand. He asked the children to make a fist and keep it closed until they arrived home. Then, they should open their fist, show their parents what was "on their fingers," and tell them that the man who taught them this five-finger exercise would be preaching that evening.

When Thomas Campbell, Alexander's father, learned of Scott's evangelistic success on the Western Reserve, he went there to hear and see precisely what

Scott was saying and doing. He reported to his son that while "we have long . . . spoken and published many things 'correctly concerning' the ancient gospel, . . . I am at present for the first time upon the ground where the thing has appeared to be 'practically exhibited' to the proper purpose."[37]

Scott was astounded at his own success and grew more and more convinced of the originality of his message. In 1828 he reported to the Mahoning Baptist Association, which sponsored his work, that he had restored "to the world the manner—the primitive manner—of administering to mankind the gospel of our Lord Jesus Christ!" Nine years later, in 1836, Scott published the book he entitled *The Gospel Restored.* There he argued that the Campbell-led movement had accomplished a complete restoration of everything vital to the Christian faith. Thomas Campbell had restored the Bible to its authoritative position, Alexander had restored the "ancient order" (the true worship and organization of the church), and Scott himself had restored the "ancient gospel" by preaching his five-point plan of salvation.[38]

Alexander Campbell did little or nothing to resist such claims for many years, and he even spoke of Scott in 1832 as "the first successful proclaimer of this ancient gospel."[39] By 1838, however, after Campbell had made his shift toward mainstream Protestantism, he was in no frame of mind to tolerate such extravagance. The issue came to a head when Francis Emmons pointed out that as far as he could tell, both Scott and Campbell had claimed credit for the restoration of the ancient gospel—Campbell in 1823 and Scott in 1827.

Campbell denied this charge. He acknowledged that the first edition of his *Christian System* (1835) was entitled *Christianity Restored*, but he labeled that title misguided and blamed his printer for the mistake. "To restore the gospel," Campbell affirmed, "is really a great matter, and implies that the persons who are the subjects of such a favor once had it and lost it," a judgment he now refused to make.

For his part, however, Scott took Emmons' assertion as a personal challenge to his own priority of achievement. He conceded that Campbell had indeed taught immersion for the remission of sins in 1823. Granting that, however, he argued that Campbell had not climbed in 1823 to the zenith Scott had attained with his five-finger exercise in 1827: "The restoration of the whole gospel in 1827, can never be confounded with the definition of a single one of its terms in 1823, or in any year preceding it."[40]

Scott's importance for the emerging Churches of Christ lay in the exclusivism implicit in his claim that he had actually restored the ancient gospel to the earth. Within a few short years this contention virtually defined the identity of this tradition.

Further, Scott helped shape one of the central theological planks of this heritage when he devised what he called "the plan" or what Churches of Christ would later call "the plan of salvation." Within a few short years, however, Churches of Christ transformed Scott's plan from a covenantal arrangement involving human activity and God's response to a plan involving human activity alone. In 1848, for example, John R. Howard published a plan that he described as the "terms of admission" into "the true church of Christ." That plan included only four requirements with which the sinner must comply: faith, repentance, confession, and baptism.[41] In later years Churches of Christ would add to that list the requirement of "hearing" the gospel. That five-point plan of salvation—hear, believe, repent, confess, and be baptized—has been a cornerstone of orthodoxy in Churches of Christ ever since.

John R. Howard and Arthur Crihfield

If Walter Scott was among the first in Churches of Christ to articulate the claim that this communion had completely restored the ancient gospel, John R. Howard extended that argument to its logical implication: the Church of Christ was the one true church outside of which there was no salvation. Taking Howard's position as axiomatic, Arthur Crihfield devoted his career to exposing heretics and heretical churches, a vocation that many in Churches of Christ would adopt over the next 150 years.

In the 1830s and 1840s, John R. Howard published the *Bible Advocate* in the state of Tennessee, "perhaps the first paper published in the state for the avowed purpose of advocating a return to primitive Christianity."[42] In fact, however, Howard turned the case for primitive Christianity into the proposition that the Church of Christ was the one true church. In this way, he badly distorted the ecumenical vision of Alexander Campbell and thoroughly denominationalized the concept of nondenominational Christianity.

While Howard penned numerous articles that argued the exclusive claims of the Churches of Christ, his single greatest contribution was a sermon originally entitled "Identification of the Church of Christ," first published in 1848 and often reprinted in later years under the title "The Beginning Corner; or, The Church of Christ Identified."[43] This sermon is a classic statement of the growing exclusivist identity of a sect called the Church of Christ that was emerging especially in the American South. Howard's sermon did not define that identity so much as it reflected an orthodoxy that was emerging among these people. For these reasons, it deserves to be explored in somc detail.

Like many Americans of his time, Howard worried over the growing religious pluralism in the United States. In the midst of that situation, he asked, "Where is the true church now to be found?—and how shall we be enabled to know it?—to identify and recognize it?"

In good homespun fashion, Howard answered that question by telling a story about an old pioneer who went west and laid claim to a parcel of land. According to Howard, pioneers in the old days established claims to the land by cutting marks into trees that marked the boundary of the property. First, the pioneer would place three marks on the tree that would mark the beginning corner of the property, with each mark facing one of the other three corners of the tract, then line the property out from that point. After staking his claim in this way, the pioneer in question returned east for a number of years, then finally went west again to settle on the land he had staked out years ago. Much to his chagrin, however, he could not locate the "beginning corner," since vines and undergrowth had completely obscured its location. In the meantime, others had settled on his land. The old pioneer finally located a man who knew the location of his "beginning corner," enabling him to claim his land. The more recent settlers fought to prevent him from occupying his property, but in the end the courts upheld his claim.

To Howard, this tale perfectly illustrated the work Alexander Campbell had performed in reclaiming the "old Jerusalem" gospel. In the centuries following Jesus and the apostles, a variety of illegitimate "squatters" had settled the "land," permitting undergrowth to obscure the "old Jerusalem trunk." But Campbell

> exposed and tore away the human additions and appendages, the traditions, mysticism, and error with which the marks on the Jerusalem trunk—the corner of primitive Christianity—had been covered over, obscured, and hidden from the view of men; and identified it, by the original marks, to be the same one made by Peter.

But what were the "original marks" that would always identify the true Church of Christ? In identifying these marks, Howard provided one of the first creedal statements to emerge from this noncreedal tradition.

> I. The Church of Christ originated . . . in the days of the Apostles, and was founded by them. . . .
>
> II. The Church of Christ is known and recognized in the New Testament, by such appellations as . . . "Church of God," and "Churches of Christ." . . . Hence we may with propriety call it the "CHRISTIAN CHURCH," or "CHURCH OF CHRIST." . . .
>
> III. The Church now which has no creed but the Bible . . . is, all things else being equal, the true Church of Christ. . . .
>
> IV. The Church of Christ is catholic. . . . The word catholic means universal, and the Church of Christ is the only true catholic or universal Church; all others are only sectarian parties. . . .
>
> V. A fifth mark of the true church of Christ, is its TERMS OF ADMISSION. These are Faith, Repentance, Confession, and Baptism, in the order here presented, and in their Biblical import and application. . . .
>
> VI. Another mark of the true church of Christ is its ORGANIZATION and [congregational] INDEPENDENCE . . . [with] certain officers [including] . . . 1. Bishops, or elders; 2. Deacons and deaconesses; 3. Evangelists.
>
> VII. The congregations thus organized met together every Lord's day to . . . partake of the Lord's supper, and to attend to the public worship of God. . . . The GOVERNMENT of these congregations, was strictly that of the New Testament form. . . . The church now having this worship and this government, is, all things else being equal, or having all the other marks, the true church of Christ.[44]

It is important to recognize that Howard used the phrase "Church of Christ" to designate a particular, flesh-and-blood ecclesiastical tradition, not a disembodied nondenominational ideal. He made this point especially clear in 1843. By then Howard had abandoned the postmillennial, ecumenical vision of Alexander Campbell, having been captivated by the premillennial speculations of William Miller. In the midst of the millennial excitement of those years, Howard warned "sectarians" to

> cast away all your unscriptural names, forms and practices; and return back to the true faith—the pure, original Gospel. . . . The coming of the Lord, in vengeance to destroy his enemies, cannot . . . be very far off. . . . And should you not be found among his true people—his genuine disciples—but arrayed in opposition against them, he will "destroy" you "with the breath of his mouth, and with the brightness of his coming."[45]

If John R. Howard devoted his energies to proving the Church of Christ the one true church, Arthur Crihfield devoted his time and talents to exposing other denominations as heretical. Crihfield published his journal, the *Heretic Detector*, in Middleburgh, Ohio, from 1837 to 1842. For Crihfield, the task of restoration inevitably involved the detection of heretics: "Any effort to reinstate the Apostles upon their thrones, and the gospel to its honors, is an effort to detect heresy."[46] Working from that foundation, he routinely attacked Presbyterians, Methodists, Baptists, Episcopalians, Universalists, Deists, and all other denominations that came within his view. According to him and those who wrote in his paper, denominationalism was nothing more than a species of infidelity, and all those who refused to unite with the Church of Christ but maintained allegiance to other Christian traditions simply would not be saved.[47] In due time Crihfield's paper became immensely popular in the region that would soon become the heartland of Churches of Christ, so much so that members of Churches of Christ in Kentucky invited him to move to Harrodsburg and to bring his *Heretic Detector* with him.[48]

Since Crihfield began his journal the year after Campbell made his decision to defend Protestantism, one would think Campbell would have condemned the *Heretic Detector* out of hand. Surprisingly, he praised it in 1837 for "its spirited defence of the gospel." Two years later Crihfield even coaxed Campbell to submit an article for his paper.[49] One can only surmise that Campbell recognized his position as leader of a sizable and diverse body of people and did what he could to appease the various factions of his movement.

Campbell's attitude toward Crihfield turned 180 degrees, however, in 1843. By then Crihfield was editing his third religious journal, which he called the *Orthodox Preacher*. Like John R. Howard, Crihfield had also fallen under the spell of Millerite millennialism. Rejecting Campbell's ecumenism and postmillennial optimism altogether, he no longer hoped that the restoration of the ancient church would bring to the Christian world much significant change. "Slight topical ameliorations will be effected by the reproclamation of the gospel," he wrote. "A few from the different parties will be induced to leave; but the Sects, as such, will never become extinct till 'the sign of the Son of Man is seen in the heavens.' " Campbell ridiculed Crihfield's newfound premillennial position. He noted that "from being a Heretic Detector and a Christian Family Library [Crihfield's second journal] keeper, our versatile brother Crihfield has become all at once an ORTHODOX PREACHER; and has taken up his abode . . . under the banners of the much exciting subject of the immediate second advent of Messiah."[50]

Dr. John Thomas

As a last example of the kind of sectarian Campbell encountered within his own movement in the 1830s, it is important to mention Dr. John Thomas, an English physician who began to follow Campbell in 1833. Soon, however, Thomas began publishing in his own journal, the *Apostolic Advocate*, speculations regarding the resurrection, the nature of the human soul, and the afterlife—notions that hardly fit the context of the Campbell movement. More than this, Thomas claimed that Baptists could not belong to the Church of Christ without reimmersion, since Baptist immersion was immersion into Antichrist. He even argued that the entire Protestant movement was headed for perdition, and he scolded Campbell for "the sinfulness of defending Protestantism."

Campbell was not happy. "To Calvin's honors," Campbell lamented, Thomas had "superadded that of 'the Arch Perverter of the Faith of Christ.' . . . Some of the Methodistic clergy he has dubbed 'Draconic Lambs,' in honor of the Old Serpent, I presume. And all the Protestant churches and sects are elevated to the rank of 'Synagogues of Satan.' " Accordingly, Campbell ranked Thomas with "these infallible dogmatists, so supremely devoted to his own opinions," and called on him to repent.[51] Thomas, however, refused to bow to Campbell's demands and eventually deserted Campbell to become the founder of the Christadelphians.

Some twenty years later Jeremiah Jeter, one of Campbell's most outspoken Baptist critics, noted the positive changes he had witnessed in Campbell since 1837. "He has been a careless observer of Campbellism who has not perceived its effort to get rid of the odium theologicum by conforming its teachings, more and more, to the popular views." And significantly, Jeter ascribed Campbell's change to his encounter with Dr. John Thomas. "From the rise of Thomasism," Jeter noted, "may be dated the decline of the vaunting, pugnacious spirit of the Reformation."[52]

Jeter was both right and wrong. Campbell had indeed changed, and one may certainly date the beginnings of the change to the year 1837. But Jeter was mistaken when he ascribed Campbell's change to his dispute with John Thomas. Rather, Thomas was but one among many in Campbell's flock who saw in Campbell's agenda a mandate for sectarian condemnation of the entire Christian world outside the boundaries of the Church of Christ, and he behaved accordingly.

In 1837 Campbell confessed that it was precisely this spirit of sectarianism within his own movement that drove him to join and defend the Protestant alliance against papal power in the United States. "Some of our brethren," he acknowledged, "were too much addicted to denouncing the sects and representing them en masse as wholly aliens from the possibility of salvation—as wholly antichristian and corrupt. . . . [Therefore], we have been always accused of aspiring to build up and head a party. . . . On this account I consented the more readily to defend Protestantism."[53]

THE CONSERVATIVE RESPONSE TO CAMPBELL'S CHANGE

It is easy to detect the emergence of two separate traditions within the Campbell fold—Churches of Christ and Disciples of Christ—when we take seriously the scale of the conservative protest against Campbell's efforts to defend Protestantism and to develop a more consistently ecumenical position. In 1840, for example, T. M. Allen wrote a scathing critique of Campbell to John Allen Gano: "I wish he would cease the duties of an editor. He is through with every thing important to this reformation, & now I fear he is to do harm by speculating, & going deep into the 'language of Ashdod,'—there is plenty of it in his 'Christian System'—on account of which I would not purchase it."[54]

Even more important was the depth of resentment toward Campbell developing in Tennessee—the region rapidly emerging as the Church of Christ heartland—especially on the part of the most significant leader of Churches of Christ in that region: Tolbert Fanning. In 1845 Fanning lamented the spirit of compromise he now saw in the leadership of the movement. Although he never singled out Campbell by name, it is clear whom he had in mind.

> When reformers begin to boast of their respectability, they have started to the city of confusion,—when they court the smiles of corrupt denominations, they are at the very gates, and when they shake hands with the sects, they are in the midst of "Babylon the Great." The charge has been made, that the disciples are inclining to the denominations, and judging from the tone and spirit of some of the periodicals, whose editors stood forth first to advocate the cause of primitive Christianity, I fear there is more sober truth than poetry in the allegation.[55]

Further evidence of resentment of Campbell's change on the part of conservatives emerges in the recollections of old men who looked back with considerable regret on events they had witnessed over the years. One such person was James L. Thornberry, who recalled in 1878 that he had attended a state meeting of the Stone-Campbell movement in Kentucky about 1850. There, he reported, he had heard Campbell say that "it was not enough, to hand a man the New Testament and say, That is my creed. We would have to explain a little. Also that the name Christian would not do now; if we say we are the Christian church, we are saying others are not; and that we must now have an educated ministry, who could pronounce the language properly. . . . I was vexed."[56]

In 1877 Jacob Creath, Jr., a man who had been a close friend and colleague of Alexander Campbell especially in the *Christian Baptist* period, also decried the ways Campbell had moderated his position in his later years. He asked his readers to "compare the Alexander Campbell of the Christian Baptist, and first 20 years of the Harbinger with . . . the A. Campbell of organs, big suppers, conventions and all the other human inventions." Although Creath misread the date of Campbell's change, he was nonetheless on target in his judgment that the emerging Disciples of Christ, with their organs and conventions, had descended from an older Alexander Campbell, not from the Campbell one finds in the *Christian Baptist.* "That the human inventions now practiced by those who claim to be the Reformation . . . are not in the Bible nor the Christian Baptist," he affirmed, "is as clear as a sunbeam, and therefore no part nor parcel of it."[57]

THE MYTH OF THE SINGULAR CAMPBELL

Although leaders among the emerging Churches of Christ denounced Campbell's latter-day moderation in no uncertain terms, it is striking that they typically protected Campbell from blame. Instead, they argued that Campbell remained consistent in his commitment to the principles of the *Christian Baptist* so long as his mind was clear, and that he wavered only when the strength of his mental powers declined and when he therefore succumbed to the efforts of some of his liberal Bethany College associates to control him.

Tolbert Fanning apparently began this report in 1857 in the course of a bitter dispute over the nature of the Bible with Robert Richardson, Campbell's personal physician, close friend, and colleague at Bethany College. David Lipscomb later recalled that Fanning traveled to Bethany that very year to speak directly with Campbell regarding Richardson's theology and other developments at Bethany.

> I remember well, on his return he stated that he was shocked to find his mind was so shaken that he could, with difficulty, keep it on one subject; that he could converse in general terms on things he had studied in the past, but that all power of close, connected reasoning was gone; that he had to be continually prompted to keep up an ordinary conversation. He said while A. Campbell, while his mind was directed to it, could reiterate and agree to his former positions, that he was merely a child in the hands of his friends.[58]

Lipscomb embellished this story considerably. Campbell "failed in his mental and will power early in life," he wrote. "His later years were years of a second childhood." Indeed, Lipscomb suggested that Campbell's mental decline began in 1847, a particularly tragic year for Campbell when his son Wyckliffe drowned and when Campbell himself was incarcerated in Scotland. From then on Campbell was "credulous, trusting, and was mainly controlled by his friends." It was no wonder, thought Lipscomb, that he therefore "violated his own principles, built again the [missionary] society he destroyed and destroyed that supreme and undivided respect for the word of God, and his [God's] appointments which he [Campbell] had vindicated."[59]

Lipscomb obviously failed to recognize that Campbell's change was underway a full decade prior to 1847. Nonetheless, the myth he and Fanning spawned served Churches of Christ well. It allowed them to protect the integrity of their leader while at the same time condemning the changes he made in his later years.

It is entirely possible that the story Fanning and Lipscomb told possessed elements of truth. Even Robert Richardson concurred. In a letter addressed to Philip S. Fall in 1857, Richardson noted that "Bro. Campbell is now advanced in years and too susceptible of the influence of designing and selfish persons who want to make use of the college for their own purposes. He ceases to know his true friends and the true friends of the reformation and of the college." At the same time, Benjamin Franklin, an important leader among the emerging Churches of Christ, wrote in 1856 that Campbell's "intellect is as clear, vigorous and giant-like as ever."[60]

For our purposes here, it is irrelevant whether Campbell failed in his mental powers or not. The important point is that many key leaders of Churches of Christ believed that he did, and in this way they preserved their memories of an Alexander Campbell who was singular in his commitment to the ideals he expressed in the *Christian Baptist.*

CONCLUSION

The notion that Alexander Campbell capitulated to more ecumenical Protestant views only when senility diminished his mental powers has been the basis for substantial misunderstanding of the movement that he led. In this view, apostasy came to the movement only in Campbell's later years, was fostered by people other than Campbell, and took root in opposition to Campbell's most deeply held beliefs. This reading of the Campbell movement has allowed historians to imagine that the division between Churches of Christ and Disciples of Christ had nothing to do with ambiguities in the thought of Campbell himself, but everything to do with such late-nineteenth-century issues as the propriety of missionary societies and instrumental music in the worship.

The failure to discern the shift in Campbell's thought also reflects a failure to discern the heart of Campbell's reform. Partisans of the Churches of Christ have typically argued that the restoration of primitive Christianity stood at the core of Campbell's agenda. In contrast, partisans of the Disciples of Christ have generally sought to portray Campbell as a man chiefly concerned for the unity of Christendom. Ultimately, neither of these views is correct. Campbell concerned himself first and foremost with the dawn of the millennial age. For him, restoration and unity were but means to that end. Yet, when it became apparent that recovery of the ancient church would not provide a sufficient basis for either his ecumenical or his millennial vision, Campbell turned to that Protestant "common Christianity . . . in which all good men of all denominations are agreed." This suggests that Campbell's millennial dream remained his constant, lifelong goal, the fulcrum upon which his other commitments shifted and changed.

It is important to recognize that the other constant factor in Campbell's thought was his belief that authentic Christians were scattered throughout the various Christian denominations—a notion intimately related to his millennial vision. In the aftermath of conservative complaints over his "Lunenburg letter," Campbell himself pointed to his own consistency on this point. "Why should we so often have quoted and applied to apostate Christendom what the Spirit saith to saints in Babylon—'Come out of her, my people, that you partake not of her sins, and that you receive not of her plagues'—had we imagined that the Lord had no people beyond the pale of our communion!"[61] There was a time when Campbell had thought that the movement he led would provide "a nucleus around which may one day congregate all the children of God."[62] By 1837, however, he had his doubts. Increasingly, his movement seemed too narrow to accommodate "all the children of God," and he therefore pinned his hopes for the millennial dawn on the broader Protestant movement. He thanked God that "among them all [i.e., the various Protestant sects], . . . there are many who believe in, and love the Saviour, and that, though we may not have Christian churches [i.e., churches built on the primitive pattern], we have many Christians."[63] That conviction was sufficient to nourish, for the balance of his life, Campbell's dream of a millennium on earth.

For most of his career, Campbell's millennial vision was sustained by the general spirit of optimism, if not millennialism, that had spread throughout the United States. By the 1850s, however, the debate over slavery had dampened the millennial dream throughout the larger culture. By the 1860s few would have pointed to the United States as the birthplace for the millennial age. With the collapse of the postmillennial vision in the larger culture, it was inevitable that Campbell's followers would abandon that vision as well. They seized instead on his penultimate concerns—unity and restoration—and formed themselves into hostile and competing camps around those banners, each camp claiming for its banner the place of honor in the Campbellian legacy. To a significant degree, the Disciples of Christ are the legitimate offspring of the later Campbell who moved, following 1837, toward a more consistently ecumenical, Protestant faith. To the extent that Churches of Christ descend from Alexander Campbell, they descend from the Alexander Campbell of the *Christian Baptist* period who sought to unify Christendom by restoring the ancient faith and destroying illegitimate Christian denominations wherever they could be found.

NOTES

1. For a comparison of Mormons and Churches of Christ regarding these issues, see Richard T. Hughes, "Two Restoration Traditions: Mormons and Churches of Christ in the Nineteenth Century," *JMH* 19 (Spring 1993): 34–51.

2. Alexander Campbell, "Introductory Remarks," *MH* 3 (2 January 1832): 6.

3. Campbell, *The Christian System*, 5th ed. (1835; reprint, Cincinnati: Standard Publishing, 1901), p. ix; and "Christendom in Its Dotage: A Hint to Reformers," *MH* 5 (August 1834): 374.

4. Campbell, *The Christian System*, p. 154, xi–xii.

5. Campbell, "Prefatory Remarks," *MH* 1 (4 January 1830): 8.

6. Campbell developed these themes in a series of articles he entitled "A Restoration of the Ancient Order of Things," which ran in the *Christian Baptist* in thirty separate installments from February 1825 to September 1829.

7. John Rogers, "The Life and Times of John Rogers, 1800–1867," *Lexington Theological Quarterly* 19 (January–April 1984): 76; and Jeremiah Jeter, *Campbellism Examined* (New York: Sheldon, Lamport, and Blakeman, 1855), pp. 83–84.

8. Campbell, quoted by Robert Richardson in *Memoirs of Alexander Campbell*, vol. 2 (1897; reprint, Nashville: Gospel Advocate, 1956), p. 90. Campbell held five particularly notable debates—with the Seceder Presbyterian John Walker in 1820, with the Presbyterian W. L. McCalla in 1823, with the social reformer Robert Owen in 1829, with the Roman Catholic bishop of Cincinnati John Purcell in 1837, and with the Presbyterian Nathan L. Rice in 1843. On these debates, see Bill J. Humble, *Campbell and Controversy* (Rosemead, CA: Old Paths Book Club, 1952).

9. Campbell, "Remarks," *MH*, n.s., 4 (November 1840): 492–93; and Christianos, "Baptism," *MH*, n.s., 4 (May 1840): 198.

10. Campbell, *The Christian System*, pp. 153, 166.

11. See William J. Richardson, "Ecumenical Perspectives in the Thought of Alexander Campbell," *RQ* 40 (3d Quarter 1998): 153–69.

12. Campbell, "Prefatory Remarks," *MH* 1 (4 January 1830): 8; and "Religious Controversy," *MH* 1 (4 January 1830): 41, 44.

13. Campbell, "A Restoration of the Ancient Order of Things, No. 4," *CB* 2 (6 June 1825): 221.

14. Campbell, "A Restoration of the Ancient Order of Things, No. 1," *CB* 2 (7 February 1825): 136; and Campbell and Robert Owen, *The Evidences of Christianity: A Debate* (St. Louis: Christian Board of Publication, n.d.), p. 385.

15. Samuel H. McCorkle, "Signs of the Times," *MH* 4 (October 1833): 483.

16. A Reformed Clergyman [Campbell], "The Millennium–No. 3," *MH* 5 (October 1834): 549–50; "The Millennium–No. 7," *MH* 6 (March 1835): 105; and "The Millennium-No. 8," *MH* 6 (April 1835): 148.

17. Campbell, "The Millennium," *MH*, 5th ser., 1 (June 1858): 335–36.

18. Campbell, "Schools and Colleges–No. 2," *MH*, 3d ser., 7 (March 1850): 172. On "Baconianism," see T. Dwight Bozeman, *Protestants in an Age of Science: The Baconian Ideal and Antebellum American Religious Thought* (Chapel Hill, NC: University of North Carolina Press, 1977).

19. Campbell, *The Christian System*, pp. 6, 103–4.

20. Campbell, "Catholic Controversy. No. 1," *MH* 4 (November 1833): 538–39.

21. Don Haymes has told this story in considerable detail. See Haymes, "A Battle of Giants: Alexander Campbell and Bishop John Baptist Purcell in Cincinnati, 1837," unpublished manuscript in possession of the author.

22. See Thomas H. Olbricht, "Alexander Campbell as an Educator," in *Lectures in Honor of the Alexander Campbell Bicentennial, 1788–1988* (Nashville: Disciples of Christ Historical Society, 1988), p. 82.

23. Campbell, "Essay on the Importance of Uniting the Moral with the Intellectual Culture of the Mind," *MH* 7 (Extra, December 1836): 579, 597.

24. Campbell quotes the text of the petition in "Roman Catholic Discussion," *MH* 7 (December 1836): 551–52.

25. Haymes, "A Battle of Giants."

26. Campbell, "On Common Schools" (1841), in *Popular Lectures and Addresses* (St. Louis: John Burns, 1861), p. 259.

27. Campbell, "Address on the Anglo-Saxon Language: Its Origin, Character, and Destiny" (1849), in *Popular Lectures and Addresses*, p. 44.

28. Campbell, "Any Christians among Protestant Parties," *MH*, n.s., 1 (September 1837): 411–14. When his readers complained, Campbell denied that his response to the woman from Lunenberg represented any shift in the position he had always held. "Any Christians among the Sects?" *MH*, n.s., 1 (December 1837): 561.

29. M. Norvel Young, *A History of Colleges Established and Controlled by Members of the Churches of Christ* (Kansas City: Old Paths Book Club, 1949), p. 28.

30. Campbell, "To an Independent Baptist," *CB* 3 (1 May 1826): 204.

31. Eva Jean Wrather has assessed the radical dimensions of Scott's thought in " 'My Most Cordial and Indefatigable Laborer': Alexander Campbell Looks at Walter Scott," *C-E* 84 (23 October 1946): 1044–48. Wrather suggested to me some years ago that in many ways Scott stands at the fountainhead of Churches of Christ.

32. Campbell, "Elder Walter Scott's Demise," *MH*, 5th ser., 4 (May 1861): 296–97.

33. For the influence that Sandeman and the Haldane brothers exercised over Churches of Christ, see Lynn A. McMillon, *Restoration Roots* (Dallas: Gospel Teachers Publications, 1983).

34. Walter Scott, "The State-System," *Chr* (February–March 1837): 25–72. See also "United States' System: An Address" (1837), *College of the Bible Quarterly* 23 (April 1946): 4–44.

35. Scott, *To Themelion: The Union of Christians, on Christian Principles* (Cincinnati: n.p., 1852), pp. 78–79; "Address Given before the American Christian Missionary Society" (Cincinnati, 1854), p. 26; and *A Discourse on the Holy Spirit* (Bethany, VA: n.p., 1831), pp. 20–21.

36. Scott [pseud., Philip], "On Teaching Christianity–No. 11," *CB* 1 (3 November 1823): 67.

37. Thomas Campbell quoted by William Baxter in *Life of Elder Walter Scott* (Cincinnati: Bosworth, Chase & Hall, 1874), pp. 158–59.

38. Scott, *The Gospel Restored* (Cincinnati: n.p., 1836), pp. v–vi. See also Scott, "Circular Letter," *C-E* 1 (2 January 1832): 17–18.

39. Campbell, "To Epaphras–No. 1," *MH* 3 (2 July 1832): 298.

40. Campbell, "Events of 1823 and 1827," *MH*, n.s., 2 (October 1838): 466ff.

41. John R. Howard, "Identification of the Church of Christ,"*CMag* 1 (September 1848): 267ff.

42. J. W. Grant, "A Sketch of the Reformation in Tennessee," c. 1897, typescript in Center for Restoration Studies, Abilene Christian University, p. 83.

43. First published under the title "Identification of the Church of Christ" (*CMag* 1 [September 1848]: 267ff.), the sermon was expanded and republished under the title "The Beginning Corner; or, The Church of Christ Identified" (*ACR* 1 [August 1856]: 225–36), then republished again under its second title in *Biographical Sketch and Writings of Elder Benjamin Franklin*, ed. John F. Rowe and G. W. Rice (Cincinnati: G. W. Rice, 1880), pp. 206–28. The 1856 version, published in *ACR*, is the one used here.

44. Howard, "The Beginning Corner; or, The Church of Christ Identified," pp. 226–35.

45. Howard, "A Warning to the Religious Sects and Parties in Christendom," *Bible Advocate* 1 (January 1843): 82.

46. Arthur Crihfield, "Preface," *HD* 2 (January 1838): 5; and "To T. M. Henley," *HD* 1 (15 May 1837): 132.

47. Crihfield, *HD* 3 (January 1839): 15f; Thomas Henley, "Sectarianism, Catholicism, Asa Shinn, &c.," *HD* 1 (July 1837): 173–74; and G. A. Patterson, "Heaven," *HD* 2 (April 1838): 108.

48. See Campbell, "Various Notices," *MH*, n.s., 5 (August 1841): 384.

49. Campbell, "The Heretic *Detector*," *MH*, n.s., 1 (September 1837): 432; and "Essay on Heresy," *HD* 3 (October 1839): 241f.

50. Crihfield, "Coming of the Lord-No. III," *OP* 1 (February 1843): 25–31; and Campbell, "The Orthodox Preacher," *MH*, n.s., 7 (February 1843): 83.

51. Campbell, "Extra, No. 1," *MH* 1 (December 1837): 578, 587–88, 581.

52. Jeter, *Campbellism Examined*, pp. 340–41. For additional judgments regarding Campbell's change, see pp. 338–53, 357–58.

53. Campbell, "Any Christians among the Sects?" *MH*, n.s., 1 (December 1837): 564–65.

54. Letter from T. M. Allen to John Allen Gano, Boon Co., Missouri, dated 25 May 1840, in Gano papers, Center for Restoration Studies, Abilene Christian University.

55. Tolbert Fanning, "The Crisis," *CRev* 2 (October 1845): 10.

56. James L. Thornberry, "Conventions, Organizations, &c.," *GA* 20 (28 March 1878): 200.

57. Jacob Creath, Jr., "Old and New Things Contrasted," *GA* 19 (6 December 1877): 756.

58. David Lipscomb, "A. Campbell and the Societies," *GA* 26 (4 June 1884): 358.

59. Lipscomb, "A. Campbell and the Society," *GA* 26 (14 May 1884): 315; and "Solid Thoughts by Ernest Men," *GA* 26 (23 April 1884): 262.

60. Richardson in a letter to Philip S. Fall dated 24 August 1857, in Philip S. Fall Collection, microfilm in Center for Restoration Studies, Abilene Christian University; and Franklin, "Anniversaries of Our Societies in Cincinnati," *ACR* (November 1856): 346.

61. Campbell, "Any Christians among the Sects?" *MH*, n.s., 1 (December 1837): 561.

62. This was the wording in the first edition of Campbell's *Christian System*, which bore the title *Christianity Restored*, published in 1835. For clarification of this sentence, see Campbell, "Any Christians among the Sects?" *MH*, n.s., 1 (December 1837): 562.

63. Campbell, *Christian Baptism* (1851; reprint, Nashville: McQuiddy Printing, 1913), p. x.

3
THE LEGACY OF ALEXANDER CAMPBELL

In the previous chapter we saw how some of Campbell's followers failed to discern his ecumenical intentions, focused instead on the sectarian side of his agenda, and in that way laid the foundations for a new, identifiable denomination known as Churches of Christ.

In this chapter we will explore the contours of Churches of Christ as they emerged in the mid-nineteenth century, especially as we find those contours reflected in three of the most important leaders of that period: Tolbert Fanning, Moses Lard, and Benjamin Franklin. As editors of influential papers circulated widely throughout this communion, these three men not only helped to create an orthodoxy for Churches of Christ; they also reflected in their work a popular orthodoxy that was emerging all around them.

TOLBERT FANNING

From 1844 through 1874, Tolbert Fanning edited three highly influential publications that served Churches of Christ in the South. These included the *Christian Review* (1844–47), the *Gospel Advocate* (1855–61), and the *Religious Historian* (1872–74). Fanning also founded Franklin College, the first educational institution related to Churches of Christ in the South, and served that school as president from 1845 until just prior to the Civil War. These roles made Fanning perhaps the most powerful second-generation leader of Churches of Christ in the South.

Born in 1810, Fanning grew up in northern Alabama and received his earliest training in the Christian faith from preachers associated with the movement led by Barton W. Stone. Not surprisingly, he bore the influence of Stone in significant ways throughout his life, and we will explore that dimension of Fanning's work in the following chapter. In this chapter, we will confine our discussion to the ways in which Fanning embraced—and failed to embrace—the perspectives of Alexander Campbell.

Fanning came under the indirect influence of Alexander Campbell while still a young man. When he first met Campbell in the late 1820s or early 1830s, he was deeply impressed with what he saw and heard.[1] Then, in 1835 and 1836, Campbell invited Fanning to accompany him on two successive preaching tours. In the course of their travels together, Campbell doubtless exerted considerable influence over the thinking of this young man.

Like other early leaders in Churches of Christ, however, Fanning seemed essentially oblivious to the ecumenical dimensions of Campbell's thought. Instead, he focused his work throughout his career on two objectives: (1) explaining and defending the Church of Christ as the one true church outside of which there was no salvation, and (2) defending the Bible, read through Lockean and Baconian lenses, as the only legitimate source of religious truth and understanding. By defining these issues as he did, he contributed greatly to the major motifs that would shape Churches of Christ for the next 100 years and more.

Defining the True Church

Throughout his career Fanning confused the universal ideal of nondenominational Christianity with a specific religious movement of his own time and place called the Church of Christ. He systematically nurtured that confusion even in the midst of his travels with Alexander Campbell. In 1836, for example, Fanning and Campbell traveled to New England, and while in Boston, Fanning delivered an address that sheds substantial light on his early religious views. He virtually ignored in that speech the Campbellian theme of the unity of Christians, but revealed instead his own frustration with the extent of religious pluralism in the United States. Because so many people of his age believed that "if you are not pleased with one religion, select another," he described the nineteenth century "as the most remarkable era, for . . . aberrations from the truth, in the annals of time." Nonetheless, he assured his audience that there were still people in the United States who had rejected such nonsense out of hand and who had restored to the earth the original, apostolic faith. "Do my sectarian friends ask me for an example, now in the world, of apostolic order? In the United States, there are over a hundred thousand, mostly in the western country, who have taken the Bible, untrammelled by human philosophy and scholastic extravagances, and made a bold and solemn march for primitive ground and practices."[2]

Precisely the same concerns prompted Fanning to begin his first publication, the *Christian Review*, in 1844. He hoped the *Review* would enable him to explain to his contemporaries the beliefs and practices of the Church of Christ, which he felt was "woefully misrepresented" among the various sects and denominations. "Something for self-defense," he affirmed, "is absolutely required."[3] So Fanning published in the *Review* a lengthy series of articles that described the nature of the true church, its worship, its organization, and its requirements for admission. In their historical naivete these articles prefigured "The Beginning Corner," John R. Howard's classic sermon that we considered in the previous chapter.

"Historical naivete" is a key phrase, for unless we understand the meaning of that term in this context, we will altogether miss what Fanning sought to achieve in these articles. Simply put, Fanning believed that the Churches of Christ had remained immune from the corrupting influences of history, culture, and tradition. For this reason, he described Churches of Christ in negative rather than positive terms. The Church of Christ, he argued, was not a denomination, since it traced its roots to God, Christ, and the apostles, not to any ordinary human being in the course of ordinary human history. For that reason, the Church of Christ had no humanly devised creed, no theology that represented tinkering and fine-tuning on the part of human beings, and no human history, since it was, after all, a divine, not a human, institution. Fanning granted that all other churches originated in the course of a particular history and in the context of a particular culture. Lutherans, for example, originated in the sixteenth century in the context of the German Reformation and therefore continued to bear the marks of that particular history and culture. The Churches of Christ, in contrast, originated in Jerusalem under the preaching of the apostles, who in turn articulated an ideal imparted to them from the mind of God. This sense of historylessness was perhaps the most distinguishing characteristic of Tolbert Fanning's understanding of the Church of Christ, and partly because of the pervasive influence of his writings, it remained a distinguishing feature of Churches of Christ well into the twentieth century.

Baconian and Lockean Primitivism

The historical naivete that Fanning promoted did not result from his Christian primitivism per se. Rather, it grew from the *kind* of primitivism that he embraced, that is, a primitivism informed almost entirely by his understanding of two philosophical perspectives: Scottish Baconianism on the one hand and the philosophy of John Locke on the other. Moreover, Fanning virtually equated the two, claiming that "John Locke [was] the *real* author of the Baconian philosophy."[4]

From Locke, Fanning learned that the human mind is incapable of originating new and original ideas, since the mind is essentially a *tabula rasa* or a blank tablet on which ideas, originating from outside itself, stamp their content. For Fanning, this meant that the faithful Christian is content to receive on his or her mind the impress of divine revelation. David Lipscomb, editor of the *Gospel Advocate* after Fanning, recalled how Fanning "denied earnestly that man is possessed of any intuitive knowledge of God or of good and evil." Instead, Lipscomb said, Fanning believed that human beings were "wholly dependent upon teaching from external sources to determine what is right and what is wrong."[5] Since God conveyed His revelation in a book, Fanning believed that the truth contained in that book remained unchanged from one age to another. Any speculation or theologizing about divine revelation, therefore, was foolish and inevitably gave birth to corrupted human traditions.

From the Baconian tradition, Fanning learned to read the Bible as if it were a scientific text, gathering from the biblical text all the facts on any given subject before drawing final conclusions. Based on his understandings of Locke and Baconianism, therefore, Fanning believed that one undertook the project of restoring primitive Christianity first by allowing biblical facts to impress themselves on one's mind. If one rightfully gathered all the biblical facts and faithfully followed biblical instructions in precise detail, one could then claim—as Fanning did—that one had no theology but the Bible, no creed but the Bible, and no worship or organizational schemes other than those sanctioned by the biblical pattern. Indeed, if one followed all the Bible's instructions in precise detail, one would inevitably restore the ancient Church of Christ.

No one incident illustrates Fanning's philosophical presuppositions more faithfully than his quarrel in 1857 with Robert Richardson, Campbell's personal physician and colleague at Bethany College. In 1856 Richardson wrote a series of articles for the *Millennial Harbinger*, claiming that the rationalism of the Campbell movement had squelched authentic spirituality. He rebuked those in the movement who "glory in its [the Bible's] 'letter' [and] . . . rejoice in its facts," who regarded the Bible "as a system of external or outward communication, terminating upon the ordinary understanding." He thought those people had transformed the spiritual life into "a process of reasoning" or a "simple sequence of cause and effect, as in physical science." They failed to understand, he charged, that the "Divine word . . . addresses itself to our higher spiritual nature."

Richardson laid the blame for this problem squarely at the feet of Lockean thought, a philosophical perspective that many in the Campbell movement revered. At the same time, Richardson observed, those who most revered the Lockean perspective typically failed to recognize the extent to which that perspective shaped their thinking. For this reason, he argued, those most captivated by philosophical systems ironically claimed to reject those systems and to adhere to the Bible alone.[6]

Richardson's articles provided all the bait that was needed to draw Tolbert Fanning into print and to expose him as a prime example of the species of thinking Richardson had described. In the *Gospel Advocate*, Fanning rebuked Richardson for elevating the Spirit above the written biblical text. For Fanning's money, Richardson was an infidel who had embraced speculative and "*Transcendental philosophy*." "We declare our solemn conviction," he intoned, "that no one who respects the Bible can believe in any system of philosophy in existence." Nonetheless, he distinguished between "speculative philosophy" and Lockean epistemology: "John Locke [was] the *real* author of the Baconian philosophy and all correct thinking in England since his day."[7]

Fanning's articles provided Richardson with a concrete illustration of the kind of illusory thinking he had been describing in the *Harbinger* all along.

> If John Locke is the author of all correct thinking in England since his day, . . . he is . . . also the author of all correct thinking in America during the same interval. Surely, then, unless President F. thinks *in*correctly or *not at all*, it must be admitted that John Locke is the author of *his* thinking, and that he is, however *unconscious* of it, a philosopher of the School of Locke, or, what is usually termed A SENSUALISTIC DOGMATIST.

He concluded that Fanning was "an excellent representative of a considerable class who habitually inveigh against philosophy, yet are . . . its victims."[8]

Distressed at Richardson's accusations, Fanning sought to defend himself. But the more he erected his defenses, the more he confirmed Richardson's charges. He flatly denied that "our belief through the word is our system of philosophy." At the same time, what if he did rely on John Locke? he asked. After all, "John Locke denied all theories and speculations, and therefore was, strictly speaking, no philosopher."[9] Fanning imagined he occupied precisely that same ground.

Seeds for Division in the Campbell Movement

The Fanning-Richardson controversy would not be so important had it been only an academic, philosophical dispute, confined to its protagonists and with no further ramifications. As it turns out, however, this dispute not only sheds considerable light on the ahistorical outlook of Tolbert Fanning. It also sheds light on the ambiguity in the thought of Alexander Campbell and on the seeds for division in the Campbell movement that took root precisely in that ambiguity. Finally, it casts considerable light on the emergence within the Campbell movement of a separate tradition that increasingly claimed the designation "Church of Christ."

Richardson knew that Fanning represented a numerically significant faction within the Campbell movement. He hinted at this fact when he observed, if "one [who] is of some reputation for education and intelligence" could be as historically and philosophically naive as Fanning, "how much reason there is to fear that the genius of Locke holds its secret councils in the hearts of multitudes who are still less capable of detecting its presence!"[10] The truth is that by this date, there were already two ideological factions in the Campbell movement, one that drew its inspiration from the Alexander Campbell of the *Christian Baptist* period, and another that had followed Campbell into the more intentionally ecumenical course upon which he embarked in 1837.

The charges and countercharges that Fanning and Richardson leveled at each other bear this out. Richardson believed that Fanning and the thousands who shared his outlook, mainly in the South, had brought "reproach upon the cause of the present Reformation by their unbecoming love of controversy, and by the crude and erroneous exhibitions which they make of the real purposes of this religious movement."[11] At the same time, Richardson blamed Campbell and his *Christian Baptist* for the inspiration that guided the ahistorical primitivists farther South.

> The philosophy of Locke with which Bro. Campbell's mind was deeply imbued in youth has insiduously mingled itself with almost all the great points in the reformation and has been all the while like an iceberg in the way—chilling the heart and numbing the hands, and impeding all progress in the right direction.[12]

For Fanning's part—as we recall from the previous chapter—already in 1845 he had attacked Campbell for seeking to "court the smiles of corrupt denominations." We recall as well Fanning's conviction that Campbell in his later years had become "a child in the hands of his friends" who sought to change the course of the movement Campbell had founded. Fanning believed that Richardson was preeminent among those friends. For that reason, he publicly expressed his conviction that Richardson "is not of us," and that unless he changed his course, "we cannot anticipate a continuance of Christian harmony."[13]

The depth of the division emerging at that time became more obvious still when Campbell allowed himself to be drawn into the controversy. Strikingly, Campbell had difficulty deciding which of these two men to uphold. After all, they both represented authentic Campbellian impulses, one from the early period of his career and the other from the later. Campbell's involvement began when Fanning traveled to Bethany to seek Campbell's support in the controversy. Initially, Campbell acknowledged the legitimacy of Fanning's complaint and publicly scolded his old friend Richardson for "placing *faith* and *philosophy* in any real or formal antagonism."[14] Richardson thought Campbell's attacks on him were so severe and so unwarranted that after twenty-eight years of writing for the *Millennial Harbinger*, he resigned his connection with that paper. He even resigned his teaching position at Bethany College and accepted a post instead at the new Kentucky University.[15]

Inexplicably, however, following a journey to Kentucky in 1858, Campbell completely reversed himself. He wrote in the *Harbinger* that he thought Fanning's behavior "an outrage upon both editorial and Christian courtesy and upon the rules of church order and discipline."[16] If that were not enough, he wrote in a private letter to Fanning's brother-in-law, Philip S. Fall, in 1858,

> I have . . . ever since my late tour to Mississippi viewed Elder Fanning as intent on a war with us under some pretence or other. And I still must regard him as hostile to Bethany and indeed I know not why—or wherefore unless an unsanctified ambition lurks within him. He is a very vulnerable man, and ought not to expose himself. Unfortunately, however, such men cannot be dispossessed of that unclean spirit.[17]

Clearly, Campbell had spawned followers who sat at opposite sides of the table from one another at many critical points. Inevitably, Campbell stood at the center of their disputes, but precisely for that reason, he could do practically nothing to reconcile them. Ironically, the Fanning-Richardson episode suggests that the ecumenical movement launched by Alexander Campbell had now given birth to two new religious movements on the American scene—Disciples of Christ and Churches of Christ—though neither was yet recognized as a denomination, separate and distinct from the other.

BENJAMIN FRANKLIN

Shortly after Benjamin Franklin's death in 1878, David Lipscomb wrote that Franklin had "a larger number of readers than any man that has written in the effort to restore primitive Christianity." No wonder. Six of Franklin's roughly twenty-five debates saw the light of publication, as did two volumes of his sermons, one progressing through thirty-one editions and the other through nineteen. In addition, he edited or coedited four different journals that served Churches of Christ, the most important being the *American Christian Review*, which he edited for almost a quarter of a century, from 1856 until 1878.[18]

If Tolbert Fanning contributed to Churches of Christ a systematic defense of that tradition as the one true primitive and apostolic church, along with an historical naivete informed by Lockean and Baconian primitivism, Franklin's greatest contribution lay in the way he identified the ancient gospel and church with poverty, plainness, simplicity, and a democratic social order. Further, Franklin identified all these characteristics with the *Christian Baptist* and earnestly believed that the values of the *Christian Baptist* characterized Campbell throughout Campbell's life.

Clearly, Fanning also espoused poverty, simplicity, and plainness as the apostolic way. And Franklin routinely made exclusivist claims regarding the Churches of Christ and nurtured an historical naivete regarding the influence of history and culture on biblical faith. Both men shared all these characteristics. Still, it is safe to say that Franklin's greatest contribution to Churches of Christ lay in his identification of plainness and poverty with genuine Christian faith, with Alexander Campbell, and with the *Christian Baptist.*

Franklin and the *Christian Baptist*

Benjamin Franklin apparently never grasped the fact that Campbell had undergone a substantial reorientation in the mid-1830s. As late as 1856, he praised Campbell as the single man who had "made such a defense of Christianity against the assaults of Infidels, Romanists—such an effort to separate it from everything else, and preserve it in its purity, as no other man on earth has made in the last thousand years." Then, only months before Franklin's death in 1878, he pictured Campbell as a plain and simple man who never sought "the *prestige* of the great city" or climbed "on the *shoulders of rich men.*" Instead, from "the hills of Brooke County, Virginia . . . , then a place of no note, and comparative obscurity," Campbell issued a simple and straightforward publication, free from ostentation, intended only to "be read and understood." From that plain and simple platform Campbell "assailed the popular clergy" and "made issue on the principal men and movements of the country, claiming to be religious." This was precisely the kind of publication Franklin sought to produce throughout his editorial career. Of his *American Christian Review* Franklin declared in 1872, "If you want to 'undo what Alex Campbell did,' the REVIEW is not the paper for you. . . . [But] if you are for maintaining our distinctive plea and all the ground we have gained, the REVIEW is the paper you want."[19] From Franklin's perspective, the *Christian Baptist* always defined "what Alex Campbell did."

With his bias toward the *Christian Baptist*, Franklin found models in editors and preachers who also conformed their ministries to the principles of that publication. His biographers inform us that Franklin had especially high regard for Fanning's *Christian Review*. In addition, Franklin personally acknowledged his debt to Arthur Crihfield and published his very first article in Crihfield's *Heretic Detector*.[20]

He therefore launched his *American Christian Review* with a proclamation worthy of any of his mentors.

> [Our cause] is the cause of God, and if any man proves recreant to it, he will be destroyed. . . . Better were it for a man that he had never been born, than that he should trifle with this mightiest and greatest of all causes. Men may leave one human establishment and go to another, without affecting them much; but men who leave this cause, leave Christianity, the church of God, and the Head of the church; and all such men are ruined.[21]

Clearly, Fanning took his stand on the sectarian side of Campbell's *Christian Baptist* and never fathomed Campbell's ecumenical intent.

A Plain and Simple Gospel

The high value that Franklin placed on poverty, simplicity, and plainness must be understood against the backdrop of the region in which he lived. Franklin lived and worked in the North, especially Indiana and Ohio. That fact was crucial, especially in the years following the Civil War when postwar prosperity brought to that region an emphasis on economic progress, education, and culture. Franklin, however, never shared in those benefits. Because he felt estranged from these developments, he defined both himself and the church that he labored to promote in terms that stood in marked contrast to those more popular values.

Two incidents illustrate especially well this dimension of Franklin's life and career. The first took place when Franklin entered into a partnership with David Staats Burnet, a wealthy, influential Disciples leader in Cincinnati, to publish the *Christian Age*. That partnership was a mismatch from the beginning. In order to finance his share in this venture, Franklin sold his small farm in Milton, Indiana. Then, without sufficient funds to purchase a home in Cincinnati, he had to rely on Burnet's generosity for housing. Burnet first supplied a log house, then part of an unoccupied school building. Years later, Franklin's son Joseph recalled,

> The temporal surroundings of the two families were so different that free social intercourse was impossible. Mr. Franklin had always been poor, and had a large family to maintain. Their living was necessarily of the plainest kind. Mr. Burnet's family had always been accustomed to the social manners indulged in by wealthy people. . . . Mr. Franklin's family could not rise above a feeling that they were somehow subordinate and merely tributary to Mr. Burnet's splendid establishment.

The Franklins felt the disparity especially on Sunday mornings "when Mr. Burnet's family rolled off in a fine carriage to the city to worship, while they [the Franklins] went on foot to the village of Mt. Healthy, one mile in the opposite direction."[22]

Construction of a new church building for the Central Christian Church of Cincinnati, Ohio, in 1872 provides a second window into Franklin's sense that poverty and simplicity should characterize the Christian faith. Built to seat some 2,000 worshippers and erected in French Gothic style, this building was a radical departure from the plain sort of architecture that had generally characterized buildings serving the Disciples of Christ and Churches of Christ movement. With a nave some 34 feet wide, 125 feet long, and 103 feet high, this building housed an organ, a choir loft, and a stained-glass window that some thought the largest in the United States. When the building was dedicated, the pastor W. T. Moore preached on Jesus' words from the cross: "It is finished."[23] Benjamin Franklin lost no time in directing a scathing attack against Moore and the values this building represented.

To appreciate the significance of this episode, one must view it in the context of the much larger rift between conservative and progressive Protestants in the northern states during the Gilded Age. In the midst of the prosperity that increasingly characterized the North following the Civil War, many urban Protestant denominations moved upscale. They often constructed lavish buildings that alienated their rural, more traditional, and more impoverished constituents. Methodism provides perhaps the best single case study of this development. Estranged from developments in the mainstream of the Methodist Church and convinced that their protests fell on deaf ears in the Methodist establishment, many conservatives and traditionalists finally moved outside Methodism altogether and established separate Holiness denominations. In much the same way, Benjamin Franklin was scandalized by this new building of the Central Christian Church, which, he claimed, was a satire on the spirit of the Christian faith.

This building, with its "fine effect of light, warmed and tinted as it passes through the stained windows," Franklin complained, ran completely contrary to the "ancient order" that Campbell's followers, he felt, had always prized. Further, Moore's sermon was a satire on "that forsaken book, the 'Christian Baptist.' " Franklin recalled that when the Episcopalians of Cincinnati built a building for $100,000, "we talked of it as an example of extravagance beyond all endurance." And now this. The new building of the Christian church, he affirmed, would alienate even the Lord Himself, who "is not attracted by imposing temples, worldly show, nor fine entertainments."[24]

Franklin's attack brought down on his head the full wrath of the pastor who lambasted Franklin for the poor breeding that Moore thought his dogmatism and grammar reflected. "Your last reply," Moore wrote, "is a curious combination of ugly epithets, irrelevant matter, evasion of the real issue, uncharitable insinuations, bad grammar, and worse rhetoric."[25] In the aftermath of the Central Christian Church affair, young progressives increasingly dismissed Franklin as an "old fogey," "a legalist," and "an alarmist."[26]

Perhaps no single critique of Franklin sheds more light on the growing rift between the progressives and the primitivists within the Campbell movement than an article published in the *American Christian Review* over the name "Carl Crabb." It may well be that Franklin wrote this article himself in order to satirize the progressives. In any event, it stands as telling testimony to the dynamics overtaking the Campbell movement. Crabb explained that he intended the title of his article, "Franklinian Stupidity," to describe both Franklin and "a large class of the brotherhood, of whom the editor of the REVIEW is almost a perfect specimen." Attacking the *Christian Baptist* tradition head-on, Crabb affirmed that Franklin and those who shared his outlook seemed "wholly incapable of appreciating anything that rises above the first plain, plodding ideas of Bro. Campbell and his co-laborers forty years ago." Then Crabb asked, "Who can not see the difference between this 'cramped, cribbed and confined' discipleship and that more liberal theology now advocated by our more advanced scribes?" He therefore called for "a renunciation of the old paths of stupidity, and the adoption of . . . practices more in accord with the spirit of the times."[27]

Perhaps nowhere does one find Franklin's emphasis on plainness and simplicity more graphically portrayed than in his sermons. In one particular sermon, tellingly entitled "The Simplicity of the Divine Economy," Franklin contrasted fashionable clerics and churches with the plainness of the ancient order as he understood it.

> The idea of a modern great man is to get rid of the Jerusalem Church, as a model, and get Spurgeon or Beecher in view; mass the Lord's people, build a great temple; imitating Paganism more than Christianity. . . . [But] the plain and unassuming congregations of the Lord, with their humble overseers and deacons . . . does [*sic*] not suit the ambition of those who are, or would be, promoted to great popularity, distinction and power.[28]

From this perspective, Franklin argued in 1870 that a division in the Campbell movement had been in process for "fifteen years or more." The opposing sides, he thought, were "entirely alien to each other [and] at war,"[29] a rupture Franklin traced to fundamental differences in the Campbell movement regarding wealth, poverty, and the simplicity of the ancient church.

Franklin's Critique of an Educated Ministry

In part because of the long shadow Franklin cast over certain segments of Churches of Christ for years to come, it is important to take account of his rejection of an educated ministry. Simply put, he feared that he and his kind would be rendered irrelevant by younger, more educated men. That fear became apparent when he returned from the Ohio State Missionary Society meeting in 1863. He had heard some at that meeting argue that preachers in the movement should equip themselves with a better education. In particular, Franklin reported, they should "be versed in history, chronology and other extended fields of knowledge, or attain to some certain degree in the languages, or even English literature, before they can be accredited preachers of the gospel of Christ." Franklin was incensed. "We have no patience with this mere butterfly twaddle, toploftical, aircastle, highfalutin and empty thing," he declared. Then, in a sarcastic defense of the Bible and the *Christian Baptist*, he complained,

> We are a long way ahead of these old books, read and admired by old fogies. These were good books in their time, and plain, old-fashioned men did their work in their day; but we are philosophers, geologists, astronomers, historians and reasoners, not going by the *Word*, but *general principles*; not confined to the *letter of Scripture*, but the *spirit*.[30]

Franklin's rejection of educated ministers also reflects his fear that country preachers would soon be displaced by urban dandies. "Aged men . . . are now sneered at as 'common,' 'old fashioned,' 'fogies,' that may do to speak 'in the country,' but not in towns and cities!" he complained. But if Churches of Christ had any hope of keeping alive their vision of primitive Christianity, it would be a mistake to "confine our labors to cities, towns, and villages." Instead, "we must go out into the country among the people, and be one of them."[31]

Franklin's rejection of educated ministers translated itself into a generalized suspicion of colleges that included in their curricula the training of preachers. It was as foolish to suppose that one might train preachers in a theological school, he thought, as it was to think that one could teach "plowing, planting, sowing, reaping, threshing, &c., . . . in an agricultural school." The only way to train younger men, he argued, was to "go out into the field and work" with them "and show them . . . how the work was done."[32] Franklin's suspicion of ministerial education was important not just for the light it sheds on a sizable population within the Campbell movement in the mid-nineteenth century but also because Franklin fathered a tradition of antagonism toward church-related higher education, a tradition that would be taken up by his protégé, Daniel Sommer, who led a minority protest against colleges established by Churches of Christ later in the century. But that is a story we shall tell in chapter 5.

MOSES LARD

If Tolbert Fanning symbolized the growing preoccupation of Churches of Christ with the question of the one true church, sustained by the conviction that the Church of Christ had no roots in human history or tradition; and if Benjamin Franklin tied the identity of the true church to poverty, plainness, and simplicity; Moses Lard grounded the theology of Churches of Christ in an impenetrable defense of rationality. In doing this Lard both reflected and honed to razor-sharp precision the rationality that had characterized this movement from its beginning.[33] Further, like Fanning and Franklin, Lard disseminated his ideas through a widely circulated journal entitled simply *Lard's Quarterly*, which he published from 1863 to 1868.

Jeremiah Jeter, one of Campbell's most biting critics, provided an early occasion for Lard to develop his rational framework. In his 1855 book entitled *Campbellism Examined*, Jeter hammered on two of the claims that had characterized the Campbell tradition: the notion that there were no Christians outside the Church of Christ, and the notion that Churches of Christ simply took the Bible at face value, apart from any human interpretation.

Alexander Campbell invited Moses Lard, a graduate of Bethany College, to respond to Jeter on Campbell's behalf. Although Lard published a volume specifically designed to defend the Campbell movement against Jeter's attacks,[34] he returned to the issues Jeter had raised again and again for the duration of his career.

Lard denied Jeter's charge that Campbell thought his movement the one true church outside of which there were no Christians. "Mr. Campbell does not claim for himself and his brethren that they, as a body, exhaust the meaning of the term *the church*," Lard objected. Yet, demonstrating his own failure to comprehend Campbell's ecumenical intent, Lard quickly added, "So far as the body of Christ has on earth *a denominational* existence, they are that body."[35]

It was Jeter's other charge, however, that Lard had to take most seriously. When Jeter ridiculed the notion that Churches of Christ took the Bible at face value, without any human interpretation, he struck a potentially devastating blow at the very heart of the theological system that increasingly defined Churches of Christ. To this charge, therefore, Lard would respond time and again over the coming years.

In 1863 Lard published in *Lard's Quarterly*, a classic statement of the rational structures characteristic of Churches of Christ. He entitled the article "The Reformation for Which We Are Pleading—What Is It?" Informed by the Baconian notion that all human beings can understand a given phenomenon precisely as it is, without differences of interpretation, Lard stated the philosophical starting point for Churches of Christ: "The Bible, then, being assumed true, we hold that its contents may be so apprehended that the mind has . . . the highest possible assurance that its knowledge is correct." With that assumption nailed down, Lard then explained what he thought Churches of Christ were all about.

The reformation for which we are pleading consists 1st. *In accepting the exact meaning of Holy Writ as our religious theory.* . . . 2d *In the minute conformity of our practice to the revealed will of Christ.* . . . Hence all practices having their origin in tradition, human reason, or expediency, are utterly eschewed. . . . Thus it is proposed continually to construct the body of Christ after the Divine model.[36]

A few months later in another key article, Lard used the Baconian underpinnings of Churches of Christ to assess the legitimacy of other professed Christians. Once again he started from the premise that all Christians can see the Bible alike. He thought it "a humiliating fact . . . they *will* not . . . , [and] a grand lie that they cannot." Then, in a single, masterful stroke, he used that Baconian presupposition to undergird the exclusivism increasingly characteristic of Churches of Christ: "If a man knowingly holds one false doctrine, or one which with reasonable effort he might know to be false . . . , it is simply certain that he cannot be saved if he remains in this condition."

At the same time Lard contended that Churches of Christ had conformed *their* doctrine and practice precisely to biblical teaching. "Have we introduced into the church any foreign element or doctrine unsanctioned by the Bible?" Lard asked. If so, "forty years watching and labor upon the part of our opponents who have lacked neither ability nor industry, have been wholly insufficient . . . to detect that element." Because "we accept as the matter of our faith precisely and only what the Bible teaches, rejecting everything else," Lard concluded that Churches of Christ had conformed themselves precisely to the model of the ancient, apostolic church.[37]

Of all the "elements" of biblical teaching, none took a more honored place among Churches of Christ than the requirement of adult immersion for entry into the church and for forgiveness of sins. This had been true since 1828 when Alexander Campbell, after vacillating on that question for several years, finally affirmed unequivocally that immersion was essential to the remission of sins. That doctrine quickly became the proverbial line in the sand that Churches of Christ drew between themselves and other Christian traditions, and no one drew that line more deeply or with more precision than did Moses Lard. "I mean to say distinctly and emphatically," Lard wrote,

that Martin Luther, if not immersed, was not a Christian. . . . If a man can be a Christian without immersion, let the fact be shown. I deny both. Immovably I stand here. But I shall be told that this is Phariseeism, that it is exclusivism. Be it so; if it be true . . . then am I so far the defendant of Phariseeism and exclusivism. . . . I recognize no human being a Christian who is not immersed.[38]

Finally, Lard was responsible for making explicit a method of biblical interpretation that had been at work among Churches of Christ for many years, in spite of his denial that Churches of Christ interpreted the Bible. Lard argued that a biblical doctrine or practice could be established "by being actually asserted [in the biblical text]" or "by being necessarily implied."[39] Members of Churches of Christ had long assumed that a doctrine or requirement could be "asserted" in the biblical text by either an explicit command or a clear example. Lard now contended that they could also discern biblical requirements by paying special regard to what the text "necessarily implied," that is, to necessary inferences. This threefold hermeneutic—command, example, and necessary inference—has characterized Churches of Christ since the days of Lard, becoming orthodoxy especially in the twentieth century.[40]

MISSIONARY SOCIETIES AND INSTRUMENTAL MUSIC

When Benjamin Franklin wrote in 1870 that the Campbell movement was dividing between those who had been seduced by the spirit of the Gilded Age and those who maintained their commitment to the simplicity of the apostolic faith, he noted that the issues in which the two factions "manifest themselves . . . are not the *cause*, but only the *occasion* for manifestation."[41] He was making the point that the issues over which the two factions fought had not caused the division but were symptoms of much deeper issues. And he was right.

On the surface, the two most prominent issues over which the emerging Churches of Christ and the emerging Disciples of Christ did battle were missionary societies and the use of instrumental music in the worship. But we must ask about the more fundamental concerns that these two issues symbolized.

The society issue predated the music controversy by at least thirty years and grew especially from the teachings of Alexander Campbell. With his strong democratic bias, Campbell had opposed missionary societies in the days of the *Christian Baptist*, claiming they supplanted the integrity of the local congregation. By 1849, however, he had changed his tune and in that year became president of the American Christian Missionary Society, a development we noted in chapter 2.

We can discern in the writings of many mid-nineteenth-century leaders of Churches of Christ the significance of the missionary society issue during that period, but perhaps nowhere can we detect that significance more clearly than in the thought of Tolbert Fanning and Benjamin Franklin. Fanning opposed the societies for several reasons. First, as far as he was concerned, his rejection of these organizations grew purely and simply from his fidelity to the biblical text. Yet, as Robert Richardson explained, Fanning's allegiance was not only to the biblical text but also to the principles of Baconianism and Lockean epistemology. Since Fanning thus felt that the Bible was the only source of information available to human beings regarding the will of God, he sought to structure both his own life and that of the church according to strict biblical principles. Speculation on the biblical text, he felt, would lead inevitably to human inventions such as missionary societies.

Second, one cannot understand Fanning's opposition to missionary societies apart from his deeply held democratic biases in favor of "the people." Indeed,

Fanning supported the societies so long as he saw their purpose as one of consultation and support, but when he finally thought he saw in the leadership of the societies an effort to control the local churches, he turned against them.

This change in attitude should likely be seen in light of a development in Fanning's own home church in Nashville. For many years congregations of the Church of Christ in Nashville had employed no full-time preachers, using instead a system of mutual ministry. In 1846, however, Fanning's congregation hired as its minister Jesse B. Ferguson, a suave and fashionable man with a commanding pulpit presence. In due time Ferguson split the congregation with his claims of spiritualism.[42] Because Fanning turned against the societies precisely during this period, we might well conclude that he saw both located preachers and missionary societies as threats to the self-determination of the local congregation.

Third, Fanning opposed societies because of his extraordinarily high view of the church. He believed that one could not place the Church of Christ in the same league with any human organization, and that the Church of Christ was in fact the kingdom of God that would one day triumph over all the earth. As he grew older, therefore, he increasingly devoted his exclusive allegiance to the church and found it difficult to support any organization that competed with this divine organization. One can discern that commitment not only in Fanning's opposition to missionary societies but also in his opposition to organizations devoted to promoting the public good. Temperance societies were a case in point. He granted that temperance societies "have had a good influence in the world." At the same time he declared his intention "to advocate temperance from my Divine commission," not from a human platform. "If I plead temperance from human authority," he explained, "I own I have not confidence in God's plan to reform the world."[43] His commitment to the church as the ultimate kingdom of God, which should preclude allegiance to human organizations, however, grew not from Fanning's association with Alexander Campbell but from his connection to another powerful tradition at work within Churches of Christ, a tradition shaped chiefly by Barton W. Stone. We will examine that tradition in detail in the next chapter.

As with Fanning, Benjamin Franklin's opposition to missionary societies also reflected his democratic bias, though his opposition began in earnest only in 1867, the year Alexander Campbell died. Beginning in that year, it became apparent to Franklin that younger men would now turn the course of the Campbell movement in directions quite different from those charted by Campbell's *Christian Baptist*. In fact, a group of progressives launched that very year the *Christian Standard*, a journal intended to undermine the influence of Franklin's *American Christian Review*. Franklin quickly realized that the only way to preserve the simplicity of the ancient church was to keep control of the movement in the hands of local congregations, thereby preventing young, power-hungry progressives from subverting the cause to which he had given his life.

Franklin made all this clear when he wrote,

> No matter how good the men, how honest, nor how pure their purposes—their work in any kind of aggregation, or confederation, of congregations, will result in taking away the rights and liberties of the people; oppressing and enslaving them, on the one hand, and building a clerical aristocracy, who will tax the people and rule them with a rod of iron, on the other hand.

If the Church of Christ hoped to avoid such a disaster, he wrote, there was "but one remedy, and that is to follow the model found in the first church, and admit no other form or church government and management."[44] To Franklin, this policy entailed rejection of missionary societies that threatened the integrity of the local church.

The dispute over instrumental music came relatively late to the Campbell movement, but when it erupted, it did so with sound and fury and perhaps did more than any other single factor to bring to a head the division that had been festering in the movement for many years. We can best discern the dynamics of that issue in the thought of Benjamin Franklin, especially since it was he who helped trigger the dispute in 1860.

In that year Franklin responded to some of his readers who had pressed him for his opinion of the use of instrumental music in worship. His answer perhaps says more about his commitment to plainness and simplicity and his suspicion of social elites than it does about instrumental music per se. Instruments in worship might be alright, he wrote, "if a church only intends being a *fashionable* society [or] a mere place of amusement and secular entertainment." He categorized those who agitated for the instrument as "*refined* gentlemen" with "*refined ears* [who] enjoy fine music manufactured for French theatres, interspersed with *short* prayers and *very short* sermons."[45]

That article helped ignite the fuse of the instrumental music debate when L. L. Pinkerton, the preacher for a Campbell-oriented congregation in Midway, Kentucky, complained that Franklin had aimed his article at him, especially since his church was the only one in Kentucky that "has yet made a decided effort to introduce" the instrument. Further, with an eye for the facts of the matter, Pinkerton discerned in Franklin's article a commitment not just to a cappella music but to a simplicity and plainness that Pinkerton associated with crude and lower-class rustics. When all was said and done, the debate between Franklin and Pinkerton was not over music but over social class. One sees this clearly in Pinkerton's response to Franklin.

> If your article on church music reflects the notions of the Reformation as to what constitutes Christian courtesy, manly literature, logic, rhetoric, religion; nay, if any considerable portion of the Reformation can even tolerate such coarse fulminations, then the sooner it is extinct the better. I am ready and willing to discuss the subject of instrumental music in churches with any man who can discriminate between railing in bad grammar and Christian argumentation.[46]

Though the origins of the instrumental music debate appear to lie in a struggle over social class, opponents of the instrument lost no time in defending their position with appeals to the primitive church and the biblical text. Again, Franklin is a case in point. In 1870 he complained, "There is not a man anywhere who claims any [biblical] authority for the new element [the instrument]. . . . The worship in all its parts . . . is a matter of *revelation—divinely prescribed.* Nothing is acceptable worship, only that which the Lord ordained."[47]

Slowly but surely, the dispute over instrumental music broke out in congregation after congregation all over the country. By the dawn of the twentieth century, there was scarcely a local church that had escaped the ravaging effects of this controversy and scarcely a congregation that had escaped the consequent division. By the early twentieth century it became apparent even to the director of the federal religious census that a major rupture had taken place in the religious movement hitherto listed simply as "Disciples of Christ." In 1906 the first federal religious census listed "Churches of Christ" as a new denomination whose most visible characteristic was their adamant refusal to use instrumental music in their worship.

CONCLUSIONS

By the middle of the nineteenth century, Churches of Christ were emerging as a sect in their own right. Increasingly, they stood distinct from the more progressive Disciples of Christ, exhibited little if any interest in Campbell's ecumenical agenda, and defined themselves almost exclusively in terms of the restoration of the ancient order.

Their preoccupation with the primitive church, however, was sustained by a number of other themes that we easily discern in the writings of some of the major editors who served this people during that period, especially Tolbert Fanning, Benjamin Franklin, and Moses Lard. Among those themes, several were particularly important: a commitment to the common people and a rejection of wealth and status; a commitment to democratic governance of the churches and a rejection of the controlling power of elites; a highly rational worldview shaped by both John Locke and Scottish Common Sense Realism; an all-pervading naivete regarding the power of history and culture; and a radically sectarian perspective by virtue of which they commonly claimed that the Church of Christ to which they belonged was the one true church apart from which there could be no salvation.

If Fanning, Franklin, and Lard helped to flesh out these themes and give them substance, it is important to realize that the themes they discussed were ideas and commitments that were rapidly growing among a people that called themselves the "Church of Christ." Indeed, there were many other editors and preachers who voiced the same notions that Fanning, Franklin, and Lard articulated. But these three men voiced these themes so well in the papers they edited that they helped create from the ideas at work in this tradition an orthodoxy that would endure for many generations.

Finally, these were the themes—especially when juxtaposed against the progressive ecumenism of the mature Alexander Campbell and his followers—that helped to divide this movement into Disciples of Christ and Churches of Christ. The career of Benjamin Franklin especially illumines this development, for Franklin's writings reveal a veritable chasm opening up between those who celebrated the Gilded Age in their religious faith and those who sought to maintain what they viewed as the essential plainness and simplicity of the old Jerusalem gospel.

So far we have explored in depth only one major stream that fed into the emerging Churches of Christ, namely, the heritage of Alexander Campbell. The other stream that flowed into Churches of Christ with equal force and power was that defined mainly by Barton W. Stone. This is the story we must assess in the following chapter.

NOTES

1. James R. Wilburn, *The Hazard of the Die: Tolbert Fanning and the Restoration Movement* (1969; reprint, Malibu: Pepperdine University Press, 1980), pp. 26–30.

2. Tolbert Fanning, "Discourse, Delivered in Boston, July 17, 1836" (Boston, 1836), pp. 18–19 and 24–25. This lecture was published at the request of the Boston Unitarians.

3. Fanning, "The Christian Review," *CRev* 1 (January 1844): 1.

4. Fanning, "Metaphysical Discussions–No. 4," *GA* 3 (January 1857): 3–4.

5. David Lipscomb, "Tolbert Fanning's Teaching and Influence," in James E. Scobey, ed., *Franklin College and Its Influences* (1906; reprint, Nashville: Gospel Advocate, 1954), pp. 13–14.

6. Robert Richardson, "Misinterpretations of Scripture–No. 1," *MH*, 4th ser., 6 (September 1856): 505–7. The story of the Richardson-Fanning exchange is told in more detail than can be given here by Cloyd Goodnight and Dwight E. Stevenson in *Home to Bethphage: A Biography of Robert Richardson* (St. Louis: Christian Board of Publication, 1949), pp. 168–87.

7. Fanning, "Metaphysical Discussion–No. 2," *GA* 2 (November 1856): 326–27; "Metaphysical Discussions–No. 1," *GA* 2 (October 1856): 314; and "Metaphysical Discussions–No. 4," *GA* 3 (January 1857): 3–4.

8. Richardson, "Faith versus Philosophy–No. 4," *MH*, 4th ser., 7 (May 1857): 273–75.

9. Fanning, "Professor R. Richardson's Second Notice of the Gospel Advocate," *GA* 3 (July 1857): 204–5; and "Professor Richardson's Notice of the Senior Editor of the Gospel Advocate," *GA* 3 (June 1857): 189.

10. Richardson, "Faith versus Philosophy–No. 5," *MH*, 4th ser., 7 (June 1857): 328.

11. Richardson, "Faith versus Philosophy–No. 4," p. 274.

12. Richardson, in a letter to Isaac Errett dated 16 July 1857, quoted by Cloyd Goodnight in "The Life of Dr. Robert Richardson," an unfinished manuscript containing a transcript of Richardson's private papers from the Fannie R. Thompson Collection, Bethany College Library.

13. Fanning, "Professor R. Richardson's Second Notice of the Gospel Advocate," p. 204; and "Professor Richardson's Notice of the Senior Editor of the Gospel Advocate," p. 191.

14. Alexander Campbell, "Christianity the True Philosophy," *MH*, 4th ser., 7 (September 1857): 481.

15. Richardson, "Faith versus Philosophy–No. 9," *MH*, 4th ser., 7 (December 1857): 703; and Richardson, in a letter to Philip S. Fall dated 15 December 1858, in Philip S. Fall Letters, copy in Center for Restoration Studies, Abilene Christian University.

16. Campbell, "President Fanning," *MH*, 5th ser., 1 (June 1858): 353.

17. Campbell, in a letter to Philip S. Fall dated 4 January 1860, in Philip S. Fall Letters, copy in Center for Restoration Studies, Abilene Christian University.

18. Lipscomb, "Benjamin Franklin," *GA* 20 (5 December 1878): 758–59. For a catalog of Franklin's published debates, see *An Author Catalog of Disciples of Christ and Related Religious Groups*, comp. Claude E. Spencer (Canton, MO: Disciples of Christ Historical Society, 1946), pp. 113–14. His sermon books were *The Gospel Preacher: A Book of Twenty Sermons* (Cincinnati: Franklin & Rice, 1869) and *The Gospel Preacher: A Book of Twenty-one Sermons* (Cincinnati: Franklin & Rice, 1877). The journals included the *Reformer* and the *Western Reformer* (1843–49), the *Proclamation and Reformer* (1850–51), the *Christian Age* (1850–53), and the *American Christian Review* (1856–78).

Benjamin Franklin's several biographies include *Biographical Sketch and Writings of Elder Benjamin Franklin*, ed. J. F. Rowe and G. W. Rice (Cincinnati: G. W. Rice, 1880); Joseph Franklin and J. A. Headington, *The Life and Times of Benjamin Franklin* (St. Louis: Christian Publishing, 1879); Otis L. Castleberry, *They Heard Him Gladly: A Critical Study of Benjamin Franklin's Preaching* (Rosemead, CA: Old Paths Publishing, 1963); and Earl I. West, *Elder Ben Franklin: Eye of the Storm* (Indianapolis: Religious Book Service, 1983).

19. Franklin, "Anniversaries of Our Societies in Cincinnati," *ACR* (November 1856): 346; "Introduction," *ACR* 21 (1 January 1878): 4; and "The A. C. Review," *ACR* 15 (16 April 1872): 124.

20. Franklin and Headington, *The Life and Times of Benjamin Franklin*, pp. 63, 267; and Franklin, "Still Going Ahead," *Proclamation and Reformer* 1 (February 1850): 105–6. Franklin's first published article was "A Discourse to the Unconverted," *HD* (April–June 1837): 132–35.

21. Franklin, "Introductory Address," *ACR* 1 (January 1856): 3–4.

22. Franklin and Headington, *The Life and Times of Benjamin Franklin*, pp. 193–94.

23. See "Opening of the Central Christian Church," *ACR* 15 (20 February 1872): 61; and W. T. Moore, "Dedication of the Central Christian Church," *ACR* 15 (20 February 1872): 57.

24. Franklin, "Central Christian Church," *ACR* 15 (20 February 1872): 60.

25. Moore, "The Central Church Once More," *ACR* 15 (16 April 1872): 122; and "Central Christian Church," *ACR* 15 (26 March 1872): 101.

26. See West, *Elder Ben Franklin*, p. 222; and *Biographical Sketch and Writings of Elder Benjamin Franklin*, p. 43.

27. Carl Crabb, "Franklinian Stupidity," *ACR* 15 (2 April 1872): 105.

28. Franklin, "Sermon No. XXI, Theme—The Simplicity of the Divine Economy," in *The Gospel Preacher*, 2:488ff., 500–502.

29. Franklin, "What Is Sectarianism?" *MH* 41 (January 1870): 356.

30. Franklin, "Ohio State Missionary Meeting," *ACR* 6 (23 June 1863): 98.

31. Franklin, "Labors in the Gospel," *ACR*, 1st ser., 1 (January 1856): 7; and "Evangelizing," *ACR*, 1st ser., 1 (February 1856): 55–56.

32. Franklin, "Do We Need a Theological School?" *MH* 36 (August 1865): 367.

33. On Lard, see Kenneth L. Van Deusen, *Moses Lard: That Prince of Preachers* (Joplin, MO: College Press Publishing, 1987).

34. Moses Lard, *A Review of Rev. J. B. Jeter's Book Entitled "Campbellism Examined"* (Philadelphia: n.p., 1857).

35. Lard, *A Review of Rev. J. B. Jeter's Book*, pp. 31–32.

36. Lard, "The Reformation for Which We Are Pleading—What Is It?" *LQ* 1 (September 1863): 14, 22.

37. Lard, "Have We Not Become a Sect?" *LQ* 1 (March 1864): 246, 248–49, 253, 255, 258, and 259.

38. Lard, "Do the Unimmersed Commune?" *LQ* 1 (September 1863): 44, 49.

39. Lard, "Do the Holy Scriptures Authorize the Baptism of Infants?" *LQ* 1 (December 1863): 158.

40. On the development of the threefold hermeneutic, see Michael Casey, "The Development of Necessary Inference in the Hermeneutic of the Disciples of Christ/Churches of Christ" (Ph.D. diss., University of Pittsburgh, 1986); "The Origin of the Hermeneutics of the Churches of Christ, Part One: The Reformed Tradition," *RQ* 31 (1989): 75–91; and "The Origins of the Hermeneutics of the Churches of Christ, Part Two: The Philosophical Background," *RQ* 31 (1989): 193–206. See also Russ Dudrey, "Restorationist Hermeneutics among the Churches of Christ: Why Are We at an Impasse?" *RQ* 30 (1988): 34. For background to the command-example-inference formula, see Thomas H. Olbricht, *Hearing God's Voice: My Life with Scripture in the Churches of Christ* (Abilene, TX: ACU Press, 1996), pp. 122–27.

41. Franklin, "What Is Sectarianism?" *MH* 41 (January 1870): 356.

42. On the Jesse B. Ferguson affair, see Johnny Tucker, *Like a Meteor across the Horizon* (Fayetteville, TN: Tucker Publications, 1978).

43. Fanning, "Temperance and Temperance Societies," *CRev* 2 (March 1845): 49–50.

44. Franklin, "Sermon No. XXI, Theme—the Simplicity of the Divine Economy," p. 495.

45. Franklin, "Instrumental Music in Churches," *ACR* 3 (31 January 1860): 18.

46. L. L. Pinkerton, "Instrumental Music in Churches," *ACR* 3 (28 February 1860): 18.

47. Franklin, "Explanatory to Brother Franklin," *ACR* 13 (24 May 1870): 164.

4
THE RISE AND FALL OF THE APOCALYPTIC TRADITION AMONG CHURCHES OF CHRIST

In addition to Alexander Campbell and the heritage of the *Christian Baptist*, anyone seeking to understand Churches of Christ must also understand the apocalyptic heritage of this tradition. Two men were chiefly responsible for making this worldview such a prominent fixture on the intellectual landscape of Churches of Christ for the duration of the nineteenth century. Those two were Barton W. Stone, a contemporary of Alexander Campbell and the person who effectively gave birth to this outlook among Churches of Christ, and David Lipscomb, the most important single leader in this tradition during the second half of the nineteenth century. By the late nineteenth century, however, the apocalyptic orientation was unraveling, and during the World War I era, key leaders of Churches of Christ found the apocalyptic worldview a serious liability. They therefore launched a concerted campaign to drive that viewpoint from their ranks. We will explore all these developments in this chapter.

Before proceeding, we must briefly clarify what the apocalyptic perspective meant for Stone, Lipscomb, and their followers. Simply put, these two men and the thousands among southern Churches of Christ who shared this outlook lived *as if* the kingdom of God—that is, the anticipated, final rule of God over all the earth—were a reality in the here and now.

This commitment imparted to their lives two definable dimensions. First, they were profoundly pessimistic regarding the ability of human beings to bring any lasting good to this world. Because they believed that God alone could banish evil and transform the earth into a scene of peace, justice, and righteousness, they typically held themselves aloof from human schemes designed to accomplish these objectives. They rejected the claim, often heard among some of the followers of Alexander Campbell, that the church embodied the fullness of the kingdom of God. The church, in their view, did offer a glimpse of the kingdom, and for this reason, they sought to promote the values of the kingdom of God in and through the church.

Second, Stone, Lipscomb, and their followers were primitivists, to be sure, but they looked to the primitive church especially for models of kingdom ethics and righteous living. Accordingly, they typically rejected wealth and fashionable living, freed their slaves, renounced violence, embraced pacifism, refused to serve in political office, often refused even to vote, and generally separated themselves from the values of greed and materialism that characterized the culture in which they lived. Clearly, then, the substance of the apocalyptic perspective was ethical in nature and had everything to do with the question, "How should we therefore live?"

This does not mean that those who embraced this perspective were unconcerned with structural models of the ancient church. In fact, as Alexander Campbell, beginning in 1823, increasingly came to dominate the Stoneite tradition, these people grew more and more concerned with questions of ecclesiastical form and structure. This was true even for an apocalyptic thinker like David Lipscomb, and by the dawn of the twentieth century, questions of the form and structure of the ancient church increasingly crowded out the apocalyptic orientation that had defined the Stone-Lipscomb tradition for so many years.

Finally, we must emphasize again—as we did in the introductory chapter—that apocalypticism, as we use that term here, does not necessarily involve premillennial theories regarding the time and manner of the second coming of Jesus. It is true that Stone, Lipscomb, and many—though not all—of their followers did believe that the second coming of Jesus would inaugurate the universal rule of God over all the earth, and to that extent, they were premillennial in their outlook. But the reader will badly misread this tradition if he or she equates the apocalyptic worldview of the Stone-Lipscomb tradition with premillennial theories regarding the end of the world. Stone, Lipscomb, and most who looked to them for leadership were far more interested in an apocalyptic lifestyle than they were in speculation regarding how and when the millennium would occur. If we hope to understand this tradition, we must keep this distinction clearly in mind.

BARTON W. STONE

Throughout his life Barton W. Stone possessed the same keen interest in nondenominational Christianity that Alexander Campbell did, but he came to that interest by a very different route. Stone's deepest roots were sunk not in the soil of Enlightenment rationalism as with Campbell, but in the soil of American revivalism. He benefited profoundly from the spirit of the Great Awakening that swept through the American colonies in the 1730s and early 1740s, then became a major participant in the Second Great Awakening of the early nineteenth century.

When only eighteen years old, Stone came under the influence of the revival spirit when, in 1790, he enrolled in David Caldwell's "log college" in North Carolina. Caldwell had imbibed the revival spirit at Princeton, where he graduated in 1761, then established his own "log college" in North Carolina, where he promoted revivals in the South. In 1791 Stone was converted to the Christian faith in a revival led by one of Caldwell's students, William Hodge. Five years later, in 1796, Stone received his preaching license from the Orange Presbytery of North Carolina. Significantly, the man who addressed the candidates for license that day was Henry Patillo, a student of Samuel Davies, who arguably was the most influential revivalist in the American South in the years following the Great Awakening.

Stone's revivalist roots sparked an interest in nondenominational Christianity that remained with him throughout his life. This should not be surprising, since nondenominational Christianity belonged to the very essence of revivalism, which regularly played down denominational distinctions and focused instead on the one theme that all Christians share in common: the love of God for sinners.

George Whitefield, the driving force behind the Great Awakening of the eighteenth century, reflected this emphasis when he reported in one of his revivals a mock conversation between himself and Abraham.

> Father Abraham, whom have you in heaven! Any Episcopalians? No! Any Presbyterians? No! Any Independents or Methodists? No, no, no! Whom have you there? We don't know those names here. All who are here are Christians. . . . Oh, is this the case? Then God help us to forget party names and to become Christians in deed and truth.

And Samuel Davies picked up the same theme when he warned "against this wretched, mischievous spirit of party. . . . A Christian! a Christian! Let that be your highest distinction."[1] Because of his revivalist background, therefore, Barton Stone was fully prepared to ally himself with Alexander Campbell in an effort to promote nondenominational Christianity, though it is evident that the two men came to this emphasis by very different routes.

In 1801 Stone found himself at the center of the Cane Ridge Revival, which broke out at his own Presbyterian meeting house in Cane Ridge, Kentucky. This revival was an early manifestation of the Second Great Awakening and surely one of the greatest local revivals in American history.[2] Predictably, that revival prompted Stone to embrace nondenominational Christianity at the expense of his own Presbyterian connections. He and five other Presbyterians did this when the Synod of Kentucky charged one of that group, Richard McNemar, with violating the standards of the Westminster Confession of Faith through his participation in the revival. As a result, these six men withdrew in 1803 from the Synod's jurisdiction and formed instead a dissenting organization, the Springfield Presbytery. By 1804, however, they determined that even the Springfield Presbytery was a hindrance to Christian union and genuine nondenominational Christianity. As a result, they dissolved the Springfield Presbytery on June 28, 1804, and announced to the world their intention to merge into the church universal. They did this in a treatise entitled *The Last Will and Testament of the*

Springfield Presbytery, a document that clearly reflects Stone's commitment to nondenominational Christianity as that commitment was inspired by the spirit of American revivalism. Among other things, that statement affirmed,

> We *will*, that this body die, be dissolved, and sink into union with the body of Christ at large; . . . We *will*, that our weak brethren, who may have been wishing to make the Presbytery of Springfield their king, and wot not what is now become of it, betake themselves to the Rock of Ages, and follow Jesus for the future. We *will*, that the Synod of Kentucky examine every member, who may be *suspected* of having departed from the Confession of Faith, and suspend every suspected heretic immediately; in order that the oppressed may go free, and taste the sweets of gospel liberty.[3]

Not only was Barton Stone shaped by the spirit of the revivals; so were many of the converts to the movement that he led. This was especially true of the Separate Baptists who fed hundreds and thousands of converts into the Stone movement.

The Separate Baptists ultimately descended from New England Puritan stock. During the Great Awakening of the eighteenth century, many Puritans sought to revive the interest in primitive Christianity that characterized the first generation of Puritans in America. Those who took this step became known as Separates, and when many of those Separates submitted to believers' baptism, they became known in turn as Separate Baptists. Shubal Stearns and Daniel Marshall led a sizable group of Separate Baptists to Sandy Creek, North Carolina, in 1755. That group spawned some forty-two other congregations that embraced literally thousands of Separate Baptists. In due time many of those Separate Baptists joined the westward movement into Kentucky and Tennessee. There they encountered the nondenominational preaching of Barton W. Stone and his followers. Large numbers converted to that perspective, so that by 1811 Joseph Thomas could report that the movement led by Barton Stone contained over 13,000 people and over 100 preachers.[4] Those numbers, of course, may be exaggerated. Still and all, it is clear that the Stone movement encountered substantial success in its early years. Equally important, this growth occurred some twelve years before the Stoneites in Kentucky and Tennessee had even heard the name of Alexander Campbell.

Finally, we must note one more aspect of the revival influence on the Stone movement, an influence mediated through Rice Haggard. A Virginian, Haggard assiduously read the sermons of Samuel Davies and from those sermons learned the importance of the name "Christian" as opposed to denominational labels. When James O'Kelly spearheaded a revolt of dissenting preachers and abandoned Francis Asbury's Methodists in 1792, Haggard told those preachers that according to the New Testament, "The disciples were called Christians, and I move that henceforth and forever the followers of Christ be known as Christians simply." Some twelve years later this same Rice Haggard met with Stone and his dissenting colleagues in Bethel, Kentucky, in 1804. There he gave to Stone the same advice he had earlier given to O'Kelly. Stone took that advice to heart. He and his colleagues soon published a pamphlet by Haggard: *An Address to the Different Religious Societies, on the Sacred Import of the Christian Name.*[5] For the rest of his life Stone resolutely insisted—often in opposition to Alexander Campbell—that the only legitimate name for Jesus' disciples was the name "Christian."

Barton W. Stone and the Meaning of Nondenominational Christianity

Stone's understanding of nondenominational Christianity revolved around three themes: the restoration of apostolic Christianity, the unity of all Christians, and the freedom for all Christians to read and understand the Bible for themselves, apart from any "official" denominational interpretation.

Their effort to restore the ancient Christian faith stood at the heart of the nondenominational orientation of Stone and his followers. They imagined that if they took their stand exclusively on the Bible and the first Christian age, they could escape the power of history, culture, and denominational tradition. One early Stoneite, for example, brashly proclaimed, "We are not personally acquainted with the writings of John Calvan [*sic*], nor are we certain how nearly we agree with his views of divine truth; neither do we care." Another argued that "the primitive Christian never heard of the five points of Dort, nor of Calvinism."[6] For these early Stoneites bent on the task of restoring the ancient faith, denominational traditions were neither history or relevant to their agenda.

The Stoneites also believed that the restoration of primitive Christianity was the only legitimate means to Christian unity. After all, original, apostolic Christianity existed before there were any denominational traditions whatsoever. Although few denominationally oriented Christians would wish to unite with other Christians on a denominational platform not their own, all Christians of whatever stripe could claim the faith of the first Christian age.

At the same time, what would prevent primitive Christianity from becoming just another orthodoxy, bound by the interpretations of one or another denominational perspective? Put another way, how could the Stoneites be certain that their movement on behalf of primitive Christianity would not evolve, in time, into one more denominational tradition, as restrictive as all the rest?

To guard against that possibility, the Stoneites built into their program an insistence on Christian freedom: the right of every Christian to read and interpret the Bible for himself or herself. In fact, for many years they refused to develop any well-defined ecclesiastical structure, liturgy, or theological tradition. Instead, they kept their movement flexible and open-ended.

Their commitment to Christian freedom was quite self-conscious, so much so that many Stoneites drew parallels between their own religious movement and the American revolution. One Stoneite, for example, wrote in 1827 that "the present conflict between the Bible and party creeds and confessions . . . is perfectly analogous to the revolutionary war between Britain and America; liberty was contended for on the one side, and dominion and power on the other." Another Stoneite used the Jeffersonian phrase "certain inalienable [*sic*] rights" to describe what the Stone movement was all about. He insisted that these "inalienable [*sic*] rights" pertained to "free investigation, [and] sober and diligent inquiry after [religious] truth."[7]

We can discern the Stoneite commitment to freedom especially in their ideas regarding the Holy Spirit on the one hand and baptism on the other. In their judgment, openness to the power of the Holy Spirit was a fundamental safeguard for Christian freedom. After all, the Holy Spirit was the spirit of the sovereign God that stood in judgment on every orthodoxy, every constraint, and every means of spiritual bondage devised by the human imagination.

This explains why Stone grew so distressed in the 1830s and 1840s with the increasingly orthodox position on the Campbell side of the movement that the gifts of the Holy Spirit had ceased with the apostles. While Campbell firmly believed in the power of the Holy Spirit in the life of the Christian, he denied that the Spirit had anything to do with the conversion of a sinner, apart from the biblical text. He claimed, for example, that "if the Spirit of God has spoken all its arguments" in Scripture, then "all the power of the Holy Spirit which can operate on the human mind [in conversion] is spent."[8] This was the voice of the rational side of the Stone-Campbell movement that would, in time, tend toward the construction of various orthodoxies in the name of the primitive Christian faith.

By the late 1830s many on the Campbell side of the movement—and especially those whose allegiance was to the *Christian Baptist*—found little or no place for the Holy Spirit either before or after conversion. The Spirit was simply too unmanageable for people committed to a highly rational and orderly worldview. Arthur Crihfield was a case in point. Judging the work of the Holy Spirit by the data of human reason and experience, Crihfield scorned Stone's views. "These plants [Stone's understandings] were merely exotics," he wrote, "and experiments have proved that they cannot be acclimated to the temperate zone of Christianity." Likewise, B. F. Hall, writing in Crihfield's *Heretic Detector* in 1837, affirmed his belief that "the Holy Spirit exerts no influence on the heart of sinners over and above the word: that his influences are in the facts he has revealed in the gospel, the evidences by which he has confirmed these facts, and in the motives to obedience presented in the Scriptures of Truth."[9]

Stone, in contrast, objected to all these assessments. In his judgment, they relied far too much on scientific evidence and human experience and failed to take sufficient account of the power of a sovereign God. For this reason he quarreled with Campbell's notion that missionaries "capable of confirming their testimony by working miracles" had ceased with the deaths of the apostles. "By what authority," Stone asked, "have we concluded that no more such men with miraculous powers may be expected in the present dispensation or age?" He even claimed that Christians in his own day and age might well work miracles through the power of the Holy Spirit were it not for disbelief.[10]

One also finds the Stoneite commitment to Christian freedom displayed in their position on baptism. While immersion for the forgiveness of sins soon became the defining mark of a Christian on the Campbell side of the movement, the Stoneites typically resisted orthodoxies on this matter for many years. After Joseph Thomas visited the Stoneites in Kentucky in 1810–11, he reported that "those that have, and those that have not been 'buried with Christ in baptism,' do not divide and contend about the subject; but they continue upon the plan which they set out upon—to let nothing divide them but Sin, and all search the scriptures for themselves, and act according to their understanding in the fear of God."[11]

In 1823 the Stoneites in Kentucky and Tennessee first laid eyes on Alexander Campbell, who had traveled to Kentucky to debate W. L. McCalla. In the course of that debate, Campbell developed the notion of immersion for the forgiveness of sins. From that date on, the Stoneites slowly adopted Campbell's position on this issue. Nonetheless, they still refused to make immersion a test of Christian fellowship. In 1830 Stone criticized Campbell himself for a doctrine of baptism that struck Stone as narrow and exclusive.

> Should they make their own peculiar view of immersion a term of fellowship, it will be impossible for them to repel, successfully, the imputation of being sectarians, and of having an authoritative creed (though not written) of one article at least, which is formed of their own opinion of truth; and this short creed would exclude more christians from union than any creed with which I am acquainted.[12]

Time and again Stone made this point. "To denounce all not immersed as lost, and to cut them off from salvation however holy and pious they may be," Stone wrote in 1831, "appears to dethrone charity and forbearance from our breast." If Campbell's position were true, he maintained, "countless millions of the fairest characters in the profession of Christianity for many centuries back, have been swept from joyful hope to gloomy despair."[13] More than this, Stone complained, the effort to make immersion the *sine qua non* of the Christian faith had "steeled the breasts of our brethren of all denominations against us." He especially lamented the efforts of many younger Christians in the movement who sought "to concentrate religion in immersion and weekly communion" to the neglect of a daily demonstration of Christian love. Without that dimension, Stone wrote, "religion is not worth a straw."[14]

It therefore came as a great shock to many of Stone's friends and associates to learn that only two years before his death, Stone apparently embraced the Campbellian position on immersion for the forgiveness of sins, lock, stock, and barrel. "We must believe, repent, and be baptized," he wrote, "before we get into Christ, and therefore before we become new creatures, before we are saved, before we are justified, or sanctified, or redeemed—before we receive the Spirit, or bear the fruits of the Spirit, as love, joy, peace, &c. and before we become members of one body of Christ, and one in him."[15]

When Stone's old friend, John Rogers, read these words, he could not believe his eyes.

> I have just read, with astonishment, a piece from your pen. . . . I have read it over and over again, and still my astonishment increases. I have been ready to say, '*This* surely is a misprint, or *that* was a slip of the pen'; and yet I fear I am mistaken. What! I have said to myself, can these be the sentiments of Father Stone? Is it possible, that he who has looked upon a number of us as a little too straight, upon some points—who has regarded bro. Campbell as rather ultra upon these points, is it possible, that *he* has gone beyond us all—has quite out Campbelled bro. Campbell himself?

Stone assured Rogers that he had read the article precisely as Stone had intended it.[16] If anything, this exchange between Stone and Rogers highlights the point I have sought to establish here: Stone's followers always understood him to teach that they should hold in fellowship the pious unimmersed as Christian brothers and sisters.

The truth is that for most of his career, Stone's understanding of nondenominational Christianity had far more to do with ethics than with orthodoxies of any kind. If some in the Campbell movement increasingly defined nondenominational Christianity in terms of those who had been immersed and who therefore belonged to the "true church" rather than to a "denomination," Stone typically defined nondenominational Christianity in terms of a distinctly Christian lifestyle that made denominational boundaries and distinctives meaningless. He thought it wrong to restrict the label *Christian* exclusively to the immersed, since "we see no more fruits of the Spirit in them—no more holiness in their lives—no more humility and self denial" than in the unimmersed. "Do we not see as much conformity to the world manifested [in the immersed]—as much pride—as much injustice—as much avarice?" he asked. And he counseled those who had been immersed but who refused to conform their lives to kingdom values, "Talk no more of being washed from your sins by immersion, when we see you living in sin; and many of you living on the gains of oppressing the poor African."[17]

For most of his career, Stone argued that an openness to the power of the Holy Spirit and a commitment to Christian freedom, even on issues like baptism, belonged to the very essence of nondenominational Christianity. This is why he protested so strongly when he found some in the movement erecting orthodoxies and abridging the freedom of individual Christians, all in the name of nondenominational Christianity. Put another way, some in the movement, Stone believed, were using the nondenominational ideal for denominational purposes. He made this point when he noted in 1836 that some in the combined Stone-Campbell movement were for some time zealously engaged to do away [with] party creeds, and are yet zealously preaching against them—but instead of a written creed of man's device, they have substituted a non-descript one, and exclude good brethren from their fellowship, because they dare believe differently from their opinions, and like other sectarians endeavor to destroy their influence in the world.[18]

Far from excluding any committed and pious Christian from his fellowship, Stone sought to nurture relationships with Christians from a variety of denominational traditions. He insisted that he could "pray with unimmersed, holy people, and praise, and perform every act of divine worship with such." He "found nothing in scripture to forbid me to commune with them at the Lord's table," and he noted in 1841 that "it is common with us that Baptists, Methodists and Presbyterians commune with us, and we with them."[19] This, at least in part, was the meaning of nondenominational Christianity for Barton W. Stone.

Barton W. Stone: Apocalyptic Sectarian

Many historians of the Disciples of Christ, finding this ecumenical emphasis in Stone, have portrayed him chiefly as an advocate of Christian unity and as a forerunner of the modern ecumenical movement. From this perspective, Stone emerges as fundamentally similar to the mature Alexander Campbell who celebrated in his later years a "common Christianity [on] which all good men of all denominations are agreed."[20]

Such a view, however, altogether misses the true genius of Barton W. Stone, since it ignores the single theme that stood at the heart of all that Stone was about: his apocalyptic orientation. We noted both in the introduction to this volume and in the beginning of this chapter the meaning of Stone's apocalyptic worldview: he lived his life *as if* the final rule or kingdom of God were present in the here and now. Once we fully understand this apocalyptic perspective, we can more fully grasp Stone's nondenominational orientation, since the latter makes very little sense if not understood in the context of the former.

Stone never advocated Christian union on the grounds that one denomination is just as good as another. To the contrary, Stone held that the entire denominational system was corrupted by sin and was nothing more than a temporary accommodation to this fallen world. He therefore labeled the denominational system as "Babylon" and "a wilderness of confusion." He believed that when the kingdom of God finally arrived, all denominations would be swept away and all Christians would be united into one church, namely, the primitive, apostolic church that one reads about in the New Testament documents.

His apocalyptic worldview, therefore, prevented Stone from developing a denominational and triumphalist perspective on his own movement. He believed that the complete restoration of the ancient church would emerge only in the context of the final kingdom of God. In the meantime, humility, not triumphalism or dogmatism, should characterize those who worked for the restoration of the ancient faith.

Stone readily granted that there were Christians in all denominations. Moreover, he prized fellowship with those Christians and thereby *seemed* to recognize the legitimacy of their denominations. This is the point, however, at which we can most easily misread Stone. Stone never recognized the legitimacy of any denomination. He actively sought out fellowship with Christians of various stripes *in spite of* their denominational affiliations because he knew that the final rule of God, though a promise, was not yet a reality in this fallen world. At the same time he regularly preached that all Christians of whatever stripe should abandon denominational Babylon and unite, as he put it, on the New Testament alone. In this way Stone's apocalyptic worldview provided the foundation for his understanding of nondenominational Christianity.

But there were other facets to Stone's apocalyptic worldview, and we will miss the genius of this man and of the movement he led unless we explore them in some detail.

Separation from the World

The notion that Christians must separate themselves from the world and its values stood at the center of Stone's apocalyptic orientation. One finds this theme, in one form or another, on almost every page of his *Christian Messenger*, which he published from 1826 through 1844. Quite simply, separation from the world meant for Stone the abandonment of self-interest and material possessions coupled with a life of service both to one's neighbor and to the kingdom of God. As he wrote in 1842, "No Christian lives for himself—not self but the Lord is the great end of his living. . . . Like an obedient servant, he says, Lord what wilt thou have me to do? And when that will is known, he flies to do [it], not regarding how great the sacrifice of wealth, ease, or reputation."[21]

This commitment played itself out in several ways in Stone's own life. At one point, he aimed for a law career, but he abandoned that goal in the interest of preaching. Then, following the Cane Ridge Revival, he turned his back on monetary support for his preaching ministry and committed himself instead to a life of poverty in the service of the kingdom of God. "Having now no support from the congregations, and having emancipated my slaves," he later recalled, "I turned my attention . . . cheerfully, though awkwardly, to labor on my little farm. . . . I had no money to hire laborers, and often on my return home, I found the weeds were getting ahead of my corn. I had often to labor at night while others were asleep, to redeem my lost time."[22]

Stone and many who looked to him for leadership prized the ideal of the impoverished preacher. Abner Hill was a case in point. An early Stoneite preacher in Tennessee, Hill recalled, "I had a good farm, a good house, . . . and a good prospect for living independent." But after coming to terms with the New Testament, "I determined to give up my worldly prospects and to do all I could to turn people to righteousness." Stone affirmed the lifestyle Hill adopted when he wrote that "decency in plain, coarse apparel displeases none but fops and dandies. We read of no rich preacher in the New Testament, nor in the best days of the church, before they were made rich by Constantine, when Heaven's order was prostrated by that deed."[23]

One might argue that the Stoneites' commitment to separate themselves from material possessions was to some degree, at least, a reflection of the widespread, oppressive poverty that many were virtually powerless to escape. John Rogers, for example, recalled that the southern pioneer preachers "were mostly men of small means" who "knew nothing of the luxuries and refinements of modern society." Writing of his experience in Middle Tennessee and south central Kentucky, Isaac Jones recalled that the preachers in that area were "poor men, (some having no homes of their own) having but little education." B. F. Hall shed additional light on the economic plight that characterized both preachers and lay people in Tennessee and Kentucky in the early years of the nineteenth century. "No one now can have any idea of the sacrifices which were made by the veteran [*sic*] pioneers of the present great religious movement," Hall wrote in his autobiography. "[Their] adherents . . . were generally of the poorer class, and without great personal influence. The preachers too were poor, and received but little pecuniary aid. They had, consequently, to resort to some secular pursuit to make a living."[24]

It is difficult to believe, however, that economic deprivation was the only factor prompting these people to embrace an apocalyptic orientation. Since other impoverished people rejected that orientation, and since some people of means embraced it, one must conclude that other factors were at work here as well. Although we can never know what all those factors may have been, we can know that the apocalyptic worldview gave to these people a sense that they were pilgrims on this earth, passing through to a better land. As Stone himself admonished his readers, "You must not mind earthly things, nor set your affections on them—not to be conformed to the world. . . . Here you have no abiding place, but are as strangers and pilgrims seeking a better country."[25]

We have already noted on several occasions that the Stoneites' apocalyptic worldview did not translate automatically into premillennial sentiments. After all, their apocalypticism had far more to do with a countercultural lifestyle than it did with millennial theories of any kind. Nonetheless, their sense that they were pilgrims in this world did lead many Stoneites to embrace an explicitly premillennial perspective. Stone himself is only a case in point. In the early 1830s, for example, he wrote in the *Christian Messenger* that "the second coming of Christ is at the commencement of his millennial reign on earth—here on earth he will reign till the 1000 years be finished—nor will he cease to reign on earth till he has raised from death the wicked, and judged them according to their works."[26] It is true that William Miller's notoriously well known millennial predictions in the early 1840s fueled Stone's interest in the millennial theme. Yet, because of his radical sense of being separate from the world and its values, Stone's premillennial sentiments predated Miller's predictions by many years.

Rejection of Politics, Violence, and War

Stone's apocalypticism also bore fruit in the attitude he took toward politics. Simply put, he held that all civil government, including the government of the United States, was fundamentally illegitimate, and that Christians should reject all political involvement, even voting. This position was not unique to Stone, but came to characterize many in Churches of Christ until well in the twentieth century, as we shall see.

Stone and his colleagues who bolted from the Synod of Kentucky following the Cane Ridge Revival explained the rationale for this position in their *Observations on Church Government.*

> It will be granted that he who *creates* has a right to *govern.* Upon this principle God is acknowledged to be the governor of the world. . . . [But] men have been generally fond of mending what they supposed God had left imperfect, filling up and supplying what they judged deficient, and making plain what divine wisdom had left in the dark. Thus have they wandered from the plain simple rule of God's word, and taken the reins of government into their own hands.[27]

The Stoneites generally grounded their rejection of civil government and political activity in Daniel's interpretation of King Nebuchadnezzar's dream, recorded in Daniel 2:31–45. In that vision the king saw a great image with a head of gold, chest and arms of silver, belly and thighs of bronze, legs of iron, and feet of iron and clay. Then he saw a stone, not cut by human hands, that smashed the image to pieces and then became a great mountain that filled the whole earth. According to Daniel's interpretation, the stone that became a great mountain that filled the earth was the kingdom of God, a kingdom that would crush the kingdoms of this world and then endure forever.

The Stoneites typically understood this vision to mean that the day would come when the kingdom of God would prevail over all the earth and, in the process, destroy all human government. Interestingly, they often tied this understanding to an explicitly premillennial sentiment, claiming that all these things would transpire when Christ began his 1,000-year reign on earth. The critical point, however, is this: if the Stoneites sought to live their lives *as if* the final rule of God were already present in the here and now, their understanding of Daniel 2 demanded that they refuse all political involvement even in the present age. Stone himself provides a clear statement of that position.

> The lawful King, Jesus Christ, will shortly put them [human governments] all down, and reign with his Saints on earth a thousand years, without a rival. . . . Then shall all man made laws and governments be burnt up forever. These are the seat of the beast. . . .

Christians have no right to make laws and governments for themselves . . . [and] all should submit to the government and laws of our King. . . . We must cease to support any other government on earth by our counsels, co-operation, and choice.[28]

Based on this conviction, the Stoneites routinely enjoined total noninvolvement in civil government except for paying taxes and obeying legitimate civil laws. James M. Mathes of Indiana provided a classic illustration of this position in a letter he wrote to Stone in 1836. There Mathes complained that some preachers "forget themselves" and "become candidates for posts of honor and profit in the civil department." Mathes pointed out that one could not justify such political activity by the example of the primitive Christians. "They were subject to every ordinance of Caesar's government, for conscience sake, but took no part in law-making," he observed. "Let us profit by their example." A year earlier, in 1835, an ad hoc committee representing several congregations within the Stone movement submitted the following to the *Christian Messenger*: "Cease, cease, dear Brethren to be numbered among the Political aspirants—partake not of the evil of their midnight corruption. . . . While we take sides in the Political contests of this evil day, . . . we virtually renounce the laws of our King."[29]

If the Stoneites were this committed to a posture of political noninvolvement, one might expect that they would also advocate a complete renunciation of violence and war. Indeed, they did, and they grounded that renunciation in their commitment to lead their lives *as if* the final rule of God were present in the here and now. Stone made the point as well as anyone: "If genuine christianity were to overspread the earth, wars would cease, and the world would be found together in the bonds of peace. This is Christ's kingdom—the kingdom of peace." At the same time he pointed out that "a nation professing christianity, yet teaching, learning and practicing the arts of war cannot be of the kingdom of Christ."[30]

Finally, since the question of the legitimacy of missionary societies played such a significant role in the nineteenth-century history of Churches of Christ, we should observe that the Stoneites rejected missionary societies for the same reason that they rejected participation in civil government: both missionary societies and civil governments challenged the ultimacy of the kingdom of God. The only organization on earth that in any way embodied the values of the kingdom of God, they contended, was the church. They therefore gave their undivided allegiance to the church as the penultimate expression of God's kingdom on earth and refused to participate in any humanly contrived organization whatsoever. In this way the Stoneites grounded even their rejection of missionary societies in their apocalyptic worldview.

Barton W. Stone and Alexander Campbell

It will be instructive at this point to contrast Barton Stone with Alexander Campbell on several of the issues we have explored thus far in this chapter. We have already noted that Campbell was a child of the Enlightenment whereas Stone was a product of the revivals. Fundamentally, that difference meant that Stone geared his life to the *power* of God at work in the human heart, whereas Campbell sought to discern with near-scientific precision the *will* of God as that will was expressed through the data of an ancient text. This point is not intended to downplay Stone's interest in the biblical text, for it was that text that defined his understanding of the power and the kingdom of God. Nor does this point suggest that Campbell had no interest in the power of God at work in the human heart. The difference here is one of degree, not of kind.

Second, Stone's radical allegiance to the power of God made him susceptible to an apocalyptic worldview and rendered him highly pessimistic regarding the possibility of genuine human progress in matters of peace, justice, and righteousness. Indeed, for Stone, the glories of human progress seemed to pale when compared with the glories of the kingdom of God. On the other hand, Campbell's intense rationality oriented him more toward human progress than toward the consummation of the kingdom of God, breaking into human affairs from outside the bounds of this world. One finds this contrast between Campbell and Stone symbolized especially well in their respective interpretations of Daniel 2, the passage that so thoroughly informed the Stoneites' apocalyptic understandings. Far from finding in that passage an apocalyptic worldview, Campbell placed the meaning of the passage squarely in the context of human history and progress. The little stone that would become a great mountain and fill the whole earth was not for Campbell the coming kingdom of God but, rather, the Protestant Reformation of the sixteenth century. And the image that the stone destroyed was not human government but the Roman Catholic Church.[31] From Campbell's perspective, the kingdom that would fill the whole earth and last forever was a kingdom that would be erected, at least in part, by human instrumentality.

In addition to their different intellectual backgrounds, Stone's poverty and Campbell's wealth helped to sustain and confirm the very different spiritual commitments of these two men. The poverty Stone experienced for most of his life rendered him less reliant on human progress and achievement and more reliant on the power of God. In contrast, Alexander Campbell plowed an inheritance from his father-in-law into farming, land speculation, book publishing, and educational enterprises, and according to one biographer, "died the wealthiest man in West Virginia."[32] Campbell's Enlightenment orientation coupled with his sizable material wealth made it highly unlikely that he would have much use for Stone's apocalyptic worldview.

These fundamental differences between Campbell and Stone bore fruit in a number of ways. We have already noted the difference between these two men regarding the power of the Holy Spirit. We should also note the different ways they discerned moral and ethical guidance. If Barton Stone found ethical guidance in his understanding of the coming kingdom of God, Campbell found that guidance both in the pattern of the primitive church and in the rules and regulations he discovered in the New Testament. Put another way, if Campbell looked to a rationally discernible legal pattern, Stone looked to the kingdom of God that stood in judgment on this world and its values. Evidence of this difference abounds, but nowhere more clearly than on the question of war and violence. If Stone rejected war because he sought to live his life *as if* the final kingdom of God were present in the here and now, Campbell rejected war "BECAUSE CHRISTIANITY FORBIDS IT" and because the Christian faith enjoined pacifism "in its uncorrupted, unsophisticated youth."

Finally, it is important to note the difference in demeanor and temperament that separated these two men, a difference nowhere more apparent than in their respective attitudes toward argumentation and debate. Campbell prized rational argument and held five particularly notable debates. He debated the Seceder Presbyterian John Walker in 1820, the Presbyterian W. L. McCalla in 1823, the social reformer Robert Owen in 1829, the Roman Catholic bishop of Cincinnati John Purcell in 1837, and the Presbyterian Nathan L. Rice in 1843. Following the McCalla debate, he concluded that "a week's debating is worth a year's preaching . . . for the purpose of disseminating truth and putting error out of countenance."[33]

Unlike Campbell, Barton Stone rejected debate, claiming that "debates tend to strife, deaden piety—destroy the spirit of prayer—puff up the vain mind, . . . and destroy the comforts of true, heavenly religion." He thought it rare to find "in the same person, a warrior and an humble and devoted christian." And he questioned the spiritual depth of those converted by debate and argumentation: "The children are like the parents, lean and pigmy things."

On the eve of Stone's death in 1844, however, the Campbellian tradition of rationality and debate was slowly choking out the apocalyptic spirituality that Stone had sought to nurture in his followers for so many years. Stone therefore complained that many of his brothers and sisters increasingly placed factual knowledge of the Bible, religious controversy, and debate above "godliness, piety and brotherly love." Rhetorically he asked, "Do we see genuine christianity promoted by such controversies and debates? Look around and enquire for these fruits. Do you know of any person spiritually renewed or refreshed with spiritual understanding? Do you find brotherly love and christian union advanced? On the contrary, do you not find their opposites promoted?"[34]

In spite of all these differences, the Campbell and Stone movements began to explore common ground in 1823, the year that Alexander Campbell made a foray into Kentucky to debate the Presbyterian W. L. McCalla. Prior to that debate, few Stoneites had even heard of Campbell. Now they not only heard him but found themselves intensely attracted to his message.

There were several reasons for Campbell's appeal. First, he actively promoted the restoration of primitive Christianity as a means to Christian union, a theme already dear to the Stoneites. Second, Campbell developed in his debate with McCalla the notion of immersion for the forgiveness of sins. This doctrine brought great comfort to the hearts of many Stoneites whose Calvinist background prompted great anxiety over the possibility of their salvation. After all, how could one know if one had been predestined to heaven or hell? Campbell's new doctrine, however, meant that sins were forgiven and salvation was assured at the very moment of one's immersion. And third, where the Stoneites, in the interest of Christian freedom, had resisted developing any formal theology or ecclesiastical practices, Campbell outlined in detail the pattern of the primitive church that should be restored. This structure promised security to a people who had known the insecurities of freedom for so many years.

Following that visit to Kentucky in 1823, Campbell's influence among the Stoneites grew more and more pronounced until in 1832, some of the followers of Campbell and Stone formally united in a grand ceremony in Lexington, Kentucky. Although substantial common ground justified that union, the hype that accompanied the union effectively obscured the fundamental differences between the two groups. A number of Stoneites, however, perceived those differences and refused to enter the union. A case in point was the Ohio preacher Matthew Gardner, who complained that the Campbellites "seem to labor more especially to reform the churches of other denominations over to their views than they do to reform the wicked from the error of their ways." While noting how the Stone movement "arose upon the liberal ground of each individual enjoying and exercising his own private opinion," Gardner claimed that "Mr. Campbell has obviated all these difficulties."[35]

Those who did agree to the union inherited the daunting task of reconciling the two opposing worldviews that had characterized the Stone and Campbell movements for so many years. No one accomplished that task with more finesse than did the great third-generation leader of Churches of Christ, David Lipscomb.

DAVID LIPSCOMB

Without a doubt, David Lipscomb was the single most influential person among Churches of Christ from 1865 until his death in 1917. To a great extent that influence grew from his role as editor of the Nashville-based *Gospel Advocate*, an extraordinarily prestigious journal among Churches of Christ for all those years. But Lipscomb's influence also derived from his own personal integrity, from his unswerving allegiance both to the Bible and to the kingdom of God, and from his ability to weave into a single, coherent vision the legal tradition of Alexander Campbell and the apocalyptic tradition of Barton W. Stone.

Lipscomb's Debt to Tolbert Fanning

Lipscomb owed a great debt to his mentor, Tolbert Fanning. In chapter 3, we explored how Fanning embraced the rational and legal perspectives of Alexander Campbell. At the same time Fanning drank deeply from the apocalyptic heritage of Barton W. Stone. This should not be surprising when we realize that Fanning received his earliest religious instruction from several Stoneite preachers in his home state of Alabama.[36] Clearly, he learned his lessons well. Sounding much like Stone, he expressed his disillusionment with sectional strife and national politics when he wrote in 1861 that the "church of Christ" would " 'break in pieces and consume' [the] kingdoms of the world." Fifteen years earlier, the very month in which the United States declared war on Mexico, Fanning criticized democracies along with monarchies and aristocracies, and he affirmed his conviction that the only legitimate sphere in which Christians should labor was "the kingdom of [God's] dear son."[37] Like Stone, Fanning also refused to vote. Lipscomb recalled in 1867 that Fanning had not voted in some twenty years, "holding it to be incompatible with the Christian profession." Likewise, Fanning embraced pacifism and counseled members of Churches of Christ to refuse to participate in war, even in times of national emergency.[38] We can only surmise that Fanning must have shared all these lessons with his younger colleague, David Lipscomb.

Yet, there was one fundamental point on which Lipscomb shared far more in common with Barton W. Stone than he did with his more immediate mentor, Tolbert Fanning. Typically, Fanning particularized the transcendent kingdom of God and then identified that kingdom with the very tangible and temporal sectarian movement known widely in Middle Tennessee as the Church of Christ. For Fanning, there was little or no difference between the two. In this way, Fanning allowed the very tangible ecclesiastical concerns of Alexander Campbell to swallow the apocalyptic legacy of Barton W. Stone.

David Lipscomb, however, refused to interpret Campbell in the light of Stone or Stone in the light of Campbell. Instead, he nurtured both traditions simultaneously and drew from them both in ways that enabled him to emerge as the single greatest third-generation leader of Churches of Christ.

Lipscomb, Campbell, and Stone

In fact, the genius of David Lipscomb lay in the way he was able to blend the perspectives of Alexander Campbell with the perspectives of Barton W. Stone without sacrificing either emphasis in the process. In many ways a thoroughgoing disciple of Campbell, Lipscomb embraced a highly rational view of Scripture that tended inevitably toward legalism. Nurtured by Common Sense Realism, he flatly declared, "The Bible is science, is knowledge, classified by God." While contending that the Bible was "addressed to the common sense in man," he was determined to make the *Gospel Advocate* "more perfectly the reflex of the Divine Will as revealed in the Bible than any human production now in existence." Accordingly, Lipscomb seemed never to doubt the truth of his convictions or the accuracy of his understanding of Scripture. Although capable of dialogue with his adversaries, he was convinced that he was right and they were wrong. With this perspective, Lipscomb typically stood at the very core of the doctrinal disputes that erupted between Churches of Christ and Disciples of Christ over issues like missionary societies, instrumental music in worship, the role of women in the church, and basic attitudes toward Scripture. The year before his death, he took comfort in the fact that "we have opposed all innovations and changes upon his [God's] order at every point along the line of duty drawn by him."[39]

But there was far more to Lipscomb than Baconianism or legalism. He was also an apocalyptic sectarian whose commitment to the final rule of the kingdom of God rivaled that of his mentor, Tolbert Fanning, or even that of Barton W. Stone. Although evidence of this perspective abounds throughout Lipscomb's career, nowhere did he make his apocalyptic orientation more apparent than in a little book he published in 1889 called simply *Civil Government*. This small volume consisted of a series of articles Lipscomb wrote shortly after the Civil War regarding the Christian's relation both to government and to the world. There, he picked up many of the themes that characterized Barton W. Stone half a century before: the ultimacy of the kingdom of God, the imperative that Christians separate themselves from the values of the world, and a refusal to engage in politics or war. If one doubts that the apocalyptic orientation stood at the center of Lipscomb's thought, one need only hear Lipscomb's own appraisal of this book: "Nothing we ever wrote affects so nearly the vital interests of the church of Christ and the salvation of the world as this little book."[40] What, then, were the contours of Lipscomb's apocalyptic orientation?

Apocalyptic Eschatology

Lipscomb's apocalyptic understandings grew from his assessment of human government as a departure from God's original design. He argued in *Civil Government* that God intended from the beginning to rule over all the earth, but His designs were frustrated by the rebellion of Adam and Eve. That rebellion "culminated in the effort of man to organise a government of his own, so that he himself might permanently conduct the affairs of the earth, free from the control of God." Humanity rejected God's sovereignty once again when the Jews clamored for a king. For that reason Lipscomb took very seriously God's words to Samuel on that occasion: "For they have not rejected thee, but they have rejected me, that I should not be king over them." In Lipscomb's judgment human beings had simply transferred their allegiance from God to Satan.[41]

Nonetheless, Lipscomb looked for the day when God would destroy all human governments, the best along with the worst, and reestablish His control over the earth. Like Stone and Fanning before him, he rooted this anticipation in Daniel 2:

> The end of all conflicts and strifes of earth, will be the complete and final destruction, the utter consuming of the last vestige of human governments and institutions, and the giving of the dominion, and power, and authority of the whole earth to the people of the saints of the Most High. . . . All these kingdoms are to be broken in pieces, and *consumed*

> . . . but the little stone cut out of the mountain without hands is to become a great mountain, and fill the whole earth.

Lipscomb thought these themes the very "key notes . . . of the Old and New Testaments." Without them, he contended, the Bible was "without point or meaning."[42]

It is important to recognize, however, that unlike Tolbert Fanning, Lipscomb refused to equate the eschatological kingdom of God with the church. "The kingdom in its present stage," he wrote in 1903, "is not called 'the everlasting kingdom,' but it will grow into it. It is the same kingdom in a lower stage of development."[43]

This point raises the question, did David Lipscomb embrace premillennial views? On the one hand, Lipscomb never contended that Jesus would one day return to earth to rule on the throne of David for a literal thousand years. On the other hand, Lipscomb firmly believed that "the one purpose of God was to re-establish his authority and rule on earth." Lipscomb could not imagine that God's purposes would forever be frustrated. In addition, Lipscomb clearly thought that God's final, sovereign rule over the earth could not occur apart from the second coming of Jesus. In 1898, for example, Lipscomb spoke of the "reign of Jesus on earth" and argued that " 'the times of restoration of all things' must be when Jesus returns again to earth—the restoration of all things to their original relation to God."[44]

Acknowledging Lipscomb's premillennial views, however, risks confusing the central with the peripheral in Lipscomb's thought. Although Lipscomb firmly anticipated that God would finally reestablish his authority over all the earth, he sought to live his life *as if* God's sovereign rule were present in the here and now. Thus, although questions of lifestyle and ethics stood at the heart of his apocalyptic orientation, he seldom spoke of his millennial understandings and resolutely refused to speculate regarding when and how the millennium might commence. He made this position abundantly clear when he replied in 1898 to a *Gospel Advocate* reader who asked for Lipscomb's position on the millennium. Lipscomb responded,

> We cannot write a commentary on the New Testament under the head of "Queries," nor do we understand much about the millennium. The best way to bring about the millennium is to teach and practice obedience to the practical precepts of the Bible. Practice the precepts and follow the example of the Savior, and this will do a thousandfold more to fully bring about the reign of Jesus on earth than a thousand discourses and theories about what the millennium is or when it begins or ends.[45]

If premillennial thinking played such a minor role in Lipscomb's thinking, it is fair to ask why it should be mentioned in this text at all. The reason is simple. In the early twentieth century, Churches of Christ fought a major battle over premillennialism and sought to expel premillennial advocates from the mainstream of the tradition—a story we will consider later in this chapter. The real, underlying issue in that fight, however, was not premillennialism at all but, rather, the apocalyptic worldview of the nineteenth century which had, by World War I, become an embarrassment to many in mainstream Churches of Christ and a liability to their aspirations to become a respectable denomination. Opponents of premillennialism sought to make it appear that millennial thought was foreign to the heritage of Churches of Christ. For this reason, it is important to recognize that although premillennial thinking never played a major role in the history of Churches of Christ, it nonetheless accompanied the apocalyptic worldview of many nineteenth-century leaders of Churches of Christ, including Barton Stone and David Lipscomb.

Separation from the World

Lipscomb argued throughout his life that the Christian's allegiance must be to the kingdom or rule of God, not to kingdoms erected by human beings. In his view this bedrock principle demanded a complete rejection of the values of the world. This perspective played itself out in Lipscomb's life in a variety of ways. First, Lipscomb sought to live a simple life, free from ostentation, materialism, and greed. As Benjamin Franklin reported in 1875, Lipscomb was "a plain and unassuming man, with the simplicity of a child. . . . He lives in utter disregard of the notions of the world, puts on no airs, [and] wears just a coat, hat and pants as suit him."[46]

In addition, Lipscomb made it clear that by separation from the world, he did not mean mere morality. He had not the slightest doubt that "the devil is willing to turn moral reformer and make the world moral and respectable." Rather, Lipscomb called for "a full surrender of the soul, mind, and body up to God," leading to "the spirit of self-denial, of self-sacrifice, the forbearance [*sic*] and long suffering, [and] the doing good for evil."[47]

One finds an especially notable example of the spirit of self-denial to which Lipscomb was committed when a cholera epidemic struck Nashville in 1873. During the month of June alone, almost 500 people died. Blacks were especially hard hit. Many who had the means to flee the city did so. Lipscomb was not well and had every reason to escape the plague by retiring to his farm at Bell's Bend, outside the city. Lipscomb believed, however, that his citizenship in the kingdom of God required him to go into houses where the plague had struck, to clean and feed the victims, and to do everything in his power to help restore their health. He urged members of Churches of Christ in Nashville to follow suit. "It is a time that should call out the full courage and energy of the church in looking after the needy," he wrote. "Every individual, white or black, that dies from neglect and want of proper food and nursing, is a reproach to the professors of the Christian religion in the vicinity of Nashville."[48]

Like Stone and Fanning before him, Lipscomb also refused to participate in political activity. His reason was clear: since God's sovereign rule would one day destroy all human governments, "how could the individual citizens of the kingdom of God found, enter into, and become part and parcel of—upbuild, support, and defend that which God's kingdom was especially commissioned to destroy?"[49]

Likewise Lipscomb committed himself to a life of rigorous pacifism, a commitment that once again reflected his devotion to the kingdom of God as opposed to human governments. "All human government," he wrote, "rests for authority upon the power of the sword."[50] In contrast, the kingdom of God was a kingdom of peace. How, then, Lipscomb wondered, could a Christian participate in acts of violence? In 1881 Lipscomb contrasted the brutality that characterized human governments with the spirit of peace that ruled the kingdom of God.

> In the beginning of the late strife that so fearfully desolated our country, much was said about "our enemies." I protested constantly that I had not a single enemy, and was not an enemy to a single man North of the Ohio river. . . . Yet, . . . thousands and hundreds of thousands who knew not each other . . . were made enemies to each other and thrown into fierce and bloody strife, were embued with the spirit of destruction one toward the other, through the instrumentality of human governments.[51]

As a final measure of Lipscomb's commitment to countercultural values, we should note his consistent bias toward and concern for the poor. In fact, Lipscomb thought that poverty was a fundamental characteristic of the kingdom of God. In his judgment, the church was "the especial legacy of God to the poor of the earth. . . . It is the rich that are out of their element in Christ's Church." In 1906 he confirmed this judgment when he argued that "Christ intended his religion for the poor, [and] adapted it to their necessities."[52]

It would be easy enough to argue that Lipscomb's devotion to the poor was nothing more than a function of his own meager circumstances—if only that were true. In point of fact, Lipscomb inherited substantial means from a moderately wealthy father. The truth is, David Lipscomb, for whatever reason, was a man driven by his vision of the coming kingdom of God—a kingdom that would someday rule with righteousness and justice over all the earth and that would finally destroy human governments along with popular values based on self-indulgence. Lipscomb therefore committed himself to live *as if* that kingdom were present in the here and now. This was his apocalyptic worldview.

The Genius of David Lipscomb

It must by now be obvious that Churches of Christ of the nineteenth century built their spiritual house not only on the legal and rational foundation bequeathed to them by the early Alexander Campbell but also on an apocalyptic orientation rooted in Barton W. Stone. The strength of the apocalyptic vision is testimony to the fact that Churches of Christ nurtured in the nineteenth century a strong countercultural dimension that played itself out in pacifism, refusal to participate in politics, separation from popular values and mores, and a commitment to the poor.

More than anyone else, David Lipscomb successfully combined the Stoneite and Campbellite perspectives. He was a legalist, to be sure, but his legalism pointed beyond itself to his apocalyptic orientation: acutely conscious of the coming kingdom of God when God's rule would be complete, Lipscomb simply sought to conform his life to God's rule even in the here and now.

By combining these two visions, Lipscomb was able to hold together in a single movement members of Churches of Christ whose piety had been chiefly informed by Campbell and those whose piety drew on Stone. But Lipscomb was the last major leader in the history of this tradition who held these two perspectives together so well. In fact, even before Lipscomb's life was done, the Stoneite heritage was rapidly eroding. Lipscomb complained in 1880, for example, that fewer and fewer *Gospel Advocate* readers shared his rejection of political involvement.[53] Ever since 1823 when Alexander Campbell had gone to Kentucky to debate W. L. McCalla, Campbell's influence had gradually preempted that of Barton W. Stone among Churches of Christ. In the waning years of the nineteenth century, that process accelerated, and by the time of World War I, progressive leaders of Churches of Christ launched a deliberate campaign to drive the apocalyptic legacy of Barton Stone and David Lipscomb from their heritage. For the next third of a century, this campaign focused on the premillennial theories of a German immigrant named R. H. Boll. More than anything else, the effort to discredit Boll set Churches of Christ on their evolutionary course from nineteenth-century sect to twentieth-century denomination and, for that reason, is a watershed in the history of this tradition.

THE R. H. BOLL AFFAIR

After emigrating from Germany to settle in Ohio in 1890, R. H. Boll made his way to Smyrna, Tennessee, where he worked as a farmhand, possibly from 1892 to 1895. He converted from his ancestral Roman Catholic faith to the restoration plea of the Churches of Christ in 1895 and enrolled that same year in the Nashville Bible School.[54] David Lipscomb and his close friend and colleague, James A. Harding, had established the Nashville Bible School only four years earlier in 1891. For many years thereafter this institution promoted an apocalyptic perspective and trained scores of preachers who embraced that outlook.

We have already seen the intensity with which David Lipscomb embraced that viewpoint. Much the same can be said of his coworker at the Nashville Bible School, James A. Harding. Harding maintained a level of trust in God that awed many of his contemporaries. One of his students at the Nashville Bible School, R. C. Bell, later recalled that "Brother Harding possessed more fully than any other Christian I have known Paul's absolute confidence and unqualified trust in God's promise to supply every need."[55] Indeed, Harding refused to rely on salaries, contracts, or any other humanly devised means that might have guaranteed his financial security. Instead, he trusted God to provide for his needs. What little he had, he typically gave away. When a progressive Texas preacher challenged Harding's lifestyle as impractical, Harding defended his behavior and explained,

> For thirty-six years I have endeavored to follow the directions of Jesus literally. I have avoided the accumulation of property. There have been few, if any, times in these thirty-six years that I have had money enough to bury me if I had died. I have owned two horses, at different times, and a buggy. I have owned two cows, at different times, and a calf. . . . I doubt if there has been a time in these thirty-six years when all of my possessions would have brought as much as five hundred dollars if they had been sold at public auction.[56]

Harding's extraordinary level of trust in the providence of God was part and parcel of his apocalyptic orientation. He sought to live his life squarely within the framework of the kingdom of God. For him, God's coming kingdom was so profoundly real in the here and now that he simply refused to place his faith in human schemes, human institutions, or human progress. He relied on God to triumph over all the earth in the final days, and he relied on God to provide for all his needs in the here and now.

Not only did Harding maintain a staunchly apocalyptic orientation. He also embraced a classic premillennial perspective.[57] In fact, perhaps no one among late-nineteenth-century Churches of Christ held more firmly to premillennial thinking than did he. As with Lipscomb, however, Harding's premillennialism was not an end in itself but testified instead to the apocalyptic framework in which Harding sought to live his life.

Lest one imagine that the apocalyptic orientation was the only important dimension of Harding's thought, it must be said that Harding—like Lipscomb—also embraced the legal outlook and debating spirit that characterized those who radicalized Alexander Campbell's *Christian Baptist*. "Our business," Harding trumpeted, "is to fight everything and everybody that impedes the success of our Master's cause." Harding sought especially to debate those within his own fellowship who refused to draw the line against instrumental music in worship. When the popular preacher T. B. Larimore, for example, refused to line up with Harding on this issue, Harding refused Larimore permission to speak at the Nashville Bible School of which Harding was president at the time.[58]

Once we understand the intellectual worlds of David Lipscomb and James A. Harding, we also understand the world that R. H. Boll entered when he enrolled in the Nashville Bible School in 1895. Clearly, Boll learned his apocalyptic lessons from these two men, but perhaps especially from Harding, who viewed Boll as a model student and once remarked, "I wouldn't take a million dollars for him."[59]

Boll's apocalyptic outlook manifested itself in many ways. Convinced that the rule of God was the only means to genuine progress, Boll doubted that "the boastful splendor of the twentieth century" and "the roar of its civilization" represented any meaningful progress at all. When the United States declared war on Germany in 1917, Boll advised young Christians to refuse to fight. He questioned the conventional wisdom that World War I was "a struggle . . . to make the world safe for democracy" and grounded his pacifist counsel in his conviction that Christians do not belong to the kingdoms of this world.[60]

Boll's apocalypticism found expression not only in the conventional kind of premillennialism he sometimes encountered at the Nashville Bible School but also in an explicitly dispensational variety of premillennial thought.[61] The theory of dispensational premillennialism held that God had sought to inaugurate His rule on earth on several occasions, but in each instance had been frustrated by human resistance. In particular, He had sought to establish His kingdom through the ministry of Jesus, but because of Jewish hostility, settled for the church instead. By the early twentieth century this thinking had become standard fare among American fundamentalists with whom Boll increasingly identified.[62]

It goes without saying that dispensational premillennialism was altogether foreign to Churches of Christ. Moreover, this theory—if taken seriously—would completely undermine the restorationist premises of Churches of Christ. After all, the ancient church, which Churches of Christ labored so diligently to restore, was in this scheme of things a mere accident. For this reason J. C. McQuiddy, publisher of the *Gospel Advocate*, charged in 1919 that Boll's doctrine "belittles the church of Christ" and was "calculated to destroy every congregation of disciples."[63] From this perspective, it is little wonder that mainstream Churches of Christ found fault with R. H. Boll.

Yet, when one surveys the evidence and the sequence of events in the war against R. H. Boll, it is clear that Boll's dispensational premillennialism was only one factor—and perhaps not even the major factor—that prompted mainstream Churches of Christ to launch such a thorough-going crusade against him and his teachings.

Even before that crusade got under way, Boll had difficulties with the owners of the *Gospel Advocate* who, in 1909, had made Boll the paper's front-page editor. For several years, his apocalyptic and premillennial ideas appeared in the paper, though his editorial colleagues at the *Advocate* were none too pleased, for several reasons. First, the *Advocate* editors typically rejected speculation on millennial themes. And second, they found the dispensational variety of millennial thinking altogether foreign to the commitments of Churches of Christ. Finally, after Boll persisted in publishing his millennial views in the *Advocate*, his superiors dismissed him from his position as front-page editor. At that point, Boll became editor of an explicitly premillennial paper published in Louisville, Kentucky, called *Word and Work*. That paper became the voice of premillennialism among Churches of Christ for the next several decades; it also became the object of an increasingly vehement attack from most mainstream leaders of Churches of Christ.

The question that nags is, why? It addition to Boll's dispensational theories, several other reasons suggest themselves.

Grace versus Works and Self-Reliance

First, Stanford Chambers, one of the early leaders of the premillennial movement among Churches of Christ, suggested that "the real issue [was] not prophecy but grace."[64] In a real sense Chambers was right, since apocalyptic and premillennial thinking were for Boll but additional ways of speaking of the unmerited grace of God. After all, the apocalyptic outlook pointed directly to the insufficiency of humankind to build the kingdom of God and looked instead to the merciful intervention of a gracious God.

Yet, many in Churches of Christ had built their theological house on a foundation of human initiative, self-reliance, and good works. Accordingly, we noted in chapter 2 Alexander Campbell's contention that human beings appropriated the grace of God only by obeying His commands. This Campbellian assumption soon became a centerpiece in the theology of Churches of Christ. In 1878, for example, F. D. Srygley argued, "By obedience to his [God's] requirements man may walk 'the way that leadeth unto life.' . . . Everything God has done in preparing the *city*, and revealing the *way* is of grace. . . . Hence salvation is of grace and not of works." Or again, in 1920 C. R. Nichol and R. L. Whiteside published a four-volume work entitled *Sound Doctrine*, a set of books that circulated widely among Churches of Christ. "The greatest exhibition of God's grace," the authors claimed, "is seen in the gift of his Son, Jesus Christ," but "next to that, his greatest favor to man is seen in the very command he has given for man's guidance." For this reason, they argued, those who heard the first gospel sermon on the day of Pentecost "could save themselves only by performing the conditions upon which salvation was so graciously offered."[65]

At the same time a few preachers in Churches of Christ in the early to middle years of the twentieth century held out strongly for a biblical theology of grace. Perhaps the most notable of this group was G. C. (Grover Cleveland) Brewer. Growing up in Tennessee and North Alabama, Brewer at an early age came under the influence of T. B. Larimore, an influential preacher known for his kind and generous spirit. He also attended the Nashville Bible School, where, according to Stanford Chambers, "salvation 'by grace . . . through faith' rather than by 'works' or deeds of merit was a cherished truth."[66] The lessons he learned about grace shaped his ministry for the rest of his life. Yet, Brewer often found himself standing alone, resisting the legalistic theology of so many in Churches of Christ at that time. In 1945, for example, he rebuked his brothers and sisters who placed their faith in the "plan of salvation," a lynchpin in Church of Christ theology (see chapter 2). To have "faith in faith, faith in repentance, faith in confession, [and] faith in baptism," he wrote, "is to build according to a blueprint; and if you meet the specifications your building will be approved by the great Inspector!" He insisted that such a notion was fundamentally unbiblical. "We are saved by a *person*, not by a ceremony" or "a plan."[67]

Another preacher widely known for his theology of grace in the early to middle years of the twentieth century was K. C. Moser, who preached in Texas and Oklahoma from the 1920s through the 1970s. When Moser argued in 1934 that the grace of God was free and undeserved, a storm of controversy erupted. Three years later Moser complained that the gospel of grace was seldom preached from pulpits in Churches of Christ. Typical of the many sermons he had read and heard, he said, was one on John 3:16, where the preacher argued that in the cross, God "simply showed man how to save himself."[68]

It is little wonder, then, that so many found Boll's apocalyptic orientation so disturbing and threatening. In truth, unmerited grace held the place of honor in Boll's theology. "Can we ever have a minute's real peace with God," Boll asked, "or feel anything more than anxiety and fear toward Him so long as we stand upon this miserable plan of salvation by works?" But Boll rejoiced that there was "a way in which we may have present peace and assurance . . . *right now.* . . . *'Being therefore justified by faith we have peace with God through our Lord Jesus Christ. . . .'* (Rom. 5:1,2)." Based on this confidence, Boll resolutely affirmed, " 'Even so, Come Lord Jesus!' "[69]

The Threat to Respectability

Second, Boll's apocalyptic theology threatened mainstream Churches of Christ in their quest for respectability and denominational standing during and following World War I. To understand this development, one must realize that during the course of their separation from the Disciples of Christ during the 1880s and 1890s, Churches of Christ lost thousands of members and hundreds of church buildings. Especially in urban areas, they emerged at the end of the division as a straggling band of largely lower-class members, more often than not meeting in a storefront or a ramshackle building in a part of town that most prominent southerners would have regarded as the wrong side of the tracks. As J. N. Armstrong recalled in 1940, "Not only did the defection leave us without schools, but those who introduced the music carried with them, also, the best church property, most of the wealth, big businesses, banking, and so forth. All colleges, scholarships, church property, wealth, and big businesses became the inherited asset of the Christian Church."[70]

This state of affairs was unacceptable to many leaders of Churches of Christ, who for years had taken pride in belonging to one of the largest and fastest-growing religious movements in the United States. America's entry into World War I only compounded the problem. Citizens throughout the country were suddenly subjected to unprecedented pressure to support the war effort in every way possible. If Churches of Christ had been relegated to a degree of social marginality by virtue of their division from the Disciples, their marginality would only intensify if they responded to the war with affirmations of pacifism.

It quickly became apparent to many church leaders that if Churches of Christ hoped to regain a measure of respectability, they would have to abandon what remained of their nineteenth-century pacifist heritage and present a united front in support of the war effort.

Churches of Christ, however, could in no way reconcile support for the war with the old apocalyptic theology of the nineteenth century. They needed, instead, a theology far more progressive, far more amenable to militarism, far more centered on the concerns of this world, and far less focused on the coming kingdom of God. Such a theology was close at hand in the form of Alexander Campbell's rational, progressive primitivism.

The issue of pacifism came to a head when Lee Douglas, U.S. Attorney General for Middle Tennessee, threatened *Gospel Advocate* publisher J. C. McQuiddy with arrest if he persisted in publishing in the *Advocate* "seditious" articles that discouraged "registration of young men under the Selective Service . . . Act." McQuiddy straightaway expunged from the *Advocate* all promotion of pacifism and criticism of militarism.[71]

The changes in the *Advocate*, however, ran far deeper than the loss of the pacifist sentiment. Instead, one finds in the *Advocate* during those years an almost complete reversal of worldview based on a reappraisal of human potential. Many found no longer useful the apocalyptic worldview of Stone and Lipscomb, which downplayed human ability to usher in the kingdom of God. Instead, they more and more embraced the progressive optimism that had always characterized that strain of the movement that owed its greatest debt to Alexander Campbell. In fairness, it must be said that this shift had been in process for many years, but the crisis associated with World War I accelerated the transition and made it complete.

Accordingly, McQuiddy severely criticized those who had doubts about the ability of human beings to usher in the kingdom of God. "It is not Christlike, it is not manly, it is not noble," McQuiddy complained,

> to sit down and whine that it is impossible to bring about such a condition [as the end of all war]. . . . The same spirit would never have broken the Hindenburg line; the same spirit would never have conquered Germany and made her sue for peace. . . . The same spirit will never overcome the world, the flesh, and the devil, and bring the crown that is sure to come to the faithful.[72]

The shift in worldview was perhaps most apparent in the attitude the editorial staff of the *Advocate* adopted toward Woodrow Wilson's proposed League of Nations. If virtually all the southern luminaries of Churches of Christ throughout the nineteenth century—Stone, Fanning, Lipscomb, and Harding—had thought human institutions incapable of renovating the world and had looked to God alone as the source of millennial peace, the *Advocate*'s editors now suggested that the League might do God's work for him. "I ask those who are pessimistic, I ask those who are fighting the policy of our President [regarding the League],"

J. C. McQuiddy demanded, "how do they know but that this is the time of which the prophet prophesied and that the day is soon to dawn when nation shall not lift up sword against nation?" M. C. Kurfees argued even more pointedly. Quoting directly from the biblical prophecies, he asked, "Who knows but . . . [that the League's] adoption may be a long step toward the glad time when the nations 'shall beat their swords into plowshares, and their spears into pruning hooks'; and when 'nation shall not lift up sword against nation, neither shall they learn war any more.' "[73]

Many of the followers of R. H. Boll thus concluded that the League was nothing more than the "last form of the Gentile power . . . that men are looking for as the Golden Age but which God . . . shows us will be the climax of all the world's great wickedness."[74]

THE CHANGE IN R. H. BOLL

Ironically, as Michael Casey has discovered, even Boll finally compromised the more rigorous dimensions of the apocalyptic heritage of Churches of Christ, and he did so in several ways. First, he abandoned David Lipscomb's position that human governments were fundamentally diabolical. Accordingly, he refused to criticize the government of the United States for its decision to enter into World War I. Second, although he consistently argued that it was wrong for a Christian to fight in carnal warfare, he also argued that the Christian owed allegiance to his government and should therefore engage in alternative service during wartime. Third, the "Red Scare" that followed immediately upon the heels of World War I convinced Boll that the world was divided between good and evil: Bolshevism on the one side and the United States on the other. As the years progressed, his anti-Communist rhetoric intensified, and he finally emerged as a traditional American patriot.[75]

If this dramatic transition seems almost bizarre, it makes a great deal more sense when viewed against the backdrop of a similar transition that took place within American fundamentalism during the very same period. Already we have observed that Boll embraced the dispensational premillennial theology that was a hallmark of the American fundamentalist tradition. In his articles in *Word and Work*, Boll routinely quoted from fundamentalist writers and recommended their works. Now, in the midst of the Red Scare, he followed the lead of the fundamentalist movement once again.

In his monumental study *Fundamentalism and American Culture*, George Marsden explained that fundamentalism grew from the womb of nineteenth-century American evangelicalism, a tradition committed to transforming the United States into a Christian commonwealth. By virtue of the Second Great Awakening and the "humanitarian crusade" it fostered, these people made notable strides toward achieving that goal in the early years of the nineteenth century.

By century's end, however, much had changed. Now, "modernism"—fostered by Darwinian evolution, higher criticism of the biblical text, and a new psychology that sought to explain God primarily in terms of human need—increasingly dominated the culture of the United States. Many evangelicals therefore found themselves estranged from the culture they had once thought would reflect the rule of God. In response, many turned away from the culture, embraced premillennial sentiments, intensified their allegiance to the kingdom of God as opposed to the kingdoms of this world, adopted a distinctly pessimistic perspective on human progress, and refused to participate in politics. In a word, once the dominant influence in American life, these evangelicals now discovered that they were sojourners and aliens in a foreign land. Here one finds the beginnings of American fundamentalism.

R. H. Boll's apocalyptic perspective resembled this pessimistic outlook of American fundamentalism in remarkable ways. Indeed, one might well argue that though Boll initially learned his apocalyptic lessons at the old Nashville Bible School, he found those lessons reinforced by the broader world of American fundamentalism, especially through 1917.

World War I, however, transformed fundamentalism, almost in the twinkling of an eye, into a militant, intensely patriotic, Christian tradition. The war, after all, presented conservative Christians in the United States with a scapegoat that seemed to explain the moral and religious demise of the United States. That scapegoat was the German nation, which many now identified as the source of virtually all the modern notions that threatened to undermine the supposedly Christian foundations of the United States. With this realization, fundamentalists now reaffirmed their original determination to bring America under the rule of God and therefore launched an all-out war on such German notions as evolution (which they associated with Nietzsche's *Ubermensch*) and biblical criticism. In this way, they believed, they had one last chance to transform America into an outpost of the kingdom of God. The post–World War I Red Scare only intensified the fundamentalists' determination to save the United States from the evil that threatened to engulf it.[76] When viewed against this backdrop, R. H. Boll's transition from apocalyptic pessimist to American patriot begins to make sense.

RAISING THE FIGHT TO A NEW LEVEL: THE ROLE OF FOY E. WALLACE, JR.

The fact that Boll underwent this transition did not deter his detractors, for whom Boll was a marked man from the beginning of the premillennial controversy. Not until the 1930s did the attack on Boll and his premillennial doctrines become personal and, in many instances, vicious. The man who raised the attack to those levels was Foy E. Wallace, Jr., a Texan who edited the *Gospel Advocate* from 1930 to 1934, then launched his own paper, the *Gospel Guardian*, for the express purpose of driving premillennial sentiments from Churches of Christ.

In 1938 Wallace gave birth to yet another journal, the *Bible Banner*, where he sought to discredit not only premillennialism but also pacifism and the entire apocalyptic worldview.

Wallace marshalled an enormous following. He entered life with impressive credentials as the son of another famous preacher, Foy E. Wallace, Sr. He quickly gained fame as a boy-wonder pulpiteer. Then, as he grew older, he emerged as an intimidating speaker and debater, a fighting editor, and a man with the power to crush those in Churches of Christ who resisted his opinions and leadership. Arguably, Foy Wallace, Jr., was the single most influential preacher among Churches of Christ in the 1930s and 1940s.

Wallace was in many ways a quintessential Texan who fit the rough-and-tumble mold that had dominated the Texas frontier. In earlier years perhaps no one exemplified that mold more completely than Austin McGary, who in 1884 founded the *Firm Foundation*, a Texas-based paper destined to become as dominant among Churches of Christ in that part of the country as the *Gospel Advocate* was in Tennessee.

After serving first as sheriff and then as conveying agent for the state penitentiary, McGary established the *Firm Foundation* for the express purpose of fighting David Lipscomb, editor of the *Gospel Advocate*, over the issue of rebaptism. Lipscomb and his colleagues in Middle Tennessee routinely accepted Baptists who sought membership in the Churches of Christ. McGary, in contrast, believed that baptism was legitimate only when administered "for the remission of sins." But Baptists, McGary claimed, were baptized because they believed their sins were already forgiven. McGary therefore argued that any Baptist who wished to become a member of the Church of Christ must be rebaptized. He felt so strongly about this matter that he attacked David Lipscomb's position time and again. When Lipscomb finally complained of McGary's tactics, McGary lashed out, "He richly deserves the castigation that is in store for him, and he should stand up bravely and take it. He plaited the whip with his own hands, and if he aimed it for a plaything, he should not have made it so *heavy!*"[77] McGary's style was perhaps best reflected in his assertion that "the man who proclaims 'the truth as it is in Jesus' . . . must wound a large per cent of the people."[78]

The fighting style that characterized the work of Austin McGary also defined the work of Foy E. Wallace in a later generation. Wallace contributed to the battle over premillennialism little that was substantive, but he did succeed in dramatically altering the tone of the debate. He introduced into the controversy a style that specialized in ridicule, sarcasm, name-calling, and charges that premillennialists were willfully divisive. He announced this style in the inaugural issue of the *Bible Banner*, where he complained of the "general softness" that he thought was "pervading the church" in his time. "Firm faith and plain preaching, once universal and unanimous among those devoted to the ancient gospel," he proclaimed, "are now yielding to the persuasions of the plush-mouthed and velvet-tongued moderns." He blamed this trend on "the Bollistic blight [that] has been a malignant growth in the body of Christ" and on "the spirit of pacifism . . . [which] is taking the fight out of the church." But Wallace sought to reverse that trend. He called for "militant preaching . . . and teaching and writing that defends the truth against all errors, teachers of error and institutions of error by name, make, model and number."[79]

Because few had the courage to resist Wallace or his intimidating rhetoric, he ultimately succeeded in driving premillennialism and those who embraced that position from the mainstream of Churches of Christ. By 1949, when Wallace discontinued the *Bible Banner*, the premillennial position among Churches of Christ had essentially collapsed except for a few straggling congregations in and around Louisville, Kentucky, and New Orleans, Louisiana, where the premillennial position continued to thrive. More than this, the entire apocalyptic worldview had essentially collapsed as well.

Two episodes in Wallace's onslaught against premillennialism are especially notable and deserve comment here: his attack on Harding College in Searcy, Arkansas, and his attack on David Lipscomb and the principles Lipscomb espoused in his book, *Civil Government*.

The Attack on Harding College

No twentieth-century institution associated with Churches of Christ had deeper roots in the apocalyptic orientation than did Harding College. In fact, Harding traced its lineage back through several precursor institutions and finally to the Nashville Bible School, of which, theologically at least, it was the rightful heir.

The chain of events that ultimately helped create Harding College began in 1901 when James A. Harding left the Nashville Bible School to establish a comparable institution, Potter Bible College, in Bowling Green, Kentucky. One of Harding's faculty members was his own son-in-law, J. N. Armstrong. Between 1905 and 1924, Armstrong established or helped to save three other fledgling educational institutions, the last of which—Harper College—emerged as Harding College in Searcy, Arkansas, in 1924.

One of those interim institutions, Cordell Christian College in Cordell, Oklahoma, is especially worthy of note. Armstrong, B. F. Rhodes, and R. C. Bell arrived in Cordell in 1908 to help shore up the newly established college. Armstrong quickly assumed the presidency of the institution. When the United States entered World War I, however, the local selective service board in Cordell, recognizing the pacifist sentiment that dominated the college, demanded that the "institution be so reorganized as will unreservedly conform to all military policies and requirements of the government in order to successfully carry on the war and that no half-way compliance will be tolerated." The board demanded that Armstrong, along with all faculty and trustees who shared Armstrong's pacifist sentiments, immediately resign. Cordell had little choice but to close its doors.[80]

Armstrong did not embrace premillennial sentiments, but he was deeply committed to the apocalyptic orientation he had learned from his father-in-law, James A. Harding, and from David Lipscomb. Like his mentors he believed that two forces vied for control of the world, human government and the kingdom of God. Ultimately, he argued, the kingdom of God would prevail and human governments would collapse at the feet of a sovereign God. In the meantime Harding lived his life *as if* the kingdom of God were fully present. This lent to his life a dimension of radical discipleship including, as we have seen, a commitment to pacifism and peace making. These positions made Armstrong a convenient target for Foy Wallace and others who found it difficult to distinguish between out-and-out premillennialism and an apocalyptic orientation to the world.

By the time Wallace launched his attack on Harding College, Armstrong had stepped out of the presidency and was now serving as chairperson of the Bible Department. Wallace and his lieutenant in the state of Arkansas, E. R. Harper, who preached for the Fourth and State Street Church of Christ in Little Rock, did everything in their power to discredit Harding College and to force Armstrong's resignation. Harding College, however, stood fast and refused to succumb to Wallace's efforts to intimidate the school.

The Attack on David Lipscomb

A few years later Wallace launched another attack on the person he rightly regarded as the source of both the apocalyptic worldview and premillennial thinking in Churches of Christ: the venerable David Lipscomb. In that context, Wallace criticized members of Churches of Christ who sought to portray their church as a peace church. "It is . . . a 'stigma,' " he wrote, "to have such a doctrine pinned on the churches in the records of our government and in the eyes of the world." He labeled conscientious objectors as "impractical," "misguided," "men with a dwarfed conscience," and "freak specimen[s] of humanity." His brother Cled was even more outspoken, proclaiming the doctrine of nonresistance "a screwy philosophy" and "idiotic drivel and unpatriotic rot." Pacifists themselves fared no better, emerging in Cled's rhetoric as "crackpots" and people with "dwarfed minds."[81]

At some point Wallace concluded that his efforts to destroy both pacifism and premillennialism among Churches of Christ would be abortive unless he first destroyed the apocalyptic orientation that seemed to undermine allegiance to civil government. Accordingly, he observed,

> The whole question of civil government appears to be in the background of the premillennial theory, if not in the foreground. It has a distinct connection with the premillennial scheme of things. Premillennialists generally hold that human governments belong to Satan, hence the time will come when Christ will abolish every government in the world

and set up his own. . . . Therefore, those who advocate the theory that civil government belongs to the devil are the ones who are helping the premillennialists.[82]

Realizing that David Lipscomb, and especially his little book *Civil Government*, was the root cause of considerable apocalyptic thinking in Churches of Christ, Wallace opened the pages of the *Bible Banner* to those who would discredit Lipscomb. Straightaway W. E. Brightwell pointed out that for the most part, pacifists in Churches of Christ were "those who have attended certain schools or have read a certain book [i.e., *Civil Government*]." Brightwell found completely incomprehensible Lipscomb's claim that civil government was the domain of Satan. "The purpose of civil government is good," he wrote. "The devil does not have anything to do with it. The Lord does. And the fallacy of this foolish theory ought to be patent to all."[83]

O. C. Lambert correctly pointed out that "Lipscomb recognizes no difference in the kingdoms. The United States government is just as bad as the rest. The government that gives so much freedom to Christians is no better than one that persecutes them." Lambert could not comprehend why Lipscomb would make "the devil . . . the head of the United States government." He felt "the Lipscomb book would be outlawed now if the FBI knew its contents," and called on Churches of Christ to "call all of them [copies of *Civil Government*] in and burn them."[84]

In October 1943 Wallace himself entered the fray against Lipscomb and his book, *Civil Government*. "In looking back over the years in which this book and others like it were circulated among the brethren, it is not hard to see how the theories of Premillennialism found soil in which to grow among churches of Christ," he observed. He noted that "premillennialism calls for the very things that are taught in 'Civil Government' by David Lipscomb. The two theories go together; they fit each other perfectly." Consequently, he judged that Lipscomb's book was "about as rank with false doctrine as one book of its size could be," and he lamented the fact "that any recognized leader in churches of Christ, past or present, should espouse and promote such a doctrine" as the apocalyptic worldview of David Lipscomb.[85]

In making these connections, Wallace was onto something important. In fact, Boll recalled in 1933 that Lipscomb had once said to him,

Brother Boll, your views on prophecy are not so much different from mine. I think I could apply all the prophecies concerning Israel spiritually to the church except the land promise. That is so plain and definite that I don't see any other possibility but that it will have to be fulfilled just as it reads in the Bible.[86]

CONCLUSIONS

In 1944 E. R. Harper rejoiced that "R. H. Boll has been fought by every paper, pulpit, preacher and most schools" and he and his people had been rejected "as unsound and therefore have been 'marked and avoided' by the church in general." He added, "The papers no longer allow him space to write his views and the pulpits are closed to him, . . . and most schools will not allow him to enjoy their fellowship."[87] As far as its standing in mainline Churches of Christ was concerned, the premillennial heritage was dead.

The collapse of this tradition signaled far more than the demise of premillennialism among mainline Churches of Christ. It also signaled the near-extinction of the apocalyptic orientation that had played such a major role in defining Churches of Christ in the nineteenth century. It also underscored the triumph of the rational, progressive primitivism that characterized the lineage of Alexander Campbell. And finally, it set Churches of Christ squarely on the path that would lead them from nineteenth-century sect to twentieth-century denomination.

NOTES

1. Samuel Davies, *Sermons on Important Subjects*, vol. 1 (New York: n.p., 1842), pp. 217–18; and Whitefield, quoted by Winthrop S. Hudson in *Religion in America*, 4th ed. (New York: Macmillan, 1987), p. 79.

2. On this revival, see Paul R. Conkin, *Cane Ridge: America's Pentecost* (Madison: University of Wisconsin Press, 1990).

3. Richard McNemar, Barton Stone, et al., *The Last Will and Testament of the Springfield Presbytery*, in *Historical Documents Advocating Christian Union*, ed. Charles A. Young (Chicago: Christian Century, 1904), pp. 19–23.

4. Joseph Thomas, *The Travels and Gospel Labors of Joseph Thomas* (Winchester, VA.: J. Foster, 1812), p. 90.

5. For Haggard's influence on the O'Kelly movement, see W. E. MacClenny in *The Life of Rev. James O'Kelly* (Raleigh, NC: Edwards & Broughton Printing, 1910), p. 116. The Haggard pamphlet has been reprinted as *An Address to the Different Religious Societies, on the Sacred Import of the Christian Name: Footnotes to Disciple History No. 4* (Nashville: Disciples of Christ Historical Society, 1954). See also Colby D. Hall, *Rice Haggard: The American Frontier Evangelist Who Revived the Name Christian* (Fort Worth, TX: Stafford-Lowdon, 1957).

6. Robert Marshall and John Thompson, *A Brief Historical Account of Sundry Things in the Doctrines and State of the Christian, or as It Is Commonly Called, the Newlight Church* (Cincinnati, 1811), p. 17; and Archippus, "Calvinism and Arminianism: Review of Elder D's Letter–No. III," *Christian Examiner* 1 (31 May 1830): 159.

7. T. S., "To the Editor of the Christian Messenger," *CM* 1 (25 September 1827): 249; and J. and J. Gregg, "An Apology for Withdrawing from the Methodist Episcopal Church," *CM* 1 (25 December 1826): 39–40.

8. Alexander Campbell, "Address to the Readers of the Christian Baptist, No. IV," *CB* 1 (1 March 1824): 148; see also Campbell, *The Christian System*, 4th ed. (Bethany, VA.: n.p., 1857), p. 48; and *Christianity Restored* (Bethany, VA.: n.p., 1835), p. 350.

9. Arthur Crihfield, "Incidents of a Tour to Indianapolis, Chapter III," *HD* 3 (October 1839): 267; and Hall, "Operation of the Holy Spirit," *HD* 1 (July 1837): 179.

10. Barton W. Stone, "Missionaries to Pagans," *CM* 14 (April 1845): 363 (Stone

completed this article before his death in 1844); and Stone to Walter Scott, *CM* 10 (January 1836): 13–14.

11. Thomas, *The Travels and Gospel Labors of Joseph Thomas*, p. 88.
12. Stone, *CM* (August 1830): 201.
13. Stone, "Reply to the Above," *CM* 5 (March 1831): 58.
14. Stone, "Reply," *CM* 4 (September 1830): 236.
15. Stone, "The Way of Salvation," *CM* 1 (January 1842): 77.
16. John Rogers, in a letter to Stone dated 17 February 1842, published in *CM* 12 (April 1842): 178; Stone, "Reply to Eld. J. Rogers," *CM* 12 (April 1842): 180–87.
17. Stone, "Reply to Brother Gooch," *CM* 9 (October 1835): 221–23.
18. Stone, "Desultory Remarks," *CM* 10 (December 1836): 182.
19. Stone, "Reply," *CM* 4 (September 1830): 236; and "Reply to the Above," *CM* 11 (June 1841): 340.
20. Anthony L. Dunnavant has documented this reading of Stone in his article, "From Precursor of the Movement to Icon of Christian Unity: Barton W. Stone in the Memory of the Christian Church (Disciples of Christ)," in *Cane Ridge in Context: Perspectives on Barton W. Stone and the Revival*, ed. Anthony L. Dunnavant (Nashville: Disciples of Christ Historical Society, 1992), pp. 13–14. On Stone as precursor of the modern ecumenical movement, see, e.g., Charles C. Ware, *Barton Warren Stone: Pathfinder of Christian Union* (St. Louis: Bethany Press, 1932), p. 10; and William Garrett West, *Barton Warren Stone: Early American Advocate of Christian Unity* (Nashville: Disciples of Christ Historical Society, 1954), pp. 110–31, 137–202.
21. Stone, "Christian Expositor," *CM* 12 (July 1842): 272.
22. Stone, *The Biography of Eld. Barton Warren Stone* (1847), in *The Cane Ridge Reader*, ed. Hoke S. Dickinson (n.p.: n.p., 1972), pp. 49–50.
23. Abner Hill, "An Autobiography of Abner Hill, Pioneer Preacher of Tennessee, Alabama, and Texas" (c. 1861), typescript housed in Center for Restoration Studies, Abilene Christian University, pp. 19–20; and Stone, "1,000 Spiritual Preachers Wanted," *CM* 13 (March 1844): 367–69.
24. John Rogers, "Funeral Discourse on Elder H. Dinsmore [Part 2]," *American Christian Review* 6 (17 November 1863): 181; Jones, "The Reformation in Tennessee," included in J. W. Grant's "Sketch of the Reformation in Tennessee" (c. 1897), typescript housed in Center for Restoration Studies, Abilene Christian University, p. 35; and Hall, "The Autobiography of B. F. Hall," typescript housed in Center for Restoration Studies, Abilene Christian University, pp. 67–68.
25. Stone, "Christian Union, Lecture III," *CM* 11 (May 1841): 316–17.
26. Stone, "To Elder William Caldwell," *CM* 8 (May 1834): 148. See also Stone, "The Millennium," *CM* 7 (October 1833): 314; and "Reply," *CM* 7 (December 1833): 365–66.
27. Stone et al., *Observations on Church Government, by the Presbytery of Springfield* (1808), in *The Cane Ridge Reader*, pp. 3, 8–9.
28. Stone, "Reflections of Old Age," *CM* 13 (August 1843): 123–26. See also "Civil and Military Offices Sought and Held by Christians," *CM* 12 (May 1842): 201–5; letters to and from T. P. Ware, *CM* 14 (October 1844): 163–71; and "An Interview between an Old and Young Preacher," *CM* 14 (December 1844): 225–30.
29. James M. Mathes, "Number III," *CM* 10 (May 1836): 65–66; and Jn. T. Jones, Jno. Rigdon, M. Elder, and D. P. Henderson, "Report," *CM* 9 (November 1835): 250–51.

30. Stone, "Lecture on Matt. V. VI. and VII. Chapters," *CM* 14 (July 1844): 65.

31. Campbell, "American Christian Missionary Society, President's Address," *MH*, 4th ser., 2 (March 1852): 124.

32. Benjamin Lyon Smith, *Alexander Campbell* (St. Louis: Bethany Press, 1930), p. 147.

33. Campbell, quoted by Robert Richardson in *Memoirs of Alexander Campbell*, vol. 2 (1897; reprint, Nashville: Gospel Advocate, 1956), p. 90. On Campbell's debates, see Bill J. Humble, *Campbell and Controversy* (Rosemead, CA: Old Paths Book Club, 1952).

34. Stone, "To Young Preachers," *CM* 12 (August 1842): 316–17; and Stone and D. P. Henderson, "Introduction," *CM* 14 (May 1844): 4–5.

35. Matthew Gardner in a tract published in 1836, cited by S. H. Ford in "Rise of the Current Reformation—Appendix," *CRep* 72 (March 1858): 203–5.

36. These preachers included Ephraim D. Moore, James E. Matthews, and Ross Houston. See James Wilburn, *The Hazard of the Die: Tolbert Fanning and the Restoration Movement* (Malibu: Pepperdine University Press, 1980), pp. 13–16; and Fanning, "Obituary," *GA* 3 (January 1860): 31.

37. Fanning, "Reply to Brethren Lillard, Harding, and Ransome," *GA* 7 (September 1861): 265–76; and " 'The Kingdom of Heaven': A Spiritual Empire," *CRev* 3 (May 1846): 101.

38. Fanning, "Political Strife amongst Christians," *CRev* 1 (August 1844): 184–85; "Peace," *CRev* 3 (March 1846): 65; and David Lipscomb, "The Gospel Advocate," *GA* 9 (7 March 1867): 65.

39. Lipscomb, "The Bible and Evolution," *GA* 31 (26 January 1889): 56; "Common Sense in Religion," *GA* 46 (25 February 1904): 120; "Our Subscribers," *GA* 10 (23 January 1868): 73; and "After Fifty Years," *GA* 58 (6 January 1916): 1.

40. Lipscomb, "Religion and Politics," *GA* 32 (26 March 1890): 199.

41. Lipscomb, *CG*, 8–10, 19–20, 48.

42. Lipscomb, *CG*, pp. 25, 27–28 (cf. pp. 83–84), 96.

43. Lipscomb, "The Kingdom of God," *GA* 45 (21 May 1903): 328.

44. Lipscomb, "Queries," *GA* 37 (23 June 1898): 397; and "Restoration, Times Of," in J. W. Shepherd, ed., *Queries and Answers*, 5th ed. (Nashville: Gospel Advocate Co., 1963 [orig. 1910]), p. 360.

45. Lipscomb, "Queries," *GA* 37 (23 June 1898): 397.

46. Franklin, "Visit to Tennessee," *ACR*, 18 (13 July 1875): 220.

47. Lipscomb, *CG*, pp. 145 and 133.

48. Lipscomb, "The Cholera," *GA* 15 (26 June 1873): 619.

49. Lipscomb, *CG*, pp. 28 (cf. pp. 83–84, iv) and 97.

50. Lipscomb, "Babylon," *GA* 23 (2 June 1881): 340.

51. Lipscomb, "Babylon," *GA* 23 (2 June 1881): 340.

52. Lipscomb, *GA* 8 (27 February 1866): 141; and "Tolbert Fanning's Teaching and Influence," in *Franklin College and Its Influences*, ed. James E. Scobey (Nashville: McQuiddy Printing, 1906), pp. 59–60. On Lipscomb and the poor, see Anthony L. Dunnavant, "David Lipscomb and the 'Preferential Option for the Poor' among the Postbellum Churches of Christ" in Dunnavant, ed., *Poverty and Ecclesiology: Nineteenth-Century Evangelicals in the Light of Liberation Theology* (Collegeville MN: Liturgical Press, 1992), pp. 27–50.

53. Lipscomb, "Withdrawal," *GA* 22 (16 September 1880): 597.

54. On Boll's early life, immigration to Ohio, and subsequent conversion in Tennessee

to the Churches of Christ, see Hans Rollman, "From the Black Forest to the Nashville Bible School: The Conversion of Robert Henry Boll," unpublished paper presented at Christian Scholars' Conference, Pepperdine University, 1998. This material will appear in a biography of Boll that Rollman is currently preparing.

55. R. C. Bell, "Studies in Philemon (3)," *FF* 77 (26 January 1960): 55.

56. James A. Harding, in *The Harding-White Discussion* (Cincinnati: F. L. Rowe, 1910), pp. 14–15.

57. See, for example, Harding, "The Kingdom of Christ versus the Kingdoms of Satan," *The Way* 5 (15 October 1903): 929–31.

58. Harding, "Scraps," *The Way* 1 (5 July 1899): 97; and John T. Lewis, " 'His Heart Trembled for the Ark of God,' " *Bible Banner* 1 (October 1938): 7.

59. Harding, quoted by Lloyd Cline Sears, *The Eyes of Jehovah: The Life and Times of James Alexander Harding* (Nashville: Gospel Advocate, 1970), p. 155. Stanford Chambers, also a student at the Nashville Bible School, notes that Boll had a special allegiance to Harding in "It Is to Reminisce," *Exhorter* (1 January 1968): 4.

60. Boll, "What Shall the End Be?" *The Way* 2 (April 1900): 60–61; and "The Christian's Duty as to War," *WW* 11 (December 1917): 493–94.

61. On Boll's millennialism, see Hans Rollmann, "Our Steadfastness and Perseverance Depends on Perpetual Expectation of Our Lord": The Development of Robert Henry Boll's Premillennialism (1895–1915)," *Disc* 59 (Winter 1999): 113–26.

62. Evidence abounds concerning the influence of dispensational thought on Boll. See, e.g., R.H.B., "About Books," *WW* 10 (February 1916): 88; "Bible Study Course," *WW* 10 (January 1916): 28; and "Jesus Is Coming," *WW* 10 (December 1916): 551. On Boll's dispensationalism, see Boll, *The Kingdom of God* (Louisville: Word & Work, n.d.). It is also important to note that Boll routinely ran articles in his *Word and Work* by such early fundamentalists as Arno Gaebelein, Philip Mauro, Reuben Torrey, and W. E. Blackstone.

63. J. C. McQuiddy, "Do the Kingdom and the Church Mean the Same Thing?" *GA* 61 (17 April 1919): 367; and "Is the Church the Vestibule of the Kingdom?" *GA* 61 (20 March 1919): 271–72.

64. Stanford Chambers, "It Is to Reminisce," *Exhorter* (1 January 1968): 4.

65. F. D. Srygley, "Salvation by Grace," *GA* 20 (28 November 1878): 743; and Nichol and Whiteside, *Sound Doctrine*, vol. 1 (Clifton, TX: Nichol Publishing, 1920), pp. 146, 153.

66. Chambers, "It Is to Reminisce," *Exhorter* (1 January 1968): 4.

67. G. C. Brewer, "Confession and the Plan of Salvation," *GA* 87 (26 April 1945): 233.

68. K. C. Moser, "Can the Gospel Be Obeyed?" *FF* 51 (13 February 1934): 2; and Moser, in a tract entitled "Are We Preaching the Gospel?" cited by Bill Love in *The Core Gospel: On Restoring the Crux of the Matter* (Abilene, TX: Abilene Christian University Press, 1992), p. 245. Moser's classic work was *The Way of Salvation*, published in 1932.

69. Boll, "Afraid of God and of Christ's Coming," *WW* 10 (August 1916): 34–35.

70. J. N. Armstrong, "A Piece of History," *CL* 54 (1 August 1940): 15.

71. See Michael W. Casey, "From Patriotism to Pacifism: The Emergence of Civil Religion in the Churches of Christ in World War One," *Mennonite Quarterly Review* 66 (July 1992): 376–90.

72. McQuiddy, "The Peace League," *GA* 61 (27 March 1919): 297–98.

73. McQuiddy, "The Peace League," *GA* 61 (27 March 1919): 297; see also, e.g., M. C. Kurfees, "The League of Nations and the Peace of the World," *GA* 61 (4 September 1919): 866–67.

74. Charles Neal, "The United States of the Nations," *WW* 11 (September 1917): 378–80.

75. Michael Casey, "Neither Militant nor Pacifist: R. H. Boll on War and Peace," unpublished paper presented at Christian Scholars' Conference, Pepperdine University, 17 July 1998.

76. George M. Marsden, *Fundamentalism and American Culture: The Shaping of Twentieth-Century Evangelicalism, 1870–1925* (Oxford: Oxford University Press, 1980), pp. 55–62, 102–23, and 153–56.

77. Austin McGary, "Trying to Elude Detection by Pointing to Side Issues and Dodging behind Technicalities," *FF* 1 (November 1884): 72.

78. McGary, "Personalities," *FF* 1 (February 1885): 126.

79. Foy E. Wallace, Jr., "Imprimatur—Let It Be Printed," *BB* 1 (May 1939): 2; "What the Church Must Do to Be Saved," *BB*, 1 (July 1939): 3; and " 'Jehovah-Nissi—the Lord My Banner,' " *BB* 1 (July 1938): 2–3.

80. Michael W. Casey tells this story in substantial detail in "The Closing of Cordell Christian College: A Microcosm of American Intolerance during World War I," *Chronicles of Oklahoma* 76 (Spring 1998): 20–37. See also Lloyd Cline Sears, *For Freedom: The Biography of John Nelson Armstrong* (Austin, TX: Sweet Publishing, 1969), pp. 155–57.

81. Foy E. Wallace, Jr., "The Lipscomb Theory of Civil Government," *BB* 6 (October 1943): 5; and "The Christian and the Government," *BB* 4 (March 1942): 4. Cled Wallace, "The Christian and the Government," *BB* 4 (June 1942): 4; and "The Big President of a Little College," *BB* 6 (June 1944): 3.

82. Foy E. Wallace, Jr., "The Government—Civil and Military," *BB* 4 (July 1942): 3–4.

83. W. E. Brightwell, "For the Vindication of the Cause," *BB* 4 (July 1942): 5, 7.

84. O. C. Lambert, "The David Lipscomb Book," *BB* 7 (September 1944): 9–10, 15; "Canonizing Campbell and Lipscomb," *BB* 6 (May 1944): 10; and a letter to Foy Wallace printed in Wallace, "The Lipscomb Theory of Civil Government," *BB* 6 (October 1943): 3.

85. Wallace, "The Lipscomb Theory of Civil Government," *BB* 6 (October 1943): 5–6; and " 'The Glorious Millennial Morn,' " *BB* 6 (May 1944): 5.

86. Boll, "David Lipscomb's Attitude," *WW* 27 (1933): 9. Evidence regarding Lipscomb's attitude toward Boll is mixed. James Allen reported that Lipscomb warned J. C. McQuiddy that Boll "was an unsafe man to put on the *Gospel Advocate* staff. James A. Allen, "Review of a Christian Businessman," *AT* 17 (August 1947): 170–71.

87. E. R. Harper, "Is It the Truth—or the Person?" *BB* 6 (March 1944): 7.

5
THE FIGHT OVER PROGRESS AND MODERNIZATION

Embarrassed over the negative journalistic style that Foy Wallace, Jr., had fostered, a handful of influential leaders in the 1940s and 1950s determined to move Churches of Christ in more progressive directions. In part, they sought to achieve this objective by creating kinder, gentler publications that would undermine Wallace's power and define Churches of Christ in more constructive terms.

Then, in the aftermath of World War II, a number of men—including some who had fought the negative journalistic style of Foy E. Wallace—took steps to alter the radically congregational polity that had dominated this tradition in the nineteenth century. To be sure, they continued their support for congregational autonomy, but they also erected a variety of cooperative structures aimed at providing Churches of Christ with a respectable system of higher education and a means of accomplishing effective mission work, both at home and abroad. Symbolizing this transition toward progress and modernization, Churches of Christ also embarked during this period on an aggressive building program, constructing between 1940 and 1956 over 1,000 new church buildings "representing assets of more than $147,000,000.00."[1] Most telling of all, this construction boom typically relocated congregations from ramshackle buildings, often located on the proverbial "wrong side of the tracks," to substantial and attractive physical plants, located in respectable, middle-class neighborhoods.

All this suggested that Churches of Christ were quickly moving from the status of a nineteenth-century sect to that of a twentieth-century denomination. The collapse of the apocalyptic perspective during the World War I era made this transition possible. Now, during the 1940s and 1950s, a broad mainstream of Churches of Christ quickly abandoned its countercultural orientation as it sought to take its place as one of the respectable Christian denominations in the American South.

Ironically, few if any among the mainstream of Churches of Christ fully discerned this transition to denominational standing. Instead, they continued to insist that Churches of Christ constituted no denomination whatsoever; they were, rather, the one true church authorized by the biblical text. Yet, the failure of mainstream Churches of Christ to recognize the nature of this transition in no way prevented it from occurring.

The transition from sect to denomination occasioned major, internal struggles. In fact, the dust had still not settled from the fight over premillennialism before new fights erupted over what appeared to some as a sellout to the spirit of the modern age. Some resisted constructive journalism and clung tenaciously to a fighting style that identified heretics by "name, rank, model, and number," as Foy Wallace once put it. Many more resisted efforts to create cooperative structures on behalf of colleges and missions, claiming that those efforts undermined the independence of the local congregation and therefore betrayed the model of the apostolic church. Leaders among mainstream Churches of Christ soon labeled the dissenters "anti-institutional" Christians or "antis," for short. The fight that ensued turned ugly and bitter on both sides of the aisle.

By the mid-1950s, leaders in the mainstream of Churches of Christ had lost patience with these dissenters who resisted progress, modernization, and the shift to denominational standing and virtually expelled them from the mainstream fellowship. This was the second time in the twentieth century that such an expulsion had occurred. Now alongside the mainstream Churches of Christ there stood two dissenting traditions: the premillennial Churches of Christ and the anti-institutional Churches of Christ. This chapter seeks to explore the modernization of Churches of Christ in the 1940s and 1950s and to examine how that process finally led to a major rupture between the mainstream of this tradition and the anti-institutional faction.

RESISTING THE FIGHTING STYLE

For most of the 1930s, Foy Wallace, Jr., virtually controlled the style and substance of journalism among Churches of Christ. Preoccupied with destroying the premillennial wing in this tradition, Wallace employed ridicule, sarcasm, and name calling in an effort to purge the church of its premillennial sympathizers. Convinced that Wallace's tactics would virtually destroy Churches of Christ, a small group of leaders began to search for alternatives.

The New *Christian Leader*

At the core of that group stood three men: Clinton Davidson, a millionaire insurance salesman from New York; Jesse P. Sewell, former president of Abilene Christian College (1912–1924) and now preacher for the Grove Avenue Church of Christ in San Antonio; and E. W. McMillan, former chairperson of the Bible Department at Abilene Christian College (1929–1935) and now preacher for the Central Church of Christ in Nashville, Tennessee. In their attempts to provide a constructive alternative to Wallace, these three men also enlisted the active support of E. H. Ijams, president of David Lipscomb College; George Benson, president of Harding College; J. F. Cox, president of Abilene Christian College; S. H. Hall, a Tennessee preacher noted for his constructive perspective; and G. C. Brewer, another influential preacher in this fellowship. Significantly, in one way or another, virtually all these leaders had roots in the old Nashville Bible School.

These men initially hoped that the venerable *Gospel Advocate* might provide a meaningful alternative to Wallace's brand of journalism. The fact that Wallace himself had edited the *Advocate* from 1930 through spring 1934 was grounds for considerable pessimism. But Wallace's successor, John T. Hinds, had died on New Year's Day, 1938, leaving the editorial chair of the *Advocate* vacant once again. Hopes emerged that the *Advocate* might become a powerful force for positive and constructive journalism, if only the paper's publisher, Leon McQuiddy, would choose an appropriate editor. But McQuiddy showed no signs of committing the *Advocate* to editorial reform. Finally, E. W. McMillan wrote a despondent letter to Jesse P. Sewell in August of 1938.

> Brother McQuiddy has dalleyed [*sic*] so much that I do not believe he is going to do anything toward allowing the *Gospel Advocate* to be a part of the [reform] movement. . . . It is my conviction that he is marking time in the hope that the movement may lose its momentum and allow the *Advocate* to plod on in the old rut. . . . Moreover, it is my conviction that he ultimately will lend the *Advocate* to the extreme, radical element.[2]

In the meantime Clinton Davidson had been exploring alternatives. Early in 1938 he distributed a questionnaire to a cross-section of preachers, seeking to learn their feelings regarding the current status of journalism in the Churches of Christ. Davidson reported that "97% of those who answered the questionnaire were opposed to articles in which one writer criticizes another by name," and he took that information as a popular mandate to launch a new publication. In August 1938 Davidson wrote to Sewell that he had "purchased an option on the Christian Leader. . . . I have the promise of sufficient capital to publish . . . twice monthly a magazine with better paper stock, better typography, and better cover than any paper in the brotherhood. . . . The policy will be 100% constructive."[3]

The original *Christian Leader* had first appeared in 1886. Emanating from Cincinnati, Ohio, the *Leader* had for many years served a conservative, predominantly rural, Midwestern constituency whose theological bent owed much to the influence of Benjamin Franklin (see chapter 3). It would be a stretch, at best, to transform the *Leader* into the kind of paper Davidson had in mind and to do so successfully. But Davidson and his colleagues were prepared to try.

E. W. McMillan, preacher for the Central Church of Christ in Nashville, agreed to serve as editor. Accordingly, the church building that housed the Central congregation soon also housed the *Leader*'s new editorial offices. That fact alone proved to be a serious political liability, since the Central congregation had charted for itself a course that was singular among Churches of Christ at that time. Instead of defining its mission in terms of doctrinal orthodoxy, this congregation defined itself in terms of ministry to the poor and the dispossessed. On more than one occasion the *Nashville Banner* reported how the Central Church of Christ provided facilities for homeless young people, free medical and dental care for the indigent, and free food and clothing for those in need.[4]

In 1938 N. B. Hardeman, one of the most influential preachers among Churches of Christ at that time, came to Nashville to conduct the fourth of his fabled "Hardeman Tabernacle Meetings" in Nashville's Ryman Auditorium. In 1922, 1923, and 1928 Hardeman's Tabernacle Meetings had been essentially evangelistic and supremely successful. Now in 1938, however, Hardeman directed his energies toward internal issues plaguing Churches of Christ, especially premillennialism. This was an important meeting. In fact, it is safe to say that in the 1930s there was no more significant assembly among Churches of Christ anywhere in the United States than this. Every night for two full weeks, 4,000 to 6,000 people hung on Hardeman's every word.

And yet, the Central congregation was so preoccupied with doing good works that it simply ignored these meetings, failing even to announce them publicly. Quite naturally, by this sin of omission, the Central Church made itself susceptible to charges that it was sympathetic to the premillennial heresy, a point duly exploited by Foy Wallace's *Bible Banner*.[5]

The truth is that neither the Central Church of Christ nor its minister, E. W. McMillan, subscribed to premillennial views. But both were rooted in an apocalyptic orientation that, on the one hand, compelled them to serve the poor and the oppressed and, on the other hand, helped them to appreciate the most fundamental concern of the premillennial agenda: the coming kingdom of God. Accordingly, the Central Church based

> all of its objectives as a church on the Biblical quotation, "Then shall the King say unto them on his right hand, Come ye blessed of my Father, inherit the Kingdom prepared for you from the foundation of the world, for I was hungry and ye gave me to eat; I was thirsty, and ye gave me to drink; I was a stranger and ye took me in; naked, and ye clothed me; I was sick and ye visited me; I was in prison and ye came unto me."[6]

Not only was the Central congregation a political liability for the new *Christian Leader*; so was McMillan, who had earned the judgment that he was "soft" on premillennialism when, as chairperson of the Bible Department at Abilene Christian College, he had defended R. C. Bell, one of his professors whom some accused of harboring premillennial convictions. Like McMillan, Bell was apocalyptic in his orientation, but he hardly embraced the kind of dispensational premillennialism that characterized the convictions of R. H. Boll. Widely known for his positive teachings regarding the grace of God, Bell came by his convictions naturally, having served with James A. Harding at Potter Bible College and then with J. N. Armstrong at both the Western Bible and Literary College in Missouri and Cordell Christian College in Oklahoma.

But the greatest political liability for the new *Christian Leader* was Clinton Davidson himself. A product of Potter Bible College, where he studied under James A. Harding and J. N. Armstrong, Davidson eventually settled in New York City, where he became a financial consultant to some of America's wealthiest and most significant corporate executives and, for seven years running, the world's leader in life insurance sales. Reflecting significant lower-class biases, many in the Wallace camp deeply resented Davidson's wealth. Eugene Smith, for example, characterized Davidson in the *Bible Banner* as a "man who for twenty years bowed himself in supplication and adoration at the altar of material success and there to the neglect of his soul and his God amassed a fortune." Others claimed that Davidson had deserted Churches of Christ during his time in New York and had worshiped instead with a "fashionable" and "digressive" Disciples congregation. For all these reasons Foy Wallace attacked Davidson on the grounds that he was essentially "a *business* man," not a serious Christian, and "the leading menace of the church today."[7] Most of all, Wallace believed that Davidson intended to use the new *Christian Leader* to promote the premillennial heresy.

In point of fact, however, the new *Christian Leader* typically steered clear of hotly contested doctrinal issues. Instead, those who produced the *Leader* sought to build consensus around cultural values they perceived as biblically based. The *Leader* regularly featured articles on themes like the value of a Christian home, the virtues of American democracy, Christian business ethics, love, prayer, and the power of positive thinking. This was a deliberate strategy on the part of the *Leader*, whose publishers and editor concluded that while doctrinal articles might well prove divisive and therefore generate a negative response, articles promoting biblically based cultural values might help create the kind of constructive consensus so badly needed among Churches of Christ.

This decision amounted to a second-level rejection of theological thinking in this tradition. The first-level rejection occurred in the early nineteenth century when Alexander Campbell in particular rejected theological thinking and advocated reliance on the biblical text alone. Now, in the interest of consensus among and within the Churches of Christ, key leaders were prepared to scuttle what little theological reflection had taken place in this tradition and to embrace instead a constellation of cultural values they thought consistent with the Christian faith.

Ironically, whereas the *Leader* successfully avoided the temptation to engage in doctrinal disputes in print, its publisher, Clinton Davidson, failed to heed that objective in some of his oral presentations. In spring 1940, Davidson delivered at Abilene Christian College two speeches that Jesse P. Sewell thought favorable to premillennialism. Sewell felt betrayed and refused to lend further support to the *Leader*. Without Sewell's support, the *Leader* could not continue in its current form, and in December 1940 G. H. P. Showalter, editor of the influential

Texas journal the *Firm Foundation* announced that he had acquired ownership of the *Leader*.[8]

Nonetheless, the new *Christian Leader* left a lasting legacy, even though it operated for only two years. In the first place, the *Leader*'s commitment to constructive consensus building prompted Leon McQuiddy, publisher of the *Gospel Advocate*, to embrace a similar course. Accordingly, in March 1939 McQuiddy announced that he had appointed B. C. Goodpasture as the *Advocate*'s new editor. Destined to become one of the most influential voices among Churches of Christ for the next three decades, Goodpasture used his inaugural editorial to reject in no uncertain terms the fighting, negative style that Foy Wallace had fostered during the 1930s. Appealing to the memory of Tolbert Fanning and David Lipscomb, Goodpasture wrote, "These venerable men exalted principles above persons, and sought to be free from personal bitterness and recriminations. Their example is worthy of our consideration and emulation."[9] And second, by avoiding theological reflection and doctrinal disputes, on the one hand, and by building consensus around biblically rooted cultural values, on the other, the *Leader* prefigured the emphases that would characterize a large segment of the progressive leadership of Churches of Christ for the rest of the twentieth century.

The *20th Century Christian*

Far away from New York in the city of Nashville, Tennessee, in the very same year that Clinton Davidson purchased the *Christian Leader*, four graduate students—M. Norvel Young, James D. Bales, George DeHoff, and Woodrow Whitten—also made their plans to counteract the fighting style fostered by Foy E. Wallace, Jr. Convinced that the Wallace style was completely out of touch with the concerns of their generation and therefore fundamentally detrimental to the future of Churches of Christ, these students launched from the basement of Nashville's Hillsboro Church of Christ in 1938 a new publication they called the *20th Century Christian*. Too young to possess much political clout in Churches of Christ, they prevailed upon J. P. Sanders, preacher of the Hillsboro congregation, to edit their publication. They also convinced Hugh Tiner, dean of George Pepperdine College in Los Angeles, and Athens Clay Pullias, vice president of David Lipscomb College in Nashville, to serve on an editorial council along with themselves and Sanders.

Though these students belonged to a generation much younger than Davidson, Sewell, and McMillan, they still shared much in common with their older, editorial counterparts. First, like Davidson, Sewell, and McMillan, they, too, were part of the world of higher education and therefore stood far removed in educational terms from most who supported the hard-nosed, fighting style of Foy E. Wallace, Jr. Second, like most of their older colleagues, these graduate students were heirs to the apocalyptic worldview of the nineteenth-century Churches of Christ. Bales, DeHoff, and Whitten had all been trained by J. N.

Armstrong at Harding College. Ruby Morrow Young, Norvel Young's mother, had studied under David Lipscomb, James A. Harding, and T. B. Larimore, and Young himself attended David Lipscomb College, the immediate successor of the old Nashville Bible School. Further, Young, in a very real sense, grew up in the very shadow of David Lipscomb, since his mother's father and uncle both owned farms adjoining that of Lipscomb. Not surprisingly, all four of these students were committed pacifists.

Yet, on the pages of the *20th Century Christian*, these students transformed the apocalyptic tradition in significant ways. As children of the Progressive Era, they were chiefly concerned that Churches of Christ were badly out of step with the modern world. At the same time they lamented the fact that a debating tradition and a theology rooted in Common Sense rationalism had largely severed Churches of Christ from an emphasis on genuine spirituality and practical Christian living. Accordingly, the *20th Century Christian* celebrated progress and modernization, on the one hand, and practical Christian living, on the other.

In political terms, this emphasis proved to be a stroke of genius. By embracing this approach, the students who launched the *20th Century Christian* simply removed both themselves and the journal they created from polemical or doctrinal concerns. Further, whereas Clinton Davidson's questionnaire virtually announced his intention to undermine the journalistic course of Foy E. Wallace, Jr., the four students who launched the *20th Century Christian* never gave Wallace cause to question their work. As a result, the *20th Century Christian* never attracted either the attention or the wrath of Foy Wallace, Jr. If the new *Christian Leader*, founded by older men, expired after only two years of circulation, the *20th Century Christian* survived and prospered throughout the twentieth century, by 1955 boasting a circulation to more than 50,000 members of Churches of Christ.

In the long run the new *Christian Leader* and the *20th Century Christian* exerted a significant impact on the future course of Churches of Christ. First, both publications scuttled theological thinking and doctrinal debates in the interest of a consensus built around cultural values supposedly informed by the Christian faith. Second, both publications helped move this tradition out of the backwater of nineteenth-century sectarianism and closer to the mainstream of Protestantism in the American South. Third, they helped liberate Churches of Christ from the negative, carping, and destructive journalism that Foy E. Wallace, Jr. had popularized in the 1930s. Most of all, they prompted Churches of Christ to take the modern world seriously and positioned them to embrace a thoroughly modern vision for church growth, for missions, and for church-related higher education.

THE FIGHT OVER MODERNIZATION

The process of modernization among Churches of Christ involved two strategic movements. First, if nineteenth-century advocates of the apocalyptic perspective had relied on the power and providence of God to accomplish His will in the world, those who advocated modernization did so by promoting the utilization of modern techniques and bureaucratized institutions. This was a radical shift from the perspective of, say, James A. Harding, who refused to rely on any human instrumentality to accomplish what he understood to be the Almighty's objectives (see chapter 4). Second, the effort to create within Churches of Christ a variety of institutional structures that transcended the local congregation obviously involved a transformation, however subtle, of the radically democratic and congregational polity that Churches of Christ had always identified with the primitive, apostolic pattern.

W. E. Brightwell diagnosed the problem as early as 1934. "The next religious war will be fought around the issue of institutionalism," he predicted. Two years later, in 1936, he grew more specific. He complained that many congregations of Churches of Christ were too large and too prosperous, too concerned with prestige and standing, too preoccupied with fancy church buildings and "stationed pastors," too captivated with radio preaching that inevitably diluted the simple gospel message, and too concerned with the city at the expense of their rural roots. In addition, many in Churches of Christ now sought to build colleges that would promote "human wisdom."[10] For all these reasons Brightwell cast his lot with those who would fight these various manifestations of modernization among Churches of Christ.

But in the mid-1930s Brightwell had witnessed only the tip of the iceberg. Serious modernization would not begin among Churches of Christ until after World War II, and when it began, it did so on two fronts. First, the war created among these people an awareness of parts of the world where no Churches of Christ existed, an awareness that prompted a passion for overseas missions. But how could hundreds of fiercely independent Churches of Christ, with their radically congregational polity that virtually precluded intercongregational cooperation, possibly hope to launch an effective overseas missions program? Clearly, what was needed was some way for congregations to cooperate or to pool resources in order to maximize the impact of their missions efforts. When that occurred, the war against modernization and institution building began in earnest.

World War II also prompted modernization among Churches of Christ on a second front. When the war concluded, thousands of G.I.'s returned home and flooded America's colleges and universities. During those immediate postwar years, many colleges around the nation virtually doubled their enrollments. Colleges related to Churches of Christ were no exception. Five of those colleges already were in place: David Lipscomb College in Nashville, the successor to the Nashville Bible School, founded in 1891; Abilene Christian College in Abilene, Texas, founded in 1906; Harding College in Searcy, Arkansas, founded in 1924; Freed-Hardeman College in Henderson, Tennessee, founded in 1869; and George Pepperdine College in Los Angeles, founded in 1937.

With the postwar swelling of college enrollments, the question facing colleges related to Churches of Christ was simply this: how could they provide faculties and facilities that might adequately accommodate the crush of enrollment they now faced? Previously, interested individuals, not congregations, had provided support for these schools. In fact, congregations virtually never provided monetary support for the colleges, since most feared that a college—like the dreaded missionary society of the nineteenth century—might eventually function as a parachurch organization with power—however informal—even greater than that of a local congregation.

But how could the colleges possibly provide facilities that would accommodate their surging enrollments unless they appealed to congregations, not just to individuals? When several of the colleges began to seek funds from congregations, many thought they saw the specter of institutionalized power that would inevitably subvert the autonomy and independence of the local church. This, for them, was a manifestation of modernization and a departure from the primitive, biblical standards that had always governed Churches of Christ in the nineteenth century.

Though many leaders among the mainstream of Churches of Christ routinely sought to argue that the anti-institutional people promoted novel views, the truth was quite the reverse. When judged by the nineteenth-century history of Churches of Christ, the modernizers and institution-builders were clearly the innovators in this case. After all, the entire nineteenth-century heritage of Churches of Christ had protested against the creation of parachurch organizations that might compete with the local congregation. Alexander Campbell grounded this position in his zeal for the autonomy he thought was characteristic of the primitive church, and Barton Stone concurred, rooting his position in his apocalyptic emphasis on the all-sufficiency of the kingdom of God. But now a new generation had emerged that would compromise those nineteenth-century traditions in the interest of success.

The war against institution building and modernization began in earnest in 1949 when opponents of modernization revived Foy E. Wallace, Jr.'s *Gospel Guardian*. Wallace had edited the *Guardian* in 1935 and 1936, specifically to counteract the premillennial movement in Churches of Christ. The opponents of modernization felt a strong connection to Wallace, since Wallace had warned of institutional power plays through much of the 1930s. However, when the *Guardian* reemerged in 1949 to resist institution building, Wallace was neither the journal's editor nor the most important figure in the anti-institutional crusade. Instead, the two key players were Roy Cogdill and Fanning Yater Tant. Cogdill, of Lufkin, Texas, published the paper, and Tant served as editor.

The Quarrel over Mission Work and the "Sponsoring Congregation"

A serious interest in world missions captivated Churches of Christ even before World War II had concluded. Early in 1943 the pulpit minister of the Broadway

Church of Christ in Lubbock, Texas, G. C. Brewer, invited smaller congregations throughout the United States to send funds for European missions to the Broadway congregation that would then supervise distribution of those funds in the most effective way possible. This proposal drew immediate fire from the *Bible Banner*. "Just what authority does . . . [the Broadway congregation] have to 'sponsor' a 'Plan' for somebody else?" the *Banner* queried?[11] Criticism of the "Broadway plan" would not reach its crescendo, however, for several more years.

In the meantime M. Norvel Young—one of the cofounders of the *20th Century Christian*—replaced Brewer as the pulpit minister of the Broadway congregation. Young, along with two others in that congregation—Paul Sherrod and Otis Gatewood—generated among Churches of Christ over the next few years a substantial interest in German missions in particular. Moreover, these three continued to promote the "Broadway plan" that G. C. Brewer had announced in 1943.[12] Finally, in 1947 the Broadway congregation dispatched Gatewood to the German mission field, where he served with distinction for the next ten years.

In the meantime other congregations adopted plans similar to that of the "Broadway plan," but with reference to other fields of labor. The Union Avenue Church of Christ in Memphis, Tennessee, announced that it would undertake distribution of funds for missions in Japan, and the Crescent Hill Church of Christ in Brownwood, Texas, offered to serve as a financial clearinghouse for Italian missions.

If one judges by the significant increase in mission activity undertaken by Churches of Christ over the next twenty years, one can only conclude that these various efforts were extraordinarily productive. For example, Churches of Christ sponsored only 46 missionaries worldwide in 1946–47. By 1967 that number had climbed to 724. These figures reflect several factors. They reflect, first, a greatly enhanced interest in foreign missions. They also reflect the fact that Churches of Christ, by pooling their resources in cooperative efforts, were able to accomplish more than they might have achieved otherwise. Finally, they reflect a somewhat expanded domestic base. Whereas this fellowship could count only 682,000 stateside members in 1946–47, it had grown to some 835,000 members by 1965.[13]

All was not peace and light, however, for many in the anti-institutional camp were growing increasingly concerned over what they perceived as the denominational machinery through which Churches of Christ were achieving such success. Their concerns finally erupted in a public way in 1950, when reports filtered back to the States that a group of Italian Catholics had attacked missionaries from Churches of Christ in a rock-throwing incident. Leaders and members among mainstream Churches of Christ were incensed and, following mass meetings in both Houston and Dallas, filed formal protests with the Congress and the State Department.

From the perspective of the anti-institutional people, these protests simply betrayed the extent to which mainstream Churches of Christ had made their peace with the larger culture and thereby had evolved into a denomination among other denominations. Cled Wallace, brother of Foy, made this point clear in a satirical article he published in the *Gospel Guardian.*

> Maybe if we keep our shirts on and our hats on straight, "our" denomination may be able to appoint enough committees and draft enough resolutions to influence the pope to call off his rock throwing. . . . I am not very optimistic over the prospect of persuading the President and the State Department to bomb the Vatican. It is doubtful that "our" denomination is that popular in Washington at the present time.[14]

Nothing illustrated more profoundly the extent to which Churches of Christ had evolved from nineteenth-century sect to twentieth-century denomination than their behavior in this particular incident. Yet, few among mainstream Churches of Christ were able to comprehend the point Cled Wallace sought to make. Numerous people objected to Wallace's reference to "the church of our Lord as our denomination" and therefore sought to set the record straight: "We're not a denomination, even in fun."[15] Finally, the *Guardian* editor, Fanning Yater Tant, felt he had no choice but to explain to those without ears to hear what was really at stake in Wallace's article. Cled's article, he wrote,

> shocked many brethren into taking a "breather" in their wild rush toward a typical denominational pressure campaign on our State Department. For the turn the campaign was taking—mass protest meetings, drawing of resolutions, forming of committees, appointment of representatives, etc., etc.—was so typically denominational procedure that it might have been lifted right out of the "Methodist Handbook for Political Action."[16]

This incident prompted the anti-institutional people to sharpen their attack on the "Broadway plan" for missions that, in their view, symbolized more than any other development the decline of congregational autonomy and the transition toward denominational standing that they felt Churches of Christ had embraced. Roy Cogdill put the question starkly, "If the Broadway elders at Lubbock can supervise the 'mission' work in Germany for two congregations could they not supervise it for two hundred? Or for all the churches throughout the world? Why don't we just elect them our 'missionary society' . . . and let Lubbock be our denominational headquarters?"[17]

Cecil N. Wright of Denver, Colorado, responded to this criticism in a series of scholarly articles that many in the mainstream thought definitive. Wright's articles appeared in every major doctrinal publication associated with Churches of Christ at that time, including the *Gospel Advocate*, the *Firm Foundation*, and even in the *Gospel Guardian* where Fanning Yater Tant reviewed them. Wright charged that the anti-institutional people had sought "to leave a sinister impression . . . that maybe congregational autonomy is being violated by the 'sponsoring' church method of cooperation, and [that this method] is therefore unscriptural." The *Gospel Guardian*, in contrast, thought Wright's work "as full of sophistry as it is lacking in scriptural proof."[18]

Relations between the mainstream of Churches of Christ and their anti-institutional critics continued to deteriorate. From the perspective of the anti-institutional dissenters, the mainstream of Churches of Christ had abandoned their nineteenth-century birthright for the sake of respectability, success, and worldly advantage. Indeed, the mainstream acknowledged that changes were taking place, but even in the midst of those changes, they continued to identify their work with the model of the primitive, apostolic church. Moreover, they typically dismissed the anti-institutional dissenters as troublemakers and cranks. It was inevitable that the two groups would eventually come to a parting of the ways.

The Quarrel over Colleges

In the meantime, a second issue drove a wedge between the mainstream of Churches of Christ and the anti-institutional dissenters: a quarrel over the legitimate place of church-related colleges and the proper—and scriptural—method of funding them.

This was not the first time that colleges related to Churches of Christ had been the focus of controversy. In the late nineteenth century Daniel Sommer, a protégé of Benjamin Franklin of Indiana (considered in chapter 3) and an influential editor in his own right, launched a devastating attack against church-related colleges. Like Franklin, Sommer was a plain and rustic man and resisted progress, wealth, educated preachers, and any hint of ostentation. Nothing more accurately reflects Sommer's commitments in this regard than a book he published in 1913 entitled simply *Plain Sermons*. There, he promised "plain truth . . . in plain sentences." In another volume published the same year, Sommer argued that "Christ was a plain man, the apostles and other Christians were all plain people, the gospel is a plain document, and the Church is a plain institution."[19] Not surprisingly, Sommer ascribed the virtue of plainness to simple, rural living, which, he thought, stood in marked contrast to cities, wealth, progress, and higher education.

This is the context in which we must understand Sommer's opposition to church-related colleges. In the first place, Sommer worried that the colleges might usurp the power of the local church. But more than that, Sommer worried that college-bred preachers might make simple rustics like himself obsolete. "It is interesting," he observed, "to watch the moves of self-importance among young men and women when they come home from college. . . . They look down upon the ones who are not educated as they are." Accordingly, "the poor preacher who has had few school advantages, and so knows nothing but the Bible, is a back number and is ostracized." He even feared that college-trained clerics might "PUSH ASIDE THE GOD-GIVEN ELDERS" and dominate the local congregation.[20] Clearly, Sommer's condemnation of church-related colleges had much to do with the struggle he perceived between a lower class of self-taught preachers like himself and a rising middle class among Churches of Christ.

One discovers in the anti-institutional movement of the 1940s and 1950s some of the same lower-class fears and biases one finds in Daniel Sommer half a century earlier. Roy Cogdill, for example, worried that if church-related colleges were allowed to proceed too far, unlettered preachers of the old school would soon be displaced. "How many of those men," Cogdill asked, "even if they were in their prime, would be acceptable to the churches today? In many of the congregations would they appear too uncouth, uneducated, unpolished to fill the need now? How many of them could fill a place teaching the Bible in one of 'our' schools?" No wonder that J. D. Tant, father of Fanning Yater Tant, found in Sommer a spiritual ally. "It was thought that you were 'extreme' on the college work," Tant wrote, "but of late years I have said the time will come that we will go so far from Bible Christianity that we can well say, 'We had a prophet among us but did not know it.' "[21]

Although the anti-institutional movement shared Sommer's lower-class biases with reference to colleges, they focused their energies on another issue that was even more pivotal in this particular dispute: how should the colleges be funded? In order to avoid the bare appearance of parachurch organizations, the anti-institutional people insisted that colleges be funded just as they had always been: by interested individuals only.

Nonetheless, Abilene Christian College launched a development program in 1947 seeking $3,000,000 for college expansion. Significantly, leaders of that campaign appealed in part to the local congregations, an effort that failed to go unnoticed by the anti-institutional watchdogs. Roy Cogdill, at that time the publisher of Foy Wallace's *Bible Banner*, responded to Abilene Christian College: "We are old fashioned . . . down here in East Texas" and "we are not in sympathy in any way with your efforts to enlist the churches to support your school."[22]

That same year—1947—N. B. Hardeman, president of Freed-Hardeman College in Henderson, Tennessee, launched his own appeal for congregational funding for the school over which he presided. Hardeman's appeal far transcended that of Abilene Christian College in the extent to which it disrupted the tranquility of Churches of Christ. After all, for many years Hardeman had been a close ally of Foy E. Wallace, Jr. Hardeman's efforts in this regard, therefore, caught everyone off guard, including Wallace. Still, Hardeman had a school to run and was not about to sacrifice the fiscal well-being of Freed-Hardeman College to orthodox opinion on the "college-in-the-budget" question. People who reject congregational support for colleges, Hardeman wrote, would gladly erect "a beautiful meeting house, . . . put carpets on the floor, fans in the ceiling, install a baptistry, provide for the water to be heated, buy baptismal robes, hire a janitor, buy fuel, provide nurseries, and hire baby sitters." Strangely, he thought, they refused "to make a donation to a school in which the Bible is taught. If we are not careful, we will be straining out gnats and swallowing camels."

A serious feud soon erupted between Hardeman and Wallace. Both men lost sight of the doctrinal issues at stake as they sought to discredit each other in personal ways.[23] In our context, this conflict would not be particularly significant except for the fact that Wallace was sufficiently hurt by Hardeman's attacks that he essentially withdrew his leadership from the anti-institutional movement, thereby paving the way for younger men like Roy Cogdill and Fanning Yater Tant to fill the gap.

In the meantime N. B. Hardeman sought to press the issue even further. If congregations could support orphans' homes, he asked, why could they not support colleges?[24] By raising this question, however, Hardeman only succeeded in making orphans' homes another target in the sights of the anti-institutional critics. Indeed, congregational support for orphans' homes finally became a key issue around which the anti-institutional quarrel swirled.

With this tactic, the anti-institutional people offended many in the mainstream of Churches of Christ. How could they possibly imagine, people asked, that the gospel of Jesus Christ precluded local congregations from supporting orphans' homes? To many, this position seemed patently ludicrous and even pharisaical. Indeed, G. C. Brewer, preaching at the Harding College lectureship in 1951, compared the anti-institutional advocates on this particular point to "the Pharisees who gave a tenth even of their garden herbs but showed no *mercy* to the suffering, cared nothing for *justice* . . . and had no real *faith* in God."[25]

Three years later B. C. Goodpasture, editor of the *Gospel Advocate*, took steps to isolate the anti-institutional dissenters and to make them *persona non grata* among the mainstream of Churches of Christ. In truth, Goodpasture possessed neither the legal means nor the formal institutional machinery by which he could implement this decision in a binding way. But the *Advocate* was, after all, the preeminent gospel paper circulated among Churches of Christ, and influential editors had traditionally wielded the power that bishops wielded in other traditions. If Goodpasture, therefore, determined that the anti-institutional people should be expelled from the fellowship of the mainstream of Churches of Christ, there was little doubt that the majority of those who read the *Advocate* would respect his decision.

The series of events that finally triggered the expulsion began in 1951 when the Church of Christ in Lufkin, Texas, home of the *Gospel Guardian*, suffered a serious division. Cled Wallace, Foy's brother, remained to preach for the original congregation, and Roy Cogdill, editor of the *Guardian*, became the preaching minister of the breakaway congregation. Upon learning of this situation, Goodpasture ridiculed in print what he perceived as the fundamentally divisive nature of the anti-institutional dissenters. He wondered about "the exact technique for starting a new congregation according to the 'Lufkin plan,' " and asked how it might be done " 'without circumventing the elders.' "[26]

Understandably, Cogdill took offense. "The editor of the *Gospel Advocate*," he wrote, "seems to have a disposition that makes it difficult for him to refrain from casting slurs, and trying to discredit those who differ from him." Goodpasture, for his part, dismissed Cogdill as "bombastic, blusterous, and bitter,"[27] prompting Cogdill to assail Goodpasture's character, and that of the *Gospel Advocate*, in no uncertain terms.

> *Never in her long history has the Advocate stood for so little, and never has she given her influence to so many false and hurtful doctrines as during the present administration.* . . . The fact that she is "enjoying the largest circulation in her history" only means that her influence for evil and compromise is more widely extended.[28]

This acrimonious dispute between the *Guardian* and the *Advocate* smoldered for the next two years until, finally, Goodpasture published a letter calling for mainstream Churches of Christ to "quarantine" the anti-institutional people.[29] The effect of this letter was decisive. William Wallace, son of Foy E. Wallace, Jr., later commented,

> The spirit of quarantine swept the country and the Guardian movement was subjected to the same kind of pressures which had been exerted on the premillennial movement in previous years. Churches were divided, preachers had their meetings cancelled, some left the movement making confessions of their "error" in the journals, and the Guardian movement hardened into a strong minority entity.[30]

Soon, the anti-institutional Churches of Christ took their place alongside the premillennial Churches of Christ as the second major dissenting wing of this tradition. By 1990 they could boast some 2,000 congregations found mainly in Texas and Alabama.

FURTHER ADVANCES TOWARD MODERNIZATION

In the meantime mainstream Churches of Christ pressed ahead with additional attempts to create parachurch organizations and to take their place as a respectable denomination in the American South. Two of these attempts are especially noteworthy.

The "Herald of Truth"

First, in an effort to proclaim the message of Churches of Christ to a broad domestic audience, two midwestern preachers—James Walter Nichols in Cedar Rapids, Iowa, and James D. Willeford in Madison, Wisconsin—merged their radio ministries in 1950 and in 1952 created a national radio program called the "Herald of Truth."[31] By 1954 the "Herald of Truth" had expanded to television. From its inception, the Highland Street congregation in Abilene, Texas, emerged as the sponsoring congregation for this particular ministry, receiving funds from other congregations around the country that wanted to contribute to this project.

Naturally, the anti-institutional wing of Churches of Christ protested this arrangement. By focusing on the shopworn issue of the "sponsoring church," however, the anti-institutional people missed the real significance of the "Herald of Truth." The real significance of this ministry lay in the fact that it sought to frame a message that would be palatable to a cross-section of the American public. In so doing, the "Herald of Truth" slowly but surely redefined the nature of acceptable preaching in this tradition and weakened the sectarian, exclusivistic message that had been a staple of Churches of Christ since the 1830s.

In its early years speakers on the "Herald of Truth" sought to portray the Church of Christ as the true church authorized by the biblical text and condemned the various "false teachings" promoted by Catholics and Protestants alike. By the late 1950s, however, a more positive message began to replace the older sectarian content. One can scarcely understand this transition if one fails to understand the unique strain of American piety that dominated the American media in the 1950s and that promoted religion—almost any religion—as indispensable to mental health and peace of mind. Judaism provided an American reading audience with an early glimpse of such piety in 1946 when Joshua Liebman published his book *Peace of Mind*. By 1949 the Roman Catholic television personality Fulton J. Sheen published his *Peace of Soul*, and in 1952 Protestants jumped on the bandwagon when Norman Vincent Peale published his immensely successful *Power of Positive Thinking*.

With this pervasive emphasis on positive thinking and peace of mind, it would be difficult, at best, for the "Herald of Truth" to succeed on a national scale if it persisted in its traditional, sectarian critique of other Christian traditions and its presentation of the Church of Christ as the one true church outside of which there was no salvation. Changes had to be made.

Those changes began to be heard on "Herald of Truth" in the early 1960s with the preaching of Batsell Barrett Baxter, a man who served as the primary radio and television preacher for "Herald of Truth" from 1960 through 1981. Baxter, a professor at David Lipscomb College and a preacher with extraordinary standing among Churches of Christ, never completely abandoned the traditional themes that defined the historic identity of Churches of Christ. But he brought to his radio and television preaching a kind and understanding style, and he often framed his message with the kinds of issues popularized by Liebman, Sheen, and Peale throughout the 1950s. Accordingly, Baxter explained that the gospel of Jesus Christ could bring meaning to life, foster peace of mind, contribute to better family relationships, and help Christians cope with anxiety and fear.[32] Baxter always concluded, however, with a presentation of the five-step plan of salvation, culminating with immersion for the forgiveness of sins, that had characterized preaching among Churches of Christ for so many years.

By redefining acceptable preaching in this way, Baxter and the "Herald of Truth" stood squarely in the tradition of consensus building that the new *Chris-*

tian Leader and the *20th Century Christian* had pioneered in the late 1930s and early 1940s. Further, the "Herald of Truth" shared with the *Leader* and the *20th Century Christian* in their common attempt to embrace cultural values that seemed somehow compatible with the Christian faith. The difference was this: the *Leader* and the *20th Century Christian* sought to build consensus only among Churches of Christ themselves. Baxter and the "Herald of Truth," in contrast, sought to appeal to a spiritual and moral consensus that already existed in the larger American public. In this way, preachers on the "Herald of Truth" inevitably imported public values into the theological framework of Churches of Christ.

Further, by redefining acceptable preaching as they did, the preachers on "Herald of Truth" wielded enormous symbolic power among Churches of Christ. In previous years powerful editors among Churches of Christ performed the role that bishops might have played in other Christian traditions. W. T. Moore pointed to this phenomenon in 1909 when he wrote that "the Disciples of Christ do not have bishops, they have editors."[33] As national media personalities, however, preachers on the "Herald of Truth" exerted a level of symbolic power that far transcended the power of the older "editor-bishops." In fact, one might profitably think of the preachers on "Herald of Truth" as "electronic bishops" who modeled acceptable preaching for countless local ministers in this tradition. As a result, by the late 1970s one scarcely heard from the pulpits of many large urban congregations the traditional distinctives that had defined Churches of Christ for 150 years. Instead, many preachers offered a steady stream of sermons that explained the relationship of Christian faith to meaning in life, family relationships, happy marriages, and self-esteem.

All this suggests that the anti-institutional people were likely correct when they worried about the power that cooperative arrangements and parachurch organizations might exert over the local church. The "Herald of Truth" exerted enormous power over local congregations throughout the United States, but in a far more subtle and symbolic way than anyone in the anti-institutional coalition had ever expected.

Church Buildings as Symbols of Modernization

Nothing more fully symbolized the transition of Churches of Christ from nineteenth-century sect to twentieth-century denomination than the hundreds of new church buildings they erected, especially in the late 1940s and the 1950s. Always attractive, sometimes elaborate, and typically well situated in a solidly middle-class neighborhood, these houses of worship performed several functions. First, they proclaimed to the surrounding community that Churches of Christ had come of age and should no longer be viewed as an offbeat sect on the wrong side of the tracks. Second, these buildings were functional, often equipped with offices for the minister and the secretary, Sunday school classrooms, a cry room, a kitchen and fellowship room, a sound and projection room, and other facilities that might support an increasingly institutionalized religious organization. These new houses of worship, in other words, stood as tangible symbols of the trends and transitions the anti-institutional dissenters rejected.

No one helped promote these new houses of worship more effectively than M. Norvel Young. Young had served as a cofounder of the *20th Century Christian* when he was still a graduate student in Nashville, Tennessee. Then, in the post–World War II era, he helped promote the Broadway Church of Christ in Lubbock, Texas, as a sponsoring congregation for German missions, thereby triggering the wrath of the anti-institutional dissenters. Now, in the midst of the national religious revival that followed on the heels of World War II, Young correctly predicted that Churches of Christ would be forced to build new buildings to accommodate a swelling membership.

If new church buildings were virtually inevitable, Young surmised, Churches of Christ might as well construct facilities that would serve the needs of modern, institutionalized congregations, on the one hand, and present to the public an attractive physical plant, on the other. Young presented this case at the Abilene Christian College lectureship in 1947, and again in print the following year. Modern church buildings, Young contended, should include not only a sanctuary but also a minister's study, a secretary's office, a fellowship room with adjacent cooking facilities, a storeroom that would house "food and clothing for the poor," a mimeograph room, and ample classroom space. Moreover, Young contended, "the building should be designed so that it 'looks like a church.' . . . The exterior should be attractive, though simple, without unnecessary ornamentation, but with good lines of architecture." Symbolically most important, Young advised congregations to "locate the new building on a prominent site—one that will advertise the meetings of the church. . . . Do not tuck it away in a secluded spot."[34]

Eight years later, in 1956, Young and James Marvin Powell published a book they called *The Church Is Building*, a volume that served Churches of Christ as a virtual handbook on the construction of new buildings. Most of all, it encouraged attractive, upscale facades and functional plants. Covering everything a church leader might need to know, from securing an architect to finalizing the design, this book stood as a striking symbol of the changes that were rapidly overtaking this tradition.

Appealing to a distinctly middle-class clientele, Burton Coffman, minister for Houston's Central Church of Christ, claimed in the book's introduction that attractive, well-designed church buildings provide effective advertising for the gospel. "There is no better advertisement of one's faith," he asserted, "than that provided by a modern, beautifully constructed church edifice in a prominent location." Young and Powell concurred, focusing especially on the importance of attractive landscaping.

> Church lawns that are well kept will bring many people to the church services who would not otherwise come. On the other hand an ill-kept, slovenly appearing lawn will

drive many people away who might otherwise come. . . . Many people have the erroneous impression that in order to be orthodox we must be downright "tacky."

Coffman also celebrated the modern trends that were rapidly overtaking church construction among Churches of Christ. Thoroughly modern facilities, he argued, will generally include

parking lots, public address systems, germicidal lights for nurseries, rugs, draperies, venetian blinds, art windows, spires, crosses, buttresses, heating, plumbing, air-conditioning, elevators, kitchens, dining rooms, Bible school rooms, visual aid equipment, baptisteries, flannel graphs, movie projectors, cinema screens . . . , etc.

In spite of these modern developments, Coffman was convinced that Churches of Christ still conformed to the model of primitive Christianity. Accordingly, he noted with considerable satisfaction that in buildings serving this tradition, one finds "no choir lofts, no high altars, no instruments of music. . . . In short there is nothing for use as an innovation in the pure worship of Jesus Christ according to the New Testament."[35]

In 1950 Young himself led the Broadway congregation in Lubbock, Texas, where he served as pulpit minister, in constructing a magnificent new plant boasting the largest auditorium among Churches of Christ at that time, capable of seating 2,100 people. Conforming to all the advice Young had given over the years, this new building was a beautiful and thoroughly modern facility, situated on one of Lubbock's most prominent thoroughfares. On the evening of the building's inaugural Sunday, G. C. Brewer preached on the topic "The Undenominational Nature of the Lord's Church." In spite of the changes and modern trends so visible on that Sunday, Brewer argued, the attempt "to restore New Testament simplicity, [and] to bring back to earth the ancient order of things" remained the defining characteristic of Churches of Christ.[36]

CONCLUSIONS

In the 1920s Churches of Christ threw off the shackles of the apocalyptic perspective, freeing themselves to join the modern world. In the 1940s and 1950s they capitalized on that possibility in a variety of ways. First, they created for themselves publications, radio programs, and television broadcasts that were kind, gentle, and constructive, and that sought to build consensus around widely held cultural values that many in Churches of Christ imagined were biblically based. In this way, these various initiatives radically transformed the content both of theology and preaching in this tradition. Second, in the interest of more effective missions and viable church-related colleges, Churches of Christ created a variety of cooperative arrangements that reflected a preoccupation with modern, bureaucratic structures. Symbolizing all these changes, hundreds of congregations sought to relocate themselves from ramshackle buildings, often found on the wrong side of the tracks, to shiny new physical plants, often strategically located on major thoroughfares in middle-class neighborhoods. In making these transitions, Churches of Christ shared much with other conservative Christian denominations, especially fundamentalists, who sought to achieve—or in some instances to regain—respectability in the larger culture.

Many in Churches of Christ, still devoted to the nineteenth-century sectarian model and especially to the radically democratic polity that had characterized their movement from its inception, resisted these modern developments. From their perspective these trends reflected, first, an accommodation to the values of the larger culture and, second, the transformation of Churches of Christ into a modern denomination. Their protests, however, were of no avail. In the end, leaders of the mainstream of this tradition expelled these dissenters, just as they had expelled the premillennial dissenters a quarter century before.

In the 1960s Churches of Christ would face a host of new challenges from unexpected sources: their own children. Though otherwise sharing little in common with the anti-institutional protesters, many in the counterculture generation agreed with the anti-institutional dissenters of the previous generation that Churches of Christ had, indeed, accommodated themselves to the values of the larger culture. Because of that accommodation, they argued, their religious heritage was ill-equipped to address the major ethical issues of that period: war, poverty, and racism. This is the story we seek to tell in the next chapter.

NOTES

1. M. Norvel Young and James Marvin Powell, *The Church Is Building* (Nashville: Gospel Advocate, 1956), pp. ix, 2–3.

2. E. W. McMillan, in a letter to Jesse P. Sewell dated 28 August 1938, in Sewell Papers, Center for Restoration Studies, Abilene Christian University.

3. Clinton Davidson, in a letter to all the preachers who had responded to his questionnaire, dated 30 June 1938, in Sewell Papers; and Davidson, in a letter to Sewell dated 24 August 1938, in Sewell Papers.

4. "Unique Work of Church Attracts Wide Attention," *Nashville Banner*, 30 May 1926; and "Welfare Program Including Social Service Emphasized by Central Church of Christ," *Nashville Banner*, 24 December 1941.

5. See J. L. Hines, "Questions Asked E. W. McMillan," *BB* 1 (May 1939): 21.

6. "Welfare Program Including Social Service Emphasized by Central Church of Christ," *Nashville Banner*, 24 December 1941.

7. Eugene S. Smith, "Deliverance Has Come," *BB* 1 (March 1939): 16; and Wallace, "The Man with a Program," *BB* 1 (July 1939): 9; "Will There Be an Armistice?" *BB* 2 (January 1940): 3; and "The Accent on Love," *BB* 2 (May 1940): 2.

8. Jesse P. Sewell in a letter to Davidson dated 3 May 1940, in Sewell Papers; Sewell in a letter to McMillan dated 3 May 1940, in Sewell Papers; and Showalter, "Future of the Christian Leader," *CL* 54 (15 December 1940): 6, 14.

9. B. C. Goodpasture, "The Future Policy of the Gospel Advocate," *GA* 81 (2 March 1939): 196.

10. W. E. Brightwell, "A Religious Depression," *GA* 76 (29 November 1934): 1151; "The Crisis We Are Facing," *GA* 78 (18 June 1936): 587; "The Crisis We Are Facing (No. 2)," *GA* 78 (25 June 1936): 611; and "The Crisis We Are Facing (No. 3)," *GA* 78 (2 July 1936): 635.

11. G. C. Brewer, "Evangelizing the World in the Post War Period," *FF* 60 (16 February 1943): 1–2; and Cled Wallace, "Sighting-in on 'Post-War Plans,' "*BB* 6 (August 1943): 7.

12. The Broadway Church of Christ, for example, produced in October 1949 a pamphlet promoting the German work and entitled, "Germany for Christ: A Report on the German Mission Work." This pamphlet received wide distribution throughout the fellowship of Churches of Christ.

13. Phillip Wayne Elkins, *Church Sponsored Missions: An Evaluation of Churches of Christ* (Austin: Firm Foundation, 1974), p. 6; for a summary of domestic growth rates of Churches of Christ, see Michael Casey, "Church Growth: New Information," *Image* 3 (1 May 1987): 14–15, and "Church Growth: New Information," *Image* 3 (15 May 1987): 20–21.

14. Cled Wallace, "That Rock Fight in Italy," *GG* 1 (19 January 1950): 1.

15. See, for example, the protest registered by Mr. and Mrs. Oscar Paden, parents of two of the Italian missionaries, "A Letter from the Padens," *GG* 1 (23 February 1950): 5.

16. Fanning Yater Tant, "Surveying the Scene," *GG* 1 (23 February 1950): 2.

17. Roy Cogdill, "Now It Is All Settled," *GG* 2 (11 May 1950): 9; and "Centralized Control and Oversight," *GG* 1 (20 April 1950): 1.

18. Cecil N. Wright, "The Cooperation Controversy (3)," *GA* 93 (21 June 1951): 391; and Cogdill, "Brother Wright's Self Justification," *GG* 2 (17 August 1950): 9.

19. Daniel Sommer, "Preface," *Plain Sermons* (Indianapolis: Daniel Sommer, 1913), n.p.; and "The Simple Life," in *The Church of Christ* (Indianapolis: Octographic Review, 1913), pp. 354–55, 348–49.

20. Sommer, "The Perpetuation of the Clergy through Theological Seminaries, Bible Schools, and Colleges," in *The Church of Christ*, pp. 285, 290, and 305.

21. Cogdill, "The Simplicity of the Gospel," *BB* 10 (June 1948): 4; and Tant, *Apostolic Review* 81 (7 December 1937): 5, cited by Steve Wolfgang, "A Life of Humble Fear: The Biography of Daniel Sommer, 1850–1940" (master's thesis, Butler University, 1975), pp. 115–16.

22. Cogdill, "An Answer to the Announcement of Abilene Christian College for District Rallies for the Churches," *BB* 9 (May 1947): 6.

23. See, for example, N. B. Hardeman, "The Banner Boys Become Enraged," *GA* 89 (23 October 1947): 845; reprinted in *FF* 64 (28 October 1947): 1–3; and Wallace, "Reply to the N. B. Hardeman 'Hit and Run' Attacks," *BB* 8 (September 1947): 24.

24. Hardeman, "The Banner Boys Become Enraged," *GA* 89 (23 October 1947): 844; and "Foy versus Roy, Cled, and Himself," *GA* 89 (28 August 1947): 656–57, 661. See also "Foy versus Roy, Cled, and Himself," *FF* 64 (9 September 1947): 4–7.

25. Brewer, "Christ and the Problem of Orphans and Other Dependents in the Present Day World," *Harding College Lectures, 1951* (Searcy, AR: Harding College Press, 1952), p. 99.

26. Goodpasture's commentary appeared under the heading, "The Voice of the Turtle," *GA* 93 (12 July 1951): 434.

27. Cogdill, "What Is That to Thee?" *GG* 3 (2 August 1951): 1; and Goodpasture, " 'What Is That to Thee,' " *GA* 93 (23 August 1951): 530.

28. Cogdill, "You Can See What I Meant," *GG* 3 (20 September 1951): 10.

29. "They Commend the Elder Who Wrote," *GA* 96 (9 December 1954): 962.

30. Wallace, "Onward Processes of the Movement (1)," *Vanguard* (June 1984): 20.

31. On the "Herald of Truth," see John Marion Barton, "The Preaching on Herald of Truth Radio, 1952–1969" (Ph.D. diss., Pennsylvania State University, 1975); and Robert Wayne Dockery, " 'Three American Revolutions': A Study of Social Change in the Churches of Christ as Evidenced in the 'Herald of Truth' Radio Series" (master's thesis, Louisiana State University, 1973).

32. See Barton, "The Preaching on Herald of Truth Radio, 1952–1969," pp. 131–69.

33. W. T. Moore, *Comprehensive History of the Disciples of Christ* (New York: Fleming H. Revell, 1909), p. 12.

34. Young, " 'So You Are Going to Build,' " *GA* (29 January 1948): 104–5.

35. Young and Powell, *The Church Is Building* (Nashville: Gospel Advocate, 1956), pp. 144–45; and Coffman, "Introduction," pp. ix–x.

36. Brewer, "The Undenominational Nature of the Lord's Church," sermon preached at dedication of the new building of the Broadway Church of Christ, Lubbock, Texas, 1950, transcript in possession of the author.

6
THE CHALLENGES OF THE 1960s

The decade of the 1960s presented Churches of Christ, just as it presented all other American churches, with a host of ethical challenges pertaining to race, urban poverty, and war. One might expect that Churches of Christ, with their legacy of poverty, alienation, suspicion of human governments, and countercultural behavior, might have resisted the war in Vietnam, embraced the civil rights movement, and aligned themselves with the poor of whatever racial, ethnic, or religious background.

This, however, was not to be. In fact, the decade of the 1960s functioned as a mirror for Churches of Christ, reflecting for those with eyes to see how far this tradition had come from its nineteenth-century apocalyptic roots. By the 1960s many leaders in mainstream Churches of Christ aligned themselves with a variety of right-wing political and cultural causes, undertook campaigns against both communism and Catholicism, embraced the war in Vietnam with considerable enthusiasm, and rejected the civil rights movement as a Communist-inspired threat to Anglo-American values and institutions.

In addition, the 1960s also helped create a major cultural and doctrinal division between the extreme right and the extreme left that stood on either side of the mainstream Churches of Christ. On the one hand stood a sizable group of younger, college-educated people who sought to respond in a positive way to the ethical challenges of the 1960s. On the other stood a core of hyperconservative reactionaries who railed not only against the young progressives but even against the liberalism they thought they saw in the mainstream of this tradition.

RESPONDING TO CULTURAL AND ETHICAL ISSUES

The mainstream of Churches of Christ responded to the ethical issues posed by the 1960s essentially by seeking to preserve the cultural status quo. But how could that be? How could Churches of Christ have come so far from their point of origin? Answers to this question are not difficult to find. In the first place, the roots of Churches of Christ grew not only from the apocalyptic soil of Barton W. Stone but also from the progressive, this-worldly soil cultivated by Alexander Campbell. In the second place, Churches of Christ effectively severed their apocalyptic roots in the World War I period when they purged their ranks of premillennial sympathizers. Third, in the 1940s and 1950s progressive leaders of Churches of Christ determined to halt the vicious doctrinal disputes of the 1930s and instead to build consensus around cultural values they thought inspired by the biblical text. In this way they divested theological discourse of what little legitimacy it ever possessed in this tradition and embraced instead the conservative values of Anglo-American culture, especially as those values were celebrated in the American South. Most striking of all, even in the midst of these transitions, Churches of Christ continued to regard themselves as the latter-day reincarnation of the ancient Christian church, established by the apostles. Almost unavoidably, therefore, they tended to shroud the cultural values they had embraced with the mantle of the Christian faith. For the most part, then, Churches of Christ emerged in the 1960s, not as Christian critics of traditional cultural values, but as Christian defenders of the cultural status quo.

DEFENDING AMERICA FROM THE COMMUNIST THREAT

One can scarcely understand how these positions played themselves out in the 1960s unless one first understands how certain key leaders in this tradition encouraged Churches of Christ in the 1930s to embrace a Christian anti-Communist crusade on behalf of old fashioned Americanism.

In 1936 George S. Benson returned from China, where he had served as a missionary for eleven years, to assume the presidency of tiny Harding College in Searcy, Arkansas.[1] As we noted in chapter 4, J. N. Armstrong had founded Harding College in 1924, but Armstrong was a visionary, not a businessman, and by 1936 the school faced serious fiscal difficulties. Armstrong, therefore, resigned that year, picking Benson as his successor. Had the apocalyptically oriented Armstrong understood, however, the nationalistic directions in which Benson would take his college, he might well have selected someone else.

There can be no doubt that Benson understood well the apocalyptic tradition of Churches of Christ. He studied under Armstrong at Harper College in Kansas, graduating in 1923, then served on Armstrong's faculty at Harding College during the 1924–25 academic year, prior to his departure for China.[2]

His eleven years in China produced numerous unpleasant confrontations with the Chinese Communist government. In addition, upon his return to America in 1936, Benson sensed that President Franklin Roosevelt's program for economic recovery had put the United States on the road to socialism and that respect for the American government and economic system had badly eroded during the eleven years he had been abroad.[3] These factors led Benson to embrace a stridently patriotic, procapitalist, and anti-Communist agenda. Benson institutionalized that agenda on the Harding campus in the National Education Program (NEP), an organization that specialized in the production of anti-Communist propaganda and that Benson used as a means to cultivate potential donors to the college. Both the NEP and Harding College, during the Benson presidency, routinely sought to portray the Christian faith as a natural ally of Americanism and the principles of free-enterprise capitalism.

Though Harding was closely related to the Churches of Christ, Benson directed his fund-raising efforts and his anti-Communist crusade not so much toward the church as toward conservative, wealthy entrepreneurs who knew little about Harding's religious heritage. Benson chose this course partly in response to the fact that Foy E. Wallace, Jr., and his colleagues had been so effective in their efforts to portray Harding as a bastion of premillennial sentiment (see chapter 4). As a result, many in Churches of Christ who might have supported Harding financially now refused to do so.

There can be no doubt that Benson was crucially important in the right-wing political influence he exerted upon Churches of Christ. Yet, since Benson directed his anti-Communist crusade mainly toward those outside this tradition, he was not the principle figure to lead Churches of Christ in pro-American, anti-Communist directions. That honor belongs to G. C. Brewer, whom we have already met in other contexts. Like Benson, Brewer also had roots in the apocalyptically oriented Stone-Lipscomb tradition. He studied for six years at the old Nashville Bible School, then resisted military service during World War I. He later recalled,

> I had been reared under the teaching of Brother David Lipscomb and I believed it was wrong for Christians to participate in civil government in any sense. I didn't want to buy bonds or savings stamps or contribute one penny toward the shedding of blood. This was the teaching under which all of us had been reared and no member of our family had ever voted.[4]

All that began to change for Brewer in the early 1920s. During the "Red Scare" that overtook the United States immediately following World War I, Brewer grew more and more interested in defending American ideals and institutions against foreign aggression, and less and less interested in the apocalyptic orientation of his youth.

In 1936 Brewer delivered to the Nashville American Legion a stridently patriotic address in which he called "upon all 'red-blooded' American citizens to fight communism—if need be—to the last ditch; [and] to spill every last ounce of blood—if need be—in defense of our government." He told the Legionnaires that "if and when this nation must fight to prevent the overthrow of Americanism, I, for one, am ready to give the last drop of blood in my veins in the cause my forefathers fought and died for."[5]

Brewer's speech received substantial publicity, both in the Nashville press and in periodicals related to Churches of Christ. The response from the church press was especially critical. F. D. Srygley, writing in the *Gospel Advocate*, complained, "The attitude of the entire speech was to glorify America rather than the teaching of Christ and the apostles."[6]

Srygley, however, should not have been surprised at the content of Brewer's speech. During the months leading up to his American Legion presentation, Brewer had already taken his case to his brothers and sisters in the Churches of Christ in a series of eight articles, published in the *Gospel Advocate*, that explained the menace he thought communism posed to American liberties. By the end of 1936, the *Gospel Advocate* had published those articles in a book entitled *Communism and Its Four Horsemen*. There, Brewer argued "that the communists already have an alarming hold on the United States; that they are in our schools and universities and even in the churches; that communism is in many text-books and that millions of high-school students are enrolled in the party."[7]

The most striking aspect of Brewer's book was his contention that one of the "four horsemen" by which communism sought to subvert the United States was its promotion of pacifism. Pacifist sentiments did, of course, flourish in the United States in the aftermath of World War I. For example, one 1934 poll reported that more than 60 percent of American clergy had advised their congregations not "to sanction or support any future war."[8] In addition, many embraced pacifism during this period out of political rather than religious conviction.

One would think that Brewer, with his apocalyptic and pacifist background, would have rejoiced over these developments. The truth is, his apocalyptic perspective, eroded though it was by this stage of his career, was likely directly responsible for his rejection of these post–War pacifist sentiments. At least on the part of secularists, Brewer thought, and even on the part of liberal mainline Protestants, such sentiments grew not so much from an allegiance to the kingdom of God as from an allegiance to political principles and convictions.[9] Further, he saw in most of these pacifist trends only the influence of international communism. The Communist effort to pacify the United States, he argued, "accounts for the great hue and cry against war in our country—not among Christians, but among atheists. This accounts for the oath that so many college professors and students are taking not to fight, even if our country is invaded. The colleges are full of communism."[10]

Brewer's transition from apocalyptic pacifist to strident patriot and anti-Communist agitator makes sense against the backdrop of American fundamentalism, a backdrop that we explored in the previous chapter. In this context it is perhaps sufficient to add that although members of Churches of Christ were never card-carrying fundamentalists, they did share many of the fundamentalists' chief concerns. They could not formally join the fundamentalist crusade, since their sectarian exclusivism prevented them from aligning themselves in any formal sense with other Christian traditions or movements. But they frequently attacked biblical criticism, defended theories of biblical inerrancy, praised the work of William Jennings Bryan, and ridiculed notions of Darwinian evolution. For all these reasons Brewer, and many others in Churches of Christ, felt a kinship to fundamentalism, even if most would never formally identify themselves with the fundamentalist crusade.[11]

Given this kinship, there can be little doubt that the fundamentalist affirmation of American nationalism, particularly in the wake of their own apocalyptic sojourn—a development considered in the previous chapter—encouraged Brewer and many others in Churches of Christ, including R. H. Boll, to move in comparable directions. Yet, there was one critical difference between fundamentalism and Churches of Christ: when fundamentalists embraced American nationalism, they simply returned to the God-and-country alliance that most evangelicals had sought to promote for most of the nineteenth century. But when Brewer and others with roots in the apocalyptic tradition of Churches of Christ embraced a nationalist ideology, they turned their backs on a separatist, countercultural heritage that had served many members of Churches of Christ in the American South since the days of Barton W. Stone.

By the 1950s hyperpatriotism and anticommunism had become staples in the ideology of Churches of Christ. A new publication called the *Voice of Freedom*, for example, emerged within this fellowship in 1953. Its masthead carried the slogan "An undenominational, nonsectarian publication devoted to telling the truth, the whole truth, and nothing but the truth, about the threat to our freedom from Catholicism and Communism." The *Voice of Freedom* was no off-the-wall venture. Instead, six of the most influential leaders in this tradition gave it birth: G. C. Brewer; B. C. Goodpasture, editor of the *Gospel Advocate*; Batsell Barrett Baxter, who within a few years would become the primary speaker on the national radio and television ministry the "Herald of Truth"; and three noted evangelists in this tradition, Alonzo D. Welch, H. A. Dixon, and J. M. Powell. With leaders like these sustaining the patriotic, anti-Communist stance of Churches of Christ in the 1950s, it is little wonder that by the 1960s few among the older generation of Churches of Christ would question America's role in the Vietnam War or the campaign against communism that the Vietnam War represented.

DEFENDING AMERICA FROM THE CATHOLIC THREAT

Churches of Christ in the 1960s also fought to save America from a perceived Catholic menace when they campaigned to prevent the election of John F. Kennedy to the presidency of the United States. The anti-Catholic stance of Churches of Christ was rooted deeply in the history of this tradition. In the first place, the Christian primitivist posture of Churches of Christ was inherently anti-Catholic, since it rested on the assumption that the church had fallen from its original purity with the establishment of the papacy, the Catholic hierarchy, and a variety of Catholic doctrines and practices. Further, we noticed in chapter 2 Alexander Campbell's efforts to portray Catholicism as fundamentally un-

American and to expose what he thought were the Pope's designs on the United States.

In 1953 the anti-Catholic sentiment emerged in the *Voice of Freedom*. Defending that journal's anti-Catholic stance, G. C. Brewer explained that "Catholicism is another form of totalitarianism and . . . our freedom would be lost if the Catholics gained power."[12] By 1960 virtually the entire editorial leadership of Churches of Christ—from the *Gospel Guardian* to the *Gospel Advocate*, from the *Firm Foundation* to the *20th Century Christian*—joined the crusade to prevent the election of John F. Kennedy in 1960. In taking this position, however, Churches of Christ were hardly unique. Conservative Protestants throughout the United States, from the National Association of Evangelicals to the Southern Baptist Convention, engaged in similar efforts.

No one articulated the concern of Churches of Christ any more succinctly than did the Austin, Texas, based *Firm Foundation*. Its editor, Reuel Lemmons, argued that Catholicism and democracy were antithetical ideologies. Yet, Communism and Catholicism were fundamentally similar. "Structurally the two are identical. Philosophically they are identical. Militantly they are identical. Their aim at world domination is identical." B. C. Goodpasture, editor of the Nashville-based *Gospel Advocate*, raised the specter of Catholic-sponsored executions. "Those who think no danger to our religious freedom is involved are evidently not acquainted with history," Goodpasture observed. "They do not know about the fires of Smithfield, the horrors of the Spanish Inquisition, the bloody Massacre of St. Bartholomew's Day, and the frightful slaughter of the Waldenses and Albigenses." Goodpasture therefore challenged Kennedy "to prove that your Church does not claim the right to put Protestants, Jews, and liberals and other heretics to death, and that your becoming President would not hasten this happy day. . . . Do you intend to help the church put to death any and all heretics and evangelicals when 'Der Tag' arrives?"[13]

The most notorious incident involving the challenge that Churches of Christ posed to John F. Kennedy occurred in September 1960, when Kennedy met with the Houston Ministerial Association. On that occasion Church of Christ radio evangelist V. E. Howard rose to his feet, publicly confronted Kennedy with selections from the *Catholic Encyclopedia* on "the doctrine of Mental Reservation," and then pressed Kennedy to declare whether he did or did not accept "these authoritative Catholic declarations." Kennedy told Howard, "I have not read the *Catholic Encyclopedia* and I don't know all the quotations you are giving me. I don't agree with the statements. I find no difficulty in saying so, but I do think probably I could make a better comment if I had the entire quotation before me." In spite of Kennedy's forthright answer, Howard wrote in the *Gospel Advocate* that Kennedy had sought to evade the issue. The *Christian Chronicle*, a newspaper serving Churches of Christ, concurred: "The Catholic doctrine of mental reservation was placed squarely in Kennedy's path here Sept. 12 and he dodged it."[14]

By joining the national campaign to defeat John F. Kennedy on the grounds of his religion, Churches of Christ demonstrated yet again how far they had come from their apocalyptic, apolitical origins of the nineteenth century. More than this, their anti-Kennedy campaign on behalf of a Protestant America made it obvious that they were now prepared to join hands—at least politically—with the conservative Protestant culture of the American South.

RESPONDING TO THE RACIAL CRISIS

In 1955 the Rev. Martin Luther King, Jr., led blacks in Montgomery, Alabama, in a massive bus boycott after Rosa Parks, a black woman, had been arrested for refusing to give up her seat on a bus to a white man. That event triggered a national civil rights movement, waged on behalf of equal treatment under the law for blacks and other American minorities. The reaction to the Freedom Movement on the part of most white members of Churches of Christ ranged from resistance to apathy.

Background

The fact that white, mainstream Churches of Christ had, indeed, joined hands in substantive ways with the conservative Protestant culture of the American South sheds some light on why this tradition expressed virtually no support for the work of civil rights activists in the 1960s. But this is not the only explanation.

Theological considerations also played a role. In the first place, most white members of Churches of Christ ignored the Freedom Movement, since they found no *explicit* support for the civil rights movement in the biblical text. One can easily illustrate this mindset with a reference to Alexander Campbell. With his passionate concern for the unity of all Christians, Campbell had long argued that unity could be realized only if Christians focused on those beliefs and practices for which the Bible provided clear and explicit instructions. Because the Bible never condemned thc institution of slavery in so many words, Campbell refused to make slavery an issue directly related to the Christian faith. It is true that Campbell freed his own slaves, but he did so mainly because "*in this age and in this country it* [slavery] *is not expedient.*" He thought slavery "not in harmony with the spirit of the age nor the moral advancement of society"; nor was slavery "favorable to individual and national prosperity." Yet, Campbell refused to label slavery "sinful," simply because, as he wrote in 1845, "there is not one verse in the Bible inhibiting it, but many regulating it. It is not, then, we conclude, *immoral.*" To the contrary, he suggested, "in certain cases and conditions," slavery might be viewed as "morally right."[15]

This perspective bore substantial fruit among Churches of Christ. Benjamin Franklin, for example, wrote of slavery in 1859,

1. If those who labor on the subject will show where the Lord ever gave a decision or opinion, we will publish and maintain it.
2. The same goes for the Apostles.
3. If they will show where the Lord or the Apostles ever discussed the subject, we will discuss it.
4. If they didn't discuss it, we won't.
5. Those who condemn us for ignoring it condemn Jesus and the Apostles. We follow them.[16]

The Campbellian tradition of Churches of Christ undermined a systematic concern for social ethics in other ways as well. First, although Campbell concerned himself with questions of ethics and social justice, he placed extraordinary emphasis on the process of individual conversion and on what many in this tradition have called the "first principles" of the Christian religion—faith, repentance, confession, and immersion for the forgiveness of sins. In this way, Campbell privatized the Christian faith and rendered questions of ethics and social justice far less important than the process of conversion itself.

Second, Campbell implicitly argued for what Eugene Boring has called "a canon within the canon." In other words, Campbell claimed that one finds the essentials of the Christian faith only in those parts of the New Testament that were written *after* the apostles established the church on the Day of Pentecost, recorded in Acts, chapter 2. Although Campbell valued the Old Testament and the Gospels for various purposes, he argued that none of that material provided instructions for the Christian church in the Christian age. For all practical purposes, therefore, Campbell had rendered both the Gospels and the Old Testament—the biblical materials that speak most clearly to questions of social justice—irrelevant to the restoration project of Churches of Christ.[17]

Standing in substantial contrast with the Campbell tradition, the Stone tradition in its early years generated substantial passion on behalf of social justice—and especially on behalf of the liberation of slaves—as a distinct Christian virtue. For example, the North Carolinian Joseph Thomas, who visited Kentucky in 1810–11 for the express purpose of assessing the size and nature of the Stone movement, reported that

> the christian companies in this settlement and about Cane Ridge have been large; but within a few years, many of them, who held black people as slaves, emancipated them, and have moved to the state of Ohio. I will observe that the christians of these parts *abhor* the idea of *slavery*, and some of them have almost tho't that they who hold to slavery cannot be a christian.[18]

There can be little doubt that the abolitionist sentiment found among the old Stone Christians at this very early date grew, to a great extent, from their apocalyptic orientation. Those who embraced the values of the world might well hold slaves and scramble for wealth, position, and power at the expense of other human beings. This, however, was precisely the sort of behavior in which those committed to the principles of the kingdom of God could not engage.

Yet, the commitment to racial justice that characterized the Stone communities in the early years had badly eroded among many Churches of Christ in the aftermath of Reconstruction. David Lipscomb, for example, learned in 1878 that some members of a congregation in McKinney, Texas, had resisted the efforts of a black man to become a member of that church. In a scathing article published in the *Gospel Advocate*, Lipscomb challenged the Texas congregation in no uncertain terms.

> God saves the believing negro or white through his obedience, and can one claiming to be a child of God say no? . . . How dare any man assume such power and authority? How dare a church tolerate the persistent exhibition of such a spirit? Such a church certainly forfeits its claims to be a church of God. . . . For our part we would much prefer membership with an humble and despised band of ignorant negroes, than with a congregation of the [most] aristocratic and refined whites in the land, cherishing such a spirit of defiance of God and his law, and all the principles of his holy religion.[19]

In 1907 Lipscomb had occasion to address the issue of racism again, though this time in context of the Bellwood Church of Christ in Lipscomb's own city of Nashville. Several members of that church had sought to bar from its services a young black girl who had been adopted by Mr. and Mrs. E. A. Elam, who belonged to that congregation. S. E. Harris, spokesperson for the segregationist group, told Elam that many were "sore" over the fact that this girl presumed to attend this otherwise all-white congregation when she could just as easily attend "the colored church." Once again, Lipscomb was incensed.

> No one as a Christian . . . has the right to say to another "Thou shalt not," because he is of a different family, race, social or political station. . . . To object to any child of God participating in the services on account of his race, social or civil state, his color or race, is to object to Jesus Christ and to cast him from our association. It is a fearful thing to do.[20]

Yet, when all was said and done, the Stone-Lipscomb tradition finally marginalized questions of social justice, at least in the context of the public square. After all, their allegiance was to the kingdom of God, not to this world. It was all too easy, therefore, to argue that Christians should take social ethics seriously in the context of the church, but need not concern themselves with these issues in the larger society. Thus, even Lipscomb himself, though objecting to racism in the church in no uncertain terms, was reluctant to oppose slavery in the broader culture.

> Slavery is a political relation, established by political governments. . . . Christ did not propose to break up such relations by violence. He recognized the relationship, regulated

it, and put in operation principles that in their workings would so mold public sentiment as to break down all evil relations and sinful institutions.[21]

Many factors, therefore, finally undermined a strong concern for social justice among Churches of Christ, especially with reference to race. Alexander Campbell helped undermine that concern when he argued that slavery was not a biblical issue, that the steps one took toward conversion were the true "first principles" of the Christian faith, and that the Old Testament and the Gospels had little or nothing to do with the restoration of the ancient church. The Stone-Lipscomb tradition further undermined a concern for social justice by virtue of its contention that the kingdom of God had little to do with the affairs of a mundane world, thereby relegating the role of kingdom ethics to the confines of the church.

These theological factors crippled the ability of Churches of Christ to address the racial divide in any meaningful way. But looming larger than all these theological factors combined was the fact that Churches of Christ lived and moved and had their being in the American South. Without a theological orientation that affirmed the importance of social justice in the larger world, it was inevitable that Churches of Christ would absorb the values of the culture in which they lived.

Churches of Christ and Martin Luther King, Jr.

When all was said and done, therefore, perhaps it should not be surprising that the mainstream press of Churches of Christ virtually ignored the Freedom Movement from its inception in 1955 until 1968, when death claimed both Martin Luther King, Jr., and Marshall Keeble, the leading African American evangelist within this tradition. Indeed, one might never know by reading the *Gospel Advocate* and the *Firm Foundation* between 1955 and 1968 that a civil rights movement had transpired in the United States at all.

The passing of Keeble, however, prompted both these papers to break their silence on the question of race in the United States. The eulogies for Keeble, however, almost invariably mixed praise for the evangelist with harsh criticism for Martin Luther King, Jr., and the Freedom Movement that he led. In the *Advocate*, for example, Karl Pettus noted that Keeble "never led a march or a demonstration, peaceful or otherwise. He was never connected with a riot. . . . He didn't march for school integration, but he worked and spent himself for most of his life for Christian education." In the *Firm Foundation*, editor Reuel Lemmons took a similar position. Keeble, he wrote, "never led a riot; he never burned out a block of buildings; he never marched on Washington. But he marched toward heaven from the day he obeyed the gospel."[22]

Most of the leadership of mainstream Churches of Christ viewed activism on behalf of social justice as fundamentally unbiblical. When Rex Turner, president of Alabama Christian College during the Selma marches in 1965, learned that some among Churches of Christ were sympathetic to Martin Luther King and his nonviolent protests, he charged that these people sought "to displace the gospel of Christ with a social gospel . . . that has little or no concern for the fundamental doctrines of Christianity." Editor Reuel Lemmons agreed. "A lot of people wanted to compare Martin Luther King to Jesus Christ. In reality, King was a modernist, and denied faith in Jesus Christ as taught in the Bible."[23]

In addition, the leadership of Churches of Christ often charged that King and the movement he led was Communist inspired. "If he [King] was not an outright Communist," wrote Reuel Lemmons, "he certainly advocated Communist causes." James D. Bales, a Bible professor at Harding College, wrote an entire book to make this point. There, Bales charged that King's "contribution to anarchy within the United States, his cooperation with Communists within the United States, and his efforts to render us defenseless in the face of external Communist aggression all add up to defeat for freedom and victory for communism if he and others like him prevail."[24]

Marshall Keeble and Patterns of Institutionalized Racism

Long before the 1960s, however, it was obvious that Churches of Christ had absorbed the racial values of the dominant southern culture. Nowhere was this reality more apparent than in the life and work of Marshall Keeble, the African American evangelist already mentioned, and the relationship he sustained to the white power structure of this tradition. For most of the twentieth century until the mid-1960s, Keeble preached to large and enthusiastic black audiences across the American South, routinely converting hundreds in a single week. By any measure he was the most successful twentieth-century evangelist among Churches of Christ, white or black. Keeble also served as president of the Nashville Christian Institute, a school that offered elementary and secondary education for blacks in Churches of Christ from 1941 to 1967. Yet, because Keeble remained almost completely dependent on the white power structure of Churches of Christ for fiscal support, he also felt constrained to conform to the racial norms that prevailed within the white Churches of Christ and the larger culture of the American South.

A single illustration makes this point. In 1941 Foy E. Wallace, Jr., attacked Keeble in print for allowing the southern racial divide to grow blurred and indistinct in his gospel meetings. Too many whites attended those meetings, Wallace complained. Even worse, "reliable reports have come to me of white women, members of the church, becoming so animated over a certain colored preacher as to go up to him after a sermon and shake hands with him *holding his hand in both of theirs.*" Wallace thought it shameful "for any woman in the church to . . . forget her dignity, and lower herself so, just because a negro has learned enough about the gospel to preach it to his race."

Instead, Wallace commended the behavior of N. B. Hardeman as a model for race relations in Churches of Christ.

> When N. B. Hardeman held the valley-wide meeting at Harlingen, Texas, some misguided brethren brought a group of negroes up to the front to be introduced to and shake hands with him. Brother Hardeman told them publicly that he could see all of the colored brethren he cared to see on the outside after services, and that he could say everything to them he wanted to say without the formality of shaking hands.[25]

In the following issue of the *Bible Banner*, Keeble expressed his contrition.

> I have tried to conduct my work just as your article in the *"Bible Banner"* of March suggested. Taking advice from such friends as you have been for years has been a blessing to my work. So I take the privilege to thank you for that instructive and encouraging article. I hope I can conduct myself in my last days so that you and none of my friends will have to take back nothing they have said complimentary about my work or regret it.[26]

Wallace quickly and publicly commended Keeble for the attitude he had displayed in this statement. "This letter is characteristic of the humility of M. Keeble. It is the reason why he is the greatest colored preacher that has ever lived." Keeble and other acceptable black preachers, Wallace suggested, "know their place and stay in it, even when some white brethren try to take them out of it." This is because they understand their "relationships . . . in the church in the light of . . . [their] relationships with society."[27] Wallace's views reflect the dominant perspective of white southerners during that time.

In 1968, the year of Keeble's death, Howard A. White, a former history professor at David Lipscomb College, reflected on the course of Keeble's life. In spite of Keeble's stature as the preeminent evangelist of this tradition, White nonetheless recalled that he

> was the victim of discrimination *most* of the time. During the five years I taught at David Lipscomb College, he came every year to speak at the lectures. Not once was he invited to join a luncheon or a dinner or to do anything else beyond speaking. His students and associates from the Nashville Christian Institute were segregated in one corner of the balcony. Because of his great and generous spirit, Brother Keeble suffered all these indignities in silence and without any observable resentment.[28]

Dewayne Winrow, another African American preacher in Churches of Christ, knew Keeble well and worked with him as an apprentice minister for a number of years. Winrow contends that Keeble should not be mistaken for "an 'Uncle Tom' for whites." Instead, Winrow writes, Keeble was "a preacher ahead of his time" who ingeniously used for his own purposes a racist system that he felt powerless to overcome.[29]

Understanding the Heritage of African American Churches of Christ

The truth is, ever since the abolition of slavery, Churches of Christ have nurtured two distinct fellowships, one white and one black. For many years blacks read their own gospel paper, the *Christian Echo*, sent their children to the all-black Southwestern Christian College in Terrell, Texas, and enthusiastically attended their own all-black Bible lectureships. By the 1960s nothing in this regard had changed. The *Christian Chronicle* noted in 1968,

> The average white member of a local church knows less about his Negro fellow-Christians than he does about local politics or the latest TV heroes. There have been, indeed, two separate brotherhoods with their own leaders, schools, missionaries, lectureships, and geographical areas of strength. Even the white churches who have supported Negro mission work and building projects are largely unaware of life on the other side of the "middle wall of partition."[30]

Yet, African American Churches of Christ shared much in common with their white counterparts theologically. They were conservative, embraced the legacy of Campbellian rationalism, and read the biblical text from a literalist perspective. Even their liturgy was more subdued than what one might find in many African American Christian traditions. As Marshall Keeble explained, "The gospel can take the dance out of the man, stop him from dancing, pull him out from under a mourner's bench, and set him up on a seat."[31]

For most of the twentieth century two pioneers loomed large in the history of African American Churches of Christ. One was Marshall Keeble. The other was G. P. (George Phillip) Bowser. A preacher and an educator, Bowser established a preacher-training school in Nashville in 1907; he then moved the school to Silver Point, Tennessee, in 1909, where it became known as the Silver Point Christian Institute. By 1938 Bowser was living in Fort Smith, Arkansas, where he ran another school—the Bowser Christian Institute—out of his homc. If Keeble made his greatest contribution through his preaching, Bowser made his greatest contribution by training in these various schools a core of black evangelists who provided significant leadership for African American Churches of Christ for much of the twentieth century. Among those evangelists were J. S. Winston, R. N. Hogan, Levi Kennedy, and G. E. Steward.

In addition, Bowser was an editor who founded a publication that served the black Churches of Christ in much the same way that the *Gospel Advocate* and the *Firm Foundation* served the white Churches of Christ. He launched that paper in 1902 and called it the *Christian Echo*.

Bowser obviously suffered the same racial discrimination that befell Keeble and all other blacks in the American South. Yet, Bowser refused to align himself with the white power structure of Churches of Christ in the way that Keeble did. This strategy allowed him and those who followed his leadership to maintain a measure of independence from white domination and exploitation. For example, A. M. Burton, a white Nashville businessman, attempted to establish a school for blacks in 1919. He called this school the Southern Practical Institute, secured a white man named C. E. Dorris as its principal, and asked Bowser to assist with its administration. When the new school opened, Dorris insisted that the students enter the school through the rear door. Without compromising with Dorris in the least, the students simply "packed up and went home."[32] Burton's school quickly collapsed.

This tradition of dissent also loomed large in Bowser's paper, the *Christian Echo*. In the 1960s R. N. Hogan, one of Bowser's students, served as the *Echo's* editor. Hogan especially attacked the tradition of segregated educational facilities that had prevailed for so long among Churches of Christ. Even though the Supreme Court declared segregation in America's public schools unconstitutional in 1954, and even though many church-related institutions quickly followed suit, Church of Christ–related institutions lagged behind. Abilene Christian College admitted blacks to its graduate programs in 1961 and to its undergraduate programs in 1962. Harding College integrated in 1963. And David Lipscomb College waited for a full ten years after the Supreme Court ruling to open its doors to black students—a step it finally took in 1964. Even then, many black leaders felt that segregation might have persisted among some of these schools had it not been for government threats to cut off federal funds. G. P. Holt, for example, expressed in the *Christian Echo* his skepticism regarding most white educators among Churches of Christ. Holt was not impressed

> when some college president or Dean or representative of a (quote) "Christian College" tells black brethren, "Look at us, we are not segregated; we have ten Black students at our College. See we love you." We know and you know and God knows that our Colleges have not had a *Change of Heart*—but that the Government of our land is responsible for these ten Black students in the College.[33]

It was in this context that R. N. Hogan launched his attack on Church of Christ–related colleges that refused admission to blacks. Hogan lamented the fact that black students were "admitted to Denominational schools as well as State schools, but cannot enter a christian (?) school operated by members of the church of Christ." To Hogan, the issue was simple: those who ran these schools should "stop calling themselves Christians, stop calling their schools christian schools, and stop calling their churches, churches of Christ." In the summer of 1963, Hogan praised Abilene Christian College for opening its doors to African American students, but he continued his attack on the other schools.

> It is almost an insult for a Negro to ask to be admitted into the David Lipscomb College in Nashville, Tenn. Yet it is supposed to be operated by Christians; what reason can David Lipscomb, Harding, Freed Hardeman, Florida Christian (?) and other such schools

who are refusing to allow Negroes to be trained in their schools, give for such practice, but sheer prejudice and hate? [34]

Hogan found it especially difficult to believe that the school that wore the name of David Lipscomb—the man who had worked so hard to overcome segregation and racial prejudice in Churches of Christ—should be the last bastion of segregation in this tradition.[35]

Even Abilene Christian College might not have integrated when it did had it not been for a courageous white professor of Bible named Carl Spain who spoke prophetically on this issue at the college's annual Bible lectureship in 1960. Before a large crowd assembled for his speech, Spain wondered why Churches of Christ were so slow to embrace racial justice. "God forbid," he said, "that churches of Christ, and schools operated by Christians, shall be the last stronghold of refuge for socially sick people who have Nazi illusions about the Master Race." He went on,

I feel certain that Jesus would say: "Ye hypocrites! You say you are the only true Christians, and make up the only true church, and have the only Christian schools. Yet, you drive one of your own preachers to denominational schools where he can get credit for his work and refuse to let him take Bible for credit in your own school because the color of his skin is dark!"[36]

The Nashville Christian Institute

Nowhere can the struggle for equal rights, waged by African American members of Churches of Christ, be seen more clearly than in the story of the Nashville Christian Institute, often known simply as N.C.I. With black money, with an all-black board of directors, and with a stated purpose of serving black youth, black members of Churches of Christ opened this elementary and secondary school in Nashville, Tennessee, in 1941.

Shortly after the school opened, however, the school added several whites to its board. In 1943 several key figures at David Lipscomb College joined the board as well, including Lipscomb president Athens Clay Pullias and Lipscomb board members A. M. Burton and J. E. Acuff. Over the years Burton proved to be a staunch benefactor of N.C.I. As the founder and president of Life and Casualty Insurance Company of Nashville, Burton contributed perhaps half a million dollars to N.C.I. over the years and was eventually selected as president of its board of directors.[37] Upon Burton's death in 1966, however, Athens Clay Pullias, still president of David Lipscomb College, assumed the presidency of the N.C.I. board.

By then N.C.I. had fallen on hard times. The integrated public schools of Nashville now competed with N.C.I., which had seen its enrollment fall from a high of 683 students in 1947–48 to a low of 138 in 1967. N.C.I. teachers now received only half the wages being paid in the public schools, and the N.C.I.

building was in poor repair.[38] With insufficient funding to correct these deficiencies, the predominantly white board decided in 1967 to close the school and use its assets of some $500,000 to establish at David Lipscomb College the Burton-Keeble Scholarship Fund for African American youth.

Some blacks agreed with this decision. Marshall Keeble was one of them. "While Sister Keeble and I regret to see Nashville Christian Institute close her doors, we wholly support what we thought had to be done."[39] Many others, however, felt betrayed, and a group of N.C.I. alumni filed a suit in federal court, seeking an injunction against the N.C.I. board. They secured as their attorney for this case an African American lawyer and minister in Churches of Christ from Tuskegee, Alabama, a man who was widely known in the black community in the South as the attorney for the civil rights movement. Indeed, Fred Gray had first come to national prominence when he defended both Rosa Parks and Martin Luther King, Jr., in the movement's early years.

In the suit he filed, Gray emphasized the irony that David Lipscomb College took money from an all-black school in order to establish a scholarship fund for black youth when, historically, the college had denied admission to black young people altogether. It appeared to Gray, and to others in the black community, that David Lipscomb College simply sought to enrich itself at the expense of N.C.I. and the black community N.C.I. had served.[40] Clearly, these were the sentiments of R. N. Hogan, who charged that "under the guise of wanting to help the Negro, some white brethren, who claimed to be Christians, became members of the Board of Directors of this Negro School" and finally "decided to grab the assets of N.C.I. and close it's [*sic*] doors." As far as Hogan was concerned, "these men who claim to be Christians are guilty of robbing poor Negroes who struggled and gave of their meager income in order to build a Christian School for their children who were denied the privilege of attending the white so-called christian school." Hogan encouraged blacks to contribute as generously as possible to the legal effort on behalf of N.C.I.[41]

The effort to secure an injunction against the N.C.I. board finally failed. The N.C.I. property remained closed, David Lipscomb College retained the assets, and the chasm that had separated black and white Churches of Christ for so many years now opened up even wider than before. Many blacks no doubt shared the sentiments of G. P. Holt, who lamented that "a great brotherhood had been stabbed in the back. . . . (We have felt the power structure of the Nashville hierarchy.)" And Jack Evans, president of Southwestern Christian College, remarked as late as 1990 that "because the Institute was closed against the will of the black churches of Christ . . . , a feeling of an injustice and unfairness still exists among some black people."[42]

Prophetic Calls for Change

In spite of the prevailing patterns of segregation and discrimination, there were nonetheless some powerful voices, both black and white, that challenged the status quo and called for change. The most important development in this regard was the series of race relations workshops that occurred between 1966 and 1968. The first of the workshops took place in January 1966 in Nashville, Tennessee. An "underground," by-invitation-only event, this workshop was engineered by a group of white activists including Walter Burch, a public relations consultant then living in Abilene, Texas; George Gurganus, a professor at the Harding Graduate School of Religion in Memphis, Tennessee; Ira North, minister of the Madison Church of Christ, Madison, Tennessee; Dwain Evans, minister for the Church of Christ in West Islip, New York; and John Allen Chalk, the dynamic young evangelist for the "Herald of Truth" radio ministry.[43]

In March 1968 the predominantly black Schrader Lane Church of Christ in Nashville, Tennessee, hosted the second workshop, with leadership provided by David Jones, the congregation's minister. White Churches of Christ in Nashville offered only meager support for that workshop, though the *Christian Chronicle*—at the prompting of Walter Burch—sought to give the substance of the workshop broad exposure by publishing the workshop's proceedings in a special tabloid supplement.[44]

Two whites, Burch and Dwain Evans, along with two black ministers, Roosevelt Wells of Harlem and Eugene Lawton of Newark, New Jersey, met in Harlem in February 1968 to plan the third race relations workshop, scheduled for Atlanta, Georgia. These four hoped that the Atlanta workshop could attract influential leaders from the white and black communities of Churches of Christ. The activism of Burch and Evans, however, rendered both of them a political liability with many in Churches of Christ. They therefore removed themselves from any further planning of the Atlanta event. In the meantime Wells and Lawton invited Jimmy Allen, a noted white evangelist and Bible professor at Harding College, to help in the final coordination of the project.

A variety of influential leaders from virtually every spectrum of Churches of Christ, white and black, attended the conference that took place in June 1968 in an Atlanta suburb, hosted by the predominantly black Simpson Street Church of Christ and its minister, Andrew Hairston. Delegates were sufficiently convicted that most—though not all—signed a statement confessing "the sin of racial prejudice which has existed in Churches of Christ and church-related institutions and businesses."[45]

John Allen Chalk found these conferences so encouraging that he addressed the problem of racial prejudice on the nationally broadcast "Herald of Truth" radio ministry for which he regularly spoke. Racial prejudice, he charged, was simply incompatible with the Christian faith. Chalk's sermons provoked a largely positive response, suggesting that attitudes were slowly changing within Churches of Christ.[46]

Yet, a sizable residue of racial prejudice remained, reflected in the fact that the circulation of the *20th Century Christian* dropped by half—from 40,000 to 20,000—following publication in July 1968 of a special issue entitled *Christ and Race Relations*, featuring articles by black and white leaders within

Churches of Christ. Little wonder that black minister G. P. Holt lamented in 1969 that the black and white Churches of Christ were "growing farther apart each day."[47]

In November 1999, however, Dr. Royce Money, president of Abilene Christian University, traveled to Southwestern Christian College in Terrell, Texas, to issue on behalf of Abilene Christian University a formal apology to African American members of Churches of Christ for the years of racial discrimination. "Abilene Christian University has been a Christian institution of higher learning for more than 90 years," Money said. "Its doors were not open to African-Americans for well over half that time. We are here today to confess the sins of racism and discrimination and to issue a formal apology to all of you, to express regret and to ask for your forgiveness."[48]

THE GREAT IDEOLOGICAL DIVIDE

Not only were black and white churches drifting farther and farther apart; so were liberals and conservatives within the predominantly white Churches of Christ. Reuel Lemmons offered telling evidence of this split when he criticized both extremes in a series of editorials published in the *Firm Foundation* in 1969 and 1970. Lemmons was an important person to reflect on this development, since he was widely known for his moderation on many issues.

The progressives, Lemmons complained, contained both "modernists" and "liberals" who had little use for the traditional restoration vision, who concerned themselves primarily with "education and social change," and who felt that the primary task of the church was "to foster race relations and better housing." Moreover, Lemmons claimed that many liberals had embraced theological modernism and viewed the Church of Christ as nothing more than another denomination. At the same time Lemmons warned that in reacting against the liberals, the conservatives had abandoned the historic commitment of Churches of Christ to "liberty in the realm of opinion" and often had confused their traditions with biblical truth.[49]

In order to understand this ideological divide, we will first explore the emergence of a progressive movement among Churches of Christ and then consider the conservative reaction that followed.

The Progressive Movement

In a real sense Carl Ketcherside and Leroy Garrett helped to launch the progressive movement among Churches of Christ in the 1950s. Both men had roots in radically sectarian wings of Churches of Christ. Though raised in the mainline Churches of Christ, Garrett had embraced the anti-institutional position as an adult, and since 1920 Ketcherside had aligned himself with the Sommerite wing of Churches of Christ. By the 1950s, however, both men had grown disillusioned with the narrow sectarianism that increasingly defined the modern version of the Stone-Campbell tradition. Both, therefore, determined to resurrect the passion for ecumenical relations with other Christians that had characterized Barton W. Stone and Alexander Campbell in the early nineteenth century. From 1952 through 1958, Garrett published a periodical called *Bible Talk* that promoted an ecumenical understanding of the Christian faith and that chastised Churches of Christ for having obscured the ecumenical side of their heritage. In 1959 he launched a second, more influential journal called *Restoration Review* that pursued the same agenda. In 1939 Ketcherside launched his *Mission Messenger*, a journal that served the Sommerite wing of Churches of Christ. In 1957 he made that journal a voice of ecumenical understanding among Christians, appealing especially to the memory of Thomas and Alexander Campbell. Although Ketcherside and Garrett encountered substantial resistance among Churches of Christ in the short run, it is difficult to overestimate the influence that these two men exerted among Churches of Christ over the long term. At the very least they helped create a theological climate that would prove favorable to the progressive tradition that emerged among Churches of Christ in the 1960s.

In that decade a veritable ideological chasm opened up between progressives and conservatives in this tradition. That chasm resulted in part from the influence of higher education among Churches of Christ, but it was then exacerbated by the revolutionary temper of the times. If we wish to understand that chasm, therefore, we must first explore the development and significance of higher education in the heritage of Churches of Christ.

Higher Education within Churches of Christ

Two factors initially prompted members of Churches of Christ to establish colleges that would serve this tradition. First, they sought to shield their youth from the corrupting influences of state-supported institutions. Second, they hoped the colleges would confirm their young people in the theological tenets of this tradition. Ultimately, however, most of the colleges proved to be genuine centers of higher learning, prompting thought, reflection, and self-criticism on the part of their students—precisely the qualities that would eventually lead many students to question various denominational orthodoxies.

Beyond this, higher education inevitably widened the world of Churches of Christ. It exposed students to new and challenging ideas, and then, upon graduation, many of those students entered the brave new world of urban, corporate cultures, where they were forced to interact with people quite different from themselves. At the very least, therefore, higher education helped to break down some of the parochial exclusivism that had characterized Churches of Christ for so many years.

Perhaps even more important, in the 1940s Churches of Christ began to experiment with graduate theological education. In 1944 W. B. West launched the first graduate program in religion at George Pepperdine College in Los Angeles, then established a comparable program in 1952 at Harding College. In 1953 Abilene Christian College followed suit.[50] In order to sustain these programs, these pioneering institutions were forced to employ substantial numbers of professors with doctoral degrees in biblical and related studies. Abilene Christian's LeMoine G. Lewis left a defining legacy in this regard. After completing course work for his doctorate in church history at Harvard, Lewis began teaching at Abilene Christian in 1949 and served in that capacity until 1986, the year before his death. Shortly after he began his teaching career, Lewis completed his doctorate, and subsequently encouraged many students to pursue doctoral work in religion at Harvard and comparable institutions. "By the mid-1950s," Don Haymes has written, "the first generation of 'LeMoine's boys' had arrived at Harvard—Everett Ferguson, Pat Harrell, and Abraham Malherbe." Others quickly followed, though not all were "LeMoine's boys." Roy Bowen Ward from Abilene Christian along with Thomas H. Olbricht and Don McGaughey from Harding College attended Harvard while Harold Forshey, also from Abilene Christian, attended Boston University.[51] LeMoine Lewis was by no means single-handedly responsible for the flow of bright, young Church of Christ students to major theological centers during those years. Also responsible for this trend were Jack Lewis, LeMoine's brother and a professor at the Harding Graduate School of Bible and Religion, and J W Roberts and Paul Rotenberry at Abilene Christian.

Ferguson, Malherbe, and Olbricht were particularly important as second generation scholars, since all three eventually accepted teaching positions at Abilene Christian and continued to nurture at that institution a tradition of high-level theological scholarship. Their students, in turn, earned doctoral degrees in biblical and related studies at many of America's finest centers of higher learning. Through this process a core of top-flight scholars in biblical and related studies emerged from the very bosom of Churches of Christ.

New Publications

This development in higher education was critical for the development of a progressive tradition in Churches of Christ that would challenge conventional orthodoxies in a variety of ways. After all, Harvard-trained scholars were not likely to rest content with traditional in-house debates as they played themselves out in papers like the *Gospel Advocate* and the *Firm Foundation.* In 1957, therefore, two of "LeMoine's boys," Abraham Malherbe and Pat Harrell, created the *Restoration Quarterly*, a scholarly journal that sought to put Churches of Christ in touch with the larger world of biblical and theological scholarship and to "create a community of scholarly discourse" among scholars with roots in that fellowship. Ultimately, the work of the *Restoration Quarterly*, grounded as it was in modern genres of biblical criticism, raised serious questions about the legitimacy of the old Baconian hermeneutic (see chapter 2) that had served Churches of Christ for almost one hundred and fifty years.

Such questions exerted little impact on the broad mainstream of Churches of Christ, however, until a journalistic medium emerged that could translate high-level, critical scholarship into a language that specifically addressed the pew.

Two journals fitting that description appeared in the late 1960s—*Mission* in 1967 and *Integrity* in 1969. Although both these journals generated substantial controversy, it is perhaps safe to say that *Mission* became the preeminent symbol among conservatives of the presence of theological liberalism among Churches of Christ.

Dwain Evans, a man we have already met in the context of the racial struggle, provided leadership for the creation of *Mission* when he invited several colleagues to explore the need for a journal that would address the relevant issues of that period in thoroughly biblical terms. Several strategic meetings followed Evans' initiative. One participant in those meetings explained why a new journal was so badly needed.

> No extant publication is speaking to our brotherhood in bold, fresh, and relevant terms. No periodical exists which deals with the most pertinent issues of modern life. . . . Many are hungry for such a publication. . . . They are more concerned in searching than in perpetuating the illusion that we have utterly restored pure Christianity.[52]

Walter Burch, an activist along with Evans in the racial struggle, canvassed congregations from coast to coast for sixteen months in order to raise funds for the new journal, but received little encouragement from most in mainstream Churches of Christ. Still, the new journal made its debut in July 1967. Several of the scholars who had worked to launch the *Restoration Quarterly*—Thomas H. Olbricht, Roy Bowen Ward, Abraham Malherbe, Everett Ferguson, Carl Spain, Frank Pack, and J W Roberts—now contributed to the production of *Mission* in a variety of ways.

Essentially, writers for *Mission* sought to redirect the traditional theology of Churches of Christ toward a more theological reading of the biblical text, enhanced tolerance for other Christians, and a greater sensitivity toward ethical issues, especially social justice and racial equality. An article by Don Haymes, published in 1968, symbolized the heart of *Mission*'s agenda. Because Churches of Christ had allowed their preoccupation with the book of Acts to marginalize the Gospels, Haymes charged, they had "managed to sidetrack the real issues in a desperate search for gnats to strain."

> The basic issue is whether we can do the Gospel on Jesus' terms; whether we will serve God or mammon, and not, unfortunately, whether we will sing without an instrument, or say "thee" or "you" in prayer or even baptize by immersion. . . . So long as we harbor the illusion that God cares more about what transpires within the hallowed walls of church buildings than about the sickening bloodshed of Vietnam, or the struggle for freedom of men and women in the chains of poverty, or the willful treachery of governmental bureaucracy, or even the routine of our offices, classrooms, farms or factories, then we are still kidding ourselves.[53]

The response to *Mission* was swift and certain. Guy N. Woods, a leading Tennessee evangelist and debater, typified many when he charged that *Mission* was leading the church into "digression and apostasy. Men who forsake the truth, as many of your writers have done, under the guise of scholarship, disgrace both truth and scholarship." *Mission* became such a flash point of controversy that the board of trustees at Abilene Christian College, bowing to criticism, sought to force four Abliene Christian College faculty to resign from *Mission*'s board.[54]

Mission kept its voice alive, however, for twenty years. By 1987 its editorial board determined that the mainstream of Churches of Christ had sufficiently internalized *Mission*'s agenda that there seemed little compelling reason to keep the journal in operation.

The Conservative Movement: New Journals and New Schools

It is not quite accurate to say that a conservative movement emerged among Churches of Christ in the 1960s, since this tradition had been conservative, both theologically and socially, for most of the twentieth century. It is fair to say that when faced with the relativistic and revolutionary temper of the 1960s, many allowed their traditional conservatism to harden into a rigid, reactionary posture. On the cultural front they committed themselves to defending law, order, and traditional social structures. On the religious front they attacked every vestige of liberalism in the interest of sustaining the traditional orthodoxies of Churches of Christ. Some even abandoned the venerable claim, long associated with the restoration tradition, that members of Churches of Christ were "Christians only" and argued instead that members of Churches of Christ were the "only Christians." Others exchanged the search for truth for the conviction that they now understood "absolute truth absolutely." Most in this camp resisted higher education, blaming Church of Christ-related colleges for the "liberalism" that threatened, they thought, to undermine the heritage of this tradition. And in their efforts to defend the church from a variety of cultural and theological demons, many embraced the tactics popularized by Foy E. Wallace, Jr., in the 1930s and 1940s.

Confident that the old mainstream journals like the *Gospel Advocate* and the *Firm Foundation* were either unable or unwilling to defend the church from the inroads of liberalism, modernism, and relativism, several enterprising conservatives launched new, competing journals between 1967 and 1970. Roy Hearn of Memphis, Tennessee, and Franklin Camp of Birmingham, Alabama, established the *First Century Christian* in 1967. Two years later, in 1969, the *Spiritual Sword* appeared, under the editorial guidance of Thomas B. Warren, a Bible professor at Freed-Hardeman College in Henderson, Tennessee, and Rubel Shelly, one of his former students.

The *Spiritual Sword* is worth special consideration because it sought to attack the progressives from *within* their own stronghold—the citadel of higher learning. Warren held a doctorate in philosophy from Vanderbilt University and his protégé, Rubel Shelly, would earn the same degree in 1981. Both men embraced the presuppositions of Lockean empiricism and Common Sense Realism and routinely employed a variety of logical arguments to discredit the relativistic understandings that had, in their judgment, captured both the culture and the church. From their perspective the restoration heritage of Churches of Christ was founded on the proposition that human beings can know absolute truth absolutely. Warren therefore explained in his opening editorial, "This journal is launched both in determined opposition to skepticism, liberalism and relativism and in strong affirmation that the Bible is the infallibly inspired word of God and that men can learn and obey the truth."[55]

If the editors of the *Spiritual Sword* had borrowed their tactics of logic and philosophical analysis from the world of higher learning, a third—and far more typical—conservative journal took the opposite approach. Ira Y. Rice, a former missionary to Singapore, established *Contending for the Faith* in 1970 and routinely used that journal to discredit the enterprise of higher education. Indeed, Rice quickly grew convinced that the world of higher learning was a primary source of "liberalism" and "modernism" filtering into Churches of Christ.

Rice returned from Singapore to study Mandarin Chinese at Yale University in 1965. In the Church of Christ that served the Yale community, he encountered attitudes and theological perspectives that troubled him greatly. "I kept hearing reference," he later wrote, "to 'the best divinity schools'; and kept asking myself how a *denominational* or *secular* so-called 'divinity' school could be even *good*, much less *better* or *best*!" One of the students Rice encountered "used the word 'Christendom' in such a way that the true church was lumped with those in error." Another "made it appear that *Martin Luther* was a *Christian*" and that "churches of Christ are *just another denomination*."[56]

Rice found especially troubling the perspectives of three individuals—Robert M. Randolph and Derwood Smith, both divinity students, and Bob Howard, a local preacher. Once Rice determined that Randolph, Smith, and Howard held theological positions that were increasingly common among Churches of Christ, he published in 1966 a widely circulated volume that he hoped would counteract these trends. He called that volume *Axe on the Root* and quickly followed with two additional volumes bearing the same title. There, he concluded that it was likely impossible for Christian students to attend "secular or sectarian 'divinity' school[s], and to come out untainted."[57]

Then, in 1970, Rice launched *Contending for the Faith*, where he shifted his attack from "secular or sectarian" schools to colleges related to Churches of Christ. He argued, for example, that the "primary source of infiltration by liberalism/modernism" into Church of Christ–related colleges was "academic accreditation." He thought that "ACC's [Abilene Christian College] seduction by accreditation is practically complete. And what is true at ACC . . . largely either has already become true at several of our other campuses or rapidly is heading in that direction."[58]

Rice was hardly alone in his suspicion of higher education during those turbulent years. Even in mainstream publications like the *Firm Foundation* and the *Gospel Advocate*, articles critical of graduate education—and especially of graduate *theological* education—frequently appeared. Articles in the *Gospel Advocate*, for example, blamed "graduate education" for the growth of "liberalism" in Churches of Christ and criticized "sermons filled with quotations from [Reinhold] Niebuhr, [Karl] Barth, [Harvey] Cox, [and] [Dietrich] Bonhoeffer."[59]

The fact that such an outcry was common should not cause one to imagine that the pulpit of Churches of Christ in the 1960s and 1970s was theologically illiterate. Quite the reverse was true. The frequency of the outcry only testified to the fact that more and more pulpit preachers in this tradition *had* benefited from graduate theological training. The problem lay in the fact that many congregations were simply unprepared to hear from their pulpit ministers conclusions drawn from critical biblical scholarship. After all, these were people who had been weaned on biblical literalism and demanded book, chapter, and verse for every theological assertion. But Churches of Christ were in the midst of a theological reorientation that prompted tension and struggle at almost every step along the way.

To fully understand the backlash within Churches of Christ against the world of higher education, one must also recall that these were the years when conservatives throughout the United States viewed America's college campuses as seedbeds for unorthodox ideas, violent protests, and revolution. In this context it would be strange, indeed, if conservatives in Churches of Christ had failed to challenge the role of higher education within their own tradition.

Of all the schools related to Churches of Christ, Abilene Christian College received the lion's share of criticism during those years. In part this was because its Bible Department had assembled an unusually sterling faculty, filled with Ph.D.s from Harvard and comparable institutions. And because the college was sending so many of its graduates to graduate-level study at those same institutions, many drew the conclusion that it was less interested in preparing ministers for the pulpit than it was in preparing scholars for the academy. And finally, many conservatives felt that none of the colleges related to Churches of Christ were turning out preachers who were sufficiently orthodox in the faith. Glenn Wallace summed up the complaint against the colleges when he wrote, "Our Bible departments—in some colleges—are being overloaded with Harvard specialists. . . . Many are tainted with sectarian philosophy and are totally ignorant of the sickness in our land. They speak—not in a relevant message—but in intellectual nothingness or just plain denominational terms."[60]

For all these reasons a number of local congregations throughout the United States took it upon themselves to establish "schools of preaching," intended to produce preachers who were "orthodox" according to the traditional standards of Churches of Christ. Fitting this category were the Memphis School of Preaching, the Brown Trail School of Preaching in Fort Worth, and the Bear Valley School of Preaching in Denver. Other schools of preaching had somewhat different emphases. For example, the Sunset School of Preaching in Lubbock, Texas, and the White's Ferry Road School of Preaching in West Monroe, Louisiana, embraced a warm, evangelical pietism; Sunset in particular taught its students a strong theology of grace.

It must be said that these schools exerted an enormous impact on a sizable segment of Churches of Christ. According to Batsell Barrett Baxter, ten schools of preaching trained over 25 percent of all students studying for the ministry in Churches of Christ in 1970. Typically, these schools offered courses in Bible, Bible geography, church history, homiletics, and Christian evidences, but they did little or nothing to provide students with a liberal arts background for their ministry.[61] In the years to come, the narrow orientation of many of these schools would contribute to a growing gulf between the conservative Churches of Christ, on the one hand, and the growing number of progressive congregations, on the other, that often relied on ministers who combined liberal arts training with graduate theological education.

THE LOSS OF A GENERATION

Because it appeared to many in the younger generation that Churches of Christ exhibited greater interest in fine points of doctrinal orthodoxy than they did in the pressing moral and ethical issues of the 1960s, large numbers of young people simply dropped out of Churches of Christ during that period. Some went to other Protestant denominations; many dropped out of organized religion altogether. As Thomas H. Olbricht observed in *Mission* in 1973, "It is no secret that a whole generation born between 1930 and 1950 has become Church of Christ dropouts. Visit churches in St. Louis, in Houston, in Nashville and you won't see them. Oh, there are some, but they aren't the bright [and] the creative."[62]

At the same time another group of young people argued that Churches of Christ had become too acculturated to articulate and promote a radical vision of the Christian faith. Many of these people joined a revitalization effort within the Churches of Christ that was known from 1967 through the end of the 1970s as the Crossroads Movement.[63] Led by Charles H. (Chuck) Lucas, a campus minister at the University of Florida, this movement implemented "discipling" strategies that called for nothing less than "total commitment" to the task of "discipling" converts. Its numerical growth stunned most observers who quickly realized that the Crossroads Movement, though nominally affiliated with Churches of Christ, was fast becoming a new sectarian organization in its own right.

In 1979 the Crossroads Movement took a major step in that direction. In that year one of Lucas's student converts, Kip McKean, accepted a call to preach for the Church of Christ in Lexington, Massachusetts, the mother church of what would soon be known as the Boston Church of Christ and, later, as the International Church of Christ.[64] With thriving congregations in major cities around the globe, the Boston Church of Christ was by 1992 "one of the world's fastest growing" Christian movements,[65] sustaining virtually no fellowship with the older Churches of Christ from whence they had come.

But the major point is simply this: young people who had been radicalized by the revolutionary ethical and moral visions of the 1960s deserted Churches of Christ during that period in droves. Some went to mainline Protestant denominations. Some left organized religion altogether. And some cast their lot with the Crossroads Movement that would soon become the International Church of Christ.

CONCLUSIONS

The decade of the 1960s was a difficult period for Churches of Christ, just as it was for the nation at large. During the preceding thirty years Churches of Christ had increasingly embraced a panoply of conservative cultural values, replete with anti-Catholic and anti-Communist sentiment, and had scuttled what little remained of their historic apocalyptic perspective. Having abandoned virtually every vestige of their countercultural heritage of the nineteenth century, they were poorly prepared to face the ethical and moral issues that convulsed the nation during the 1960s.

Nothing more graphically illustrates that point than the way Churches of Christ responded—or failed to respond—to the racial crisis of that period. Mainstream publications of Churches of Christ virtually ignored that crisis until 1968, when the death of Marshall Keeble prompted unfavorable comparisons of Martin Luther King, Jr., to Keeble, the great African American evangelist for the Churches of Christ. In addition, educational institutions aligned with Churches of Christ were among the slowest of all church-related institutions in the South to embrace racial integration. Yet, calls for change emerged from a relatively small group of both blacks and whites who sought to address the racial crisis in constructive ways. Race relations workshops offered the most visible manifestations of these efforts.

In addition, the 1960s witnessed a growing rupture between a younger generation of college-educated progressives, on the one hand, and an older generation of conservatives on the other. Moderates, perhaps best represented by Reuel Lemmons, editor of the Texas-based *Firm Foundation*, sought to mediate between the two extremes.

From the progressives' point of view, the conservatives' agenda, focusing as it did on questions like instrumental music and the identity of the one true church, was simply irrelevant to the pressing social questions that defined the age in which they lived. And from the viewpoint of the conservatives, the progressives had completely abandoned the historic restoration commitment of Churches of Christ.

Several new journals emerged to mark this ideological divide. *Mission* and *Integrity* served the progressives, while publications like the *First Century Christian* catered to the most conservative elements of Churches of Christ. At the same time, conservatives grew disillusioned with the increasingly academic orientation of the colleges, especially their Bible departments. They therefore took steps to establish "schools of preaching" that could produce pulpiteers who were sound in the traditional theology of Churches of Christ.

In the face of these divisions over issues they thought irrelevant to the world in which they lived, hundreds and perhaps thousands of college-educated young people deserted Churches of Christ in the 1960s. Some dropped out of organized religion altogether, some went to other denominations, and others cast their lot with the Crossroads Movement, later to become the International Church of Christ.

By the time the decade of the 1960s had run its course, Churches of Christ, like the larger nation, appeared to be in a serious crisis. Yet, from the ashes of that period emerged considerable renewal. In the concluding chapter, we will briefly trace some of the outlines of that renewal.

NOTES

1. On Benson, see John C. Stevens, *Before Any Were Willing: The Story of George S. Benson* (n.p.: n.p., 1991); and L. Edward Hicks, *"Sometimes in the Wrong, but Never in Doubt": George S. Benson and the Education of the New Religious Right* (Knoxville: University of Tennessee Press, 1995).

2. Benson recalled this in an interview with the author on 11 June 1990 at Searcy, Arkansas.

3. See chap. 1 of Hicks, *"Sometimes in the Wrong, but Never in Doubt."*

4. G. C. Brewer, *Autobiography of G. C. Brewer* (Murfreesboro, TN: DeHoff Publications, 1957), p. 60.

5. This quotation was reported by F. D. Srygley in "G. C. Brewer's Lecture," *GA* 78 (26 November 1936): 1133, 1141.

6. Srygley, "G. C. Brewer's Lecture," *GA* 78 (26 November 1936): 1133, 1141; see also the *Nashville Banner*, 9 November 1936.

7. Brewer, *Communism and Its Four Horsemen: Atheism, Immorality, Class Hatred, Pacifism* (Nashville: Gospel Advocate, 1936), p. 3.

8. Cited by Edwin S. Gaustad in "The Pulpit and the Pews," in *Between the Times: The Travail of the Protestant Establishment in America, 1900–1960*, ed. William R. Hutchinson (Cambridge: Cambridge University Press, 1989), p. 38.

9. I am grateful to Michael Casey for this insight. See Casey, "Neither Militant nor Pacifist: R. H. Boll on War and Peace," unpublished paper presented at Christian Scholars' Conference, Pepperdine University, 17 July 1998, p. 17.

10. Brewer, *Communism and Its Four Horsemen*, pp. 10 and 36–39.

11. On the relationship of Churches of Christ to American fundamentalism, see Michael Casey, "The Interpretation of Genesis One in the Churches of Christ: The Origins of Fundamentalist Reactions to Evolution and Biblical Criticism in the 1920s" (master's thesis, Abilene Christian University, 1989); and James Stephen Wolfgang, "Fundamentalism and the Churches of Christ, 1910–1930" (master's thesis, Vanderbilt University, 1990).

12. Brewer, "Our Purpose and Our Method of Attack," *Voice of Freedom* 1 (January 1953): 2.

13. Reuel Lemmons, "Editorial—Religion and Politics," *FF*, (1 November 1960): p. 690; Lemmons, "Can a Roman Catholic Be a Good President?" *FF*, 19 April 1960, p. 242; B.C. Goodpasture, "Some Corrections," *GA* 102 (25 August 1960): 530; and Goodpasture, "An Unusual Book," *GA* 102 (22 September 1960): 595.

14. V. E. Howard, "Kennedy Refuses to Deny Doctrine of Mental Reservation on Houston TV Program," *GA* 102 (22 September 1960): 593, 603; and "Kennedy Sidesteps Questions," *Christian Chronicle* 17 (20 September 1960): 1.

15. Alexander Campbell, "Our Position to American Slavery–No. VIII," *MH*, 3d ser., 2 (June 1845): 258–59 and 263; "Our Position to American Slavery–No. V," *MH*, 3d ser., 2 (May 1845): 193; and "Our Position to American Slavery–No. VIII," *MH*, 3d ser., 2 (June 1845): 258. On Campbell and slavery, see Robert O. Fife, *Teeth on Edge* (Grand Rapids: Baker Book House, 1971); and Jess O. Hale, Jr., "Ecclesiastical Politics on a Moral Powder Keg: Alexander Campbell and Slavery in the *Millennial Harbinger*, 1830–1860," *Restoration Quarterly* 39 (2d Qr 1997), pp. 65–81.

16. Benjamin Franklin, "Our Position Called For," *ACR* 2 (March 1859): 42, cited by James Brooks Major in "The Role of Periodicals in the Development of the Disciples of Christ, 1850–1910" (Ph.D. diss., Vanderbilt University, 1966), p. 97.

17. See Campbell, *Familiar Lectures on the Pentateuch*, ed. W. T. Moore (St. Louis: Christian Publishing, 1867), pp. 266–304. On Campbell's "canon within the canon," see M. Eugene Boring, "The Formation of a Tradition: Alexander Campbell and the New Testament," *Disciples Theological Digest* 2 (1987): 5–62.

18. Joseph Thomas, *The Travels and Gospel Labors of Joseph Thomas* (Winchester, VA, 1812), p. 56.

19. David Lipscomb, "Race Prejudice," *GA* 20 (21 February 1878): 120–21.

20. Lipscomb, "The Negro in the Worship—a Correspondence," *GA* 49 (4 July 1907): 425.

21. Lipscomb, *A Commentary on the New Testament Epistles: Ephesians, Philippians, and Colossians*, ed. J. W. Shepherd (Nashville: Gospel Advocate, 1939), p. 121.

22. Karl Pettus, "The Memorial to Marshall Keeble," *GA* 110 (18 July 1968): 449; and Lemmons, "Marshall Keeble," *FF* 85 (14 May 1968): 306.

23. Rex Turner, "The Attitude of a Christian in the Midst of a Race Crisis," March 1965, pp. 1, 4, cited by Lynn Perry in "The Church of Christ and Racial Attitudes," unpublished manuscript; and Lemmons, in a letter to Jennings Davis dated 23 May 1968, in John Allen Chalk Files in the library of the Harding Graduate School of Religion, Memphis, Tennessee.

24. Lemmons, in a letter to Jennings Davis dated 23 May 1968, in John Allen Chalk Files; and James D. Bales, *The Martin Luther King Story* (Tulsa: Christian Crusade Publications, 1967), p. 199.

25. Foy E. Wallace, Jr., "Negro Meetings for White People," *BB* 3 (March 1941): 7.

26. Marshall Keeble, "From M. Keeble," *BB* 3 (April 1941): 5.

27. Wallace, addendum to Keeble, "From M. Keeble," *BB* 3 (April 1941): 5.

28. White, in a letter to Reuel Lemmons dated 10 June 1968. Letter in possession of author.

29. Winrow, statement concerning Marshall Keeble, January 1995, in possession of Richard T. Hughes.

30. "The Other Brotherhood," *CC* 25 (8 March 1968): 2.

31. Keeble, "The Church among the Colored," *Abilene Christian College Lectures, 1950* (Abilene: ACC Bookstore, 1950), 145–46.

32. R. N. Hogan, "The Grab of the Century," *CE* 63 (December 1968): 1–2.

33. G. P. Holt, "Tension between the Black and White Church," *CE* 63 (June 1969): 4, 9.

34. Hogan, "The Sin of Being a Respecter of Persons," *CE* 54 (June 1959): 5; "Brother David Lipscomb Stood with God on Race Prejudice in the Church of Christ," *CE* 55 (June 1960): 2; "Is It the Law or Down-Right Prejudice?" *CE* 58 (June 1963): 3.

35. Hogan, "Brother David Lipscomb Stood with God on Race Prejudice in the Church of Christ," *CE* 55 (June 1960): 2.

36. Carl Spain, "Modern Challenges to Christian Morals," in *Christian Faith in the Modern World: The Abilene Christian College Annual Bible Lectures, 1960* (Abilene: Abilene Christian College Students Exchange, 1960), p. 217.

37. Brief for Defendant 5 at 10, *Obie Elie et al. v. Athens Clay Pullias et al.*, case 18,402 (6th Cir., 1967), pp. 10–11.

38. *Elie v. Pullias*, p. 12.

39. Keeble, "Nashville Christian Institute to Close," in Annie C. Tuggle, *Another World Wonder* (n.p.: n.p., n.d.), p. 142.

40. Complaint of Plaintiffs in *Obie Elie et al. v. Athens Clay Pullias et al.*, case 4794 (U.S. District Court, Middle District of Tennessee, Nashville Division, 1967), p. 9. On Gray's civil rights work, see Fred Gray, *Bus Ride to Justice: Changing the System by the System* (Montgomery: Black Belt Press, 1995).

41. Hogan, "The Grab of the Century," *CE* 63 (December 1968): 1–2.

42. Holt, "The Tragedy of Complacency," *CE* 63 (December 1968): 3; and Evans, "Outreach," *GA* 132 (January 1990): 19–20.

43. Watter Burch described this event as "underground" in a statement in the author's possession.

44. See "Background of Race Relations Workshop," in *Report on Race Relations Workshop: Supplement to Christian Chronicle*, 10 May 1968, p. 3; and Burch, "Statement of Response to Bob Douglas Re: Race Relations in Churches of Christ in 1960s," unpublished manuscript dated 6 February 1979, p. 11, in Walter Burch Files; files in possession of Walter Burch.

45. Dwain Evans, "The Meeting at Atlanta," *Milestone* (bulletin of Church of Christ, West Islip, New York), 1 July 1968, n.p.; interview by the author with Walter Burch, 11 October 1992; and "Conference on Race Relations," *Mission* 2 (September 1968): 24–29.

46. For the sermons, see John Allen Chalk, *Three American Revolutions* (New York: Carlton Press, 1970), esp. pp. 85–86, 105; for the response, see "Analysis of Mail Received from Radio for 'Three American Revolutions,' " John Allen Chalk Files.

47. On the *20th Century Christian* special issue, see Carroll Pitts, Jr., "A Critical Study of Civil Rights Practices, Attitudes and Responsibilities in Churches of Christ" (master's thesis, Pepperdine University, 1969), p. 104, and interview by the author with Steven Lemley, 8 May 1994; on Holt, see Holt, "Tension between the Black and White Churches," *CE* 63 (June 1969): 4, 9.

48. "Words and Wounds: Abilene Christian University Apologizes for Racist Past," *Dallas Morning News* (24 December 1999), 21A.

49. Lemmons, "Modernism," *FF* 86 (12 August 1969): 498; "Liberalism," *FF* 86 (19 August 1969): 514; "Wise Up or Go Under," *FF* 87 (24 February 1970): 114; "Traditionalism," *FF* 86 (26 August 1969): 530; "The Church and Its Young People," *FF* 87 (8 December 1970): 770; and "In Opinions Liberty," *FF* 87 (10 February 1970): 82.

50. See *The Last Things*, ed. Jack P. Lewis (Austin: Sweet Publishing, 1972), pp. 25–29; and Don H. Morris and Max Leach, *Like Stars Shining Brightly* (Abilene: Abilene Christian College Press, 1953), p. 229.

51. Don Haymes, "The Silence of the Scholars," *Mission* 8 (September 1974): 8–9.

52. "Statement Outlining Proposed New Christian Journal," 25 June 1966, in files of Walter E. Burch.

53. Haymes, "The Christ of the Gospels," *Mission* 2 (December 1968): 11 and 9.

54. Guy N. Woods, letter to editor, *Mission* 6 (September 1972): 27; and Thomas H. Olbricht, "New Journals for the Sixties: *Restoration Quarterly* and *Mission*," unpublished paper, 1992, in possession of the author, pp. 25–26.

55. Thomas B. Warren, "Our Aim," *SS* 1 (October 1969): 2.

56. Ira Y. Rice, *Axe on the Root*, vol. 1 (Dallas: n.p., 1966), pp. 8–9, 24.

57. Rice, *Axe on the Root*, 1:72.

58. Rice, "Restoration Movement Is at the Crossroads: Whither in the '70s?" *Contending for the Faith* 1 (January 1970): 2.

59. Ross W. Dye, "Waybill for Decline," *GA* 110 (30 May 1968): 337; and Malcolm L. Hill, "What Breeds Liberalism?" *GA* 112 (12 March 1970): 170.

60. Wallace, "A Voice of Concern," *FF* 85 (26 March 1968): 198.

61. Batsell Barrett Baxter, "The Training of Preachers," *FF* 87 (23 June 1970): 387; and Hearn, "Getwell Road School of Preaching," *GA* 110 (1 February 1968): 68–69.

62. Thomas H. Olbricht, "Is There a Message?" *Mission* 6 (June 1973): 5. For other acknowledgments of the flight of the young from Churches of Christ, see Perry C. Cotham, "Freedom of Expression: Is It Really Necessary in Our Churches?" *Mission* 4 (April 1971): 12–13; and Frank Holden, "The New Children," *Mission* 5 (September 1971): 3–4.

63. See Martin Edward Wooten, "The Boston Movement as a 'Revitalization Movement' " (master's thesis, Harding University Graduate School of Religion, 1990).

64. For the philosophy of the Boston Movement, see Kip McKean, "Revolution through Restoration: From Jerusalem to Rome, from Boston to Moscow," *UpsideDown* 1 (April 1992): 1–13.

65. Richard N. Ostling, "Keepers of the Flock," *Time*, 18 May 1992, p. 62.

7
RENEWAL

Throughout the 1970s and well into the 1980s, Churches of Christ found themselves in a deep malaise. Nothing contributed to that malaise more effectively than the rapid erosion of this tradition's historic identity. For over a hundred years that identity had been crystal clear: the Church of Christ was not a denomination with human roots but, rather, the one true church, described in the biblical text, outside of which there was no salvation. Now many in this tradition were not so sure.

Compounding the malaise were new, more accurate statistics regarding both the growth rate and the size of Churches of Christ. It seemed reasonably clear that Churches of Christ were no longer experiencing the rapid growth they had enjoyed since the Great Depression.[1] Instead, they were likely holding their own or perhaps experiencing numerical decline. Moreover, earlier estimates that Churches of Christ had a membership in excess of 2,000,000 now seemed unfounded. By 1994 Mac Lynn, the preeminent statistician among Churches of Christ, estimated the total membership of Churches of Christ at roughly 1,250,000.[2]

These numbers, and the perception that Churches of Christ were no longer experiencing rapid growth, caused considerable distress in the ranks of the faithful. After all, nondenominational Bible churches, built on a vision remarkably similar to the one that informed the Stone-Campbell movement in its earliest years, enjoyed enormous success in communities throughout the United States at the very time Churches of Christ seemed to be stagnating. Celebrating the success of conservative Protestant Christianity in general, Dean M. Kelley published in 1972 his noted book *Why Conservative Churches Are Growing*. And *Newsweek* magazine proclaimed 1976 "The Year of the Evangelical."[3] Many wondered why Churches of Christ apparently no longer experienced the kind of success that similar religious movements had enjoyed since the 1970s.

In addition, the venerable restoration vision—the single notion that had defined the essence of Churches of Christ since the early nineteenth century—was rapidly falling on hard times—and for a variety of reasons. First, although many in Churches of Christ still used the countercultural language of restoration and primitive Christianity to define what this tradition was all about, Churches of Christ increasingly behaved like a denomination that had made its peace with the surrounding culture. The growing dissonance between the rhetoric of restoration and the reality of cultural accommodation helped to discredit the restoration vision in the minds of many in this tradition. Second, the widespread failure of Churches of Christ to respond in a positive way to the ethical crises of the 1960s convinced many, especially among the young, that the restoration ideal was ethically impotent. Third, observing trends in the history of their own tradition, many in Churches of Christ concluded that the restoration ideal was inherently legalistic and exclusionary and, for that reason, rejected the restoration ideal out of hand. And finally, Churches of Christ for almost two hundred years had employed the premises of the eighteenth-century Enlightenment—especially Lockean empiricism and Scottish Common Sense Realism—to define the meaning of the restoration ideal. Yet, the postmodern climate that emerged in the aftermath of the 1960s triggered in the general culture a widespread rejection of Enlightenment epistemologies. The pressing question for Churches of Christ, therefore, was this: how could a modern (i.e., Enlightenment-based) religious tradition like Churches of Christ survive in a postmodern world?

Churches of Christ responded to these challenges in a variety of ways. Some thought Churches of Christ had simply failed to advertise themselves sufficiently and responded with a promotional campaign.[4] The Crossroads (Boston) Movement, considered in the previous chapter, diagnosed the problem as the natural result of widespread acculturation and therefore called for a renewal of radical discipleship. The most enduring response, however, came in the form of a widespread attempt to renew and even reinvent this tradition.

By no means, however, did these renewal efforts characterize every congregation in the fellowship of Churches of Christ. Many congregations, especially in small towns and rural areas, resisted these attempts. But renewal did bring significant change to many of the larger, urban congregations that stood in the mainstream of this tradition.

THEOLOGICAL RENEWAL

In the 1960s many preachers among Churches of Christ began to proclaim a major biblical motif that had rarely been heard in this tradition: a theology of grace. We have already observed at various points throughout this book that Churches of Christ had, for most of their history, promoted a legal approach to the Christian faith. This peculiar understanding of the Christian religion grew in part from the fact that most in this tradition understood the biblical text as a divinely given law book. It also grew from the fact that most in Churches of

Christ understood the restoration vision as a mandate to obey without equivocation all New Testament commands and to implement all New Testament examples, even those that only reflected nothing more than a necessary inference.

Yet, it must be acknowledged that here and there, Churches of Christ had kept alive a minority report that affirmed a theology of free and unmerited grace. As we noted in chapter 4, G. C. Brewer and K. C. Moser, among others, actively promoted this conception in the 1930s, 1940s, and 1950s. When, therefore, a Harding College Bible professor named Jimmy Allen proclaimed the message of grace to his students in 1963, he drew on a tradition that was not altogether foreign to Churches of Christ. Yet, whereas Moser and Brewer had encountered stiff resistance when they preached a doctrine of grace, Allen's teaching ignited not controversy but a campuswide revival.[5] The truth is, Allen's proclamation was but the tip of the iceberg, for in the 1960s, preachers in Churches of Christ were rapidly recovering the biblical doctrine of grace, a theme that would increasingly define this tradition for the remainder of the century.

How can we explain this development, especially in light of the tendencies toward legalism that had characterized Churches of Christ from the earliest years of this tradition? First, it is fair to say that if a Christian movement focuses its attention on the biblical text for long enough, it will eventually discover the heart of the gospel message, and Churches of Christ have always been relentless in their fidelity to the biblical text. This fact alone, however, does not fully explain why the discovery of a theology of grace occurred in the 1960s and not earlier—or even later.

One must also consider the fact that the 1960s was a dynamic decade that prompted a reconsideration of virtually all questions, not just in Churches of Christ but throughout the culture. A new generation was impatient with time-honored tradition and demanded a reassessment of assumptions a previous generation took for granted. In this context many who embraced a theology of grace in the 1960s were also revolting against the legalism, the exclusivism, and the hard style that had dominated Churches of Christ for so much of the twentieth century. Beyond this colleges related to Churches of Christ were, by the 1960s, increasingly reaping the benefit of biblical and theological scholarship. Much of that scholarship pointed students to the heart of the biblical message, not to peripheral concerns, and inevitably affected the pulpits of this tradition. In addition, religious programming on radio and television increasingly opened Churches of Christ to a world that had essentially been closed to this tradition for many years, allowing them to hear the message of grace from other Christians, especially from conservative evangelical Protestants. Most decisive of all, perhaps, was the newly emerging postmodern climate that emphasized the subjective dimensions of human experience and downplayed strict objectivity. In that postmodern context, many young people in Churches of Christ abandoned the objective, legal approach to the Christian faith that they had learned from this tradition and embraced instead a relational paradigm that made abundant room for the grace of God, for a subjective experience of the Holy Spirit, and for a relationship with other Christian believers that was grounded in a relationship with the Divine.

By the 1980s another phase of theological renewal was well underway, a phase often described as a reassessment of the traditional hermeneutic of Churches of Christ. In chapter 2, we noted Alexander Campbell's intensely rational approach to the biblical text. Campbell viewed the Bible as a kind of constitution—or pattern—that should govern the church, and he argued that Christians should discern that pattern scientifically, employing the Baconian method of induction. One of Campbell's protégés, Moses Lard, helped introduce into Churches of Christ a hermeneutic—or a method of reading the biblical text—that elevated biblical commands, biblical examples, and necessary inferences, all discerned with scientific precision.

That threefold hermeneutic—command, example, and necessary inference—was both subject and object of the hermeneutic debate that engulfed Churches of Christ in the 1980s. Indeed, it is fair to ask how such a rigorously scientific approach to the biblical text could survive in the postmodern world that had emerged in the United States by that time. In hindsight, therefore, the "hermeneutic crisis," as it was often described in the literature of Churches of Christ during that period, was perhaps inevitable.

The "hermeneutic crisis" was a "*crisis*," since it raised questions about the very heart and soul of the historic identity of Churches of Christ. What kind of book was the Bible, after all? Was it a constitution? A pattern? A blueprint? Or was it a theological treatise, describing the relationship God seeks with humankind and the kind of relationship humans should therefore sustain with one another? Increasingly, leaders in mainstream Churches of Christ defined the Bible in these latter terms.

In 1985, for example, moderates among Churches of Christ launched a new journal called *Image*. There can be little doubt but that the very creation of this new journal reflected the hermeneutic changes that were already redefining this tradition. Those responsible for the creation of *Image* employed Reuel Lemmons as the journal's inaugural editor. We recall from an earlier chapter that Lemmons was a powerful leader among Churches of Christ who had for almost thirty years edited the Austin-based *Firm Foundation*. In his very first editorial for *Image*, Lemmons said nothing about the Bible as a blueprint or pattern or constitution. Instead, he reflected on the theme implicit in the title, *Image*. "This magazine," he wrote, "shall have one goal and one purpose—to mould men more perfectly into the image of Jesus Christ."[6]

If Lemmons addressed the hermeneutic crisis only implicitly, others addressed it head-on. Perhaps no one emerged with greater visibility in this regard—or addressed the question with greater precision—than Thomas H. Olbricht, professor of Bible and biblical theology at Abilene Christian University for nineteen years (1967–86) and then at Pepperdine University for another ten (1986–96). As early as 1965, Olbricht candidly wrote,

Campbell got us headed in the wrong direction. . . . I think he was wrong in seeing it [the Bible] as a collection of facts, the unity of which emerges from the individual facts themselves. What he should have done is to raise the question of what are the great themes of the scriptures of God's love shown in his deeds of sin and salvation and then interpreted the individual facts in that light.

In 1991, in a presentation at Princeton Theological Seminary, Olbricht summarized the arguments he had made for many years when he contended that "the focal point in scripture is the mighty loving action of God on behalf of man made in his image and the universe he has created." The starting point for hermeneutics, therefore, should be "God, Christ, and the Holy Spirit, rather than commands, examples, and necessary inferences, regardless of how helpful these may be in regard to specific matters of church order."[7]

Younger scholars also entered the fray. Russ Dudrey, for example, claimed that what was at stake in the hermeneutic debate

is not merely the success of Restorationism; at stake is our knowledge of the Father. Hardline patternism approaches Scripture as a revelation of propositional truths rather than of the heart of the Father. Surely we subvert our model of the character of God if we require our hermeneutic to address such scholasticizing issues as . . . how we should read the blueprint of New Testament case law.[8]

In September 1989 the *Christian Chronicle* ran a banner headline that proclaimed, "Bible Interpretation Controversy Smoulders." In the story that followed, the *Chronicle* observed that "one subject keeps cropping up in sermons, articles, retreats and lectureships these days—how to interpret the Bible." It is not surprising that the "hermeneutic crisis" received such sustained and systematic attention, since by virtue of this "crisis" many in Churches of Christ were seeking to renew and even redefine the meaning of this tradition, but to do so in terms that squared with the allegiance Churches of Christ had always given to the biblical text.

RENEWAL IN WORSHIP

Renewal was not confined to theology and hermeneutics. It also emerged in the realm of corporate worship. There, renewal pertained both to liturgy and to the role that women might legitimately play in the public worship services of Churches of Christ.

For most of the twentieth century, Churches of Christ embraced a musical repertoire that might have characterized most evangelical denominations in the United States. Yet, their musical tradition was distinctive in several ways. First, singing was always a cappella, a practice grounded in the conviction of Churches of Christ that instrumental music was neither authorized by the New Testament nor utilized in the golden age of primitive Christian faith. Second, Churches of

Christ never utilized choirs in their formal worship. Instead, the entire congregation participated in the singing, which was invariably led by a single male member of the church.

By the 1990s these patterns were changing dramatically. First, in many congregations one seldom heard the old gospel songs like "The Old Rugged Cross" or "I Come to the Garden Alone," much less the stately, traditional hymns that one might have heard a generation earlier. Instead, contemporary Christian music, popularized by evangelical artists, increasingly dominated the worship experience. Older members often denigrated this music as "camp songs," a perception supported by the fact that hymn books were rapidly being displaced by lyrics (minus musical notation) that were projected onto a screen or on a wall at the front of the church auditorium.

In addition, in many congregations a "praise team" or "worship team" had displaced the traditional male song leader. Typically composed of six to eight members, half male and half female, all on individual microphones, these praise teams brought new vibrancy and life to a new generation of worshippers.

It is difficult to overemphasize the significance of the fact that praise teams typically included women and therefore placed them in a position of leadership of corporate worship. Historically, at least in the twentieth century, Churches of Christ had never permitted women to occupy a leadership role in any capacity whatsoever. Women did not serve as elders. Women did not serve as deacons. Women seldom or never taught Bible classes in which men were their students, and some congregations barred women from teaching classes in which males of any age were present. And finally, women never led in the public worship.

To be sure, there is evidence that women both preached and led in public worship in congregations related to the Stone movement in the early years of the nineteenth century. But when the Stone and Campbell traditions joined forces in 1832, most of the congregations that utilized women refused to join that union and, in time, became a part of the Christian Connection that descended from Elias Smith and Abner Jones in New England and James O'Kelly in Virginia. Accordingly, none of those congregations made their way into the stream that eventually became known as Churches of Christ.[9]

Although some women in the Disciples of Christ pressed for greater involvement in the late nineteenth century, the door remained firmly closed to women who sought a leadership role in the public worship of Churches of Christ. David Lipscomb, for example, not only claimed that female leadership in worship was contrary to the law of God. He also feared what he described as the "strong emotional nature" of women that "demands whatever strikes her fancy, whether authorized by the Lord or not." In 1892 two auxiliary societies that served the Disciples of Christ—the Christian Woman's Board of Missions and the General Christian Missionary Society—met jointly in David Lipscomb's own hometown of Nashville, Tennessee. Lipscomb clearly perceived the Christian Woman's Board of Missions as a threat to male leadership and responded accordingly. "Every man," he inveighed, "who encourages [the woman's board] works against God, the church, womanhood, the interest of the family, motherhood, and against true manhood itself."[10]

Although the classic position of Churches of Christ on the role of women in church affairs surely reflected the values of a patriarchal American South, it also reflected the church's allegiance to a scientific and literal reading of the biblical text. Defenders of this position, for example, routinely pointed to I Corinthians 14:34, where Paul writes that "women should remain silent in the churches. They are not allowed to speak, but must be in submission." They also argued from I Timothy 2:12: "I do not permit a woman to teach or to have authority over a man; she must be silent."

By the 1980s and into the 1990s, the "women's question" had surfaced with a vengeance among Churches of Christ. Elderships throughout the country were discussing and reconsidering the church's traditional position on this issue. One can hardly doubt that this development was triggered, in part, by the fact that women were playing a far more prominent role in the broader American culture than ever before. But one must also attribute this development to the hermeneutic shift that was rapidly overtaking Churches of Christ. If the Bible was essentially a divinely authorized rule book, and if one rightly discerned those rules in commands, examples, and necessary inferences, then there was little doubt that passages like I Corinthians 14:34 and I Timothy 2:12 severely restricted the role that women might play in the governance and the public worship of the church. But if the Bible was a theological document, not a legal document, then there were passages that seemed to reflect the core of the biblical message and for that reason, some felt, might well take precedence over texts like I Corinthians 14 and I Timothy 2. One of those texts was Galatians 3:28: "There is neither Jew nor Greek, slave nor free, male nor female, for you are all one in Christ Jesus."

As congregations of Churches of Christ undertook a reconsideration of this issue, change was inevitable. By the late 1990s a number of congregations had opened the door to a greater participation by women in the public worship of the church,[11] though those congregations still constituted a distinct minority in the overall scheme of things.

CONCLUSIONS

By the close of the twentieth century, Churches of Christ had come a very long way from their beginnings almost two hundred years before. No longer confined to the original heartland of Middle Tennessee and the surrounding environs, Churches of Christ could now be found throughout the United States and in virtually all parts of the world, thanks both to migration patterns and believers' devotion to evangelism.

As the third millennium dawned, they no longer constituted a struggling sect harboring a countercultural mentality. Instead, they had evolved into a major denomination that had accommodated itself in many ways to the values of the larger culture. No longer even acquainted with the apocalyptic perspective of the nineteenth century, Churches of Christ, by the late twentieth century, were in the process of rethinking their other major theological support—the restoration vision. Indeed, many congregations had embraced the process of renewal and even redefinition of their tradition.

At the same time there was serious resistance to renewal in many quarters. Some in this tradition were reluctant to relinquish the traditional Baconian hermeneutic and especially the distinctive Church of Christ version of that hermeneutic that emphasized commands, examples, and necessary inferences. In many congregations legalism and exclusivism still prevailed. Although the question regarding the role of women in the corporate worship was under widespread consideration, it was by no means a foregone conclusion that any significant change on this issue was inevitable.

Only time would tell how deeply renewal would finally run and how far the redefinition of this tradition would extend. In the midst of this uncertainty, however, one thing did seem clear: Churches of Christ would likely continue their almost two hundred-year-old allegiance to the New Testament as their final court of appeal. If past history was any indicator, renewal would come only after serious engagement with scripture and only insofar as change could be justified by the biblical text. The fundamental question facing Churches of Christ as the twenty-first century dawned was this: What kind of book was the Bible, after all? The extent of renewal would depend to a very great extent on how Churches of Christ would finally answer that question.

NOTES

1. Michael Casey argues that Churches of Christ experienced their greatest rate of growth between 1926 and 1946. See Casey, "Church Growth: New Information," *Image* 3 (1 May 1987): 14–15, and "Church Growth: New Information," *Image* 3 (15 May 1987): 20–21.

2. Mac Lynn, comp., *Churches of Christ in the United States* (Brentwood, TN: Morrison and Phillips Associates, 1994; first published 1989), p. 15.

3. Dean M. Kelley, *Why Conservative Churches Are Growing: A Study in Sociology of Religion* (New York: Harper & Row, 1972); and "Born Again," *Newsweek*, 25 October 1976, pp. 68–78.

4. On this theme, see Richard T. Hughes, *Reviving the Ancient Faith: The Story of Churches of Christ in America* (Grand Rapids: Eerdmans, 1996), pp. 354–57.

5. The author was a student in Allen's class—a class on the book of Romans—and recalls both Allen's emphasis on a biblical theology of grace and the student revival that resulted.

6. Reuel Lemmons, "The Emergence of IMAGE," *Image* 1 (1 June 1985): 4.

7. Thomas H. Olbricht, "The Bible as Revelation," *RQ* 8 (1965): 229; and "Is the Theology of the American Restoration Movement Viable?" paper presented at Restoration Colloquium, Princeton Theological Seminary, December 1991.

8. Russ Dudrey, "Restorationist Hermeneutics among the Churches of Christ: Why Are We at an Impasse?" *RQ* 30 (1988): 37–42.

9. Bill Grasham, "The Role of Women in the American Restoration Movement," *RQ* 41 (4th Quarter 1999): 211–39.

10. David Lipscomb, cited by Fred Arthur Bailey in "The Status of Women in the Disciples of Christ Movement, 1865–1900" (Ph.D. diss., University of Tennessee, 1979), p. 67; and Lipscomb, "Woman and Her Work," *GA* 34 (13 October 1892): 644.

11. For example, the Brookline Church of Christ in the Boston area employed women as leaders of public worship by the late 1970s and in a preaching role by 1983; in 1987 the congregation made Micki Pulley a co-minister with pulpit responsibilities. By the mid-1970s the Church of Christ in Chapel Hill, North Carolina, utilized women in every worship capacity other than preaching and serving communion. In 1982 the West Islip Church of Christ in West Islip, New York, formally decided to allow women an equal role in the worship services and leadership of the congregation. By 1989 the Bering Drive Church of Christ in Houston involved women in the leadership of public worship, though not in a preaching capacity. By 1994 the Cahaba Valley Church of Christ in Birmingham, Alabama, had opened up all aspects of public worship to women, including preaching; Katie Hays, a recent graduate of the Yale Divinity School, became one of three ministers who regularly filled the pulpit. In 1998 the elders of the Malibu Church of Christ in Malibu, California, after several years of biblical study on this issue, opened the door for women to participate in all aspects of the worship service except for preaching. And in 1999 the elders of the Dayspring Church of Christ in Edmond, Oklahoma, made a similar decision. (This information was drawn from personal observation of the situation both in Malibu and at Dayspring; from a letter to the author from Paul Casner, former minister of the West Islip Church of Christ, West Islip, New York; from telephone interviews by the author with Robert M. Randolph, Brookline, Massachusetts; Bobbie Lee Holley, Chapel Hill; Bill Love, Houston; and Lance Pape, Birmingham; and from a congregational statement entitled "The Role of Women at Cahaba Valley," January 1990.)

Part Two
A BIOGRAPHICAL DICTIONARY OF LEADERS IN CHURCHES OF CHRIST

By R. L. Roberts

A

Note that the "A" and "B" references in the Bibliographies refer to primary and secondary works.

ADAMS, JOHN (1770–1858, OH). *Career*: Exhorter; itinerant preacher.

John Adams seems to have been the first in Tennessee to follow the lead of Barton W. Stone and David Purviance at Cane Ridge in 1803 when the Stone preachers separated from the Presbyterians. John Adams and his wife were members of the Cane Ridge church, where he was active as a gifted singer and possibly a licensed Presbyterian exhorter. In 1802 Adams sold his Kentucky farm and moved to Wilson County, Tennessee. The Purviance family had settled in Kentucky in 1790, immigrants from Iredell County, North Carolina; but when Native Americans killed a son of Colonel John Purviance, the family moved to Cane Ridge, Kentucky, and returned to Tennessee after the revival. Adams seems to have had an attachment to the Purviance family and possibly this caused his move to Tennessee and his subsequent move to Ohio, where David Purviance also lived. Adams' second wife (married in 1816) was a sister of David Purviance. Adams became a traveling evangelist in Tennessee and was probably the first Stone movement preacher in Tennessee. Only brief mentions of his early activity in Tennessee remain. Adams is possibly the evangelist who started the Rock Springs Church of Christ in Clay County, Tennessee, in January 1805, the oldest congregation of Churches of Christ in Tennessee that continues to meet. Adams also started a church that met on Stone's River in Wilson County. Joseph Thomas met Adams in Tennessee in December 1810 while preaching on Stone's River and later wrote, "Here I was met by brother Adams, who took me home with him. I found him to be a servant of the most high God, and a man of information and learning. He is a preacher of the Christian church. . . . I preached at his house to a solemn and attentive people."

In 1816 Adams moved to Preble County, Ohio, one of many families in the Stone movement from Tennessee and Kentucky who moved to new states north of the Ohio River to free their slaves. Along with David Purviance and Levi, his son, Adams opposed the Stone-Campbell union. A brief note reprinted by Stone from the *Christian Palladium* says that "Elder John Adams says he cannot go with nor fellowship the Reformers any longer." Stone responded, "This I could not have expected from one, who always before professed fellowship for Christians.—But names and opinions are powerful things." Although John Adams did not join in the ongoing Stone-Campbell movement, evidence that his ministry helped initiate the Christian movement in Middle Tennessee seems unquestionable.

Bibliography

B. Joseph Thomas, *Travels and Gospel Labors* (Winchester, NC, 1812), p. 12; Evan William Humphreys, *Memoirs of Deceased Christian Ministers* (Dayton, OH, 1880), pp. 9–11; Isaac N. Walters, "Extract from the recent journal . . . ," *CM* 9 (1842), 158.

ALLEN, THOMAS MILLER (21 October 1797, VA–10 October 1871, Columbia, MO). *Education*: Law School, Transylvania University, 1819–22. *Career*: Lawyer, minister.

From 1835 when he came from Kentucky to Missouri until his death in 1871, Thomas Miller Allen was the most influential preacher in the Stone-Campbell movement in Missouri. After marriage in 1818 Allen studied law at Transylvania University and briefly practiced in Bloomington, Indiana, in 1822. Upon becoming a Christian he quit law practice and returned to Kentucky, where the Allens became charter members of Old Union church in Fayette County and where Allen began preaching. In 1825 Barton W. Stone ordained Miller along with B. F. Hall. During his ten-year ministry in Kentucky, Miller started churches at Paris, Antioch, Clintonville, and Cynthiana. After moving to Missouri in 1835, he established churches near his home in Boone County and in other parts of the state. T. P. Haley refers to T. M. Allen's move to Missouri as the beginning of an epoch in the history of the few struggling churches in that state. Allen and other associates of B. W. Stone, including John Allen Gano, were reluctant to accept many of Alexander Campbell's positions for a number of years after the Campbell and Stone merger in 1832. Favoring the name "Christian," Allen wrote to Gano in 1840 regarding the controversy over the designation "Disciples": "The brethren throughout all my travels stand firm for the name Christian. Bro Alex [Alexander Campbell] has missed it this heat. The fact is, I wish he would cease the duties of an editor. He is through with every thing important to this reformation, & now I fear he is to do harm by speculating, & going deep into the 'language of ashdod',—there is plenty of it in his 'Christian System'—on account of which I would not purchase it." His opposition to Campbell in the late 1830s and early 1840s reflects a strong sentiment among those preachers who had worked in harmony with Barton W. Stone. Allen was very generous in supporting education, especially Bethany College and the University of Missouri. He strongly urged patronage of the church's early publications, especially *Lard's Quarterly*, the *American Christian Review*, and the *Millennial Harbinger*. To John Gano at the time of Stone's death, Allen characterized the life of Barton W. Stone as "a commentary on the blessed gospel of Christ" and his ministry as the best example of the cause of restoration. He echoed the feelings of many nineteenth-century restorers when he wrote, "I believe that no person now living has done more for the Union of Christians—the peace of Zion—and the salvation of Sinners than father Stone did."

Bibliography

A. Letters to John Allen Gano, May 26, 1858; October 7, 1859; and December 6, 1844, in Gano Papers, microfilm in Center for Restoration Studies, Abilene Christian University.

B. Alvin R. Jennings, *T. M. Allen, Pioneer Preacher of Kentucky and Missouri* (Fort Worth: Star Bible and Tract Corporation, 1977).

ANDREWS, SARAH SHEPHERD (26 November 1893, Dickson, TN–16 September, 1961, Japan). *Education*: Dickson College. *Career:* Missionary.

Sarah Shepherd Andrews served from 1916 to 1961 as a missionary to Japan, where her work proved to be the most permanent among Churches of Christ in that country. She was instrumental in establishing four churches in Japan and saving them from destruction during World War II. She eventually saw those four grow into eight congregations. She remained in Japan throughout World War II, first in a prison camp, from which she was released in September 1942 because of lack of provisions, then under house arrest for the remainder of the war. Of her war experience she later wrote, "I had never experienced hunger until I was caught in the throes of war and famine as an enemy national during this war. My weight reached the low ebb of seventy-five pounds, and my body became very edematous from malnutrition. In desperation I boiled leaves from the trees for food, boiled and used water from cornstalks for sugar, used sea water for salt, and after months of meatless days I relished grasshoppers for meat, wishing I could have the same dish often." After the war a friend asked her, "Why did you stay?" Andrews responded, "If I had not been in Japan . . . the three churches in my section of the country, together with the property, would have been lost to the national federation of churches. Therefore, I rejoice to have stayed and suffered for the cause of truth." Andrews returned to the United States to regain her health from 1947 to 1949. Her last period of work in Japan featured increased activity, although she had not regained full strength. In 1952 she started work in Numazu City and erected a church building in 1954, exactly as she had earlier planned.

Upon her death the Japanese people, both Christian and non-Christian, built a memorial to Sarah Andrews. A concrete wall surrounding the site is inscribed with a tribute to her and the Twenty-third Psalm is engraved on the lid of the box that contains her earthly remains.

Bibliography

A. "My Maintenance during the War," *GA*, 90 (January 29, 1948), 100, 117; "45 Years on the Field," *CWom*, 29 (December 1961), 26–27.

B. Hettie Lee Ewing, *She Hath Done What She Could: The Reminiscences of Hettie Lee Ewing* (Dallas, 1974), pp. 152–157; Gary O. Turner, "Pioneer to Japan: A Biography of J. M. McCaleb," M. A. thesis, Abilene Christian College, 1972, pp. 88–89.

ARMSTRONG, JOHN NELSON (6 January 1870, near Gadsden, TN–11 August 1944, Searcy, AR). *Education*: West Tennessee Christian College, Union University, graduated from Nashville Bible School, 1896. *Career*: Teacher, Potter Bible College, 1901–05; president, Western Bible and Literary College, Odessa, MO, 1905–08; president, Cordell Christian College, Cordell, OK, 1908–15; president, Harper College, Harper, KS, 1916–24; president, Harding University, 1924–36.

J. N. Armstrong, probably more than any other man, continued among the Churches of Christ the heritage of James A. Harding, David Lipscomb, and the old Nashville Bible School. In addition, as president of Harding College from 1924 to 1936, he embodied the spirit of that institution, which could not have existed without him. During a very difficult financial time when the teachers could not be paid, Armstrong held a gospel meeting and shared the money he received with his faculty. Each received $5. Several controversies mark Armstrong's life and work. Like his mentors, Harding and Lipscomb, he was a strong pacifist. During his presidency of Cordell Christian College in Cordell, Oklahoma (1908–1918), conflict with the government and local citizens over pacifism forced that institution to close its doors. When president of Harding College, he engaged Daniel Sommer in public debate over the "Bible college issue." But Armstrong's friendship with the premillennial advocate Robert H. Boll caused probably the severest criticism and opposition from within Arkansas and especially from the *Gospel Guardian*. In 1935 his critics sought to pressure Armstrong to admit that he held premillennial views. The truth is, he did not hold those views, but his friendship with R. H. Boll and his embrace of pacifist sentiments made him suspect for many years in the eyes of his critics.

Bibliography

A. *Undenominational Christianity* (Cordell, OK, 191?); "Unity and Good Fellowship—How to Find It," *FF*, 52 (March 12, 1935), 5.

B. L. C. Sears, *For Freedom: The Biography of John Nelson Armstrong* (Austin, 1969); Loyd L. Smith, "J. N. Armstrong," in *Gospel Preachers of Yesteryear* (Allen, TX, 1986), pp. 11–17.

ASH, JOSEPH (1808, Canada–1895, Canada). *Career*: Minister and editor.

Joseph Ash was a pioneer leader of Churches of Christ in Ontario, Canada. One finds an early indication of the unity between several conservatives in Canada and those who held to similar views in the States in a brief mention in the *Gospel Advocate* of a visit by Joseph Ash, a Canadian preacher, to Tennessee shortly after the Civil War. He apparently sought to become personally acquainted with Tolbert Fanning, editor of the *Advocate*, to learn more of Fanning's theology. He embraced Lipscomb's view of the Christian's nonparticipation in civil government and resisted progressive innovations from churches in the northern states. Ash came to Churches of Christ from the Christian Connection, which he joined shortly after his baptism in 1829. His discovery of Alexander Campbell's *Millennial Harbinger* shortly after his baptism played an important role in his religious development. Ash wrote articles for Benjamin Franklin's *American Christian Review* and the *Bible Index*, a Canadian paper, and published the *Christian Worker* (1881–1886) at Meaford, Ontario.

Bibliography

A. "Reminiscences of the Rise and Progress of Our Cause in (Ontario)," series of nineteen articles, *CW* (November 1882–September 1884).

B. "Obituary," *ACR* (1862), 3; Reuben Butchart, *The Disciples of Christ in Canada since 1830* (Toronto, 1949), pp. 69, 143, 411–415.

B

BARKER, SQUIRE LEANDER (4 July 1847, Lea Co., VA–15 June 1930, Beulah, NM). *Career*: Farmer; frontier preacher.

Squire Leander Barker was a pioneer preacher for Churches of Christ in the mountains of northern New Mexico. Barker was baptized in Virginia by Silas Shelburne and married a niece of Joshua K. Speer, noted early Tennessee reformer. The Barkers immigrated to Texas, settling in Burnet County, and then moved to Shackleford County in West Texas, where he began preaching at Hulltown (now Moran, Texas) during the 1880s. Severe drought gripped West Texas in 1886 and many members of the Churches of Christ suffered. Barker was the principal agent for relief contributions from all over the United States. Because of Mrs. Barker's health, in 1889 the Barkers moved to the mountains of New Mexico, settling on Sapello Creek, twenty-five miles northwest of Las Vegas. The Barkers devoted the remainder of their lives to establishing Churches of Christ in that region. They received comparatively little support and rejected support from missionary societies.

Barker and his wife published accounts of their work under the title "New Mexico Mission" principally in the *Gospel Advocate, Christian Leader, Firm Foundation*, and *Octographic Review*. Preaching tours took Barker into remote areas of northern New Mexico and southern Colorado where no preacher in the Churches of Christ had ever gone. He established small churches in New Mexico at Las Vegas, Hall Peak, and Beulah, and in southern Colorado. One son, Omar S. Barker, became a well-known western writer whose works include poems about his father and an interesting chapter about the religion of the Barkers in *Little World Apart*, a fictionalized account of the Barker family experiences in New Mexico. Elliott S. Barker, another son, became a well-known forester and writer. Elliott's book *Western Life and Adventures, 1889 to 1970* (Albuquerque,

1970) contains an interesting account of the family's covered wagon journey from West Texas to the Rocky Mountains in 1889.

Bibliography

A. "Risen with Christ" in Laurence W. Scott, ed., *Texas Pulpit/by Christian Preachers* (St. Louis, 1888), pp. 248–260.

B. Omar Barker, *Little World Apart* (Garden City, 1966); Lawrence Scott, ed., *Texas Pulpit by Christian Preachers* (St. Louis, 1888); Gary Williams, "S. L. Barker: A New Mexico Pioneer," term paper at University of New Mexico, Albuquerque, 1987; and Elliott S. Barker, *Western Life and Adventures, 1889 to 1970* (Albuquerque, 1970).

BARRET, ALLEN BOOKER (15 July 1879–6 April, 1951, Henderson, TN). *Education*: West Tennessee Christian College; Nashville Bible School. *Career*: Teacher, Southwestern Christian College, 1904–05; founder and first president, Childers Classical Institute, now Abilene Christian University, 1906–08; president, Southland University, 1909; Clebarro College, 1910–15; Bible Chair, University of Texas, 1918–23.

A. B. Barret is best known as the founder of Abilene Christian University, which became the best-known educational institution conducted by members of the Churches of Christ. Barret's work is just one example of the great educational influence of the Nashville Bible School begun by James A. Harding and David Lipscomb in 1891. In September 1906 Barret founded Childers Classical Institute in Abilene, Texas, now Abilene Christian University, and served two years as president before resigning to become president of Southland University, a new school planned at Denton to succeed Southwestern Christian College. After the Denton venture failed for lack of support, Barret with Charles H. Roberson, who aided Barret in the Abilene and Denton schools, accepted an opportunity to build a college at Cleburne, Texas. The result was Clebarro College, which lasted from 1910 to 1917, when financial difficulties forced its closure. Barret then moved to Austin, Texas, where, along with Charles Heber Roberson and G. H. P. Showalter, he helped establish a Bible chair at the University of Texas. When Barret's work with the Bible chair at the University of Texas ended in the early 1920s, he returned to Tennessee. While preaching in Fayetteville, Tennessee, he became a prominent antievolution lecturer and proponent of the antievolution bill adopted by the Tennessee legislature in 1925. Barret was also known for his preaching. His first preaching work in Texas was in Sherman, beginning in 1902, but he also preached for congregations in Murfreesboro, Tennessee, and Bowling Green, Kentucky.

Bibliography

A. "Mason-Barret Debate," *Texas Missions*, June–September, 1907; "Preaching the Word," *GA*, 45 (September 10, 1903), 587; *The Shattered Chain* (Henderson, TN, 1942).

B. J. W. Shepherd, "Introduction, Allen Booker Barret," in *The Shattered Chain* (Henderson, TN, 1942), pp. iii–viii.

BARRETT, THOMAS R. (1842, TN–26 June 1916, Gainesville, TX). *Career*: Minister; farmer; doctor.

During the 1850s Thomas Barrett came to Texas, where he preached and established churches in Hopkins County (Mt. Vernon) and in various North Texas communities. Before the Civil War he moved farther west to the new town of Gainesville in Cooke County. He was perhaps best known for his role in a Civil War episode known as the Great Gainesville Hanging. Many in that region, some of whom belonged to Churches of Christ, had voted against secession. When it appeared that the South might be faced with defeat, some in this group wanted the Union army to move into that area to establish law and order. The hangings occurred when this plan became known. Some sixty men were finally hanged, many of whom belonged to the Christian Church or Church of Christ. Vigilantes forced Barrett into serving on the jury, but in that capacity Barrett was able to get a rule passed that required a two-thirds vote for conviction of any suspect. In this way the preacher justified his serving on the jury. Still, many of those who were hanged by the vigilantes were members of the Christian church at Gainesville, and many of these were relatives of the Joseph C. Matthews family. John M. Crisp said that the whole congregation was torn up; many members were killed and the rest scattered, forced to flee for their lives. Mansil W. Matthews, a prominent minister and physician, was thought to be a Union sympathizer and was almost hanged. Only the appeal of his close friend Captain Emmitt M. Daggett of Fort Worth saved him from the gallows. Barrett had to flee the area soon after the war to escape being killed. An intensive search was conducted in Central Texas, but he avoided detection and finally found his way back to Tennessee until the excitement died. He returned to Texas two years later and lived out his time as a farmer-preacher, dying as an old man. His account of the hanging was published.

Bibliography

A. *The Great Hanging at Gainesville, Cooke County, Texas* (Gainesville, 1885; reprint, Austin, 1961).

B. G. W. Diamond, *George Washington Diamond's Account of the Great Hanging at Gainesville, Texas* (1862; reprint, Austin, 1963); Richard B. McClasin, *The Great Hanging at Gainesville, Texas, 1862* (Baton Rouge, 1994).

BAXTER, BATSELL (7 November 1886, Sherman, TX–4 March 1956, Nashville, TN). *Education*: B. L., Nashville Bible School, 1911; B. A., Texas Christian University, 1917; M. A., Baylor University, 1918; doctoral work, University of Chicago. *Career*: Teacher, Cordell Christian College, 1911–13; teacher and dean, Thorp Spring Christian College, 1914–19; president, Abilene Christian

University, 1924–32; president, David Lipscomb University, 1932–34 and 1943–46; president, George Pepperdine College, 1937–39.

Batsell Baxter was closely associated with the Christian college movement among Churches of Christ, beginning with his tenure as a professor at Cordell Christian College, Cordell, Oklahoma, in 1911. Baxter also taught at Thorp Spring Christian College for five years, 1914–1919, serving as dean for three years. At the invitation of President Jesse P. Sewell, Baxter moved to Abilene Christian University in 1919 and became president in 1924. He immediately called for support for university training for ministers in the church. With limited success he sought to attract professors with doctoral degrees from recognized universities but who shared the conservative views of the mainstream of Churches of Christ on such issues as instrumental music and evolution. Baxter also served as staff writer for the *Gospel Advocate* from 1932 to 1956. Another Baxter legacy to the Churches of Christ was a son, Batsell, one of the most able ministers of the Churches of Christ in the twentieth century.

Bibliography

A. Ed., *Christian Education*, vols. 1–7, 1923–1929 (Abilene, TX); Abilene Christian University *Bible Lectures* (Austin, 1919), pp. 199–208; 1923–1924, pp. 9–20; 1933, pp. 45–56, 83–89; 1935, pp. 116–120.

B. G. A. Dunn, "Brother Baxter's 'University' Idea," *FF*, 42 (July 14, 1925), 3; Patricia Yomantas, "Batsell Baxter" in Jerry Rushford, ed., *Crest of a Golden Wave: Pepperdine University, 1937–1987* (Malibu: Pepperdine University Press, 1987), pp. 15–19.

BAXTER, BATSELL BARRETT (23 September 1916, Cordell, OK–31 March 1982, Nashville, TN). *Education*: B. A., Abilene Christian University, 1937; M. A., University of Southern California, 1938; Ph.D., University of Southern California, 1944; B. D., Vanderbilt University, 1957. *Career*: Professor of preaching and applied Christianity, George Pepperdine College, 1938–45; professor of speech and Bible, David Lipscomb University, 1945–82; head of the Bible Department, David Lipscomb University, 1956–82; minister, Whittier, CA, 1938–42; Burbank, CA, 1942–45; Nashville, TN: Belmont Church of Christ, 1945–46; Trinity Lane Church of Christ, 1946–51; and Hillsboro Church of Christ, 1951–80.

Batsell Barrett Baxter was one of the most influential preachers in Churches of Christ from the 1950s through the 1970s. He authored eighteen books, co-authored one, and coedited six, was a founding editor of *Up Reach* magazine in 1979, and served as staff writer for the *20th Century Christian* and the *Gospel Advocate*. Baxter also served as the featured speaker on "Herald of Truth," a national radio and television broadcast of Churches of Christ, from 1960 though 1981. Abilene Christian College honored Baxter as an Outstanding Alumnus in 1961 and presented him with an honorary doctorate in 1979.

Bibliography

A. *Heart of the Yale Lectures* (New York, 1947); *Speaking for the Master* (New York, 1954); *If I Be Lifted Up* (Nashville, 1956); *The Search for Happiness: Futility or Fulfillment* (Grand Rapids, 1977); *A Devotional Guide to the Bible Lands* (Grand Rapids, 1979); *Family of God: A Study of the New Testament Church* (Nashville, 1980); *Every Life a Plan of God: The Autobiography of Batsell Barrett Baxter* (Abilene, 1983).

B. Willard Collins, "Batsell Barrett Baxter," *GA*, 124 (April 15, 1982), 228; Ira North, "The Influence of Batsell Barrett Baxter," ibid., 229.

BELKNAP, ONA (16 May 1904, Oklahoma City, OK–25 February 1997, Nacogdoches, TX). *Education*: Unknown. *Career*: Teacher; writer; editor, *Christian Woman*, July 1967–72.

Ona Belknap was one of the most influential women among Churches of Christ in the mid-twentieth century, known best perhaps for her work in Christian journalism. For many years she wrote articles on religious and Biblical subjects for a variety of publications serving Churches of Christ, but she published them under a pseudonym—a man's name—because she thought that people would read articles by men more readily. Her poems and articles also appeared in *Christian Woman*, especially after July 1967, when she became the third editor of that magazine. By 1958 she was a frequent speaker to women's groups in a variety of Church of Christ settings and conducted religious seminars and training courses in creative writing in many states. Ona Belknap and Thelma Holt organized in Detroit, Michigan, in 1969 the first Black-White Christian Women's Seminar, which became a popular annual event. A member of the 12th and Drexel Street Church of Christ in Oklahoma City, Belknap and her husband led in establishing a permanent mission in a neglected area of Oklahoma City.

Bibliography

A. *CWom*, 1967–1972.

B. Yvette Stills, "Ona Belknap," *CWom*, 40 (January 1972), 25.

BELL, ROBERT CLARK (20 March 1877, Bell Buckle, TN–14 June 1964, Abilene, TX). *Education*: Nashville Bible School, 1907–08; B. A., Austin College, Sherman, TX, 1917; M. A., Southern Methodist University, 1918. *Career*: Teacher, Potter Bible College, Bowling Green, KY, 1901–05; Cordell Christian College, Cordell, OK, 1909–11; Abilene Christian College, Abilene, TX, 1919–23 and 1927–58; and Harding College, Searcy, AR, 1923–26; president, Thorp Spring Christian College, Thorp Spring, TX, 1911–16.

R. C. Bell was a popular preacher and teacher in several colleges related to Churches of Christ, including Potter Bible College, Cordell Christian College, Abilene Christian College, and Harding College. A student of David Lipscomb and James A. Harding at the Nashville Bible School, Bell came to a profound understanding of the Pauline doctrine of justification by grace through faith. Indeed, his understanding of Pauline theology was recognized as probably greater than any other among preachers and teachers in colleges supported by Churches of Christ.

Bibliography

A. *Studies in Romans* (Austin, 1957); *Studies in Galatians* (Austin, 1954).

B. "Very Personal," *FF*, 44 (October 4, 1927), 3; *Abilene Reporter-News*, March 27, 1961; June 15, 1964.

BENSON, GEORGE STUART (26 September 1898, Dewey Co., OK–15 December 1991, Searcy, AR). *Education*: Graduated in first class of Harper College, 1923; B. A., Harding College, 1925; B. S., Oklahoma A&M University, 1925; M. A., University of Chicago, 1931. *Career*: Missionary to China, 1925–36; founder and principal, Canton Bible School, 1933–36; president, Harding University, 1936–65; chancellor, Oklahoma Christian University of Science and Arts, 1956–67.

George Stuart Benson was known principally as a missionary to China for eleven years, 1925–1936, and as president of Harding College, Searcy, Arkansas, 1936–1965. Following his resignation from the presidency of Harding in 1965, he worked to develop several other Church of Christ–related institutions, including Oklahoma Christian College, Lubbock Christian College, Alabama Christian College (now Faulkner University), and George Pepperdine College. His influence on Church of Christ–sponsored education was, therefore, pervasive. Benson also exerted a significant influence on the political culture of Churches of Christ. While he was serving as a missionary in China, his experience with the Communist regime was extremely negative. After the Communists forced him out of China in 1936, he embraced a strident procapitalist, anti-Communist posture. That commitment enabled him to raise significant sums of money for Harding College. He established on the campus of Harding College the National Education Program, an organization that sought to discredit the Communist ideology. Benson also lectured to a variety of audiences, both within and without the Churches of Christ, on the evils of communism and the strengths of free enterprise capitalism.

Bibliography

A. *Missionary Experiences* (Edmond, OK, 1987).

B. L. Edward Hicks, *Sometimes in the Wrong, but Never in Doubt: George S. Benson and the Education of the New Religious Right* (Knoxville, 1994); John C. Stevens, *Before Any Were Willing: The Story of George S. Benson* (Searcy, AR, 1991); Donald P. Garner, "George S. Benson: Conservative, Anti-Communist, Pro-American Speaker," Ph.D. dissertation, Wayne State University, 1963; Ted Altman, "The Contributions of George S. Benson to Christian Education," Ed.D. dissertation, North Texas University, 1970.

BERNARD, ELIZABETH (10 October 1890, DeSoto, TX–12 December 1971, Hong Kong, China). *Education*: Nurses training, College of Industrial Arts, Denton, TX; New York University; Evergreen School for the Blind, Baltimore; physical therapy, U.S. Veterans Bureau. *Career*: Missionary.

Elizabeth Bernard began her lifelong work with Chinese orphans and blind children in 1933. The war with Japan forced a move first to Hong Kong in 1938, then to Macau, and from there she fled via a difficult and dangerous journey to Guilin, China. Finally, she was evacuated to India and to the United States in 1944. She returned to Gaungzhou, China, in 1947, repaired the damage to the Canton Bible School buildings, and resumed her care of orphan children, only to be uprooted again, this time by the Communist Revolution in 1949. By 1951 she was the only worker from Churches of Christ in Hong Kong. After suffering a stroke, she died on December 12, 1971, and is buried in Happy Valley on Hong Kong Island.

Bibliography

B. Clarence King, "Help Elizabeth Bernard," *FF*, 81 (October 6, 1964), 645; "Elizabeth Bernard's Legacy," *Hong Kong Kall* (June–August, 1991); Denton E. Scott, "Elizabeth Bernard," *FF*, 89 (January 4, 1972), 12.

BERRY, JOSEPH (1773–1834, LA). *Career*: Pioneer preacher.

Joseph Berry was apparently the leader of the Stoneite Christians who met at the Bethlehem meeting house in Wilson County, Tennessee, in 1810. Barton W. Stone knew him intimately for more than twenty years. Their first association was probably sometime between 1810 and 1814 during Stone's residence in Tennessee. The large family of Joseph's father, John Berry, of Lincoln County, Kentucky, became affiliated with the Stone movement early in the nineteenth century. James Berry, the oldest son, moved to Tennessee in 1800, and several of the Berry children followed, settling in Wilson and Maury Counties. Many in this family married into prominent families of the same faith. Joseph's daughter Hannah married Daniel Travis II about 1814. Joseph's sister Hannah married Scott Riggs (1779–1872), a preacher in Indiana by 1815. Joseph's younger brother, John P. Berry, was married the second time to Elvira Harris, a sister of Persius E. Harris, an early preacher in Tennessee and Indiana who was married to Barton W. Stone's daughter Tabitha. Joseph's daughter Mary Campbell Berry married Coonrod Kern, another early preacher, who died in 1861 at Blandinsville, Illinois. Joseph Berry died in Louisiana in September 1834 on a journey from Indiana to Texas. Upon Berry's death, Stone wrote that Berry "had been for many years a very zealous preacher in the church of Christ."

Bibliography

B. "Obituary," *CM*, 9 (January 1835), 23; *John Berry and His Children* (Georgetown, TX, 1988), pp. 51–98.

BILLINGSLEY, NANCY MULKEY (9 March 1780, TN–24 September 1850, near Pikeville, TN). *Career*: Teacher; exhorter.

John Mulkey and Philip Mulkey were famous preachers in southern Kentucky and East Tennessee, but according to Isaac N. Jones, neither father (Jonathan Mulkey) nor brothers (John and Philip) could equal Nancy's outpouring of scriptural exhortations. This youngest daughter in the talented Mulkey family was a shouter, but her style differed from the popular frontier style of shouting "Glory Hallelujah," screaming, jerking, jumping up and down, or clapping of hands till exhausted. Isaac N. Jones described Nancy's remarkable exhortations: "She would arise with zeal on her countenance and fire in her eyes, and with a pathos that showed the depth of her soul, and would pour forth an exhortation lasting from five to fifteen minutes, and which brought tears from every feeling eye." Joseph Thomas witnessed an exhorting by "a sister" in 1810 while visiting the Mulkey meeting house, near Tompkinsville, Kentucky. Although the woman's name was not given, she was probably Nancy. Thomas' record for Saturday [December] 15th and Sunday 16th reads as follows: "I held two days meeting at brother Mulkey's. . . . At night meeting commenced again; the Christians were much exercised, among whom was a sister moved, and surely by the power of the Holy Ghost, to speak to the people. I was no little astonished at her flow of speech and consistency of idea. . . . Many felt the weight of her exhortation. . . ." Nancy and her husband, Samuel Billingsley, became members of the Mill Creek Baptist church in 1805, the first church in southern Kentucky under the leadership of Nancy's brother, John Mulkey. The Billingsleys then joined with the majority of the Mill Creek members when John and the Mill Creek church united with the Christian church and Barton W. Stone in 1809. In 1818 the Billingsleys moved to Bledsoe County, Tennessee, where the family formed the nucleus of the Smyrna church, which flourished at the time of Nancy's death in 1850.

Bibliography

B. Isaac N. Jones, "The Reformation in Tennessee," in J. W. Grant, "Sketch of the Reformation in Tennessee" (c. 1897), typescript in Center for Restoration Studies, Abilene Christian University, 55; Joseph Thomas, *Travels and Gospel Labors* (Winchester, VA, 1812), p. 13; Philip Mulkey Hunt, ed., *The Mulkey Family of America* (Portland, 1983), p. 486; B. F. Manire, *Reminiscences of Eld. W. H. Stewart* (Jackson, MI, 1894), p. 14.

BILLINGSLEY, PRICE (1877, MS–1959, Nashville, TN). *Career*: Evangelist, editor, writer.

Price Billingsley began preaching in 1898 in Louisiana and became one of the most active preachers in Texas during the early decades of the twentieth century. He was probably the most successful evangelist among Churches of Christ in West Texas during the first quarter of the twentieth century. He utilized tent meetings to establish churches in many Texas communities where no

Churches of Christ existed. There is no evidence that Billingsley ever attended school, though he did spend some time with J. D. Tant, one of the strongest preachers in Texas, as his tutor. Even without formal education, Billingsley was an eloquent preacher and sometimes masterful as a writer. He published a paper, the *Gospel Advance*, while living and preaching in Tennessee. Most of his work was evangelistic, extending into many states and Canada.

Bibliography

A. Diaries and papers, housed in Center for Restoration Studies, Abilene Christian University; "Let Me Preach More Kindly," *FF*, 42 (July 28, 1925), 2; *Springs of Church Might* (Nashville, 1947).

BILLS, DANIEL GERSHAM (8 September 1790–October 1862, TN). *Career*: Physician, church leader.

Barton W. Stone visited Maury County, Tennessee, perhaps in 1810 and baptized four members of the Bills family. These baptisms led to the beginning of Wilson Hill Church of Christ on Globe Creek in Marshall County, although the precise beginning date of the congregation is unknown. Stone preached in Tennessee and possibly in Maury County, Tennessee, in 1810–1811. We do know that his itinerary included Tennessee in those years. Daniel Gersham Bills (1790–1862) and his wife, Rachel Summers Bills (1793–1883), were baptized by Stone at Wilson Hill in 1820. Daniel Bills became a significant leader of that congregation. Both Daniel and Rachel "read" medicine and ministered to the sick. Daniel was also remembered for his "effectual, fervent prayers."

Bibliography

B. W. W. Hinshaw, *Encyclopedia of American Quaker Genealogy* (Baltimore,1969), 981; "Bills Family," *Marshall County Historical Quarterly*, 4 (Summer 1973), 73–77; "Obituaries," *CM*, 9 (October 1835), 214; ibid., 8 (April 1834), 128; "Religious Conditions in Tennessee," *GA*, 51 (May 6, 1909), 552; A. G. Branham, "News from the Churches," *CRe*, 6 (March 1845), 70; B. F. Hart, "Obituaries—Bills," *GA*, 55 (October 16, 1913), 1004; and G. W. Bills, "In Memoriam," *GA*, 25 (May 9, 1883), 29.

BLEDSOE, JESSE (6 April 1776, VA–25 June 1836, Nacogdoches Co., TX). *Education*: Transylvania University. *Career*: Judge; professor of law, Transylvania, 1822–28; secretary of state, KY, 1808; U.S. Senator, 1813–15; minister, 1831–35.

When the *Kentucky Gazette* announced that Barton W. Stone would open a school in Lexington in January 1815, it listed the subjects taught—"the *Latin* and *Greek* languages, and *sciences*"—and attached a note of commendation: "From the information we have received of Mr. Stone as a moral man, and a teacher, he is excelled by none in the western country." Little wonder that men like Jesse Bledsoe—professor of law, secretary of state in Kentucky, and U.S.

senator—would be baptized by Stone and join his Christian reform movement. Jesse Bledsoe's family included some well-known Separate Baptist ministers of Virginia and Kentucky beginning with his grandfather, Joseph Bledsoe, Sr., a leading Separate Baptist in Virginia who organized the Wilderness church and brought that church to Kentucky in 1783, and his brother Moses Bledsoe. Jesse married a daughter of Nathaniel and Sarah (Howard) Gist a family associated with the Mulkey church near Tompkinsville, Kentucky. Several newspapers carried notices of Bledsoe's death including two in Lexington. The *Observer and Reporter* quoted the following from the *Mississippian*: "Judge Jesse Bledsoe is dead . . . a Senator in Congress from Ky, the rival of Henry Clay, and the most brilliant man of his time in the councils of his nation. He died at Nacogdoches, Texas, on the 25th of June last, and received every attention in his last moments which the citizens of that place could render him." The *Lexington Morning Herald* noted that Bledsoe delighted in reading the classics, held a position as professor of law at Transylvania University, and served as secretary of state in Kentucky. The article described Bledsoe as "a man of force and ability and one of the foremost forensic debaters of his time. It was said by Mr. Clay that he had found Judge Bledsoe the strongest advocate he had ever opposed." The Bledsoe family contributed significantly to the growth of Churches of Christ in Kentucky, Tennessee, Missouri, and California.

Bibliography

A. "Oration," *Kentucky Gazette*, July 9, 1811; for his letters written in Texas, see John J. Jenkins, ed., *The Papers of the Texas Revolution, 1835–1836*, 3 vols. (Austin, 1973).

B. May P. Webb and Patrick M. Estes, comp., *Cary-Estes Genealogy* (Rutland, 1939), p. 58; "Sketch of Jesse Bledsoe," *Lexington Morning Herald* (February 10, 1901), 10, col. 2; Banks McLaurin, *The Bledsoe Family in America* (Dallas, 1993).

BLUE, JOE HUBERT (18 September 1875–September 1954, AR). *Career*: Farmer, minister.

Joe Blue heads the list of Church of Christ preachers in Arkansas during the first half of the twentieth century. He was known outside of Arkansas as well, having preached in twenty-five states. He preached for fifty-eight years, sometimes in the face of threats, and sometimes while guarded by lawmen. During his ministry he conducted 107 debates, held 800 gospel meetings, and baptized 10,000 people. He loved religious books and never ceased to enjoy his library, one of the best religious collections in Arkansas. Blue preached his first sermon in 1896, working that year as a traveling preacher with the Bible and a copy of T. W. Brents' *Gospel Plan of Salvation* in his saddle bags. Typically, Blue worked on his farm and preached in the rural areas—"in the sticks"—mostly in homes and school houses. Few men could speak as forcefully as Blue, and many embraced his exclusivistic message. While Joe Blue lived and preached in Salem, Arkansas, for example, churches of Baptist, Methodist, Holiness, and

Presbyterian persuasions all ceased to exist and Salem was left with only one church—the Church of Christ. Joe Blue also helped establish Arkansas Christian College and Southern Christian Home in Morrilton, Arkansas.

Bibliography

B. Boyd E. Morgan, *Arkansas Angels* (Paragould, AR, 1967), p.p. 79–92.

BOLES, HENRY LEO (22 February 1874, Gainesboro, TN–7 February 1946, Nashville, TN). *Education*: Burritt College, 1898–1903; Nashville Bible School, 1906; M.A., Vanderbilt University, 1920. *Career*: Teacher, Nashville Bible School, 1906; president, David Lipscomb University, 1913–20 and 1923–32, after which he became a member of the board of trustees.

Henry Leo Boles was an influential preacher, educator, editor, and writer among Churches of Christ during the first third of the nineteenth century. He served as president of David Lipscomb College from 1913 to 1920 and again from 1923 to 1932. During the intervening years (1920–1923), he edited the highly influential *Gospel Advocate*, published in Nashville, Tennessee, a publication for which he wrote regularly for forty years. After being baptized by W. T. Kidwell, Boles preached his first sermon June 7, 1903. In 1904 and 1905 he conducted eighteen gospel meetings with 323 additions. During his forty-plus years of preaching and teaching, Boles trained about 1,500 young men who became preachers. He also published commentaries on Matthew, Luke, and Acts, held two debates—the Boles-Boll written debate on millennialism and the Clubb-Boles debate on instrumental music—and published a major book on the Holy Spirit.

Bibliography

A. *Commentary on Acts* (Nashville, 1941); *The Holy Spirit: His Personality, Nature, Works* (Nashville, 1942); H. Leo Boles and R. H. Boll, *Unfulfilled Prophecy: A Discussion on Prophetic Themes* (Nashville, 1928; reprint, 1954).

B. *GA*, 88 (March 28, 1946), memorial issue; Leo Lipscomb Boles and J. E. Choate, *I'll Stand on the Rock: A Biography of H. Leo Boles* (Nashville, 1965).

BOLL, ROBERT HENRY (7 June 1875, Badenweiler, Germany–13 April 1956, Louisville, KY). *Education*: Nashville Bible School, 1896–1900. *Career*: Writer, editor, minister.

Robert Henry Boll was unusual among Churches of Christ leaders when he embraced the dispensational premillennial sentiments of the American fundamentalist movement in the early years of the twentieth century. Boll's views sparked a major controversy over premillennial theology, a controversy that persisted for a third of a century and finally divided Churches of Christ into mainline congregations and premillennial congregations, the latter being centered mainly in Louisville, Kentucky, and New Orleans, Louisiana. Boll was born of Catholic parents in the Black Forest of southern Germany. When his father died, his mother married a man whom the son disliked, so young Robert at age fourteen seized an opportunity to come to the United States. Boll enrolled in the Nashville Bible School in 1895 and began preaching while a student of James A. Harding in 1896. Boll's fascination with millennial theories likely predated his arrival in the United States, however. His mother encouraged him to study for the priesthood and sent him to school at Freiburg, Germany, where young Boll may have first heard of John Albert Bengel (1687–1752), an early pietistic theologian. Bengel wrote two important eschatological works: *Exposition of the Apocalypse* and *Ordo Temporum*. This latter work explored a "holy history" principle by which the author felt that he could predict with certainty the date of the second coming of Christ. Significantly, John Nelson Darby transformed one line of Bengel's views into dispensational premillennialism, a notion later popularized by Cyrus I. Scofield, whose notes on the biblical text were first printed in Dallas, Texas, in 1904 and later in the annotated *Scofield Reference Bible*. Boll lived at Kentuckytown (Grayson County), Texas, in 1903 when the Scofield notes were published in Dallas. When Boll presented his dispensational views on the front page of the *Gospel Advocate*, the editors temporarily removed him from his position as "front page editor." A final break came in 1915 when Boll refused to refrain from teaching what he believed the Bible taught. He soon moved to Louisville, Kentucky, where he took over the editorship of *Word and Work* and made that paper the primary editorial vehicle serving premillennial Churches of Christ. He also served as minister of Louisville's Portland Avenue Church of Christ for more than fifty-two years. In 1927 he debated H. Leo Boles on the subject of the millennium. The debate was published serially in the *Gospel Advocate* and later appeared in book form under the title, *Unfulfilled Prophecy: A Discussion on Prophetic Themes*.

Bibliography

A. *WW*, 1916–1956; *The Book of Revelation* (Louisville, 1923); *The Kingdom of God* (Louisville, 1924); *Lessons on Hebrews* (Nashville, 1910); *The Church I Found and How I Found It* (Louisville, n.d.), p. 6; *Truth and Grace* (Cincinnati, 1917); *The Second Coming of our Lord Jesus Christ* (Louisville, 1924); H. Leo Boles and R. H. Boll, *Unfulfilled Prophecy: A Discussion on Prophetic Themes* (Nashville, 1928; reprint, 1954); *Lessons on Ephesians* (Louisville, n.d.); *Lessons on Romans, and Grace and Obedience* (Louisville, n.d.); "The Freedom of Simple Christians" (pamphlet; n.p., n.d.); "Why Not Just Be a Christian?" (pamphlet; n.p., n.d.).

B. E. L. Jorgenson, "A Biographical Sketch" in R. H. Boll, *Truth and Grace* (Cincinnati, 1917), pp. 6–12; Thomas G. Bradshaw, *R. H. Boll: Controversy and Accomplishment among Churches of Christ* (Louisville, 1998); Hans Rollmann, "Our Steadfastness and Perseverance Depends on Perpetual Expectation of Our Lord: The Development of Robert Henry Boll's Premillennialism (1895–1915)," *Disc*, 59 (Winter 1999), 113–126; Hans Rollmann, "From the Black Forest to the Nashville Bible School: The Conversion of Robert Henry Boll," unpublished paper; Michael Casey, "Neither Militant nor Pacifist: R. H. Boll on War and Peace," unpublished paper; and Eva Estelle Moody (ed.), *Catalog of the Boll Memorial Library: With a Short Biographical Sketch and an Account of Brother Boll's Death as Written by His Wife* (Louisville, n.d.).

BOWMAN, JOHN (d. January 1829, Murfreesboro, TN). *Career*: Minister.

John Bowman was Barton W. Stone's fellow preacher with whom Stone had "enjoyed an acquaintance of 35 years" beginning in North Carolina soon after Bowman was educated and ordained to the Presbyterian ministry. The two Presbyterian ministers were to experience similar careers, although John Bowman's is practically unknown, whereas that of Stone, the famous revivalist and reformer, is indelibly inscribed on the history of the Great Revival and the history of the Stone-Campbell restoration tradition. After their initial acquaintance Bowman followed Stone to the West. Stone recalled that "he moved his family to Tennessee, and united himself with the Church of Christ, to which he was truly a father and guide." Bowman was ordained by the Greenville Presbytery in North Carolina and received by the Transylvania Presbytery in Kentucky in 1802. In March 1809 the Transylvania Presbytery met at Glasgow, Kentucky, and cited Bowman for "propagating and encouraging Heresy and Schism . . . against our Confession of Faith and discipline and Presbytery" and called for him to answer charges at the next session. Bowman refused to attend the October session, where he was cited again and suspended along with Samuel McAdou, who helped found the Cumberland Presbyterian Church on February 4, 1810. The Presbytery cited Bowman again on April 5, 1810. Bowman joined the Stone movement about the time the Cumberland Presbyterian Church was organized in 1810. Abner Hill, a Tennessee preacher involved in the Mulkey-Stone merger, said that a good number of "distinguished preachers stood connected with us [the Mulkey movement]," and he named especially Barton W. Stone and John Bowman. Dr. W. D. Jourdan's 1825 list of Tennessee preachers begins with Daniel Travis, followed by John Mulkey, Philip Mulkey, and John Bowman. His ministry among the Christians spanned almost twenty years (1810–1829), and during that time he probably became the principal preacher of the Stone movement in Rutherford County, one of several Middle Tennessee counties where Stone's movement enjoyed notable success.

Bibliography

B. Transylvania Presbytery, Presbyterian Church in the U.S.A., Minutes, 1786–1951 (April 13, 1802; March 22, 1809; October 4, 1809), housed at University of Kentucky Library; James Smith, *History of the Christian Church Including a History of the Cumberland Presbyterian Church* (1835); William Warren Sweet, *Religion on the American Frontier: The Presbyterians* (New York, 1936), pp. 221–227; Abner Hill, "Autobiography of Abner Hill," typescript of manuscript in Center for Restoration Studies, Abilene Christian University, 16; William D. Jourdan, "Reminiscence," *CP*, 10 (April 28, 1870); "Obituary," *CM*, 3 (February 1829), 96.

BOWSER, GEORGE PHILLIP (17 February 1874, Maury Co., TN–23 March 1950, Detroit, MI). *Education*: Walden University, Nashville, 1895. *Career*: Minister, educator, editor.

George Phillip Bowser was probably the most influential black preacher in Churches of Christ at the beginning of the twentieth century. An ex-slave named Sam Davis won Bowser to the restoration movement after Bowser had been educated for the Methodist ministry. Known as "the father of Christian education" among black members of Churches of Christ, Bowser began a school in Nashville, Tennessee, in 1907, using the Jackson Street church building as a schoolhouse. Two years later he moved his school to Silver Point, Tennessee, and renamed it the Silver Point Christian Institute. Several prominent young men including R. N. Hogan were products of the Silver Point school. The school closed in 1920 because of financial problems, and Bowser became principal of the Southern Practical Institute in Nashville before moving to Louisville, Kentucky. In 1938 Bowser moved to Fort Smith, Arkansas, where his home became a training place for older men to become ministers. In 1902 Bowser founded the *Christian Echo*, a publication that for the entire twentieth century was the most important publication among Churches of Christ conducted by and for black ministers and churches. Bowser possessed an exceptional level of biblical knowledge and was often called "the walking Bible" and "a preaching wonder." He and the preachers he trained were not reluctant to speak out against racial discrimination.

Bibliography

B. R. Vernon Boyd, *Undying Dedication: The Story of G. P. Bowser* (Nashville, 1985); Annie Tuggle, *Another World Wonder* (Detroit, n.d.); Robert E. Hooper, *A Distinct People* (West Monroe, LA, 1993), pp. 255–278.

BOYD, SAMUEL (23 May 1763, VA–27 November 1835, Jacksonburg, IN). *Career*: Exhorter, minister.

Samuel Boyd was a significant frontier preacher in the restoration movement led by Barton W. Stone. Samuel Boyd was the son of James Boyd, also a Virginian. The family moved to South Carolina prior to the Revolution, and the father and three of his sons, including Samuel, fought for the Colonies. The father and one son died in a Tory prison. Twice the Tories burned their home, and during a skirmish Samuel was shot through the temple, losing his right eye and was left for dead. An old black woman found him and hid the wounded lad in brush, returning to care for him until he was able to get away. Boyd moved to Jackson County, Tennessee, before finally settling in Adair County, Kentucky. That region was known as "the Barrens" because of the absence of trees and water, but it was covered with extensive grasslands that attracted buffalo herds that watered at the famous Dripping Springs. Little and Big Barren rivers originate in this area, which had by 1799 attracted Moses Dooley, another early acquaintance of Barton Stone, and his sons. When they first arrived in the region, the Dooleys and the Boyds were Presbyterians. However, the great Kentucky revival soon reached this part of the state, and Samuel Boyd's house became a center for meetings and preaching, connecting with the early beginnings of the Christian movement. Barton W. Stone, William Kincade, Moses and Reuben Dooley, and David Purviance all held meetings there frequently. Boyd became an exhorter and was soon ordained to preach. The original ordination document is the oldest such document of the movement still extant today.

> We the underwritten do certify that according to a previous appointment on the east fork of little Barren on Monday after the third Sabbath of July 1809 Samuel Boyd was publicly set apart by ordination for the work of the Gospel ministry according to the manner of the Christian Church then present at that place.
>
> Benjamin Lyn
> Lewis Byram

The original document is in the Philips Memorial Library of the Disciples of Christ Historical Society, Nashville, Tennessee. Barton W. Stone visited "the Barrens" in 1805 according to a letter to Richard McNemar: "In a few weeks I start to fulfill a long daily string of appointments to Cumberland—by request I go—I have appointed two communions among many Christ-ians, on the heads of Little and Big Barrens." These "Christ-ians" were formerly Presbyterians, including the Dooley and Boyd families. In 1811 Samuel Boyd moved his family and a large herd of livestock to the frontier in eastern Indiana, where Jacksonburg (Wayne County) was later built. In this area Samuel continued an active ministry that included frequent preaching to the Native Americans. During a visit to preach among them, Boyd was again almost killed. A native American boy thoughtlessly ignited a powder keg, which exploded and demolished a rude hut, killing two children. Boyd was believed to be dead, but he recovered and continued to minister for more than twenty years. Elijah Martindale, his son-in-law, was also an effective minister in Indiana.

Bibliography

A. Belle Stanford, ed., *Autobiography and Sermons of Elder Elijah Martindale* (Indianapolis, 1892), pp. 126–139; Richard McNemar, *The Kentucky Revival* (reprint, New York, 1846), p. 85; Andrew W. Young, *History of Wayne County Indiana* (reprint, Knightstown, IN, 1967), pp. 238–239.

BRENTS, THOMAS WESLEY (10 February 1823–29 June 1905, Lewisburg, TN). *Education*: Macon Medical College, Macon, GA. *Career*: Teacher; physician; writer; chair, anatomy and surgery, Macon Medical College, Macon, GA; president, Burritt College, 1878–1882.

Thomas Wesley Brents was best known for his voluminous 1874 publication *The Gospel Plan of Salvation*, which both reflected and defined orthodoxy among Churches of Christ for many years to come. Soon after the Civil War Brents asked David Lipscomb to establish a department in the *Gospel Advocate* to explore the differences between sectarianism and Christianity, that is, between the popular denominations and the Churches of Christ. Brents proposed that this department focus especially on "the plan of salvation" or how to get into the kingdom of God. Selections from Brents' column, the "Alien's Department," were published as an anthology with the title *The Gospel Plan of Salvation*. Brents was especially concerned to contrast Calvinism with what he regarded as biblical teaching. In addition, Brents conducted numerous debates, especially with a Methodist champion named Jacob Ditzler, whom he debated seven times. Because of his writings and debates, many preachers in Churches of Christ looked to Brents for arguments to use against Calvinist opposition. Some preachers were said to carry the Bible in one saddle bag and Brents' *Gospel Plan of Salvation* in the other.

Bibliography

A. *The Gospel Plan of Salvation* (Cincinnati, 1874); *Gospel Sermons* (Nashville, 1891).

B. Letter to Fanning and Lipscomb, *GA*, 8 (December 25, 1866), 822–824; J. S. Sweeney, Letter from Tennessee, *AT*, 6 (January 1, 1874), 1; J. W. Grant, "Sketch of the Reformation in Tennessee" (c. 1897), typescript in Center for Restoration Studies, Abilene Christian University, p. 43; G. W. Bills, "T. W. Brents," *GA*, 47 (September 28, 1905), 618; John B. Cowden, *Dr. T. W. Brents* (Nashville, 1961).

BREWER, GROVER CLEVELAND (1884, Lawrenceburg, TN–9 June 1956, Searcy, AR). *Education*: School of the Evangelists, Kimberlin Heights, TN; B.L., Nashville Bible School, 1911. *Career*: Minister; writer; debater; editor, *Voice of Freedom*, 1953–56.

Grover Cleveland Brewer distinguished himself among Churches of Christ in the first half of the twentieth century in several ways: (1) as a proponent of the nonsectarian understanding of the restoration ideal, (2) as a proponent of the biblical doctrine of grace, (3) as an advocate for church cooperation on behalf of mission work and Christian colleges, (4) as an opponent of communism and Catholicism, and (5) as a powerful pulpit preacher. Brewer's ministry began in West Tennessee followed by summer meetings in eastern Tennessee and Kentucky in 1907–1909. He eventually served some of the largest congregations among Churches of Christ. He preached in Tennessee at Chattanooga and Memphis and in Texas at the Houston Street congregation in Sherman, the Central congregation in Cleburne, and the Broadway congregation in Lubbock. An able advocate of the early restoration tradition of nonsectarian Christianity, Brewer was recognized for his clear articulation of simple, apostolic, and catholic Christianity. He argued that men and women may become Christians and not join any sect. He criticized the careless use of terms like "we" or "our movement" to include less than all Christians. He argued that even though Churches of Christ sought to be nondenominational, they nonetheless had to live in a denominational world. Still, he argued, Churches of Christ should resist embracing a denominational identity. Brewer led Churches of Christ to embrace several changes that some, at least, regarded as progressive innovations. For example, he led churches to use the budget system of finance and individual cups in the communion. His critics attacked him for advocating church support of Christian colleges and orphan homes and for suggesting that individual congregations could pool their financial resources to support foreign mission work. His support for R. H. Boll in the midst of the premillennial controversy led some to accuse him of premillennial sympathies. A prolific writer, Brewer served on the staff of the *Gospel Advocate* for many years and was founder and first editor of the *Voice of Freedom*, a periodical devoted to attacking communism and Catholicism. He also authored more than a dozen books. Brewer lectured frequently on evolution, communism, and a variety of other civic and religious topics.

Bibliography

A. *As Touching Those Who Were Once Enlightened* (Nashville, 1946); *Forty Years on the Firing Line* (Kansas City, 1948); *A Story of Toil and Tears of Love and Laughter; Being the Autobiography of G. C. Brewer, 1884–1956* (Murfreesboro, 1957); *Foundation Facts and Primary Principles* (Kansas City, 1949); periodical: *Voice of Freedom* (Nashville, 1953–56).

B. Ron Halbrook, "G. C. Brewer: Perennial Protagonist," in the Florida College *Annual Lectures* (Temple Terrace, 1981).

BURNETT, THOMAS R. (1842, TN–26 June 1916, Dallas, TX). *Education*: Plum Grove Academy. *Career*: Writer; minister; debater; editor, *Christian Messenger*, Bonham, TX (dates unknown) and Dallas, TX (1888–94); editor, "Texas Department" of the *Gospel Advocate*, 1894–98; editor, *Burnett's Budget*, vols. 1–16, 1901–16, Dallas, TX.

Thomas R. Burnett was the most significant editor among Churches of Christ in Texas from 1875 to 1916. Converting to the Church of Christ in 1875, Burnett began the *Christian Messenger* in Bonham that same year. He traveled extensively in North and Central Texas in the interest of his paper, preaching, selling books, and occasionally debating. From September 1876 to September 1888, Burnett kept a journal of his numerous trips. Among his fourteen published works were several volumes of religious poetry and a religious dialog called *Hezekiah Jones*. A master at repartee and sharp retort, Burnett acquired a reputation as a racy editor, often combining controversy and good humor. He and Austin McGary, editor of the *Firm Foundation* of Austin, Texas, engaged in sharp controversy on the rebaptism issue. His reputation for controversy was widespread. One writer noted that Burnett "fights innovations like killing snakes"—the quickest way possible. Typical were his attacks on the missionary society and "the organ" and the advocates of both. Burnett's "Second Epistle of

Burnett" is a classic piece against the organ. When an organ advocate chided Texas conservatives as "old landmark saints" who will refuse to rise until Gabriel gives chapter and verse for his horn, Burnett retorted that Gabriel will have no trouble finding the verse. "Now let the digressive pastor find one for the organ or horn in worship of the church."

Bibliography

A. *Doctrinal Poetry* (Dallas, n.d.); *Center Shots* (Austin, 1912?); "Travel and Preaching—Journal of Preaching," 1876–1888, in Thomas R. Burnett Papers, 1875–1916, Eugene C. Barker Texas History Center, Austin, TX; periodicals: *Christian Messenger*, Bonham, TX (dates unknown) and Dallas, TX (1888–1894); *Burnett's Budget* (Dallas, 1901–1916).

B. *Dallas Morning News*, June 27, 1916; *GA*, 58 (August 3, 1916), 744; *GA*, 58 (August 7, 1916), 822; Keith L. King, "Disciples of Christ and the Agrarian Protest in Texas, 1870–1906," *RQ*, 35 (2d Qr, 1993), 81–91; Keith L. King, "Religious Dimensions of the Agrarian Protest in Texas, 1870–1908," Ph.D. dissertation, University of Illinois, Champaign-Urbana, 1985.

BUSBY, HORACE WOOTEN (21 February 1884, Lawrence Co., TN–10 December 1965, Ft. Worth, TX). *Education*: North Texas State University, Denton, TX. *Career*: Minister; evangelist; editor, *The Way of Truth*.

Horace Wooten Busby distinguished himself as a revivalist among Churches of Christ, holding more gospel meetings than any other preacher of this tradition during his lifetime. Averaging twenty-four meetings each year for a total of more than one thousand, he baptized approximately 18,000 people. At his insistence his meetings always featured two services each day, morning and evening. One indication of his popularity is the fact that he held twenty-six meetings at the University congregation in Abilene, Texas, twenty-nine in Ozona, Texas, and more than sixty in the Fort Worth area where he lived. He began full-time evangelistic work in 1910 with immediate success. His first meeting resulted in seventeen baptisms and four restorations. He served as a local preacher only once, in Fort Worth, Texas, from 1913 to 1920, then resumed full-time evangelism. Busby was a Christian salesman with a good understanding of persuasion. His positive approach and warm appeal made every sermon a revival. As a revivalist he was unexcelled, except by noted black evangelist Marshall Keeble. Busby was nationally known, having preached in almost every state. A stroke in 1952 shortened Horace Busby's long and outstanding ministry, one of the most fulfilling in the twentieth century.

Bibliography

A. *Practical Sermons of Persuasive Power* (Brownwood, TX, 1929).

B. Harriet Helm Nichol, *Preachers of Texas and Oklahoma* (Clifton, TX, 1911); Larry Nelson Calvin, "A Rhetorical Analysis of Selected Sermons of Horace Wooten Busby," M.A. thesis, Abilene Christian University, 1973.

BYRAM, LEWIS (NC–1834, near Paoli, IN). *Career*: Pioneer minister.

Lewis Byram's early life is obscure, especially before 1805, when he and Barton W. Stone established a church (now at Gamaliel, Kentucky) that is probably the second oldest Church of Christ in America. Stone and Byram were friends for more than forty years beginning about 1794, when Stone attended a Presbyterian academy at Greensboro, North Carolina. Originally Presbyterian, Byram was evidently associated with Union Church, a Presbyterian congregation on the East Fork of Big Barren River in Barren County, Kentucky. Hearing of developments at Cane Ridge, he invited Stone to come to his neighborhood and preach. Stone's visit in the summer of 1805 changed the religious history of southern Kentucky and the "Upper Cumberland" area of Middle Tennessee. The journey was "to fulfill a long daily string of appointments to Cumberland" beginning a "few weeks" after April 5, 1805. "A long daily string of appointments" suggests an extended preaching tour. Stone was still in the Cumberland in October and preached at the Union Presbyterian Church on the Big Barren River. It was then that this church, with Lewis Byram in the lead and ten others as charter members, became a part of the Stone movement. In later years this congregation was known as "Old Christian Union." Before leaving Barren (now Monroe) County, Kentucky, in 1812, Byram caused a revolution in the Upper Cumberland, especially in the Stockton Valley Baptist Association. His controversy with the Baptists included a "conference" with John Mulkey, the leading Baptist minister in southern Kentucky, that resulted in Mulkey's "reform." Mulkey's conversion culminated in the merger of a great number of Baptists and at least nine Baptist preachers with the Stone movement between 1809 and 1812. Although documented by relatively obscure sources, Stone's influence on Byram, and in turn on the Mulkeys, is very apparent. This development helps account for the Mulkey defection from the Separate Baptists and the strengthening of Stone's influence in the Cumberland and adjacent regions in the Upper South. Joseph Thomas visited Byram in 1810 and preached at "Old Christian Union," which had grown to 125 members. There were three ministers, including David Stewart, also a charter member. Thomas was impressed with Byram's study of the Scriptures and with his piety. Byram believed that Christians would not sin, a belief that may explain Stone's reference to Byram "as near perfect in character" as any man he ever knew. Byram continued an active ministry in southern Indiana, principally in Crawford County, from 1813 until his death in 1834.

Bibliography

B. B. W. Stone, "Obituary," *CM*, 8 (September 1835), 287; Transylvania Presbytery, Presbyterian Church in the U.S.A., Minutes, 1786–1951, housed at University of Kentucky Library; Joseph Thomas, *Travels and Gospel Labors of Joseph Thomas* (Winchester, VA, 1812).

C

CALHOUN, HALL LAURIE (11 December 1863, Conyersville, TN–4 September 1935, Nashville, TN). *Education*: B.A., College of the Bible, 1892; B.D., Yale, 1902; Ph.D., Harvard, 1904. *Career*: Teaching positions at Georgia Robertson Christian College, Henderson, TN, 1900–01; College of the Bible, 1904–17; Bethany College, 1917–25; Freed-Hardeman College, 1925–26; and David Lipscomb College, 1934–35; dean, College of the Bible, 1911–17; minister, Franklin and Nashville, TN, and Paducah, KY.

Hall Laurie Calhoun was one of the few university-trained scholars among Churches of Christ in the early twentieth century, having earned his B.D. at Yale and his Ph.D. at Harvard, where he studied under the distinguished Old Testament scholar, George Foote Moore. Following his graduation from Harvard, Calhoun accepted a position in the College of the Bible, a restoration movement–related institution in Lexington, Kentucky. There he taught under the presidency of J. W. McGarvey, the most distinguished biblical scholar of the Stone-Campbell movement at that time. Calhoun served the College of the Bible as dean but resigned that position in 1917 in the midst of a "heresy trial" involving the teachings of four professors and the president who had hired them. Calhoun believed that the defendants in this trial were guilty of teaching destructive criticism. In this way he alienated a majority of the students who disliked the dean's conservatism. Calhoun then moved to Bethany College—the institution Alexander Campbell had established in 1840—where he taught in that institution's new Graduate School of Religion. He returned in 1925 to a one-year associate presidency of Freed-Hardeman College. Following that assignment, Calhoun moved to Nashville, where he taught at David Lipscomb College and served as the minister for the Central Church of Christ.

Bibliography

A. Abilene Christian University, *Bible Lectures, 1927–1928* (Abilene, 1928); *Gospel Sermons* (Austin, 1927).

B. John D. Wright, *Transylvania: Tutor to the West* (Lexington, 1975), pp. 336–343; Adrian Doran and J. E. Choate, *The Christian Scholar: A Biography of Hall Laurie Calhoun* (Nashville, 1985).

CAMPBELL, ALEXANDER (12 September 1788, County Down, North Ireland–4 March 1866, Bethany, WV). *Education*: Glasgow University. *Career*: Minister; writer; debater; educator; editor, *Christian Baptist*, 1823–30; editor, *Millennial Harbinger*, 1830–66; president, Bethany College, 1840–66.

Churches of Christ have typically looked upon Alexander Campbell, and especially to the early Campbell, as the most influential restoration figure of the early nineteenth century. Dr. Nathaniel Field considered Campbell in the *Christian Baptist* era (1823–1830) the greatest religious light since the Apostle Paul. Jacob Creath, Jr., thought Campbell made his greatest contributions during his *Christian Baptist* years and the first twenty years of the *Millennial Harbinger* (1830–1850). The Campbell movement from the beginning was highly rationalistic and sometimes tended in mechanical directions. For example, Campbell argued that "in, and by, the act of immersion, so soon as our bodies are put under water, at that very instant" the old sins of true believers are all washed away. The movement has never outlived "the gospel in water" motif. By contrast, Barton W. Stone's first article in 1827 concluded, "So baptism saves us, and washes away our sins; not the water, but the grace and power of God through this act of obedience." Campbell also developed a reputation as a man of war during the *Christian Baptist* era. This reputation derived in part from the combative nature of the *Christian Baptist*, but also from the debates Campbell held with his theological opponents.

Before 1820 Campbell never dreamed that more than one congregation might be formed on the primitive model. For this reason Campbell turned to farming, but he did labor each Sunday to separate biblical truths from what he regarded as human traditions. Still, the Campbell movement created little notice outside of the Baptist associations. Buffalo Seminary, which he opened in 1818, did not succeed as expected, and no event seemed to create any momentum until he reluctantly debated the Presbyterian John Walker in 1820. The positive effects of that debate caused Campbell to hope that his movement might have a greater effect than he originally anticipated. A year later Campbell hit upon the idea of a religious publication, and in 1823 he launched his first journal, the *Christian Baptist*, which he published and mailed from his home in Bethany, Virginia. Needless to say, the iconoclastic *Christian Baptist* aroused considerable opposition. Campbell wrote to Philip S. Fall, the first Kentucky reformer, "I have got so many scoldings from Georgia to Maine for my severity that I must reform—whether I repent or not I must reform." Baptist editors in Kentucky coined the reproachful epithet "Campbellites." One Kentucky Baptist burned a copy of Campbell's translation of the New Testament, the "Living Oracles," after praying for ten days! In the meantime a second debate with Presbyterian W. L. McCalla in Washington, Kentucky, in October 1823 created a revolution in Kentucky. Campbell concluded that "a week's debating is worth a year's preaching." But a gradual change in his program was apparent by 1830. Campbell wrote, "We must change our course." Still later he wrote, "The Editor will himself endeavor to reform." By the early 1830s Campbell was moving in a more tolerant and ecumenical direction. In 1837, for example, he charged with error anyone who "infers that none are Christians but the immersed." And the man who had rejected missionary societies during the *Christian Baptist* period became president of the American Christian Missionary Society in 1849.

Campbell grounded his hermeneutic primarily in the Pauline Epistles within the historical framework of Acts. His authority was "Paul and common sense" with the book of Hebrews providing the key. He believed "that in a skillful hand the key is an infallible one." Although Campbell devised a formula of using Bible language for settling theological differences, many individuals whose allegiance was principally to Barton W. Stone felt that Campbell departed from this principle. By the 1840s Leonard J. Fleming, John Rogers, and D. Pat Henderson had joined Stone in calling upon Campbell to cease using philosophy, speculative language, and inferences instead of biblical facts as the basis of faith. The discussion between Stone and Campbell on atonement in 1841 is replete with calls from Stone for Campbell to state his "orthodox" position in biblical terms. In spite of these differences, the Stone and Campbell forces formally united at Lexington, Kentucky, in 1832.

Bibliography

A. *The Christian System* (Bethany, VA, 1839), a revision of *Christianity Restored* (Bethany, VA, 1835); *Popular Lectures and Addresses* (St. Louis, 1863); Lester G. McAllister, *An Alexander Campbell Reader* (St. Louis, 1988); letters of Campbell in the Philip S. Fall Papers, Frankfort, KY; periodicals: *CB*, 1823–1830; *MH*, 1830–1866.

B. Robert Richardson, *Memoirs of Alexander Campbell*, 2 vols. (Philadelphia, 1868–1870; reprint, Nashville, 1956); Selina Campbell, *Home Life and Reminiscenses of Alexander Campbell by His Wife* (St. Louis, 1882); Benjamin Smith, *Alexander Campbell* (St. Louis, 1930); Eva Jean Wrather, *Creative Freedom in Action: Alexander Campbell on the Structure of the Church* (St. Louis, 1968); Richard T. Hughes, "From Primitive Church to Civil Religion: The Millennial Odyssey of Alexander Campbell," *JAAR*, 44 (March 1976), 87–103; *RQ*, 30 (2d & 3d Qr, 1988), a special issue on Campbell including a list and overview of thirty-nine dissertations on Campbell from 1897 to 1986 and additional bibliography of recently published Campbell papers.

CAMPBELL, ALEXANDER CLEVELAND (1860s–July 1930, St. Louis, MO). *Career*: Minister.

Alexander Cleveland Campbell was a notable black evangelist in Tennessee and throughout the South during the first third of the twentieth century. Campbell withdrew from the Disciples of Christ in 1900 and with a few others began meeting in his home. The meetings grew larger, and when S. W. Womack, another black preacher, withdrew from the Gay Street Church in Nashville, he and Campbell purchased the Jackson Street property in Nashville in 1903. The resulting Jackson Street congregation became the most influential black congregation in the early twentieth century. In fact, Campbell and Womack were to black churches what Barton Stone and Alexander Campbell were to the larger restoration movement. David Lipscomb encouraged Campbell and Womack to write accounts of their work for the *Gospel Advocate*, and Lipscomb published many of those accounts before journalism began among the blacks. Marshall Keeble, the most noted black preacher, attributed the appreciation that many had for Campbell to his "boldness and knowledge of the Scriptures." Campbell traveled as an evangelist for twenty years and baptized hundreds until his health failed.

Bibliography

A. "Work among the Colored People," *GA*, 51 (December 2, 1909), 1523; "Jackson Street Mission," *GA*, 56 (April 9, 1914), 414.

B. M. Keeble, "Obituaries—Campbell," *GA*, 72 (August 28, 1930), 839.

CAMPBELL, SELINA HUNTINGTON BAKEWELL (12 November 1802, Litchfield, England–28 June 1897, Bethany, WV). *Education*: English school. *Career*: Mother, author. Married Alexander Campbell 31 July 1828).

The namesake of the famous eighteenth-century Methodist philanthropist and activist Lady Selina, Countess of Huntington, Selina Bakewell Campbell made important contributions to the Stone-Campbell movement. She married one of its most significant leaders, Alexander Campbell, and lent support for both an active role for women in the life of the church and the importance of missions among Christians. In 1821, at the age of nineteen, Selina Bakewell was baptized by her future husband, Alexander Campbell. After joining the Wellsburg, West Virginia, church, Selina formed such a close relationship with Campbell and his family—and especially with his wife, Margaret Brown Campbell—that as Margaret lay dying of tuberculosis, she secured her husband's promise that he would consider the young Miss Bakewell for the role of stepmother to their five daughters. On July 31, 1828, a twenty-six-year-old Selina married her former mentor, Alexander Campbell. Alexander was already two decades into his preaching and publishing career at that time. Marriage to such a prominent man brought a number of challenges for the new Mrs. Campbell. During her husband's frequent absences, Selina managed a several-hundred-acre farm, cared for four of her stepdaughters, and hosted dozens of houseguests. She also gave birth to six children of her own. The list of tasks necessary to run such a household and raise her family was staggering, but these were roles Selina apparently embraced as her contribution to her husband's life and ministry. Often, however, her most important role was mother to her husband's five daughters and her own six children. Both Alexander and Selina valued motherhood highly. In common with many others of their day, they considered it a holy vocation and an important part of forming the character of children. Selina also acted as hostess for the Campbell Mansion. As her husband's fame as a preacher, teacher, and writer grew, so did the number of people journeying to his home to visit him. The Campbell dining room table sat thirty and it was often full. Selina took pride in her ability to care for the bodies of her guests while her husband fed their minds. After her husband's death in 1866, Selina's activities shifted to a more public nature. In particular, she found time to write more than a hundred articles that appeared in various religious publications. As a more than competent author and thinker, Selina Campbell often commented on issues like dancing, the value of simple worship, and the importance of Christian biographies. In 1856 she prompted a new movement among Disciple women when she published the first female call for support for missions. The article, which appeared in her husband's journal, the *Millennial Harbinger*, represented the first public notice by a woman attempting to raise funds in support of foreign missions among the Disciples of Christ. Later Selina served as the president of the Christian Woman's Board of Missions' second chapter, the West Virginia chapter, despite her husband's lukewarm support for parachurch missionary societies during the time of their marriage.

In 1881 Selina completed one of her most beloved writing projects, a book entitled *Home Life and Reminiscences of Alexander Campbell*, which remains a valuable source for understanding the domestic life of the Campbell family and sheds light on Alexander Campbell's public life as a preacher and teacher. Selina spent the last years of her life mainly with her children and grandchildren. She rarely attended public gatherings. After her death from influenza on June 28, 1897, her funeral attracted hundreds of mourners to Bethany Mansion, a testament to the affection they held for this gentle sister in Christ.

Bibliography

A. *Home Life and Reminiscences of Alexander Campbell by His Wife* (St. Louis, 1882); *Chr*, 18 (July 21, 1881), 2; "Memphis, Tenn.," *CS*, 9 (June 27, 1874), 202; "Correspondence," *ACR*, 27 (July 17, 1884), 227; "Sister Mary R. Williams, Missionary in Jaffa," *MH*, 4th ser., 6 (April 1856), 236–237.

CAMPBELL, THOMAS (1 February 1763, Sheepbridge, North Ireland–4 January 1854, Bethany, WV). *Education*: M.A., University of Glasgow, 1786; Archibald Bruce's Seminary, Whitburn, Scotland. *Career*: Religious reformer; minister; teacher, academy near Covington, KY, 1817, Cambridge, OH, 1819, Buffalo Seminary, academy in Pittsburgh, PA.

Thomas Campbell, father of Alexander Campbell, emigrated from Ireland to southwestern Pennsylvania in 1807; two years later he drafted the *Declaration and Address*, which articulated the principles that would guide the religious movement that his son, Alexander, was destined to lead. As a young schoolmaster Campbell attended Glasgow University from 1783 to 1786. For theological training in the Antiburgher Seceder Presbyterian Church, Thomas attended five annual sessions taught by Archibald Bruce at Whitburn, Scotland, and taught during the other months to support his family. Campbell was ordained about 1797 (records are lacking) and served as minister of the Ahorey Presbyterian church near Rich Hill, Northern Ireland, until 1807, when he immigrated to western Pennsylvania. His family followed in 1809. A leader in the Antiburgher Synod of Ireland, Campbell worked to unite the Burgher and Antiburgher churches of Scotland and Ireland. With thirteen other ministers of four denominations, he helped to organize the economically oriented Evangelical Society of Ulster. Although the Synod disliked the society and reduced Campbell's role to that of a "simple subscriber," he continued his efforts to heal the division. In 1804 at a meeting of the Synod of Scotland in Glasgow, he was said to have "out-argued" the Synod but was outvoted. Nonetheless, the union for which he worked in Ireland finally materialized in 1818. No doubt Campbell's experiences in Ireland prepared him for developments in America, where his ecumenical efforts continued.

In America Campbell settled in Washington County, Pennsylvania, and was active in the Chartiers Presbytery of western Pennsylvania until censured for unorthodox practices and teaching. When the Associate Synod of Philadelphia sustained the Presbytery, Campbell renounced the authority of both courts and withdrew. Campbell seemed even more determined to unite the religious groups. He and several Irish friends formed the Christian Association of Washington by which they hoped to reform existing parties from within. At a special meeting of the Association, Campbell announced a rule by which he hoped the group would act: "Where the Scriptures speak, we speak; where the Scriptures are silent, we are silent." Campbell adapted another formula as well, a widely quoted maxim by German theologian Rupertus Meldenius: "In matters of faith, unity; in matters of opinion, liberty; in all things charity." This theme essentially became an outline followed in the *Declaration and Address*. Campbell presented the *Declaration and Address* to the Synod in May 1809, only to have it rejected. At that point the Christian Association of Washington adopted this document as its formal constitution on August 17, 1809. The heart of Campbell's message consists of thirteen propositions, statements of "original ground" that would, in the author's view, enable those who sought unity to "take up things just as the apostles left them," "to prepare the way for a permanent scriptural unity among Christians," and to "stand with evidence upon the same ground on which the church stood at the beginning." Thus, Thomas Campbell came to be called what he was for nearly fifty years: "the advocate of Christian union."

Campbell felt that the Association with its adopted principles must resolve into a church. The first church of the Campbell reform, Brush Run Church, was formed in 1812 and soon ordained Alexander Campbell as a preacher. The older

Campbell wrote for the *Christian Baptist*, signing his articles "T. W.," and contributed to the *Millennial Harbinger* occasionally as substitute editor and as a frequent writer on subjects such as slavery, the Holy Spirit, Christian union, atonement, education, and the Christian name. "Father" Campbell had a profound influence upon his son, Alexander, who said that he was indebted the most to his father. Campbell conducted or taught in several academies in Ohio, Kentucky, Pennsylvania, and West Virginia and preached in Virginia and North Carolina. In Pittsburgh, Pennsylvania, where he established an academy and a church, he met Walter Scott and taught Robert Richardson, two men who became leaders in the movement.

Bibliography

A. *Declaration and Address* (Washington, PA, 1809).

B. *DAB*, 3, 463; Hiram J. Lester, "An Irish Precursor for Thomas Campbell's Declaration and Address," *En* (Summer 1989), pp. 247–267; Hiram J. Lester, "The Disciple Birthday—a Disciple Passover," *Disc*, 44 (Winter 1984), 51–54; Hiram J. Lester, "The Form and Function of Thomas Campbell's *Declaration and Address*," unpublished paper; Hiram J. Lester, "Alexander Campbell's Early Baptism in Ecumenicity and Sectarianism," *RQ*, 30 (2d & 3d Qrs, 1988), 85–101; F. R. Scott, "History of Ahorey Congregation," typescript, 1973; David M. Thompson, "The Irish Background to Thomas Campbell's *Declaration and Address," Disc*, 46 (Summer 1986), 23–27; Jacob Creath, Jr., "The Wisdom of This World . . . ," *ACR*, 2d ser., 27 (September 4, 1884), 281; William H. Hanna, *Thomas Campbell: Seceder and Christian Union Advocate* (Cincinnati, 1935); Lester G. McAllister, *Thomas Campbell: Man of the Book* (St. Louis, 1954); Thomas H. Olbricht and Hans Rollmann, eds., *The Quest for Christian Unity, Peace, and Purity in Thomas Campbell's Declaration and Address* (Lanham, MD, 2000).

CARNES, WILLIAM DAVIS (23 October 1805, SC–20 November 1879, Spencer, TN). *Education*: B. A., University of Tennessee, 1841; M.A., University of Tennessee, 1843. *Career*: Minister; preparatory school director; professor of English and English literature, University of Tennessee; president, LaFayette Academy, 1847; president, University of Tennessee, 1857–59; president, Franklin College, 1859–61; president, Manchester College, 1865–72; president, Burritt College, 1850–57 and 1874–78; president, Water and Walling College, McMinnville, TN.

William Davis Carnes was a prominent educator in the South who had strong connections to the movement led by Barton W. Stone and who provided educational leadership for Churches of Christ between 1850 and 1878. While teaching at Woodbury, Tennessee, Carnes was baptized by Abner Hill and in 1824 began traveling and preaching with Hill and W. D. Jourdan, thus "educating himself by work." While preaching for the Church of Christ at Smyrna, Tennessee, he married Elizabeth Billingsley, a niece of the noted preachers John and Philip Mulkey. After teaching eight years at the University of Tennessee, Carnes became the first president of Burritt College, Spencer, Tennessee, for eight years (1850–1857); there he developed a curriculum modeled after the curriculum at the University of Tennessee. That curriculum consisted of courses in mathematics, physics, Latin, Greek, metaphysics and *belle lettres*. Carnes returned to Knoxville in 1857 after being unanimously elected president of the University of Tennessee, but he served only two years because of sickness and death in the family. In 1859 Carnes accepted the presidency of Tolbert Fanning's Franklin College in Nashville, which he hoped to develop into a first-class university. The Civil War destroyed that venture and ended Carnes' presidency in 1861. From 1874 to 1878, Carnes again served as president of Burritt College. Although this school began as a nondenominational institution, Carnes' leadership meant that the college was dominated by members of the Churches of Christ. Numerous preachers and leaders of Churches of Christ were educated there.

Bibliography

B. W. Y. Kuykendall, "Elder W. D. Carnes," *GA*, 22 (March 4, 1880), 149; Joseph M. Carnes, *Memoir of William D. Carnes* (Beaumont, TX, 1926); Ivy Carnes, "Biographical Sketch of President W. D. Carnes" in James E. Scobey, *Franklin College and Its Influences* (Nashville, 1954), pp. 203–213.

CASSIUS, AMOS LINCOLN (18 December 1889, Sigourney, Iowa–20 August 1982). *Education*: Tuskegee Institute, 1906–10, where he studied under both Booker T. Washington and George Washington Carver. *Career*: Hotel chef, 1910–19; restaurant owner, Los Angeles, 1919–?; general contractor, Los Angeles and elsewhere, 1922–?; minister, Compton Avenue Church of Christ, Los Angeles, 1922–57; minister, 137th and Avalon Church of Christ, Los Angeles, 1957–?; evangelist, 1919–70.

Along with his wife, Beulah Middleton Cassius, and a few others, Amos Lincoln Cassius helped establish the first African American Church of Christ in southern California—the Compton Street Church of Christ in Los Angeles, established in 1922. Cassius was born in Sigourney, Iowa, in 1889. His father was S. R. Cassius, who also spent a lifetime as a preacher for African American Churches of Christ. As a child S. R. Cassius visited the White House, where he shook hands with President Lincoln, for whom the son, Amos Lincoln Cassius, was named. A. L. Cassius grew up near Luther, Oklahoma, but he left home in 1906 to attend Tuskegee Institute, where for four years he studied under Booker T. Washington and George Washington Carver. A shortage of funds forced him to return to Oklahoma in 1910, only one semester shy of completing all requirements for his diploma. For the next several years he worked as a chef in large hotels in Dallas, Houston, and Chicago and then married Beulah Middleton in 1914. In 1919 the Cassiuses moved to Los Angeles, where Cassius immediately paid cash for the "Elite Café" in downtown Los Angeles, which he developed into the largest black-owned restaurant in the city. The Compton Street Church of Christ, which he and several others established in 1922, first met in the home of James Arnold, an ex-slave from Arkansas. Working also as a general contractor, Cassius personally built three church buildings for this congregation, the last one being constructed in 1950. In 1957 the Compton Street Church of Christ spawned another congregation, the 137th and Avalon congregation, for which Cassius also preached. As a contractor Cassius constructed church buildings for Churches of Christ in Statesville, South Carolina; Del Rey Beach, Florida; Clearview, Okmulgee, Wewoka, and Tulsa, Oklahoma; Barstow and Riverside, California; Hobbs, New Mexico; and Nassau and Long Island in the Bahamas. As an evangelist Cassius established congregations of the Church of Christ in Bakersfield and Riverside, California; Hobbs, New Mexico; El Paso, Texas; Phoenix, Chandler, and Tucson, Arizona; and Denver, Colorado. Cassius also served as a missionary to the Bahama Islands for five years.

Bibliography

B. Frank Pack, "Amos Lincoln Cassius: Pioneer Black Leader," *Disc*, 43 (Summer 1983), 25, 29–30; Jerry Rushford, "The Dean of West Coast Preachers," *FF* (August 25, 1981), 4.

CASSIUS, S. R. (d. 1920s, Minneapolis, MN). *Career*: Minister, educator, editor.

S. R. Cassius was a leading black minister in the southwestern United States, principally in Oklahoma and Texas, before moving to Chicago in 1917. He moved to Oklahoma Territory in 1891 and worked for twenty-five years, establishing the first black congregation of Churches of Christ there in 1892 and the Tohee Industrial School in 1900. In that early period he thought Oklahoma a "mecca for black disciples." "A black man feels like he is in heaven in Oklahoma," he wrote, "and a white man feels the other way. For this reason my people keep coming and the white people keep going." At the same time Cassius was preoccupied with racism both in the church and in the larger society, and he called for black Christians to separate themselves from the larger body of Churches of Christ. Perhaps as an expression of protest against racism in the Churches of Christ, Cassius organized a missionary board, something that white Churches of Christ had rejected in the nineteenth century. Toward the end of his career, however, he abandoned such organizations and returned to the congregationalism of Churches of Christ.

Bibliography

A. *The Third Birth of a Nation* (Cincinnati, n.d.); "The Race Problem," *CL* (March 12, 1901), 4; "The Race Problem: Afro-American Comments on Disfranchisement," *CL* (September 8, 1901), 9; "Among the Colored Disciples," *CL* (September 17, 1901), 13.

B. Earl Irvin West, *The Search for the Ancient Order*, 3 (Indianapolis, 1979), pp. 9–10, 183–185, 188–189.

CHISM, JEHU WILLBORN (1 April 1865, Comanche Co., TX–1935, Ardmore, OK). *Education*: Home schooled. *Career*: Minister, debater.

Jehu Chism was a popular and forceful preacher and debater in Texas during the first third of the twentieth century. Chism grew up on the Texas frontier in Comanche County, where he was baptized by Edwin Stirman in 1883 and began preaching in 1891. He never had formal schooling, though he did recall his mother teaching school in her home, where he learned to spell every word in the *Blue Back Speller* but did not know the alphabet. In later life he acquired a knowledge of Greek and Hebrew, which served him well especially during debates. He first encountered Greek when he saw a Greek grammar in the home of preacher Joe S. Warlick. He hid under a bed, where he spent the entire afternoon studying the grammar. Later he hired a Jewish Hebrew scholar to teach him the Hebrew language. The following incident illustrates his flamboyant style, some of the reasons for his popularity, and something of the rustic character of Churches of Christ during that period. When Chism attended a sectarian camp meeting in North Texas, a revivalist offered a long prayer that petitioned God to send down his spirit to rest upon sinners. Chism looked all around for evidence of a miraculous manifestation. Another petition asked for God to shake the earth. Chism reached down and felt the earth for movement. When nothing physical happened in response to the prayer, Chism—like Elijah—called out for the man to "Cry louder! Maybe your God is asleep." He was arrested for disturbing worship and jailed. The next year Chism returned to the same community and announced that he would hold a protracted meeting. People flocked to hear "the man who was put in prison like Paul," and more than forty of them were baptized.

Bibliography

A. *Campbellism: What Is It*? (Nashville, 1901); J. W. Ring and Chism, *The Great Debate* (Headrick, OK, 1908).

B. "J. W. Chism" in *The Great Debate* (Headrick, OK, 1908), pp. 279–285.

CLARK, JOSEPH ADDISON (6 November 1815, Shawneetown, IL–11 January 1901, Thorp Spring, TX). *Career*: Lawyer; journalist; educator; minister; founder, Add-Ran College, 1873.

Joseph Addison Clark was a significant educator in Churches of Christ, having established Add-Ran College in Thorp Spring, Texas, in 1879. In his early life Joseph became a skeptic and changed his name from the "biblical" name given him to Joseph Addison, the name of the British poet whose writings he admired. In 1839 Joseph came to Texas with his sisters and mother, who died soon after the family landed at Matagordo Bay. The family settled first in Austin, where Joseph worked as a printer, then in East Texas, where he found employment as a surveyor and where he met and married Esther D'Spain (1824–1894) in 1842. Through Esther's influence and after reading Alexander Campbell's debate with

Robert Owen on *The Evidences of Christianity*, Clark became a Christian and spent the rest of his career as a Christian educator, preacher, and journalist. Clark conducted schools in Titus County, Texas, in 1843; at Midway, Texas, in 1855–1856; and in Fort Worth from 1869 through 1873. Then, in 1873, Clark and his sons, Addison and Randolph, purchased Thorp College in Thorp Spring, Texas, and named the school Add-Ran in memory of Clark's first grandson, Addison Randolph Clark. Add-Ran College opened in the fall of 1873. After moving to Thorp Spring, Clark edited the *Texas Christian* and the *Add-Ran Student*. In 1879 Clark relinquished control of the school to his two sons, Addison and Randolph. Clark was a prodigious writer and published many articles in the *Gospel Advocate* and some in the *American Christian Review* and the *Firm Foundation*. He was very critical of liberal trends developing in many congregations of the Stone-Campbell movement in Texas at that time.

Bibliography

A. J. A. Clark, "Observations," *FF*, 13 (October 12, 1897), 2.

B. Randolph Clark, *Sketch of the Life of Elder J. A. Clark* (n.p., n.d.); Randolph Clark, *Reminiscences—Biographical and Historical* (Wichita Falls, TX, 1919), pp. 12–15; Joseph Lynn Clark, *Thank God, We Made It!* (Austin, 1969).

CLARK, NIMROD LAFAYETTE (26 February 1870, Brook Haven, Lincoln Co., MS–14 July 1956, Fort Worth, TX). *Education*: Mississippi College; University of Mississippi; M.A. in Greek language, University of Texas. *Career*: Minister; educator; writer; president, Lockney College, 1902–03; founding president, Gunter Bible College, 1903.

Nimrod Lafayette Clark has been called "the father of the nonclass movement in Texas," a small segment of Churches of Christ that rejected the innovation of Sunday schools in the early years of the twentieth century. At the same time Clark held a moderate view on this issue when he is compared with some of his opponents who issued the publication, the *Apostolic Way* (1913–1931). Clark moved to Parker County, Texas, and taught school in 1892–1893. He converted to the Churches of Christ in 1895 and soon began preaching. He served as president of the Texas Panhandle school Lockney College in 1902–1903, but he left Lockney College to become the founding president of Gunter Bible College, Gunter, Texas, in 1903. Clark led this school to embrace a more restrictive view than was common among most Churches of Christ regarding women serving as Bible teachers and the use of Bible classes in churches. From 1906 to 1911, Clark was one of four editors of the *Firm Foundation*. This was a period when the *Firm Foundation* was "filled with discussion, debate and division" over the Sunday school question. In 1906 he conducted a debate with R. L. Whiteside in the pages of the *Firm Foundation* that marks the beginning of a gradual division on the Sunday school issue in Churches of Christ.

Bibliography

A. Periodicals: *FF*, 1906–1911; *AW*, 1913–1931.

B. Ronney F. Wade, *The Sun Will Shine Again Someday* (Springfield, MO, 1986), pp. 33–41.

CLARKE, JENNIE EVERTON (20 July 1862, Luce Township, IN–15 January 1929, Luling, TX). *Education*: Xenia College, Xenia, IL. *Career*: Founder and director, Belle Haven Orphan Home, Luling, TX, 1899–1929.

Jennie Clarke founded the Belle Haven Orphan Home in Luling, Texas, in 1899, the first orphans' home sponsored by members of the Churches of Christ in Texas or the West. The U.S. census for 1900 shows that Clarke was directing that home and caring for five children that year. She continued to direct that institution until she died in 1929. Following her death, the *Luling Signal* recognized her as a pioneer citizen who gave thirty years of her life to orphan children. For many years Clarke reported quarterly in periodicals serving Churches of Christ, listing contributions to the home sent from individuals and churches. Clarke accepted into the home only true orphans and refused to take the responsibility belonging to a living single parent. In 1920 Clarke incorporated Belle Haven to assure its continuance for another fifty years. Nonetheless, because of her declining health, interest in the home declined during the 1920s, it closed in 1930 following her death. Likely Belle Haven Orphan Home inspired the creation of two other orphans' homes that were owned and operated by members of Churches of Christ and that endured: Tipton Home in Tipton, Oklahoma, and Boles Home in Quinlan, Texas.

Bibliography

B. Austin McGary, *FF*, 17 (1900), 446; *A Twentieth Century History of Southwest Texas*, vol. 2 (Chicago, 1907), pp. 391–394.

COGDILL, ROY EDWARD (24 April 1907, Hobart, OK–13 May 1985, Houston, TX). *Education*: Western Oklahoma Christian College, 1922–23; attended Abilene Christian University. *Career*: Minister, writer, publisher.

In the 1940s and 1950s when Churches of Christ were suffering division over the issues of congregational cooperation and support of orphan homes, Roy Edward Cogdill was a key figure, perhaps the key personality in the anti-institutional movement. A powerful preacher, Cogdill served several large congregations as a local minister during his career, including churches at Cleburne, Dallas, and Houston, Texas, and at Springfield, Missouri. A special issue of the *Guardian of Truth*, dedicated to him after his death, extolled him as a "keeper of orthodoxy" and a "keeper of the faith."

In 1938 Cogdill published the first of many printings of *The New Testament Church*, which became a popular study book for adult Bible classes among

Churches of Christ. Cogdill suggested in this book that in the New Testament period, "local Churches co-operated in doing their work but such work was always under the supervision of a local Church and its Eldership." That same year while preaching in Billings, Montana, Cogdill issued a plea for support: "I am earnestly asking for liberal cooperation from other brethren" to be sent through the church in Pampa, Texas, to support a radio program. The same cooperative arrangement was used in 1937 when Cogdill's work was sponsored by a Dallas church. Cogdill's argument at that time reflected the practice Churches of Christ had embraced for many years as a scriptural alternative to missionary organizations. However, once the anti-institutional battles erupted, Cogdill apparently realized that his arguments in the *New Testament Church* were at odds with the arguments he was making in the heat of the anti-institutional struggle. Accordingly, after 1952 subsequent editions of *The New Testament Church* deleted statements reflecting Cogdill's earlier position. He now claimed that the fundamental issue was the field or locale of the congregation or congregations and the size of the operation, that is, the number of churches that would work in a cooperative arrangement. Through the Roy E. Cogdill Publishing Company and later the Cogdill Foundation, he championed the cause against "institutionalism," that is, multiple congregations funneling funds through a sponsoring church on behalf of colleges, orphans' homes, and homes for the aged. In 1949 Cogdill launched a new publication dedicated to his anti-institutional agenda, the *Gospel Guardian*, later renamed the *Guardian of Truth*.

Bibliography

A. No title, *FF*, 55 (September 6, 1938), 4–5; *The New Testament Church* (Dallas, 1938); *Walking by Faith* (Lufkin, TX, 1957); *Woods-Cogdill Debate* (Lufkin, TX, 1958); "Centralized Control a Reality," *GG*, 4 (March 19, 1952), 1–3.

B. *Guardian of Truth*, 19 (July 18, 1985), memorial issue.

COX, JAMES FRANKLIN (2 April 1878, McLeansboro, IL–30 September 1968, Abilene, TX). *Education*: B.A., University of Texas, 1904; M.A., University of Texas, 1911; further graduate work, George Peabody College. *Career*: President, Lingleville Christian College; president, John Tarleton University, 1913–17; president, Abilene Christian College, 1911–12, 1932–40; chair, Department of Education, Abilene Christian College, 1919–23; dean, Abilene Christian College, 1924–32; professor, Abilene Christian College, 1940–51.

James Franklin Cox provided significant leadership for higher education related to Churches of Christ, especially at Abilene Christian College, throughout the first half of the twentieth century. A member of the first faculty (1906–1907) of Childers Classical Institute, forerunner of the present-day Abilene Christian University, Cox taught science and mathematics. Then, for a single year, 1911–1912, he served as president of Abilene Christian College, but took that institution's presidential reins again during the difficult depression years, serving from 1932 to 1940. Between 1913 and 1917 Cox served John Tarleton University as president before returning to Abilene Christian College in 1919 as head of the Department of Education, a position he held until 1923. Between 1924 and 1932, he served as dean of the college under President Batsell Baxter. In 1940 Cox returned to the classroom and taught until his retirement in May of 1951. Cox was one of the first educators among Churches of Christ to earn the doctorate and contributed significantly to the progress of Christian education among Churches of Christ in Texas and the South.

Bibliography

A. *A Brief Manual for a Course in Teaching God's Word* (Abilene, TX, 1933).

B. Margaret Moss, "Biography of James F. Cox," unpublished ms, Abilene Christian University Library; Batsell Baxter, "Brother Cox, Dean of A.C.C.," *FF*, 41 (June 3, 1924), 2.

CREATH, JACOB, JR. (17 January 1799, Mecklenburg Co., VA–8 January 1886, Palmyra, MO). *Education*: University of North Carolina. *Career*: Minister in KY to 1835, in MO, 1835–86.

Jacob Creath, Jr., whose life spanned the first fifty years of the combined Stone and Campbell movements, was often called the "Iron Duke" of the restoration movement. A severe critic of the missionary society and other "innovations," Creath sought to keep faith with the original visions articulated by Barton W. Stone, on the one hand, and Alexander Campbell during the years of the *Christian Baptist*, on the other. He called Stone the great missionary of the movement. A few months after the society began, he claimed that elders Francis R. Palmer, Joel P. Haden, and others, if they had no conscientious scruples about that convention, would not go into it from the regard they had for "the name, the memory, and virtues of that venerated man, Barton W. Stone." In April and May 1828 when Creath visited Bethany, Virginia, Campbell proposed to him a covenant "offensive and defensive upon the New Testament and the Reformation," which Campbell was then developing. Creath accepted, believing that Campbell's program involved his opposition to "organs, big suppers, and conventions and all the other human inventions." When Campbell later changed his emphasis from that of the *Christian Baptist*, Creath wrote, "All the angels in heaven and the men upon earth cannot find these human inventions in the Bible, nor in the Christian Baptist." Creath was also capable of blending his theology with southern sectionalism. After Campbell's death Creath dropped his subscription to the *Harbinger*. Editor William Pendleton asked him for reasons. Creath gave one: the course pursued against the South. Creath said that he would not support a paper against the southern people even if his own father were editor. Creath took special note of the fact that the *Harbinger* lingered a few years after Campbell's death, then died of the consumption.

Others viewed Creath in the same way he viewed himself, that is, as a defender of the old paths first lined out by Campbell and Stone. George E. Taylor of Franklin County, Missouri, wrote to Creath a few months after the missionary society began. "Bro. Stone is out of the way," Taylor noted, "and I fear that many things will be attempted now that was not thought off [*sic*] during his day. It is to you then Bro. Creath that we must look as a sentinel to guard from the evils which now threaten us, and which are likely to create divisions amongst us."

Creath was unrelenting against the things that he viewed as contrary to scripture. As a Baptist minister he was hung in effigy in a Mississippi camp meeting in 1827. Creath often wrote of his trial and exclusion by Baptist associations in Kentucky. He strongly criticized the Calvinistic rendering of the King James Version of the Bible, and none worked harder than he to raise support for the American Bible Union translation. He raised possibly $100,000 for this project.

Bibliography

A. Letter, *GA*, 13 (January 5, 1871), 30; "The Bible Alone Rejected by the Conventionists," *GA*, 19 (November 22, 1877), 724; "Old and New Things Contrasted," *GA*, 19 (December 6, 1877), 756.

B. Philip Donan, *Memoir of Jacob Creath, Jr.* (Cincinnati, 1872); T. P. Haley, *Historical and Biographical Sketches* (Kansas City, 1888), pp. 427–455.

CREATH, JACOB, SR. (7 February 1777, Cumberland, Nova Scotia–13 March 1857, Lexington, KY). "Sr." is used to distinguish the uncle from his nephew of the same name. *Career*: Minister.

Although Jacob Creath, Sr., was blind by 1850, thereby limiting his activity, and although he died before the movement's controversial period unfolded, his early contributions to the success of the Stone-Campbell movement made him a well-beloved figure. The two Jacob Creaths, uncle and nephew, distinguished by the Sr. and Jr. attached to their names, are favorably remembered by Churches of Christ for their defense of "the ancient order" against their perpetual nemesis, the Baptists. Jacob Creath, Jr., is especially known for his staunch style and fighting spirit. Possibly the older Creath was not as combative, but his name has been revered nonetheless.

Jacob Creath, Sr., and William Creath, father of Jacob Creath, Jr., were ordained Baptist ministers at Roundabout Meeting House in Louisa County, Virginia, in 1798, along with Robert B. Semple and Andrew Broadus. Jacob immigrated to Fayette County, Kentucky, in 1803, succeeding John Gano as pastor of Town Fork Baptist Church. A man of fine personal appearance with keen and penetrating dark eyes, he had a strong musical voice, and "though quite uneducated, [he] possessed such command of language and fertility of fancy and illustration" that Henry Clay called him "the finest natural orator he had ever heard."

Jacob Creath, Sr., was converted to the Stone movement by a young preacher, a friend and protégé of Barton W. Stone, John Allen Gano. When Gano joined the Christians in Georgetown, Kentucky, two of his older sisters were deeply distressed. They looked upon Gano's action as heretical. Accordingly, they dispatched a messenger seventy miles to Jacob Creath, Sr., a colaborer of John Gano, John Allen Gano's grandfather. The message sent to Creath asked that the older preacher come and win back their brother to the faith of their fathers. Creath gladly rode the seventy miles to comply and felt certain that his mission would be successful. When meeting with Gano, Creath said to him, "Brother John, I am glad you have determined to devote your life to the service of Christ, but I think you had better have taken your stand with the church of your fathers." He then reminded him of his Baptist heritage. Gano replied as he laid his hand upon his New Testament, "If you will show me in this Book where it says, 'Deny yourself, take up your cross and follow your grandfather,' I will follow mine while I live; but I read it, 'Deny yourself, take up your cross and follow Christ,' and I intend to follow this teaching if it separates me from all the kindred on earth." After twelve hours of discussion that day and more the next morning, Creath finally stood up, took Gano by the hand, and said, "Brother John, you are right, and I will take my stand with you and will preach the Scriptures as the only rule of faith and practice, and the name of Christ the only name to be worn by his followers, and this is to be the only ground of Christian union."

The senior Creath's contribution as a Baptist Minister to the religious development of Kentucky can be measured in part by the claim that he and fellow minister Jeremiah Vardeman could have elected any man they wanted as governor of Kentucky. Creath's defection to the Stone movement through John Allen Gano suggests that he favored Stone's emphases more than Campbell's. Both Gano and Creath, Sr., were, in fact, strong supporters of Stone and sometimes hesitant to adopt some of Campbell's new views in the 1840s.

Bibliography

B. John T. Brown, *Churches of Christ* (Louisville, 1904), pp. 422; James R. Rogers, *The Cane Ridge Meetinghouse* (Cincinnati, 1910), p. 107; A. Campbell, n.t., *MH*, 3d ser., 7 (July 1850), 403–404; *DAB*, vol. 4, 531–532; William K. Pendleton, "Quarter-Centennial Address," *CS*, 9 (October 31, 1874), 345ff; *ACR*, 2d ser., 5 (September 23, 1862), 1.

CRIHFIELD, ARTHUR (1802–2 December 1852, Harrison, OH). *Career*: Minister; editor, *Heretic Detector*, 1837–41; editor, *Christian Family Library*, 1842; editor, *Orthodox Preacher*, 1843–46.

Arthur Crihfield is significant in the history of Churches of Christ, since he did so much to transform the original ecumenical vision of the Stone-Campbell movement into an exclusivistic, sectarian agenda. Crihfield preached very successfully in Kentucky and Ohio and edited three periodicals. He called the first publication the *Heretic Detector*. This journal employed the same critical style that characterized Alexander Campbell's first serial, the *Christian Baptist*, but had a harsher tone. Campbell and Crihfield disagreed on some points, and by the late 1830s Campbell expressed his dislike for the *Heretic Detector's* approach. Crihfield obviously had considerable ability, but his "heady and opinionative" attitude hindered his influence. After almost thirty years in the movement during which he entertained views on church government contrary to congregationalism, Crihfield finally published a stinging attack upon the loose congregational order practiced in the restoration churches. He proposed, instead a biblical basis for episcopalianism or apostolic succession in church polity. This eighty-page publication, *An Address to the Disciples' Church*, was issued by the Protestant Episcopal Diocese of Kentucky. Later in his life Crihfield sought and was granted restored fellowship with his home Church of Christ in Harrison, Ohio. His friend and fellow minister in Churches of Christ, Benjamin Franklin, spoke at his funeral.

Bibliography

A. *Address to the Disciples' Church* (Covington, KY, 1849); periodicals: *HD*, 1837–1841; *CFL*, January–October 1842, Harrodsburg, KY, the first weekly publication in the movement, continued as *CJ* and *OP*, 1843–1846, Cincinnati and Covington, KY.

B. B. F., "Consider the Following," *CA*, 8 (October 21, 1852), 170; [Benjamin Franklin], "Death of Elder A. Crihfield," *CA*, 8 (December 9, 1852), 198.

CURLEE, CALVIN (1791, NC–23 October 1851, near Woodbury, TN). *Career*: Pioneer preacher.

Although Calvin Curlee is not widely known because his work was limited to Middle Tennessee near his home in Cannon County, his association with the early Campbell movement in Tennessee is important. Curlee's career also illustrates the ways in which Churches of Christ often originated in the bosom of the Baptist tradition and slowly evolved into a separate, identifiable movement. Philip S. Fall, a Baptist preacher and the first Kentucky reformer of the Campbell movement, extended that movement to Tennessee as the new preacher of the Baptist Church in Nashville in 1826. Through Fall's influence, Calvin Curlee, Peyton W. Smith, and Joshua K. Speer became the first advocates of Campbell's reform in the Elk River Baptist Association. In summer 1827 the Concord Baptist Association, which now included Fall, Curlee, and Smith, renounced Calvinism but retained the Concord name. J. H. Grime in his *History of Middle Tennessee Baptists* described Fall, Curlee, and Smith as "deeply dyed in Campbellism" and reported that nearly all the Baptist associations in the area were in "a perfect ferment by the leaven of Campbellism." J. D. Floyd counted fifty congregations of the Churches of Christ in Middle Tennessee and surrounding areas that traced their beginnings to the work of Calvin Curlee.

Bibliography

B. J. H. Grime, *History of Middle Tennessee Baptists* (Nashville, 1902), pp. 540–545; *History of Concord Association*, 41ff; John D. Ewell, *Life of Rev. William Keele* (Noah, TN, 1884), pp. 54–55; J. D. Floyd, *GA*, 43 (January 31, 1901), 80; J. D. Floyd, "Fruit after Many Days," *GA*, 52 (February 17, 1910), 217.

CYPERT, LILLIE (27 May 1889, AR–13 August 1954, Los Angeles, CA). *Career*: Missionary to Japan.

Lillie Cypert was one of three single missionary women who contributed most to establishing permanent congregations of Churches of Christ in Japan. The other two were Sarah Andrews and Hettie Lee Ewing. Cypert first arrived in Japan in 1917 when she went there to assist the venerable missionary to that country, John M. McCaleb. Cypert and her sister, Sadie Cypert, grew up "far back in the mountains" of Arkansas, where they "sought to find truth alone as they had no one to teach them." Sadie married M. C. Miller, who had studied at Freed-Hardeman College and who helped the two sisters to see the gospel message as taught by Churches of Christ. After spending four and one-half years in Japan, Lillie Cypert returned to Arkansas. J. D. Tant met her at that time and was deeply impressed. "In bygone years I have baptized more than a thousand girls, yet I do not know of one who would sacrifice all, give up father, mother, brother and sister and the hope of a happy marriage, as this girl has done, to go to far away Japan to teach the gospel there." With limited success Tant sought to stir the preachers and churches in Arkansas to support Cypert's work. With the fellowship of other congregations, the Church of Christ in Brownwood, Texas, finally took over Cypert's support. Lillie Cypert died almost unnoticed. A few short lines buried in a report constitute the only notice of her death to be found in the periodicals serving Churches of Christ.

Bibliography

B. J. D. Tant, "Lillie Cypert of Arkansas," *FF*, 40 (October 9, 1923), 6; Nellie Straiton, "Sister Lillie Cypert to Return to Japan," *FF*, 40 (September 25, 1923), 6; U. R. Forrest, "Brownwood Church Takes Miss Cypert's Care," *LM*, 3 (April 2, 1925), 220–221.

D

DAVIDSON, CLINTON V. (1888, Atlanta, GA–27 February 1967, Bernardsville, NJ). *Education*: Potter Bible College. *Career*: Life insurance salesman, businessman, benefactor of Camp Shiloh.

A man who for seven years running set a world record for life insurance sales and thereby amassed a considerable fortune, Clinton V. Davidson worked behind the scenes and helped in several ways to define the character of Churches of Christ during the first half of the twentieth century. First, Davidson felt that he owed a debt to Harding College, the successor to his own alma mater, the Potter Bible College in Bowling Green, Kentucky. In 1936, therefore, Davidson introduced George S. Benson, the new president of Harding College, to conservative capitalists and potential benefactors in New York City—the presidents, for example, of General Motors, the E. I. du Pont Company, the Baltimore and Ohio Railroad, and major steel and oil companies. Benson capitalized on those contacts, enabling Harding to liquidate its mortgage in 1939. Even more important, for the next thirty years Benson employed a conservative political ideology as the basis for fiscal development at Harding College. As a result Davidson contributed directly to the enduring political conservatism of Harding College, and indirectly to the enduring political conservatism of Churches of Christ. Second, Davidson sought to quell the divisive spirit that dominated journalism in Churches of Christ in the 1930s. To that end in 1938 he purchased an existing periodical, the *Christian Leader*, and sought to make this journal an example of positive, constructive journalism. The new *Christian Leader* got caught in the politics of premillennialism, however, and collapsed in 1940. In spite of its failure, the new *Christian Leader* provided an example of positive journalism that helped shape the progressive wing of Churches of Christ for the next fifty years and more. Third, after his retirement Davidson began a program of daily worship and church activity in his large home and estate in New Jersey, forty miles west of New York City. As this work increased, Davidson built Camp Shiloh on adjoining land. Camp Shiloh hosted young people of all nationalities who were bussed to the camp from New York City for recreation and Christian teaching. In a few years over 300 of these young people were converted to the Christian faith. In time the work of Camp Shiloh spread to New York City and other nearby urban areas, resulting in an English and Spanish congregation on the east side of the city and predominantly African American congregations in Trenton and Madison, New Jersey. Finally, in the 1950s Davidson developed an interest in latter-day miracles. He shared that interest with Pat Boone who had made his own sojourn into the world of speaking in tongues and pentecostal healings. Davidson attributed his financial success to the principles he learned from James A. Harding and J. N. Armstrong at the Potter Bible College.

Bibliography

A. *How I Discovered the Secret of Success in the Bible* (Westwood, NJ, 1961); "Influencing Religious Leaders," *FF*, 80 (June 18, 1963), 387.

B. James L. Lovell, "Church in the Wildwood," *California Christian*, 11 (February 1955), 3; Clinton Rutherford, "Clinton Davidson," *FF*, 84 (March 28, 1967), 202; Pat Boone, *A New Song* (Carol Stream, IL, 1970); John Scott, "Davidson Followed Harding's Theme in Life," *CC*, 24 (March 17, 1967), 3.

DAVIS, ANDREW PICKENS (1797, Mecklenburg Co., VA–30 June 188l, Washington Co., AR). *Career*: Farmer, preacher, 1823–81.

Andrew Davis' father was an old school Presbyterian, and Andrew was educated for the ministry of that faith. But when he heard Daniel A. Travis present "the primitive gospel" in 1816, he was baptized by Travis in Warren County, Tennessee. Davis began preaching at age twenty and in 1819 was ordained to the ministry after preaching for two years. For almost sixty-four years he lived and preached in eight different states, including Missouri and Arkansas, but most of his work was in Tennessee in the mountains of Jackson County and the Upper Cumberland and in Kentucky in the Green River country. He moved to Jackson County, Tennessee, in 1839. David Lipscomb credited this farmer-preacher with having more success than any other man in the cause of Churches of Christ in the Upper Cumberland region.

Bibliography

B. J. C. Mason, "Our Veterans," *CS*, 16 (July 30, 1881), 242; "Items, Personals, Etc.," *GA*, 21 (October 2, 1879), 634; "Items and Personals," *GA*, 18 (October 26, 1876), 1045; J. P. Whitefield, "Obituaries," *GA*, 23 (December 1, 1881), 758; David Lipscomb, *GA*, 8 (1866), 254.

DEFEE, WILLIAM (?–1869, near San Augustine, TX). *Career*: Minister, 1836–69.

William DeFee established the Antioch Church of Christ, now the oldest Church of Christ in Texas, in 1836 at about the beginning of the Texas Revolution. The DeFee family originally belonged to the French Huguenot tradition, whose beliefs were similar to those of Barton W. Stone and Alexander Campbell. DeFee became aware of the Church of Christ in Tennessee, where he was baptized in 1827 by Jesse Goodman, a preacher in the Mulkey movement. He migrated to Texas in 1831.

Bibliography

A. "Dear Brother Stone," *CM*, 7 (September, 1833), 281–282.
B. Matthews Papers, Texas Christian University Library.

DEWHITT, SAMUEL (1792–1853, Gamaliel, KY). *Career*: Minister in TN and KY, 1820s–1853.

Samuel Dewhitt was an itinerant preacher who evangelized Jackson County, Tennessee, and adjacent counties in Tennessee and southern Kentucky during the 1830s and 1840s. His work is important because Jackson County and Clay County (originally a part of Jackson County), Tennessee, have been strongholds for Churches of Christ for many years. In Clay County in 1980, for example, Churches of Christ claimed more than 79 percent of all church members, whereas Jackson County claimed 67 percent. Dewhitt, Abraham Sallee, and Andrew P. Davis were three of the principal second-generation itinerant preachers who evangelized this area. The records of the Christian Church on Big Barren River (established by Barton Stone in 1805 at Union Meeting House) indicate that Samuel Dewhitt joined in October 1821 "by experience in baptism." This suggests that his earliest religious activity was among people strongly influenced by Barton W. Stone. The old Christian Union Church moved about midcentury to Gamaliel, Kentucky, a town named by Dewhitt for the biblical rabbi. One of the first religious debates in Tennessee involving ministers of Churches of Christ was conducted by Dewhitt and Abraham Sallee, on the one hand, and John D. Lee and Alfonso Young representing the Mormons, on the other. The debate took place at the Ridge Meetinghouse in Smith County in 1841.

Bibliography

A. Written debate on Mormonism, *CFL*, 1 (July 18, 1842), 211; (July 25, 1842), 217–219; (August 1, 1842), 228–229; (August 15, 1842), 236–238.
B. "History of Church of Christ, Gamaliel, Kentucky," typescript; Richard T. Hughes, "Two Restoration Traditions: Mormons and Churches of Christ in the Nineteenth Century," *JMH*, 19 (Spring 1993), 46–47.

DOOLEY, REUBEN (14 November 1773, Bedford Co., VA–22 April 1822, Preble Co., OH). *Career:* Itinerant preacher, KY, TN, and OH, 1803–22.

Reuben Dooley helped in important ways to advance the work of Barton W. Stone in the Cumberland region of Tennessee and the Barrens of southern Kentucky following the Cane Ridge Revival of 1801. The Dooley family first settled in Madison County, Kentucky, but moved to Barren County, Kentucky, around 1800, obtaining land on the headwaters of Little Barren River. Prior to the Cane Ridge Revival, Moses Dooley, Reuben's father, attended an early revival, possibly at Red River Meeting House in Logan County, Kentucky. Apparently Moses returned home in the power of the spirit. His son, Reuben, straightaway began to exhort and warn his companions to repent and believe the gospel. A typical frontier revivalist, Dooley possessed great oratorical powers but little education. From the time of his conversion until the time of his death some twenty years later, he preached throughout the Cumberland and Barren regions. In addition, he preached among the Native Americans in North Carolina both in 1805 and again in 1810. Later in 1810 Stone and Dooley undertook a series of long preaching tours that extended from Kentucky into Ohio and Tennessee. This was a time when frightening earthquakes in the Mississippi Valley caused people to flock to their meetings. Dooley's numerous and extended preaching tours took him through uncharted wilderness areas and exposed him to the adverse elements of the weather. Those adverse conditions, coupled with the fact that he also worked hard on his farm in order to support his family, may account for the relative brevity of his life.

Bibliography

B. Barton W. Stone, *History of the Christian Church in the West* (reprint, Lexington, 1956), 2; Levi Purviance, *The Biography of Elder David Purviance* (Dayton, OH, 1848), pp. 194–201; P. Donan, *Memoir of Jacob Creath, Jr.* (Cincinnati, 1872), pp. 229–230; John Rogers, "Reminiscences of Elder Reuben Dooley," *CA*, 10 (1854), 35.

DUNN, LOUISE ELIZABETH (10 October 1846, TN–22 June, 1934, TN). *Career*: Mother of five preachers.

Jesse L. Sewell once held a gospel meeting at New Hope church near Readyville, Tennessee, which some called a failure because only one young girl was immersed. But this young girl was Elizabeth Nelson, who would eventually become the mother of five preachers. Elizabeth's parents died when she was eighteen years old. As the oldest of six children, she had to take on the responsibilities of the household during a time of extreme hardship following the Civil War. In 1867 she married Thomas Franklin Dunn and became the mother of nine children. At thirty-six years of age in 1882 Thomas Dunn died, leaving Elizabeth with all nine children, ranging in age from ten months to fourteen years, and a mortgaged farm. Dunn had become a soldier at age seventeen and had survived many of the bloodiest battles of the War between the States. By virtue of those experiences, he eventually rejected war and bloodshed and taught his boys never to be soldiers. They all became preachers instead. The oldest son, John E. Dunn, was one of five men who constituted the first class that graduated from the Nashville Bible School in 1896. True to the teachings of his father and the Nashville Bible School, John E. Dunn later wrote, "None of them [the Dunn brothers] take any part in politics or human governments. I intend to put forth my best efforts to teach my children never to vote or in any way participate in human government." The five sons who became preachers included John E. Dunn, Houston, TX; Dr. Thomas Franklin Dunn, St. Louis, MO; James Sterling Dunn, Dallas, TX; Jasper William Dunn, Ft. Worth, TX; and Gustus Albert Dunn, Dallas, TX. J. B. Nelson, another well-known minister in Churches of Christ, was also reared in the Dunn home.

Bibliography

B. "The Passing of 'Mother Dunn,' " *FF*, 51 (July 24, 1934), 2.

DURST, JOHN S. (20 October 1841, Nacogdoches, TX–31 August 1924, Junction, TX). *Education*: Baylor University. *Career*: Farmer, minister.

John S. Durst helped establish Churches of Christ on the Texas frontier in the late nineteenth and early twentieth centuries. His father was Major John Durst, who was one of the earliest Anglo settlers in Texas and who served as mayor of Nacogdoches for a time. Although the Dursts joined the Catholic Church after moving to Texas, the father asked his family to have nothing more to do with the Catholic religion after a priest refused him extreme unction. At this point John turned skeptical and indifferent toward the Christian religion. He maintained that skepticism even though he attended several frontier revivals conducted by "Campbellite" preachers. Finally, he and his wife attended a gospel meeting conducted by Benton Sweeney in Leona, Texas. At the conclusion of that meeting, both Durst and his spouse were baptized. Durst and a young schoolteacher, Basil P. Sweeney, became excellent preachers after Benton Sweeney's death left them with full responsibility for the small church at Leona, Texas. Following his ministry at Leona, Durst lived for many years in Junction, Texas, preaching in Central West Texas, where he was the best-known preacher in the area. Durst was a brother-in-law of Austin McGary, founder and editor of the *Firm Foundation*, and wrote many articles for McGary's paper. The two agreed completely on the issue of rebaptism. Durst affirmed the *Foundation*'s position in many articles and debates, including a written discussion with James A. Harding of Kentucky.

Bibliography

A. *The Faith That Qualifies for Baptism* (n.d., n.p.); Abilene Christian University *Bible Lectures, 1922–1923* (Abilene, 1923); "Reminiscences," nos. 1–3, *FF*, 24 (February 11–24, 1908).

B. Clem W. Hoover, "The Death of Brother John S. Durst," *FF*, 41 (1924), 3–4.

E

ELAM, EDWIN ALEXANDER (7 March 1855, Fosterville, TN–14 March 1929, Bellwood, TN). *Education*: Franklin College, 1871–75; Burritt College, 1876–79. *Career*: Preacher; journalist; teacher, Mars Hill Bible College near Florence, AL, 1879–80, and Nashville Bible School; president, Nashville Bible School (forerunner of David Lipscomb University), 1906–13.

Edwin Alexander Elam exerted a powerful influence on Churches of Christ from roughly 1880 to roughly 1920 through his teaching, his preaching, his administrative work in Christian higher education, his articles that appeared in the *Gospel Advocate* for some fifty years, and the Uniform Lessons for Sunday-school literature that he wrote and published for some thirty years for use in adult Bible classes among Churches of Christ. Elam wrote for the *Gospel Advocate* from 1880, the date of his first *Advocate* article, until his death in 1929. His work with the *Advocate* was so successful that he became coeditor, along with David Lipscomb and E. G. Sewell, in 1901. He also served as front page editor from 1900 to 1909. Also noted as a teacher, Elam taught at the Mars Hill Bible College (near Florence, Alabama) during the 1879–1880 school year. In 1901 he became a member of the board of trustees of the Nashville Bible School and served as president of that institution from 1906 to 1913, teaching Bible and church history during those years. From 1922 to 1929, Elam also wrote *Elam's Notes on Bible School Lessons*, the annual Bible school lessons published by the *Gospel Advocate*.

Bibliography

A. *The Bible versus Theories of Evolution* (Nashville, 1925); *Twenty-five Years of Trust: A Life Sketch of J. M. Kidwill* (Nashville, 1893).

B. *GA*, 71 (April 25, 1929), memorial issue to E. A. Elam; J. C. Choate, "E. A. Elam: A 'Rugged' Christian," *GA*, 108 (November 17, 1966), 726–728; H. Leo Boles, *Biographical Sketches of Gospel Preachers* (Nashville, 1932), pp. 421–425.

ELMORE, ALFRED (11 August 1838, near Frankfort, IN–11 December 1925). *Education*: At age 27 Elmore attended school taught by a noted historian, John C. Ridpath, 1865. *Career*: Minister; writer for *American Christian Review* and *Christian Leader*; editor, *Gospel Echo*.

Alfred Elmore developed a reputation as a persuasive evangelist and writer from the close of the Civil War until his death in 1925. He routinely preached in courthouses, opera houses, saw mills, railway depots, and a variety of other edifices. The year 1886 typified his schedule. He preached 489 sermons that year in forty-one different locations, with 260 conversions. For twenty years he wrote regularly for the *American Christian Review*, and for seven years he served on the editorial staff of the *Christian Leader*. He served as editor of the *Gospel Echo* from 1893 to 1900 and as an associate editor of the *Firm Foundation* in Austin, Texas, from 1910 until his death in 1925.

Bibliography

A. *Sermons, Reminiscences and Silver Chimes* (Austin, 1914).

B. Harriet Helm Nichol, "Alfred Elmore," in *Texas and Oklahoma Preachers* (Clifton, TX, 1911); G.H.P. Showalter, "Brother Alfred Elmore," *FF*, 42 (December 22, 1925), 2.

EWING, HETTIE LEE (11 October 1896, near Cleburne, TX–15 September 1986, Mesquite, TX). *Education*: Abilene Christian University. *Career*: Missionary to Japan.

Hettie Lee Ewing was one of three missionary women from Churches of Christ who helped establish permanent churches in Japan in the early twentieth century. Ewing's life turned out to be very different from the farm life that Mark Ewing, her father, wanted for her. A few summary lines near the end of her autobiography tell much of her story. "I can never give thanks to God enough and thank the American brethren enough for all this sustaining help to a nobody, just a girl out of the cotton fields, the daughter of a farmer who didn't even want me to have a high school education." Lillie Cypert's letter asking for someone to help with mission work in Japan appealed to Ewing. She had finished high school and was teaching near Corpus Christi. In the face of her father's opposition and with little help from others, she visited several congregations and obtained enough support to go to Japan against the wishes of most church leaders. She departed for Japan in 1927 but because of declining health, returned to the States in 1935. Shortly after World War II she returned to Japan, where she remained until 1972.

Bibliography

A. Orlan and Nina Sawey, eds., *She Hath Done What She Could: The Reminiscences of Hettie Lee Ewing* (Dallas, 1974); Hettie Lee Ewing, *Another Look at Japan: Reminiscences of Hettie Lee Ewing* (Dallas, 1977).

F

FALL, PHILIP SLATER (8 September 1798, Brighton, England–3 December 1890, Frankfort, KY). *Education*: English schools. *Career*: Minister, Baptist Church, Louisville, KY, 1821–22; Baptist Church, Nashville, TN, 1827–30; Church of Christ, Nashville, TN, 1857–77; Christian Church, Frankfort, KY, 1831–57, 1878–90; director, Popular Hill Academy, Popular Hill and Frankfort, KY, 1831–63.

Influenced by Alexander Campbell's "Sermon on the Law (1816)," Campbell's debates with John Walker (1820) and W. L. McCalla (1823), and early issues of Campbell's *Christian Baptist*, Philip Slater Fall became the first Baptist minister in Kentucky to join the Campbell movement. Campbell visited Louisville, Kentucky, in November 1824 and preached three sermons that made a strong impression on Fall. The Baptist church in Louisville voted unanimously in 1825 to abandon its Baptist confession of faith and to adopt the Bible alone as "the sole foundation on which a Church of Christ can rest." Beginning in 1827 Fall had a long relationship with the Baptist church in Nashville that by 1830 would become a Church of Christ. Fall's efforts also introduced the principles of the Campbell movement into other Baptist churches in Middle Tennessee, especially among the churches of the Concord Baptist Association and the Elk River Baptist Association. In addition, Fall won for the Campbell movement the first four Baptist preachers to abandon the Baptist faith and to cast their lot with the Christian movement, among them Calvin Curlee and Joshua K. Speer. Fall returned to Nashville in 1857 to rebuild this congregation, which had been broken up by the spiritualism of its pastor, Jesse B. Ferguson. He remained with that church until 1877.

David Lipscomb held the highest regard for Fall's scholarship. Interestingly, Lipscomb and Fall held the same views on the millennium. Following the Civil War, many rejected Alexander Campbell's postmillennial theories and embraced instead the views of Barton Stone, who looked to Christ as the only one who could reestablish the rule of God on this earth. Similarly, Fall spoke of Christ's second coming as "the pre-millennial advent." A devout conservative, Fall was closely associated with the Fannings (Mrs. Tolbert Fanning was his sister), the Lipscombs, and the *Gospel Advocate*, which published much from his pen. During his last years Fall served the Church of Christ in Frankfort, Kentucky. Once while he was absent from his pulpit, some in the congregation added an organ to "aid" the singing. Fall continued to preach but stated that he was too old to engage in controversy to try to put it out. However, he refused to sing and never called for a song. In this manner he registered his weekly protest. Fall was induced to attend one meeting of the Kentucky State Missionary Society, but spoke in opposition to such an organization.

Bibliography

A. "Letter from P. S. Fall, Nashville, Tenn.," *AT*, 8 (March 2, 1876), 134; "Interesting Reminiscences," *GA*, 21 (May 15, 1879), 310; "Reminiscences of Philip S. Fall," ms in the Philip S. Fall Memorial Library, Christian Church, Frankfort, KY.

B. W. F. Fall, "History of the Fall Family," *GA*, 32 (January 1, 1890), 15; *GA*, 58 (1916), 562; H. Leo Boles, "General History of the Church in Nashville," *GA*, 81 (December 7, 1939), 1146, 1167; D. L., "An Explanation," *GA*, 53 (April 20, 1911), 465; James A. Cox, "Incidents in the Life of Philip Slater Fall," B.D. thesis, Lexington Theological Seminary, 1951.

FANNING, CHARLOTTE FALL (19 April 1809, London, England–15 August 1896, Nashville, TN). *Education*: Philip S. Fall's Academy. *Career*: Teacher, Female Academy, Nashville, TN; director, Fanning Orphan School, Nashville, TN.

Charlotte Fall Fanning spent her life teaching the Bible and training girls for usefulness and doing good in "the domestic and useful callings of life." Her neighbors had inscribed on her tomb seven words that, in their judgment, described the kind of person she was: "I was sick and you visited me." She rightfully should share in the fame that accrued to her forceful husband, Tolbert Fanning, mid-nineteenth-century leader of Churches of Christ in the South. Probably no woman was more prominent and influential among these churches during her lifetime.

The Fall family came to America when Charlotte was nine years old. She had six brothers and four sisters. The parents died in Kentucky before their cabin in the wilderness was completed. Philip S. Fall took the younger children into his home, cared for them, and educated them in the Bible, the arts (especially music), and philosophy. Charlotte was a scholar in her own right, eventually learning Hebrew, Greek, Latin, German, and French. She taught French in the Female Academy of Nashville, Tennessee, where she met Tolbert Fanning, a graduate of the University of Nashville. Charlotte Fall and Tolbert Fanning married on December 25, 1836, and together they opened a school, which ran from 1837 to 1839, at Franklin, Tennessee. In 1840 they opened another school five miles east of Nashville called Elm Craig, which became Franklin College. While Tolbert concentrated on training young men, Charlotte started a school for young girls in her home. When the Franklin College building burned in 1865, the Fannings bought Minerva College, which they renamed Hope Institute, a school for girls that operated until Mr. Fanning's death in 1874. Charlotte Fanning then opened Fanning Orphan School in September 1884. After her death in 1896 the school continued until 1943, when the farm and school property were condemned and purchased by the City of Nashville for part of the new municipal airport.

Bibliography

A. *GA*, articles signed "C. F."

B. Emma Page, ed., *The Life Work of Mrs. Charlotte Fanning* (Nashville, 1907).

FANNING, TOLBERT (10 May 1810, Cannon Co., TN–3 May 1874, near Nashville, TN). *Education*: University of Nashville, 1832–36. *Career*: Minister; president, Female Seminary, 1837–39; president, Franklin College, 1840–61, 1865–74; editor, *Agriculturist*, 1840–45; editor, *Naturalist*, 1846–1850; editor, *Christian Review*, 1844–47; editor, *Gospel Advocate*, 1855–61; editor, *Religious Historian*, 1872–74.

David Lipscomb correctly identified Tolbert Fanning's place in the history of the Churches of Christ when he wrote, "The planting of the cause throughout portions of Tennessee, North and South Alabama and Mississippi was due to his labor more than that of all others combined." Indeed, in addition to his preaching, Fanning organized Franklin College, the first institution of higher learning related to Churches of Christ in the South, and launched the *Gospel Advocate*, the journal that by all odds was the most influential publication among Churches of Christ from its inception in 1855 until late in the twentieth century.

Fanning was in many ways a child of the movement led by Barton W. Stone. He received his earliest religious instruction from a Stoneite preacher, Ephraim D. Moore, and was baptized by another Stoneite preacher, James E. Mathews. Carroll Kendrick, who attended the camp meeting when Fanning was baptized, recalled that occasion by stating, "I do not remember that I had then ever heard of a *Campbellite*. B. W. Stone was the most prominent man then in the ranks." One can gauge the influence that the Stone tradition exerted upon Fanning by assessing one of Fanning's sermons, "The Mission of the Church of Christ." There Fanning contrasted two kingdoms—Satan's and Christ's—in a common sense dualism of spirituality on the one hand and materialism on the other. Fanning believed that all earthly kingdoms and organizations have the prince of this world (Satan) as their head and governor. In contrast, Christ is the head of His church, "his laws are spiritual and love is the only motive power." While Fanning denied holding any premillennial theories, he nonetheless believed that

Christ's spiritual church will eventually overcome the world by the gospel alone. Finally, the Lord will reign with his people a thousand years. At the end of that period of time, the Lord will defeat Satan's final effort to destroy the saints. Judgment will then take place, and "God's government will be approved." Unlike Stone, however, Fanning virtually equated the Church of Christ of his own time and place with the universal kingdom of God. For this reason, he lamented that some in Churches of Christ fraternized with the various Christian sects and denominations, all of which he viewed as human creations. At the same time he refused to deny that there might be Christians in the sects. Fanning believed that members of Churches of Christ should be morally superior to people in "denominational" organizations. "We have taken a higher ground than they, and if our spiritual character is not superior to theirs, we are of all men most culpable."

But Fanning was also a child of Alexander Campbell, a fact that can best be discerned in the unfortunate dispute between Fanning and Robert Richardson over human philosophy in 1857. In that exchange Fanning revealed the extent to which he was a devoted protégé of John Locke and a Campbellian rationalist.

Fanning and his brother-in-law, Philip S. Fall, were the two most influential leaders among Churches of Christ in mid-nineteenth-century Tennessee. When these two were growing old, Fanning called upon Fall to cooperate in training younger men to continue their work. Fanning had already chosen the young man who would receive his mantle. He told Fall that "for years past, I have taken considerable pains to enable brother David [Lipscomb] to understand what I studied and presented in writing over twenty years ago." He had already made Lipscomb the editor of the *Gospel Advocate* and thought that Lipscomb was doing a creditable job "without a line" from Fanning.

Bibliography

A. *Discourse Delivered in Boston, July 17, 1836* (Boston, 1836); "The Mission of the Church of Christ" in *The Living Pulpit of the Christian Church* (Cincinnati, 1868); "The Crisis," *CRev*, 2 (October 1845), 217–219; *True Method of Searching the Scriptures* (Philadelphia, 1857); "The Coming of the Lord," *GA*, 8 (September 18, 1866), 601–602; "Notice of Brother Elley's Essay," *GA*, 3 (February 1857), 54.

B. Carroll Kendrick, "Memories of Tolbert Fanning," *AT*, 6 (June 11, 1874), 1; James E. Scobey, ed., *Franklin College and Its Influences* (Nashville, 1906); James R. Wilburn, *The Hazard of the Die: Tolbert Fanning and the Restoration Movement* (Austin, 1969); *GA*, 4 (August 1858), 231, 265, 270.

FRANKLIN, BENJAMIN (1 February 1812, Belmont Co., OH–22 October 1878, Anderson, IN). *Career*: Minister; editor, *Reformer*, 1845–49; editor, *Proclamation and Reformer*, 1850–51; editor, *Christian Age*, 1850–53; editor, *American Christian Review*, 1st ser., 1856–57; 2d ser., 1858–78.

Benjamin Franklin exerted widespread influence among Churches of Christ especially through the journal he published from 1856 to 1878, the *American*

Christian Review, through two volumes of sermons that remained in print for many decades after his death, and through his twenty-five debates, six of which were published. A partisan of Alexander Campbell in the days of the *Christian Baptist*, Franklin favored plain preaching, and his preaching especially appealed to plain and rustic people. Few were more conservative than Franklin, who consistently championed the antiprogressive cause. For example, he refused to preach where an organ was present and announced this position before his death in 1878, almost twenty years before David Lipscomb adopted the same policy. Franklin's dilemma, however, lay in the fact that he was a plain and rustic man—in many ways a period piece—working in the post–Civil War North. As the North prospered following the war, many in the Christian movement found Franklin too backward looking in his views and altogether too cantankerous. Accordingly, in 1866 some of these Disciples established the *Christian Standard*, a progressive paper designed to compete head-on with Franklin's *American Christian Review*. From Franklin's perspective, supporters of the *Christian Standard* had abandoned the principles of primitive Christianity to conform to popular tastes. Franklin preached extensively in Indiana, Ohio, and Kentucky and in his later years traveled to more than half the states and parts of Canada. Some 8,000 people responded to his preaching during the course of his ministry.

Bibliography

A. *The Gospel Preacher*, 2 vols. (Cincinnati, 1869, 1877); *Sketches and Writings of Elder Benjamin Franklin* (Cincinnati, 1880).

B. *DAB*, vol. 6, 598–599; *ACR*, 12 (July 22, 1869), 237; M. M. Davis, "Benjamin Franklin," *CS*, 45 (August 14, 1909), 1411–1413; J. F. Rowe and G. W. Rice, eds., *Biographical Sketch and Writings of Elder Benjamin Franklin* (Cincinnati, 1880); Joseph Franklin and J. A. Headington, *The Life and Times of Benjamin Franklin* (St. Louis, 1879); Wendell Willis, "A Sociological Study of the Restoration Movement in the North, 1866–1878," M.A. thesis, Abilene Christian University, 1966; Otis L. Castleberry, *They Heard Him Gladly: A Critical Study of Benjamin Franklin's Preaching* (Rosemead, CA, 1963); Earl I. West, *Elder Ben Franklin: Eye of the Storm* (Indianapolis, 1983); Samuel Rogers, *Autobiography of Elder Samuel Rogers* (Cincinnati, 1881), pp. 141–145.

FREED, ARVY GLENN (3 August 1863, Saltillo, IN–11 November 1931, Nashville, TN). *Education*: Valparaiso University. *Career*: Founder and president, Southern Tennessee Normal College, Essary Springs, 1889; cofounder, National Teachers Normal and Business College, Henderson, TN; cofounder and president, Freed-Hardeman College, Henderson, TN; teacher, Southwestern Christian College, Denton, TX; vice-president, David Lipscomb College, 1923–31; minister, educator, debater.

Although Arvy Glenn Freed was a preacher in his own right, he devoted a large part of his career to training others for the ministry. He launched that phase of his career in 1889 when he founded the Southern Tennessee Normal

College in Essary Springs, Tennessee. He also helped establish the National Teachers Normal and Business College in Henderson, Tennessee, a school that in 1919 became known as Freed-Hardeman College in honor of the school's two founders, Freed and Nicholas Brodie Hardeman. This school would become one of the major institutions of higher learning serving Churches of Christ in the twentieth century. Freed served as president of Freed-Hardeman College from 1921 through 1923, but because of conflict with Hardeman, he left that school in 1923 to become vice-president of David Lipscomb College in Nashville.

Bibliography

A. *FF*, 5 (December 5, 1889), 1; *Sermons, Chapel Talks and Debates* (Nashville, 1930).

B. H. Leo Boles, *Biographical Sketches of Gospel Preachers* (Nashville, 1932), pp. 448–451; John Ancil Jenkins, "The Biography of a Gentleman: A. G. Freed," M.A. thesis, Abilene Christian University, 1969.

G

GANO, JOHN ALLEN (14 July 1805, Georgetown, KY–14 October 1887, Centerville, KY). *Education*: B. W. Stone's Rittenhouse Academy in Georgetown, 1819–22; studied law under Judge Warren in Georgetown, 1823–26. *Career*: Stockman, landowner, minister, 1827–87.

This Kentucky preacher was the last living link to the Stone movement of the early nineteenth century. As a young man he was schooled at Georgetown under Barton W. Stone and even lived in Stone's home. T. M. Allen baptized him in July 1827, and he began preaching almost immediately. Through marriage he inherited a large Georgian residence ("Bellevue") set in a 500-acre bluegrass farm in Centerville, Kentucky. He lived and farmed there for sixty years and devoted his ministerial labors to the four nearby Christian churches at Leesburg, Old Union, Newtown, and Antioch. As a stockman and landowner he accumulated a considerable estate and therefore never accepted any financial remuneration for his preaching. His articles in the *Christian Messenger* in 1830 in support of a weekly celebration of the Lord's Supper were endorsed by Stone and were influential in leading the Stone movement to adopt this practice. This development, in turn, helped pave the way for the merger of the Stone and Campbell movements in 1832, a process in which Gano played a prominent role. Following the merger he became a colaborer with John T. Johnson, a preacher from the Campbell movement, and they evangelized together for over twenty years. In the years 1830–1860 John Allen Gano established numerous congregations and was one of the most successful evangelists in Kentucky. A powerful and eloquent exhorter, and blessed with a melodious voice, he came to be known affectionately as "the Apollos of the West." He labored principally in Central Kentucky, but he occasionally extended into adjoining states. He made one tour into Louisiana, where he established a congregation in Baton Rouge. He baptized more than 10,000 persons during his sixty-year ministry.

His last article on "The Organ in Worship," written shortly before his death, was a solemn protest against the use of mechanical instruments in public worship, an innovation that was threatening to divide the Stone-Campbell movement.

Bibliography

A. Diaries, 1827–1887, housed at Center for Restoration Studies, Abilene Christian University; Roscoe M. Pierson, comp. and ed., *John Allen Gano: 1805–1887: A Collection Containing His Biographical Note Book No. 2, with Biographical Sketches by James Challen, Richard M. Gano, and W. C. Morrow* (Lexington, 1982).

B. James Challen, "John Allen Gano" in M. C. Tiers, ed., *The Christian Portrait Gallery* (Cincinnati, 1864); Richard M. Gano, *John Allen Gano* in John T. Brown, ed., *Churches of Christ* (Louisville, 1904); Bill J. Humble, "The John Allen Gano Papers," *FF*, 90 (March 27, 1973), 196; John T. Johnson, report, *MH*, new ser., 2 (June 1838), 285; R. B. Neal, "Elder John Allen Gano, Sr.," *GA*, 29 (October 26, 1887), 680; Jerry Bryant Rushford, "The Apollos of the West: The Life of John Allen Gano," M.A. thesis, Abilene Christian University, 1972; Roscoe M. Pierson, comp. and ed., *John Allen Gano: 1805–1887: A Collection Containing His Biographical Note Book No. 2, with Biographical Sketches by James Challen, Richard M. Gano, and W. C. Morrow* (Lexington, 1982).

GANO, RICHARD MONTGOMERY (18 June 1830, Centerville, KY–27 March 1913, Dallas, TX). *Education*: Bethany College, 1847; Medical University, Louisville, KY. *Career*: General in the army of the Confederate States of America; minister, 1865–1913.

Though a man with close ties to the pacifist legacy of Barton W. Stone, Richard Montgomery Gano served the Confederate army in the Civil War as both colonel and general. Gano was the son of John Allen Gano, who had been tutored by Barton Stone, and married Mattie Welch, one of Stone's descendents. Following the war, he served as an elder of the oldest congregation of any religious body in Dallas, Texas, now the Highland Oaks Church of Christ. Gano's religious efforts in Dallas began with a gospel meeting in 1867, a year after a steamboat exploration on the Mississippi River almost took his life. This church struggled before and after the Civil War until Gano conducted another successful revival in 1873. When Gano returned to Texas on a permanent basis in 1874, he began a long association with that congregation. He remained with the Dallas church when it was weakened by division in the early 1890s. During the war Gano served under General John H. Morgan in Tennessee and Kentucky and then in the western campaign in Arkansas and the Indian Territory. Gano, who became a full general near the close of the war, fought in seventy-two different battles. When the Dallas church divided and one group adopted the use of musical instruments, forming the Commerce Street Christian Church, Gano remained with the original congregation and served as an elder until his death. In addition to his long ministry in Dallas, Gano did evangelistic work in several states, especially in Kentucky, Tennessee, and Texas. He reportedly baptized almost 7,000 people during the course of his career.

Bibliography

A. Richard M. Gano's record of preaching, baptisms, and marriages in Center for Restoration Studies, Abilene Christian University.

B. M. M. Morrow, "From Fayetteville, Ark.," *Gospel Guide*, 2 (December 1906), 157; Jerry Rushford, "The Apollos of the West: the Life of John Allen Gano," M.A. thesis, Abilene Christian University, 1972; Jerry Rushford, "General Richard M. Gano (1830–1913)," unpublished typescript in Center for Restoration Studies, Abilene Christian University.

GATEWOOD, OTIS (27 August 1911, Meredian, TX–16 September 1999, Rochester Hills, MI). *Education*: B.A., Abilene Christian College, 1936; M.A., George Pepperdine College, 1950. *Career*: Missionary who established congregations of the Churches of Christ in Las Vegas, NM, 1937–39; Salt Lake City, UT, 1939–47; Frankfurt/M, Germany, 1947–57; and Vienna, Austria, 1978–88; founding president of Michigan Christian College (now Rochester College), 1959–63; founding president of European Christian College, Vienna, Austria, 1970; founding editor of *Contact*, a magazine for news about missions and international developments in Churches of Christ.

Otis Gatewood was by any measure the preeminent missionary among Churches of Christ in the twentieth century. In 1924, when Gatewood was thirteen years old and living with his family in Meadow, Texas, he peered through a window of the local Church of Christ during its worship service. A man invited him in, and Gatewood was baptized two years later in 1926. He began preaching that same year. He preached in Roby, Texas, while a student at Abilene Christian College between 1933 and 1935, and then at Rochester, Texas, in 1935 and 1936. In 1937 the elders of the Broadway Church of Christ in Lubbock, Texas, dispatched Gatewood to establish a congregation of Churches of Christ in Las Vegas, New Mexico. His work there was so successful that the Broadway congregation sent him in 1939 to establish a congregation of Churches of Christ in Salt Lake City, Utah. He and his wife, Alma, worked in Salt Lake City for the next eight years. With the conclusion of World War II, Gatewood was appalled that Churches of Christ essentially had no missionaries in the European theater. He brought this lack to the attention of the Broadway Church of Christ in Lubbock, and that congregation sent him and Alma to Germany, where they labored in Frankfurt/M from 1947 to 1957. During that same time Gatewood made numerous return trips to the United States, where he sought to raise funds and inspire workers for the mission project in Germany. All in all Gatewood preached in thirty-five different nations, and in 1958 he made the first of twenty-five mission trips to Russia, where, in 1992, he sought without success to convert former Soviet president Mikhail Gorbachev. Back in the United States in 1959,

Gatewood founded Michigan Christian College, and served as its president from 1959 through 1963. In 1970 he established European Christian College in Vienna, Austria, an institution he also served as president.

Bibliography

A. *The Gatewood-Farnsworth Debate on "Mormonism"* (Salt Lake City, 1942); *You Can Do Personal Work* (Los Angeles, 1945); *Lubbock Lectures on Mission Work* (Lubbock, 1946); *Wichita Forum Sermons* (Nashville, 1955); *Preaching in the Footsteps of Hitler* (Nashville, 1960); *There Is a God in Heaven* (Abilene, TX, 1970).

B. *POT*, vol. 3 (Nashville, 1964), p. 152; Harvie M. Pruitt, eulogy at Gatewood's funeral, September 21, 1999; "Father of Missions Dies," *CC*, 56 (November 1999), 1; "Otis Gatewood: Missions Legend on a New Mission in Paradise," *CC*, 56 (November 1999), 3.

GILES, SAMUEL BOLIVER (25 December 1808, Pittsylvania Co., VA–27 May 1884, Manor, TX). *Career*: Minister, TN and TX.

Samuel Boliver Giles first preached in Middle Tennessee but was one of the first preachers in the Republic of Texas, having established congregations among the people who composed the colony led by Stephen F. Austin. Giles and a Methodist preacher, O. Fisher, engaged in the first public debate in Texas soon after Giles arrived there. After the debate Giles continued to preach in South-Central Texas, baptizing some eighty people. No one contributed more to establishing Churches of Christ in Texas during the period of the Republic or during the early statehood period. Giles eventually prospered and, according to the U.S. census of 1860, owned property valued at over $100,000.

Bibliography

B. "Obituary," *ACR*, 27 (July 31, 1884), 246; *SHQ*, 71 (October 1967), 163–180.

GILLENTINE, JOHN (16 November 1797, VA?–2 July 1870, Spencer, TN). *Career*: Civic leader; president, board of trustees, Burritt College, Spencer, TN.

After working to promote the establishment of Burritt College in Spencer, Tennessee, John Gillentine served that institution as the first president of its board of trustees. Burritt College, in existence from 1849 to 1939, provided a classical education for young men preparing to preach and young women preparing to teach in public schools. Probably no early college supplied the Churches of Christ in Tennessee with more Christian teachers and ministers.

Bibliography

B. *Memorial & Biographical Record* (Chicago, 1898), pp. 298–300.

GOODPASTURE, BENTON CORDELL (9 April 1895, Livingstone, TN–18 February 1977, Nashville, TN). *Education*: Burritt College; David Lipscomb College; Southern Baptist Theological Seminary; Lit. D., Harding College; LL.D., Pepperdine University. *Career*: Minister, Shelbyville, TN; Florence, AL; Atlanta, GA; and Nashville, TN; staff writer, 1920–38, and editor, *Gospel Advocate*, 1939–77.

Benton Cordell Goodpasture served from 1939 to 1977 as editor of the *Gospel Advocate*, the most powerful publication among Churches of Christ at that time, particularly east of the Mississippi River. His work in that regard placed him in the ranks of what this book has described as the "editor-bishops." Indeed, his influence among Churches of Christ in the twentieth century compares with that of David Lipscomb in the late nineteenth century. Goodpasture effectively utilized the informal powers at his command when he "quarantined" the anticooperation faction of Churches of Christ at the peak of the institutional controversy. Goodpasture brought to the *Advocate* a style of institutional management that stood in marked contrast to the highly polemical rhetoric that had characterized journalism among Churches of Christ for most of the 1930s. In this way, Goodpasture—and the *Advocate* under his leadership—did as much as anyone to derail the destructive leadership of men like Foy E. Wallace, Jr.

Bibliography

A. *Sermons and Lectures of B. C. Goodpasture* (Nashville, 1964).

B. Julian E. Choate, *The Anchor That Holds: A Biography of Benton Cordell Goodpasture* (Nashville, 1971); David Edwin Harrell, Jr., "B. C. Goodpasture: Leader of Institutional Thought," in Florida College *Annual Lectures* (Temple Terrace, FL, 1981), pp. 241–253.

GRIFFIN, THACKER VIVIAN (1800–12 February 1853, Dallas, TX). *Career*: Minister, AL, TN, and TX.

Thacker Vivian Griffin was a little-known but very significant preacher who likely came from the Separate Baptists led by Shubal Stearns and Philip Mulkey. A Separate preacher named Thacker Vivian was prominent in the Fair Forest Separate Baptist Church in South Carolina, a church that began as a branch of Stearns' original Separate Baptist Church at Sandy Creek, North Carolina. It is likely that Thacker Vivian Griffin was named for the Separate Baptist Thacker Vivian. From reports of his preaching in the *Christian Messenger*, Griffin must have preached first in Georgia and later moved to northern Alabama and then to Middle Tennessee. He preached with James E. Matthews and other leaders of the Stone movement in the 1820s and helped cofound with Matthews the Fayetteville, Tennessee, Christian Church near the William Lipscomb farm a few miles from Huntland, Tennessee. Griffin was the first preacher in the Church of Christ whom David Lipscomb heard. Eventually the Lipscombs became members of the Church of Christ after being expelled by the Baptists. Griffin and

James Matthews helped bring the Lipscombs into the Stone and Campbell movement. This was no small contribution, considering the influence that David Lipscomb exerted on Churches of Christ. Griffin migrated in the late 1840s to Hord's Ridge (now the Oak Cliff suburb of Dallas, Texas), where he died in 1853. B. F. Hall went to Texas on a preaching journey in 1849, and there visited with Griffin. Hall wrote that "his bad health had prevented any [preaching] of consequence since he has been in Texas." Hall's report is the last mention of Griffin in restoration periodical sources. Griffin is found in the 1850 U.S. Census of Dallas County and mentioned in an early history of Dallas County.

Bibliography

A. Letter to Stone and Johnson, *CM*, 8 (October 1834), 301–303.
B. B. F. Hall, "Religious Intelligence," *CM*, 3 (January 1850), 26–27.

GUIREY, WILLIAM (?–1810). *Career*: Minister, author.

Although exact birth and death dates for William Guirey are unknown, this man was a pivotal figure in the early history of the Christian movement. Guirey's principle contributions were two. First, he wrote *The History of Episcopacy* (1799), a book that remains the most detailed firsthand account not only of the early Christian movement led by James O'Kelly but also of O'Kelly's defection from the Methodists in 1792. Second, Guirey's early advocacy of immersion apparently led to its adoption among churches in the West and in the South, although James O'Kelly and a small number of churches under his direct influence rejected this rite. Guirey and O'Kelly differed sharply not only over immersion but also over union with immersionist "Christians" of New England. At the same time Guirey was probably responsible for the fact that Barton W. Stone and most of his associates accepted immersion at an early date. When Joseph Thomas visited Kentucky and Tennessee in 1810 and 1811, he found that most in the Stone movement had been immersed. This contribution was important, since baptism by immersion came to play such a defining role in the Stone-Campbell tradition.

Bibliography

A. *The History of Episcopacy* (Raleigh, NC, 1799).
B. "Virginia in an Uproar!" *HGL*, 4 (January 1812), 355; W. E. MacClenny, *The Life of Rev. James O'Kelly* (reprint, Indianapolis, 1950); Evan William Humphreys, *Memoirs of Deceased Christian Ministers* (Dayton, OH, 1880), pp. 150–151.

H

HADEN, JOEL HARRIS (11 November 1788, VA–7 February 1862, Howard Co., MO). *Career*: Minister.

Joel Harris Haden began his career in the O'Kelly movement in Virginia. In 1814 he moved to Kentucky, where he played a significant role in the Stone movement, and then in 1836 he moved to Springfield, Missouri, where he helped establish Churches of Christ in the southwest corner of that state. While on a preaching tour to Tennessee and Kentucky from 1810 to 1812, Haden joined some fifty other preachers who rejected the attempt of Robert Marshall and John Thompson, two signers of the "The Last Will and Testament of the Springfield Presbytery" to get the "Stoneites" to adopt a creed that would place greater control over churches and preachers. By 1807 the Stone preachers had become concerned about the biblical teaching regarding the form of baptism and had rejected sprinkling in favor of immersion. The eastern Christian movement led by James O'Kelly had developed out of Methodism and accepted sprinkling with little question. In 1806, however, William Guirey raised this issue among eastern Christians, and concern over this question soon spread to the West. After Joel Haden had settled in Christian County, Kentucky, in 1817, he helped instigate "a wonderful revival" that won numerous converts. When Haden became disturbed regarding baptism, his studies led him to conclude that only immersion was scriptural. He awoke Stone in the night and demanded that Stone baptize him. Afterward he made an effort to reteach all whom he had taught that sprinkling was a legitimate mode of baptism. Joel Haden became very influential in bringing converts into the church and young men into the ministry. In April 1836 Haden moved to the "little village" of Springfield, Missouri, where he spent several years establishing and building up churches. There he converted Peter and Lansford Wilkes, who both became preachers. Haden must be given credit for the strength of the Christian movement in Southwest Missouri. In his late years Haden returned to his beautiful estate home (now called Linwood Estates) near Fayette, Howard County, Missouri, where the Hadens are buried.

Bibliography

A. "Religious Intelligence," *HGL*, 5 (January 8, 1813), 455–456.

B. T. P. Haley, *Historical and Biographical Sketches of the Early Churches and Pioneer Preachers of the Christian Church in Missouri* (Kansas City, 1888), pp. 183–192 [binder's title: *Dawn of the Reformation in Missouri*]; T. M. Allen, "Correspondence," *ACR*, 5 (April 1, 1862), 3; (May 6, 1862), 3.

HAGGARD, DAVID (n.d.). *Career*: Minister; missionary to Native Americans.

Data on David Haggard is available from only a few sources that give no information about his birth and death. A brother of Rice Haggard, David became a deacon (preacher) in the Methodist Church in 1787, serving on the Virginia and Kentucky circuits. Both David and Rice Haggard supported the O'Kelly separation from the Methodists in 1792. After a period of time in Kentucky, David spent some years preaching in Virginia and North Carolina before returning to Kentucky, where he labored for many years, dying at an advanced age. The earliest record of any religious organization in Cumberland County, Kentucky, is a record of a license to perform marriages granted to David Haggard in August 1800. That record describes Haggard as being "in regular communion with the society called the Christian Church." Reuben Dooley recruited Haggard to preach among the Native Americans of North Carolina after 1805. Joseph Thomas wrote that Haggard was among them for "years, teaching them to read the holy scriptures." William Kinkaid, one of Haggard's contemporaries in Tennessee and Kentucky, wrote that he was a charismatic person able to perform works of healing. The time and place of David Haggard's death are unknown. Several members of the Haggard family (including Mrs. Rice Haggard) are buried in The King Cemetery on Rennix Creek near Burkesville, Cumberland County, Kentucky. Another old cemetery with unreadable markers is on Haggard's Branch near Burkesville. Local historian Randolph Smith has suggested that these may be Haggard graves, since the family owned land on the small stream known by this name.

Bibliography

B. *Minutes of the Methodist Conferences . . . from 1773–1794* (Philadelphia, 1795); J. W. Wells, *History of Cumberland County* (Louisville, 1947), p. 61; Joseph Thomas, *The Travels and Gospel Labors of Joseph Thomas* (Winchester, VA, 1812), 80–81; William Kinkaid, *The Bible Doctrine of God, Jesus Christ, the Holy Spirit, Atonement, Faith, and Election* (Dayton, OH, 1829 [?]).

HAGGARD, RICE (1769, VA–1819, OH). *Career*: Author; minister, VA, KY, and OH.

Rice Haggard was the leading figure in the union of the O'Kelly and Stone movements in 1804 and the author of an influential tract, *The Sacred Import of the Christian Name*. This assessment can now be made with the support of sources long obscured, unknown or sometimes inaccessible to historians of the movement. Several factors helped perpetuate Haggard's obscurity, including his early death, the fact that his tract was published anonymously, and the fact that the early works by contemporary historians and preachers, William Guirey and Joseph Thomas, were not widely circulated and are still little known. These sources strongly imply that without Rice Haggard the history of the Christian Church in the West would have been different. John W. Neth, Jr., who discovered the pamphlet on the Christian name, suggested that Haggard's name should be added to those of Barton Stone, Thomas Campbell, Alexander Campbell, and Walter Scott to make five "founding fathers" of the Christian movement. Haggard would certainly merit consideration for such a place. He proposed to James O'Kelly and his followers in 1794 that they follow the New Testament alone and wear only the name "Christian," a proposal adopted by the O'Kelly movement in 1794. He then made the very same proposal to Barton Stone and his followers in the Springfield Presbytery in Kentucky in 1804. Like the O'Kelly movement before them, the Stone people also embraced Haggard's proposal. Indeed, Joseph Thomas indicates in his autobiography that Haggard's visit to Kentucky in April 1804 contributed to the dissolution of the Springfield Presbytery at Cane Ridge a few weeks later. Stone wrote that Haggard and two others (Clement Nance and James Reed) united with them in 1804 and that they published Haggard's tract on the Christian name that same year. Thomas wrote, "Not long after this [i.e. Haggard's visit] at a memorable meeting, held at Cane Ridge, in 1804, the Springfield Presbytery dissolved their body by a mutual and unanimous consent." Thomas also indicates that Haggard made another, even more significant proposition that also was accepted by the Kentuckians: "that the scriptures were all sufficient to govern the church of Christ, and any other written rules or laws were spurious and only calculated to separate and keep apart the lambs of Christ." The immediate result as noted by Thomas was the union of the Christians east and west, both vowing to continue searching the scripture on "the enquiring plan." Clearly Thomas accepted June 24, 1804, as the beginning of the free church idea among the fifteen Springfield Presbytery churches. "Thus," Thomas adds, the assembly at Cane Ridge "came to the Christian plan [and] from that day were made perfectly free from priestly power and from all them that would usurp authority over them."

What little we know of Haggard's childhood and youth is found in "An Elegy," also written by Joseph Thomas.

> Thy parents poor, had never taught thee then,
> To read the Bible, nor to use the pen;
> But in the smooth sand thou didst learn to write,
> And taught thyself to read by faggot light!

Haggard was "admitted to trial" by the Methodist Episcopal Church and served under presiding elder James O'Kelly in 1789. He was soon admitted to "full connection" as a "deacon" (preacher) before being ordained by Francis Asbury in 1791. Haggard rode circuits in Virginia and Kentucky before the first General Conference of the Methodist Church in Baltimore, Maryland, in 1792, which rejected the right of appeal by preachers if the appointments placed them in a difficulty. Rice Haggard's appointment became the test case. The loss of appeal led to defection of the preachers led by O'Kelly and their adoption of the name "Republican Methodists." Rice Haggard was the most influential minister besides O'Kelly to withdraw from the Methodists. Haggard moved to Kentucky in 1817, but his ministry ended in 1819 while he was on a preaching trip to Ohio. His widow, Nancy, lived until 1862 and aided in renewing the Christian church in Burkesville, where the Haggard double log home is now restored. His will, dated May 31, 1819 in Champaign County, OH, was presented to the court on September 10, 1819. Haggard's death went unnoticed in the newspapers at Dayton, OH, and Lexington, KY, which printed his books. Joseph Thomas lived in western Ohio in his later years but never learned "where lie the bones of Rice Haggard, or who buried him."

Bibliography

A. *An Address to the Different Religious Societies on the Sacred Import of the Christian Name* (Lexington, 1804); *HGL*, 1 (August 18, 1809–February 2, 1810); *An Address . . .*, 2d ed. (Dayton, 1815); *An Address . . .*, reprint of 1st ed. (Nashville, 1954); *A Selection of Christian Hymns* (Lexington, 1818).

B. *Minutes of the Methodist Conferences . . . from 1773–1794* (Philadelphia, 1795); William Guirey, *History of Episcopacy* (Winchester, VA, 1799); Joseph Thomas, *Life of the Pilgrim Joseph Thomas* (Winchester, VA, 1817), 282; B. W. Stone, "History of the Christian Church in the West" in Hoke S. Dickinson, ed., *The Cane Ridge Reader* (n.p., 1972); *Records and Pioneer Families in Ohio*, vol. 2 (1961), 50–51; J. Berkley Green, "Rice Haggard" in J. Pressley Barrett, *The Centennial of Religious Journalism* (Dayton, 1908), 269–281; Colby D. Hall, *Rice Haggard, the American Frontier Evangelist Who Revived the Name Christian* (Fort Worth, 1957); R. L. Roberts, "Rice Haggard, A Name Rever'd," *Disc*, 54 (1994), 67–81.

HALL, BENJAMIN FRANKLIN (13 June 1803, Moorefield, KY–1 May 1873, Kentuckytown, TX). *Education*: Acres Academy, KY; Philadelphia Dental School. *Career*: Dentist; editor, *Gospel Advocate*, 1835–36; editor, *Christian Magazine*, 1848; editor, *Christian Age*, 1852; chaplain, Confederate army; minister, Harrodsburg, Frankfort, and Louisville, KY; Nashville and Memphis, TN; Dallas and Fort Worth, TX.

Benjamin Franklin Hall learned from reading Alexander Campbell's debate with W. L. McCalla that baptism is for the purpose of the forgiveness of sins. Hall was then instrumental in convincing Barton W. Stone to embrace that view, even though Stone had discovered this doctrine in the New Testament several years earlier. It is largely due to B. F. Hall, therefore, that Churches of Christ made this doctrine such a central plank in their theological platform. Little wonder, then, that Hall's gravestone reads, "He was ordained to the ministry May 1, 1823, and was the first in line to preach salvation through obedience to the Gospel." Although Alexander Campbell viewed the doctrine of baptism for the remission of sins as a "perfect novelty," that judgment gave way to Campbell's embrace of this practice by 1827. Although Hall was Barton Stone's "son in the gospel," he aligned himself with Alexander Campbell as well, since the Stone people were slow to accept Campbell's views on the Holy Spirit. In these ways Hall was an early strategic link between the Stone and Campbell movements and the first "Campbellite" from among the Stone preachers. Hall's commitment to Campbell's reform gave him access to some Baptist pulpits, which he used to reform Baptist churches in Little Rock, Arkansas, and Wilmington, North Carolina.

Bibliography

A. *A Discourse on Christian Union* (Little Rock, 1832); *A Discourse on Spiritual Influence* (Louisville, 1840); *A Discourse on Four Baptisms* (Louisville, 1851); "Alexander Campbell," *ACR*, 2d ser., 2 (December 6, 1859), 193; "Nothing but the Truth," *GA*, 5 (August 1859), 245–247; unpublished autobiography, typescript copy in Center for Restoration Studies, Abilene Christian University.

B. R. L. Roberts, "B. F. Hall, Pioneer Evangelist," *RQ*, 8 (4th Qr 1965), 248–259; "Benjamin Franklin Hall, 1803–1870," *RQ*, 20 (3d Qr 1977), 156–168.

HARDEMAN, NICHOLAS BRODIE (18 May 1874, Milledgeville, TN–25 November 1965, Memphis, TN). *Education*: West Tennessee Christian College; B.A. and M.A., Georgia Robertson Christian College. *Career*: Minister; president, Freed-Hardeman College, 1923–54.

Nicholas Brodie Hardeman was a noted educator, evangelist, and debater in Churches of Christ during the first half of the twentieth century. With Arvy Glenn Freed, Hardeman cofounded Freed-Hardeman College in Henderson, Tennessee, in 1908, even though this school grew from a series of earlier institutions dating to 1869. Among his most notable contributions to the Churches of Christ were his "Tabernacle Sermons," preached to Nashville audiences on five occasions between 1922 and 1942. These sermons were published and served as primers for aspiring young preachers in Churches of Christ for almost half a century. Jesse P. Sewell argued in 1938 that Hardeman had aligned himself with Foy E. Wallace, Jr., in an attempt to foster negative preaching and journalism and in the effort to drive premillennial sympathies out of Churches of Christ. Arvy Glenn Freed helped to launch Hardeman's debating career when Freed was unable to keep an appointment to debate with a Baptist named Dr. Penick and sent Hardeman in his stead. Hardeman's style and personality soon made him a champion debater. He conducted two debates that were especially notable. The first was with a representative of the instrumental Christian churches, Ira

M. Boswell, on instrumental music, held in Nashville, Tennessee, in 1923. The second was with Ben Bogard, representing the Missionary Baptist Church, held in Little Rock, Arkansas, in 1938. Preachers in Churches of Christ debated more with Bogard than with any other man.

Bibliography

A. *Boswell-Hardeman Discussion on Instrumental Music in the Worship* (Nashville, 1924); *Hardeman-Bogard Debate* (Nashville, 1938); *Tabernacle Sermons*, 5 vols. (Nashville, 1922–1942).

B. J. M. Powell and Mary N. Hardeman Powers, *N.B.H.: A Biography of Nicholas Brodie Hardeman* (Nashville, 1964).

HARDING, JAMES ALEXANDER (16 April 1848, Winchester, KY–28 May 1922, Atlanta, GA). *Education*: Bethany College, 1869. *Career*: Teacher; minister; president, Nashville Bible School, 1891–1900; founder and president, Potter Bible College, Bowling Green, KY, 1901–12; editor, *The Way*, 1899–1907.

James Alexander Harding served as president of the Nashville Bible School from 1891 to 1900, then as founding president of Potter Bible College in Bowling Green, Kentucky, from 1901 to 1912. Through the students he trained at these institutions, he arguably became the most dominant influence on Christian education among Churches of Christ during the first half of the twentieth century. During all those years Harding's teaching was characterized by an emphasis on justification by grace through faith as opposed to justification by good works. This emphasis was rare among Churches of Christ at that time. Nonetheless, Harding's teaching in this regard bore fruit in the work of the preachers he trained. J. N. Armstrong, his son-in-law, made the doctrine of grace central to his work at Harding College, just as Robert C. Bell brought the doctrine of grace into his classes at Abilene Christian College. The theme of grace became especially important during the premillennial controversy (1915–1945), since those like R. H. Boll who argued for a premillennial vision grounded that vision in their understanding of divine grace and initiative. Harding himself translated his understanding of grace into a personal belief in divine providence—a notion that set him apart from most of his peers. Harding was baptized by Moses Lard and in 1874 began his evangelistic career. He preached mainly in Tennessee and southern Kentucky, but he preached as well in many other states and in Canada. He also established a reputation as a great debater. Between 1899 and 1907 Harding edited a publication called *The Way*.

Bibliography

A. James A. Harding and J. B. Moody, *Debate on Baptism and the Work of the Holy Spirit*, held May 27–June 11, 1889 (Nashville, n.d.).

B. F. D. Srygley, "Life of J. A. Harding," in *Biographies and Sermons* (Nashville, reprint, 1961); L. C. Sears, *The Eyes of Jehovah: The Life and Faith of James Alexander Harding* (Nashville, 1970).

HARDING, JOHNSON (4 September 1832, TN–13 July 1915, San Antonio, TX). *Career*: Evangelist, TN and TX.

Evangelist "Weeping Joe" Harding was one of the most colorful and most successful preachers among the Churches of Christ in the late nineteenth century and for several years after the turn of the century. He preached on city streets and in rural communities with spectacular results. Johnson made an impression wherever he preached. A reporter who covered Harding during a gospel meeting in Louisville, Kentucky, in 1883 described him as "a very active, earnest, go-ahead, dauntless sort of a preacher [who had] created quite a sensation in the part of the city where he is operating." According to the account, Harding advertised himself freely as "Weeping Joe" who "resurrects the natives." The churches excused "all his eccentricities" because he preached "the truth so plainly that people cannot help understanding him." Harding established at least two churches by colonization. He led one group from Gallatin, Tennessee, to West Dallas during the 1870s. On another occasion he led a congregation to Ballinger in West Texas. Harding preached everywhere he went. In spring 1885 heavy rains flooded the Trinity River, which crested at Dallas on a Sunday morning and brought thousands of spectators to the only bridge over the river. William Forester, editor of the Decatur, Texas, newspaper, who followed Harding's preaching with great interest, described the event in a news item. "Weeping Joe Harding preached today on the Trinity bridge to the measureless air congregation of divers sects and races. . . . In this way he succeeded in heading off several thousand sinners, who had undertaken to visit the two-mile-wide river instead of going to church. The sermon, full of earnestness, seemed to command devout attention, and several brands are reported rescued from the burning." Forester later reported that Weeping Joe had struck Gainesville, Texas, and preached on the street. He was arrested during his sermon, causing considerable indignation on the part of his audience. He was soon released and returned to finish his sermon. The Decatur editor reported Harding's belief that he had as much right to the street as the devil did, and as long as the devil preached there, he intended to preach there as well. In 1896 Harding reestablished a church in Gainesville that had been broken up by the war, and in 1892 he revitalized a congregation in Corsicana, Texas, with eighty-six additions during four months of preaching in the streets by day and in a hall by night. In 1897 he conducted a year-long tent meeting in San Antonio that resulted in eighty-seven conversions. Weeping Joe's later years were spent in South Texas, where he preached until about 1914 in San Antonio, in the Rio Grande Valley, and in any other places where he could attract an audience. J. W. Kelley said that Harding probably preached to as many audiences as any preacher and built more churches than any during his fifty-plus years of his ministry.

Bibliography

B. W. L. Butler, *AC* (December 1883), 23; *Wise County Messenger*, May 2, 1885, May 23, 1885; J. W. Kelly, "Harding," *FF*, 32 (October 12, 1915), 8.

HARPER, ERNEST ROSENTHAL (26 August 1897, TN–15 April 1986, Abilene, TX). *Education*: Freed-Hardeman College, Henderson, TN; Union University, Jackson, TN. *Career*: Minister, author, debater.

Ernest Rosenthal Harper began preaching in 1924 at Bemis, Tennessee, the first of several successful local ministries. Following several fruitful years in Jackson, Tennessee, he enjoyed ministries at two of the largest Churches of Christ in the South, the first at the Fourth and State Street congregation in Little Rock, Arkansas, 1934–1945, and then at the Highland congregation in Abilene, Texas, 1945–1956. While preaching in Jackson, Tennessee, in the late 1920s, Harper became one of the earliest radio preachers among Churches of Christ. After moving to Little Rock, Arkansas, he continued preaching over the radio and was probably the best-known preacher in the state. He also became widely known and received calls for gospel meetings throughout the United States. Harper's preaching was often issue oriented, especially during the premillennial controversy that reached its crescendo during the Little Rock years. Harper played an important role in that controversy as the point man of Foy E. Wallace, Jr., who charged him with purging Harding College of its premillennial sympathizers. During the anti-institutional controversy, Harper preached for the Highland Church of Christ in Abilene, Texas, the congregation that sponsored the national radio program, "Herald of Truth." Not surprisingly, he championed such evangelism against its detractors. He held debates on this issue with Fanning Yater Tant, editor of the *Gospel Guardian*, in 1955 and 1957.

Bibliography

A. *Living Issues* (Odessa, TX, 1951); *Prophecy Foretold, Prophecy Fulfilled* (Abilene, 1972); *Harper-Tant Debate* (Abilene, 1956).

B. "E. R. Harper Goes Home" (six articles), *GA*, 128 (September 4, 1986), 530–532.

HENRY, JOHN (1 October 1797, Chartiers, PA–1 May 1844, Austintown, OH). *Career*: Minister.

John Henry was baptized in 1828 by Adamson Bentley after reading *The Christian Baptist* and soon began preaching. His ministry lasted only approximately fourteen years when his life was cut short prematurely, but it is quite possible that no preacher in the early years of the Campbell movement attained as much popularity, especially among the country folk who heard him. Robert Richardson called him "a man of very singular powers" who was "universally esteemed." The people at Beeler's Station, Virginia (now West Virginia), called him "the walking Bible" who "could quote the Bible through from memory." Henry was a fast talker and a man of "great force in his discourse." Alexander Campbell said of him, "As a preacher of a particular order of preachers he had no equal or no superior." On one occasion Campbell and John Henry had appointments to preach together near Minerva, Ohio. Many people who were present had never seen either man, and when Henry preached in the morning, they thought he was Campbell. After all, the two had similar physical features and Henry possessed the gift of eloquence and a vast biblical knowledge by which he could master great audiences. Campbell preached next and some in the assembly said, "We wish that man would sit down and let Campbell get up for he knew how to preach." In 1844 Henry's wife fell ill while he was away from home preaching. In an attempt to reach his wife, he rode seventy-five miles on horseback in a single day, overexerted himself, became sick, and died. In this way one of the most brilliant preaching careers in the early Christian movement was shortened to approximately fourteen years.

Bibliography

B. Robert Richardson, *Memoirs of Alexander Campbell*, 2 (Cincinnati, 1897–1898), pp. 251–252; Jacob, "Reminiscences of the Churches of Seventy Years Ago," *OR*, 45 (June 3, 1902), 8.

HILL, ABNER (20 August 1788, TN–1873, Gainesville, TX). *Career*: Frontier preacher, TN, AL, IL, TX.

Abner Hill was a member of one of the Baptist churches that supported John Mulkey in the division that split the Stockton Valley Baptist Association in 1810. At first Hill tried to convince Mulkey of error. Instead, Mulkey answered all his arguments. Hill conceded, abandoned the Baptists, and embraced the reforming vision of the Christian movement. Hill typified many early preachers in Tennessee who had been influenced by Barton W. Stone and who therefore opposed a national conference of Christian Connection churches proposed in 1828 by preachers in the North (Indiana and Ohio) and East. His ministry included early circuits in Tennessee, Kentucky, and Alabama, brief stays in Illinois, and almost forty years in Texas. He went to Texas in 1836 during the Texas Revolution, following the large Matthews family, which had settled in Red River County earlier that year. These families formed an early church in the Lollard community of Hopkins County known originally as White Oak. The congregation later moved to Tarrant, then to Antioch, and continues today at Pine Forest, Texas. For three decades Hill was a frontier itinerant preacher in North Texas. Later in life he married Nancy (Matthews) Bailey, a sister of Mansil W. Matthews and the widow of Amos C. C. Bailey, on whose land grant the town of Gainesville, Texas, is located. Vigilantes broke up a frontier church at Gainesville, consisting of numerous relatives of Nancy and Abner Hill, killed the minister (John Crisp), and caused the families to be scattered during the Gainesville Hangings of 1864.

Bibliography

A. "For the Christian Messenger," *CM*, 2 (June 1828), 178–181; "An Autobiography of Abner Hill, Pioneer Preacher of Tennessee, Alabama, and Texas" (c. 1861), typescript housed in Center for Restoration Studies, Abilene Christian University.

HOGAN, RICHARD NATHANIEL (30 November 1902, Blackton, AR–24 February 1997, Los Angeles, CA). *Education*: Bible training at G. P. Bowser's Silver Point Christian Institute, 1916–20. *Career*: Plumber and factory worker; minister and evangelist, 1930–97; editor, *Christian Echo*, 1950 (?)–1997.

Richard Nathaniel Hogan was one of the most influential preachers among African American Churches of Christ for most of the twentieth century. He also edited a periodical that exerted substantial influence among African American Churches of Christ, the *Christian Echo*, from midcentury until his death in 1997. Hogan was baptized at the age of ten, and when he was fourteen, his mother turned him over to G. P. (George Phillip) Bowser to be trained as a preacher in Bowser's Silver Point (TN) Christian Institute. He traveled with Bowser on preaching appointments and within a few years had baptized over seventy people, earning him the nickname "the boy evangelist." He established a congregation of Churches of Christ on the South Side of Chicago in 1930, but he began his first, full-time, local preaching work in Muskogee, Oklahoma, in 1932. While in Muskogee, Hogan organized a school for preachers and trained a number of men who would become influential among African American congregations in their own right: Russell H. Moore, H. H. Gray, J. S. Winston, Walter Weathers, P. E. Walker, Calude Caperton, Jessie Porter, and others. During those same years Hogan established his reputation as an effective evangelist. In a single gospel meeting in Okmulgee, Oklahoma, in 1934, Hogan baptized 189 people, including five preachers from competing denominations. The numbers of baptisms continued to soar: 363 in 1934, 215 in 1935, and 359 in 1936. In 1938 Hogan moved to California, where he conducted evangelistic meetings throughout the state and established a storefront church at 48th Place and Compton Avenue in Los Angeles. This congregation evolved into the McKinley Avenue congregation in 1945 and into the Figueroa Church of Christ in 1953. In time, the Figueroa congregation grew to well over 1,000 members, and Hogan served as its minister until his death in 1997. This congregation was instrumental in spawning other congregations, including Myrtle Street in Long Beach, Southside in Los Angeles, Alondra Avenue in Compton, and Eastside in Los Angeles.

Hogan founded the Nigerian Foundation to assist Nigerian students to complete their education in the United States. He also established the Ethiopian Relief Fund, which for a number of years sent $1,500 monthly to Ethiopia to help feed the hungry. As an educator Hogan helped establish in 1950 Southwestern Christian College, a school for African American students in Terrell, TX, on whose board of directors he served for the rest of his life; and in 1971 the Los Angeles School of Preaching, housed at the Figueroa Church of Christ. In 1975, Pepperdine University conferred upon Hogan the degree of Doctor of Humane Letters, and in 1987 the same university recognized Hogan's life's work with the Life Achievement Award.

Bibliography

A. *Sermons by Hogan* (Austin, 1940); *Denominational Doctrines* (n.p., n.d.); articles in *CE*, 1940–1997.

B. Calvin Bowers, *A Rhetorical Analysis of the Preaching of R. N. Hogan*, M.A. thesis, Pepperdine University, 1972.

HOLMAN, SILENA MOORE (9 July 1850, TN–1915, Fayetteville, TN). *Career*: Teacher; religious writer on women's role; president, Tennessee Women's Christian Temperance Union, 1889–1915.

From 1888 to 1893, Silena Moore Holman distinguished herself as a powerful advocate of the rights of women and of an expanded role for women in the church. She presented her views especially in the *Gospel Advocate*, where editor David Lipscomb often provided a rebuttal. Silena's father died when she was only fourteen years of age, forcing her to provide for herself and her four younger siblings. She became a teacher, supported the family, and reacquired the family home, which had been sold for indebtedness. The fact that she met these responsibilities demonstrated to Silena what women could do and prompted her to advocate an active role for women in society and in the church. Her editorial career revolved around three major series of articles in the *Gospel Advocate*. Her first exchange with an *Advocate* staff writer, A. A. Bunner of Ohio, was soon over when David Lipscomb assumed the role as respondent to this "strong minded woman." Additional articles led to controversies in 1892 and 1896 and an exchange with F. W. Smith two years before Silena's death. Her first article on "The New Woman" gave Lipscomb "the blues." Silena reiterated what her grandmother had taught, that "a good wife earns her own living." She chastened those husbands who thought that they "supported" their wives and dared any man who questioned her to change places with his wife for just one week. She confidently affirmed that if such an experience did not make a husband better, it was simply because "there is no good" in him. A strong temperance advocate, Silena joined the Band of Good Templars and in 1889 she became president of the Tennessee Women's Christian Temperance Union and increased the membership from less than 200 to 4,000. In the eulogy at her death, T. B. Larimore called this effort of almost forty years "the mainspring of her life." On May 10, 1917, Silena Moore Holman's portrait was hung in the state capital building in Nashville—Silena was only the second woman to be so honored.

Bibliography

A. Articles in *GA*, 1888–1913.

B. T. B. Larimore, "Brother Larimore's Tribute to Mrs. Silena Moore Holman," *GA*, 57 (October 14, 1915), 1027–1028; C. Leonard Allen, *Distant Voices* (Abilene, TX, 1993), pp. 128–135.

HOLTON, ARTHUR REEVES (9 February 1891, Kosse, TX–6 August 1964, Abilene, TX). *Education*: Sabinal Christian College, Sabinal, TX, 1909; A.A., Thorp Spring Christian College, 1914; B. A., Howard Payne College; M.A., Texas Christian University; B.D., Southern Methodist University; LL.D., Abilene Christian University, 1964. *Career*: Preacher, Norman, OK, 1928–35; author; faculty, Abilene Christian College, 1917–18; faculty, School of Religion, University of Oklahoma, 1930s; president, Thorp Spring Christian College, 1921–28.

Arthur Reeves Holton was noted as an effective preacher, an educator, and a promotor of foreign missions. He began preaching in 1910 while attending Sabinal Christian College. During a long ministry he served churches in Oklahoma, Texas, Michigan, Tennessee, and Washington, D. C. He spoke often on lectureships at colleges related to Churches of Christ and in gospel meeting across the United States. His published articles and activities on behalf of foreign missions helped to generate an interest in missions among Churches of Christ in the 1950s. He wrote a weekly column in the *Christian Chronicle* entitled "The World View," and he spent four years working for Korea Christian College, Seoul, Korea. Holton wrote many historical articles about the heritage of Christian education in the Stone-Campbell tradition. He attended Thorp Spring Christian College (TSCC) and later served his alma mater as president from 1921 to 1928 at a time when the school enjoyed recognition as a solid junior college. As a senior college, however, Abilene Christian College gradually drew students away from TSCC. After Holton's resignation in 1928, the college remained at Thorp Spring only one year and finally ceased to exist after moving to Terrell, Texas. Holton taught at Abilene Christian University in 1917–1918 and in the School of Religion at the University of Oklahoma for four years in the 1930s. As preacher at Norman, Oklahoma (1928–1935), Holton planned one of the first meetings designed exclusively for women in Churches of Christ. It was at that meeting that Irene Young Mattox pioneered in teaching women's classes.

Bibliography

A. "As I Remember It," *FF*, 71 (August 31, 1954), 7.
B. *POT*, vol. 2 (Nashville, 1952), 205.

HOOTEN, JOHN H. (2 February 1779, VA–24 May 1852, Marshall Co., TN). *Career*: Pioneer preacher.

John Hooten was an important pioneer preacher in the reforming movement led by Barton W. Stone in Tennessee. Hooten first became a Methodist preacher and arranged the first Methodist circuit in Indiana Territory, but he disagreed with Methodist teachings and disliked the Methodist Discipline. As a result, he joined the movement led by Stone. Hooten went to Hickman County, Tennessee, about 1811; and during one eighteen-month period, he won about 700 converts to the Christian movement in that state. John and Mary (Reeves) Hooten had eleven children, four of whom became preachers: William Hooten, a well-known preacher in Tennessee; Elijah R. and Joseph Hooten, who were early Texas preachers, the latter being one of the most influential teachers and ministers in Hopkins County, Texas, for more than fifty years; and a fourth son for whom data are lacking. William Hooten was ordained in 1829; in addition to preaching in Tennessee, he also built up churches in Alabama, Illinois, Indiana, and Georgia.

Bibliography

B. J. R. Collinsworth, "Obituary Notices," *CM*, 5 (September 1852), 88; W. Jerome D. Spence and David L. Spence, *A History of Hickman County, Tennessee* (Easley, SC, n.d.), p. 138; "Obituary [for E. R. Hooten]," *GA*, 12 (December 8, 1870), 1134; W. Anderson, "The Old Soldier Mustered Out," *GA*, 34 (April 28, 1892), 265.

HOWARD, JOHN R. (20 September 1807, NC–28 February 1870, near Cobden, IL). *Career*: Minister; editor, *Christian Reformer*, 1836; editor, *Bible Advocate*, 1842–47.

John R. Howard was perhaps the leading advocate of the Campbell movement in West Tennessee for a period beginning about 1835. Howard radicalized Campbell's vision, however, and turned it in a decidedly sectarian direction. Howard was baptized by John R. McCall in 1833 and had read Campbell's writings for more than twenty years before he finally met Campbell at Paducah, Kentucky, in March 1859. He wrote that he was "carried away." Within a month Howard published in Benjamin Franklin's *American Christian Review* an article that extolled Campbell "with a peculiar feeling of *veneration*." He even suggested that Campbell "is the *subject of prophecy* we have no doubt" and, further, that Campbell and the movement he led were "preparing the church for entering upon the Millennium." In addition to building up a strong church in Paris, Tennessee, Howard edited the earliest Church of Christ–related publication in Tennessee, the *Christian Reformer*, which he produced from Paris, Tennessee, in 1836, and the more successful *Bible Advocate*, which he produced for five years, 1842 through 1847. During his last years Howard wrote extensively for Benjamin Franklin's *American Christian Review*.

Bibliography

A. *Christianity Illustrated* (Nashville, 1843); "The Beginning Corner: or, The Church of Christ Identified," in John F. Rowe and G. W. Rice (comp.), *Biographical Sketch and Writings of Elder Benjamin Franklin* (Cincinnati, 1880), pp. 206–228; "Alexander Campbell at Paducah, Kentucky," *ACR*, 2 (April 19, 1859), 61.

HUGHS, JAMES (1773–10 December 1834, IN). *Career*: Pioneer itinerant minister.

The ministry of James Hughs provides conclusive evidence that some of the preachers associated with Barton W. Stone practiced immersion for the forgiveness of sins by the first decade of the nineteenth century. Hughs preached in Kentucky, Ohio, and Illinois after moving to Sanganmon, Illinois, a few years before his death. Hughs, according to Stone, "fully preached the gospel of the Son of God, and insisted much on faith, repentance, and immersion for the remission of sins, and for the gift of the Holy Spirit." Stone indicates that James Hughs preached this message during most of his ministry. Stone's memoirs, written shortly before his death, state that "Br. J. Hughs, my fellow laborer, practiced upon this plan of baptizing till his death. . . . Into the spirit of the doctrine I was never fully led, until it was revived by bro. Alexander Campbell some years after." Stone cited James Hughs' practice of immersion for the forgiveness of sins as proof that this practice existed very early in the movement.

Bibliography

B. Barton W. Stone, *The Biography of Eld. Barton Warren Stone* (Cincinnati, 1847), 61; D. P. Henderson and John T. Jones, "A Discourse on the Death of Eld. Barton W. Stone," *CM*, 14 (February 1845), 313; Evan Williams Humphreys, *Memoirs of Deceased Christian Ministers* (Dayton, OH, 1880), 75; editor, "Obituary," *CM*, 9 (January 1835), 23.

I

IJAMS, ELVIN H. (30 May 1886, Florence, AL–13 July 1982, Memphis, TN). *Education*: B.S., State Normal School, Florence, AL, 1906; B.S., Peabody College for Teachers, Nashville, TN, 1918; M.A., Peabody College for Teachers, 1927; University of Southern California, 1931–32. *Career*: Professor, David Lipscomb University, 1923; dean, David Lipscomb University, 1932–34; president, David Lipscomb University, 1934–44; president, Georgia Christian Institute, Valdosta, GA, 1951–53; professor, Harding Graduate School of Religion, 1953–68.

Elvin H. Ijams served David Lipscomb University as professor, as dean, and finally as president. Arguably, however, he made his greatest contribution when he helped establish the Central Church of Christ in Nashville, Tennessee. The idea of the Central Church began when Ijams and A. M. Burton, founder and president of Life and Casualty Insurance Company, discussed the need for a practical demonstration of Christianity. These men established the Central Church of Christ in October 1925, with a purpose embodied in its slogan, "Service to humanity, glory to God." Burton purchased two run-down buildings in downtown Nashville, renovated them, and began church meetings there even during renovation. Ijams served as this congregation's minister for its first three years. Almost immediately this church offered daily worship, marriage and family counseling, local and radio evangelism, a home for young men wanting to be ministers or church workers, a home for 100 young single women who worked in Nashville, daily relief programs, clothing, hot meals, and free dental and medical care for the needy. Central grew rapidly, and its membership reached 1,200 by 1939.

At eighty-five Ijams was still serving as associate minister and the educational director at the Highland Street Church of Christ in Memphis. He died in 1982 at ninety-four years of age.

Bibliography

A. "History, Central Church of Christ, Nashville, Tenn.," 1974, typescript copy of ms housed at Highland Church of Christ, Memphis, TN; *Power to Survive and Surpass* (New York, [c. 1964]); *The Reality of God* (Nashville, 1978).

B. Paul Brown, "Ijams to Be Honored," *Nashville Christian News* (April 1972); *20th CC*, 41 (November 1, 1978), 25–27; *GA*, 124 (September 16, 1982), 557.

J

JONES, JOHN, JR. (d. 1835, Casey Co., KY). *Career*: Frontier preacher.

John Jones, Jr., the father of Sandy E. Jones, was the clerk of the South Kentucky Association of Separate Baptists in 1809 and 1810 and a prominent preacher in Southeast Kentucky until he, along with many other Separates, joined the Stone movement. In 1826 when Stone began the *Christian Messenger*, Jones was already identified as Elder John Jones of the South East Conference (a regional cooperation of churches) in Kentucky and was evangelizing with "brother Price, a Separate Baptist and James Lunsford, a Christian Preacher in Wayne County." Jones, Lunsford and other preachers were baptizing dozens. Jones indicates that 1819 was the earliest that the Separates began to unite with Stone. However, in 1817, the Hurricane Separate Baptist Church in Casey County, Kentucky, gave Collin McKinney and his wife letters of dismissal. McKinney had represented the Green River Church at the Separate association annual meeting as early as 1810. McKinney united with Stone about 1817 and subsequently (1824) became the first member of a restoration church to migrate to Texas. Baptist editor S. H. Ford, in a series on the "Current Reformation," ignores the large defection from the South Kentucky Separate association to the ranks of the Stone movement. However, he does note that the association had been prepared for the doctrines of the reformers long before Alexander Campbell was known in Kentucky. The key figures in that preparation had been Richard McNemar, John Dunlavy and Barton W. Stone. Ford observed that the doctrines of the Christians had been thickly scattered through Mercer, Boyle, and Garrard Counties, making it easy for Campbell's reformers to triumph. Still Ford claims that only Danville and Shawnee Run were lost by the Baptists in the South District. However, the fact that additional churches had already been won by Stone can be shown by comparing data in the South Kentucky Separate Baptist Association minutes and data given by John Jones, Jr., in the *Christian Mes-*

senger. For example, the McCormick church of Casey County was already in the Stone fold before Campbell's movement was introduced in that region. Jones' report of a conference of reformers in 1828 lists eight preachers and thirteen churches in eight counties in the Green River and Upper Cumberland section of Kentucky. By 1831 the number of those churches had grown to twenty-three. Little is known about Jones and his ministry besides the data contained in the *Messenger*, but this information indicates that he made an important contribution to the spread of the Stone movement in southern Kentucky. He was possibly the key person in the merger of the Stoneites and the Separate Baptists in southern Kentucky in the 1820s.

Bibliography

A. "Extract of a Letter from Elder John Jones," *CM*, 1 (October 1827), 275–276.
B. S. H. Ford, "Rise of the Current Reformation," *CRep* (November 1860); "Minutes of the Christian Conference in the South-east of Kentucky," *CM*, 3 (July 1829), 229–230.

JONES, SANDY E. (7 December 1804, Casey Co., KY–29 May 1878, Hustonville, KY). *Career*: Frontier preacher.

Sandy E. Jones was perhaps unexcelled as a proselyter for Churches of Christ during the middle years of the nineteenth century. He preached mainly in Tennessee, Kentucky, and Missouri, though he preached occasionally in Alabama and Mississippi as well. Basically uneducated and having read little but the Bible, he was nonetheless fond of controversy and he had remarkable success convincing individuals whom he had antagonized. An intelligent Methodist lady once told David Lipscomb that she believed Sandy Jones was much nearer right than anyone else, but she would be lost before she would unite with the Church of Christ, since Jones had abused and ridiculed her religion in the pulpit. In less than two months, however, Jones had baptized her. According to Lipscomb, "As a successful evangelist in making converts and building up churches" at the time, Jones had no equals. During 1842 he brought 1,400 into the Church of Christ. At Monticello, Kentucky in four days he took fifty confessions, forty-two in one day; and at Tompkinsville, Kentucky, he converted 147 in a ten-day gospel meeting. For fifteen years (1832–1847) he preached two sermons each day and three on Sundays and averaged 500 additions each year.

Bibliography

B. W. L. Williams, "Obituary—Jones," *AT*, 10 (June 21, 1878), 11.

JOURDAN, WILLIAM D. (31 January 1799, SC–21 January 1889, Plattsburg, MO). *Education*: Nashville Medical College, 1832. *Career*: Physician; minister, TN, 1823–27; KY, 1828–56; and MO, 1857–88.

William D. Jourdan typified the second generation of preachers in the movement inspired by Barton W. Stone. He was one of the first to accept and preach baptism for remission of sins, a doctrine he had learned from Dr. B. F. Hall in 1825–1826. As a young man W. D. Jourdan resided in Jackson County, Tennessee, where he first heard John and Philip Mulkey preach. He himself began to preach under the influence of Daniel Travis, who baptized him, and Andrew McBride, who took Jourdan into his home. When Jourdan affiliated himself with the Christian movement, his family refused further association with him for the remainder of his life. Jourdan acquired a reputation for opposing conventions, missionary societies, and any other extracongregational organization, and in this way helped to perpetuate the Stone emphasis on freedom and democratic church government for more than forty years beyond Stone's death. In 1857 Jourdan moved to Missouri, where he preached and wrote extensively until his death. In his later years he still reflected on Stone's understanding of the Holy Spirit in contrast to the view fostered by Alexander Campbell. In a letter to Carroll Kendrick in 1887, he called the "word only" view of the gift of the Spirit "the most distinctive heresy on vital piety that was ever taught! The very foundation of our hope and reliance is our spiritual relation and fellowship with our Master." Jourdan wrote for many periodicals, including the *Christian Messenger*, the *Gospel Advocate*, the *Christian Pioneer*, and the *American Christian Review*.

Bibliography

A. "Reminiscences," *CP*, 10 (April 28, 1870), 2; "Extracts from an Old Letter," *ACR*, 2d ser., 28 (June 4, 1885), 178.

B. "Conquests of the Gospel," *GA*, 2 (1836), 188; C. Kendrick, "California Letter," *CL*, 1 (July 12, 1887), 3; "Obituary of Dr. W. D. Jourdan," *OR*, 32 (February 28, 1889), 8.

K

KEEBLE, MARSHALL (7 December 1878, Rutherford Co., TN–20 April 1968, Nashville, TN). *Career*: Evangelist; president, Nashville Christian Institute.

Marshall Keeble, an African American evangelist, was the single most popular preacher, black or white, among Churches of Christ in the twentieth century. Keeble began preaching in 1897 and preached for seventy-one years until his death in 1968. No preacher among Churches of Christ filled as many auditoriums to overflowing. He spoke, for example, in both the 50,000-seat Dallas Convention Center and the Lubbock Municipal Auditorium where people were turned away for lack of seating. He often spoke to standing-room-only audiences at lectureship programs sponsored by colleges related to Churches of Christ, and he routinely held gospel meetings that resulted in over a hundred baptisms. He baptized well over 25,000 people and established at least 200 new congregations during the course of his long career. Keeble punctuated his sermons with the assertion, "The Bible's right!" One student of Keeble's preaching, Forrest N. Rhoads, has suggested that this emphasis was one of the key factors in his evangelistic success. In addition to his distinguished preaching career, Keeble also served as president of the Nashville Christian Institute, a school that served black youth in Nashville from 1941 to 1967.

Bibliography

A. B. C. Goodpasture, ed., *Biography and Sermons of Marshall Keeble* (Nashville, 1936); *From Mule Back to Super Jet with the Gospel* (Nashville, 1962).

B. Willie Cato, *His Hand and Heart: The Wit and Wisdom of Marshall Keeble* (Winona/Singapore/New Delhi, 1990); J. E. Choate, *Roll Jordan Roll: A Biography of Marshall Keeble* (Nashville, 1968); Forrest N. Rhoads, "A Study of the Sources of Marshall Keeble's Effectiveness as a Preacher," Ph.D. dissertation, Southern Illinois University, 1970.

KENDRICK, CARROLL (29 December 1815, Maury Co., TN–2 October 1891, Downey, CA). *Education*: Bacon College, Harrodsburg, KY; honorary M.A., Franklin College, 1851. *Career*: Physician; minister, AL, KY, TN, TX, CA; editor, *Ecclesiastic Reformer*, 1848–50.

Dr. Carroll Kendrick and his brilliant brother, Allen Kendrick, were products of the Stone movement in Alabama. Allen's life was shortened by sickness, but Carroll became a prominent figure in Churches of Christ, first in Kentucky while editing the *Ecclesiastic Reformer*, later in Texas as a self-supported missionary, and then as a beloved preacher in California during his final years. In 1851 Kendrick went to Texas as a missionary. He supported his family by farming and practicing medicine. Kendrick lived at Palestine, Salado, Bryan, and Bastrop, Texas, but he preached throughout the central and northern parts of the state. For roughly a quarter of a century, he was probably the leading evangelist among Churches of Christ in Texas, having been responsible for some 10,000 conversions from 1851 to 1877. Kendrick developed the camp meeting tradition for Churches of Christ in Texas, an evangelistic device patterned after the Stone-ite revivals in Tennessee and Alabama. In Bryan, Texas, in 1872, Kendrick organized the annual "Texas State Meeting," a meeting comparable in purpose and structure to the regional cooperative meetings that had been held as early as 1845 in every section of Texas. Since the churches that attended these meetings were autonomous in government, the meetings were for consultation only. After Kendrick had moved to California in 1886, however, progressives transformed the "Texas State Meeting" into the "Texas Christian Missionary Society." Kendrick returned to Texas from California to lend his support to those who opposed this development, although finally unsuccessfully. Kendrick wrote for many Christian periodicals. For two years in Kentucky, he edited the *Ecclesiastic Reformer* before becoming a missionary in Texas. After two failed attempts to publish a religious periodical in Texas, he edited a "Texas Department" in both the *Gospel Advocate* and the *American Christian Review*. Kendrick's mother was a sister of Daniel Parker, the noted Two-Seed-in-the-Spirit Predestinarian Baptist minister. Kendrick married Mary Wade Forbus near Stanford, Kentucky, in November 1841. Nine children were born to that union.

Bibliography

A. *Live Religious Issues of the Day: Rules and Principles for Bible Study* (Nashville, 1890; reprint, Kansas City, 1946).

B. Claudine M. Dollar, *Allied Families: Kendrick, Parker, Forgy, & Gage* (Blair, OK, 1983); Nimmo Goldston, "The Beginnings of the Disciples of Christ in East Texas," M.A. thesis, Texas Christian University, 1948; Kendrick Papers in Center for Restoration Studies, Abilene Christian University; Julian Kendrick, "Biographical Sketch—Carroll Kendrick," *GA*, 32 (December 10, 1891), 779; J. A. Williams, *Reminiscences* (Cincinnati, 1898).

KETCHERSIDE, WILLIAM CARL (10 May 1908, Cantwell, MO–14 May 1989, St. Louis, MO). *Education*: No formal education. *Career*: Minister; editor, *Mission Messenger*, 1939–75.

William Carl Ketcherside was raised in the Sommerite wing of Churches of Christ, advocated a narrow and exclusive understanding of the Christian faith early in his ministry, but in the mid-1950s he became an influential advocate of fellowship with Christians beyond the boundaries of Churches of Christ. Ketcherside edited and published the *Mission Messenger* from 1939 to 1975. For a little over a decade, it served to advocate Ketcherside's early sectarian position. In the 1950s, however, the *Mission Messenger* adopted a new emphasis on "brotherhood," "fellowship," and "grace." At the heart of his change was Ketcherside's discovery of the axiom, "Make nothing a test of fellowship which God has not made a condition of salvation." The rule was not new in Churches of Christ. In fact, people like "Raccoon" John Smith and later J. N. Armstrong had repeated this slogan often. What was new, however, was Ketcherside's far more ecumenical interpretation than what had been standard among Churches of Christ. In 1962 and 1963 Reuel Lemmons, editor of the *Firm Foundation* in Austin, Texas, attacked the Ketcherside unity plan, initiating a Lemmons and Ketcherside exchange in the *Firm Foundation* that totaled fourteen articles. Lemmon's attack "started a real prairie fire of interest" that caused circulation of the *Mission Messenger* to increase in Texas from "a mere handful" to the largest of any state followed by California, Indiana, Ohio, and Missouri. With his many loyal readers Ketcherside helped create a more ecumenical perspective, at least in some quarters of Churches of Christ.

Bibliography

A. *Pilgrimage of Joy: An Autobiography of Carl Ketcherside* (Joplin, MO, 1991); *Our Heritage of Unity and Fellowship* (New Braunfels, TX, 1992); periodical: *MM*, 1939–1975.

B. William L. Wilbanks, "The Contemporary Discussion concerning Fellowship in the Light of the Views of Thomas and Alexander Campbell," M.A. thesis, Abilene Christian University, 1966; Leroy Garrett, "Eulogy for W. Carl Ketcherside," *RR*, 31 (June 1989), 108–111.

KLINGMAN, GEORGE ADAM (3 September 1865, New Albany, IN–9 December 1939, San Angelo, TX). *Education*: College of the Bible, 1886–97; B.A., Transylvania University, 1994; M.A., Transylvania University, 1897; studied Hebrew at Southern Baptist Seminary, 1901; Ph.D., Carnegie University, Dover, Delaware, 1911; Hebrew language study, University of Chicago, summers, 1920 and 1921. *Career*: Minister, Portland Avenue Church of Christ, Louisville, KY, 1894–1902; Plum Street Church of Christ, Detroit, MI, 1904–07, 1909–1912; Cameron Avenue Church of Christ, Detroit, 1913–17; dean, Abilene Christian College, 1907–08; president, Potter Bible College, Bowling Green, KY, 1912–13; dean, A. M. Thornton Bible School, Abilene Christian College, 1917–23;

professor, Thorp Spring Christian College, TX, 1925–27, and Cincinnati Bible Seminary, 1933–34.

A pioneer in Church of Christ–related higher education, George Adam Klingman was probably the best-educated preacher in Churches of Christ during the first third of the twentieth century. Klingman preached in Louisville, Kentucky, from 1894 until 1902, followed by a ministry with the Plum Street Church of Christ in Detroit, Michigan from 1904 to 1907 and again from 1909 to 1912. A popular lecturer, he delivered the first series of special lectures at the newly established Childers Classical Institute in Abilene, Texas (now Abilene Christian University), in 1907. When the annual Bible Lectures were permanently established at Abilene Christian College in 1918, Klingman was the first speaker and the principle speaker in 1919 when he delivered five lectures on biblical criticism, evangelism, and cooperation of small churches. From 1917 until 1923, he served as dean of the A. M. Thornton Bible School at Abilene Christian College. He preached in Toronto, Canada, from 1923 until fall 1925, when he joined the faculty of Thorp Spring Christian College, which advertised him as "One of the Greatest Bible Teachers in the South." In 1933–34, he concluded his teaching career at Cincinnati Bible Seminary, an institution affiliated with the Christian Church.

Bibliography

A. *Church History for Busy People* (Cincinnati, 1909); co-author with Jesse P. Sewell, *The Bible Outlined in a Hundred Easy Lessons* (Cincinnati, 1920); co-author with Jesse P. Sewell, *Class Notes on the Shorter Epistles* (Abilene, TX, n.d.).

B. James F. Cox, "G. A. Klingman," *GA*, 82 (January 11, 1940), 41; Jim Mankin, "A Little Man with a Great Brain: the Story of George A. Klingman," *Disc*, 55 (Spring 1995), 25–31.

KURFEES, MARSHALL CLEMENT (31 January 1856, near Mocksville, NC–17 February 1931, Louisville, KY). *Education*: College of the Bible, University of Kentucky, 1881. *Career*: Minister; debater; author; associate editor, *Gospel Advocate*, 1908–24.

Marshall Clement Kurfees served as associate editor of the *Gospel Advocate* for sixteen years, from 1908 to 1924, and preached for a single congregation in Louisville, Kentucky—the Campbell Street Church of Christ—for forty-five years, from 1886 to 1931. Appreciated for the quality of his scholarship, he was especially known for his research and writing on the topic of instrumental music. Kurfees was also a highly respected debater, holding discussions with representatives of at least six different Christian denominations: Quakers, Lutherans, Mormons, Episcopalians, Methodists, and Baptists. Kurfees began preaching in Graves County, Kentucky, in 1875; during his early ministry he preached alternately in Kentucky, Illinois, and North Carolina. His forty-five-year tenure in

Louisville, Kentucky, is one of the longest among preachers of Churches of Christ.

Bibliography

A. *Instrumental Music in the Worship, or, The Greek Verb Psallo Philologically and Historically Examined* (Nashville, 1911); *Review of O. E. Payne's Book on "Psallo"* (Nashville, 1927).

B. H. Leo Boles, *Biographical Sketches of Gospel Preachers* (Nashville, 1932), pp. 430–434; F. D. Srygley, *Biographies and Sermons* (reprint Nashville, 1961), 374–381.

L

LARD, MOSES EASTERLY (29 October 1818, near Shelbyville, TN–17 June 1880, Lexington, KY). *Education*: A. B., Bethany College, 1848. *Career*: Minister; writer; debater; editor, *Lard's Quarterly*, 1863–68; editor-in-chief, *Apostolic Times*, 1869–72, Lexington, KY.

Moses Easterly Lard gained fame as a polemicist on behalf of Alexander Campbell when, in 1857, he issued a formal, book-length response to Jeremiah Jeter's *Campbellism Examined*. He also gained fame as one of the movement's most influential editors, editing *Lard's Quarterly* from 1863 to 1867, and the *Apostolic Times* from 1869 to 1872. His *Commentary on Romans*, published in 1875, influenced Churches of Christ well into the twentieth century. Lard also distinguished himself as a powerful preacher. During the mid- to late nineteenth century, Lard was perhaps the most unyielding opponent of instrumental music in the worship. In 1879, only a year before his death, Lard issued a small pamphlet setting forth the view that it is not possible to affirm with certainty the theory of endless punishment for those who die impenitent. He was promptly assailed by members of Churches of Christ for being a Universalist. Many even advocated that fellowship should be withdrawn from him for holding and publishing his opinion. A perusal of Lard's *Commentary on Romans* reveals a level of scholarship and original thinking not seen before in Churches of Christ. Following publication of that book in 1875, Lard increasingly manifested "a softened and mellowed spirit," a change attributable perhaps to the doctrine of grace he encountered in *Romans*.

Bibliography

A. *Review of Campbellism Examined* (1857); *A Commentary on Romans* (Lexington, 1875); *Do the Scriptures Teach the Endlessness of Future Punishment?* (Lexington, 1879); periodicals: *LQ*, vols. 1–5, 1863–1867; *AT*, vols. 1–4, 1869–1872.

B. Frederick D. Kershner, "Stars," *CS* (July 6, 1940), 645; W. L. Lard, "A Visit to the Scene of 'My First Meeting,' " *C-E* (January 5, 1905), 24; Kenneth L. Van Deusen, *Moses Lard, That Prince of Preachers* (Joplin, MO, 1987); Charles A. Day, "Moses E. Lard: A Master Builder of the Reformation of the Nineteenth Century," B.D. thesis, Lexington Theological Seminary, 1930.

LARIMORE, THEOPHILUS BROWN (10 July 1843, Jefferson Co., TN–18 March 1929, Santa Ana, CA). *Education*: An academy in East Tennessee; Franklin College. *Career*: Evangelist; teacher; president, Mars Hill Academy.

Although Theophilus Brown Larimore was the premier evangelist among Churches of Christ for many years, his style of preaching was hardly typical for preachers in that tradition. Larimore refused to debate and stood aloof from every partisan position or issue including instrumental music. David Lipscomb and James A. Harding once invited him to lecture at the Nashville Bible School. When Harding asked him to declare himself on the controversial music question, Larimore responded that he was on the Lord's side, an answer that failed to satisfy Harding. Harding replaced him with T. W. Brents. Lacking any interest in church politics, Larimore also refused to attend conventions or preachers' meetings. Instead he devoted his life to preaching. For years he preached twice daily and three times every Sunday. His conciliatory posture and commitment to preaching were reminiscent of Barton W. Stone's "spiritual" preacher who traveled through the world weeping over sinners and preaching the gospel. F. D. Srygley pictured Larimore as a young evangelist, "walking long distances over the hills of Alabama, and preaching the plain gospel to crowds of anxious hearers in school-houses, old barns, vacant store-rooms, and under the trees." A gospel meeting Larimore held in Sherman, Texas, in 1894 was probably the most famous ever held by anyone among Churches of Christ. The meeting was "protracted" for five months, during which time Larimore preached 333 sermons.

Young Theophilus as a plowboy earned four dollars a month, enough for tuition to attend an academy in East Tennessee. After the family moved to Kentucky, he was baptized in 1864 and during the fall enrolled in Franklin College, Tolbert Fanning's school at Nashville, Tennessee. He started preaching in 1866. On January 1, 1870, Larimore established a boarding school, the famous Mars Hill Academy, near Florence, Alabama, where many young men—"Larimore's Boys," as they were called—were taught and inspired to preach.

Bibliography

A. F. D. Srygley, ed., *Letters and Sermons of T. B. Larimore*, 3 vols. (Nashville, 1900, 1904, 1910); Emma Page, ed., *Letters and Sermons of T. B. Larimore* (Nashville, 1904); Emma Page Larimore, ed., *Life, Letters, and Sermons* (Nashville, 1931); T. B. Larimore, "How to . . . Close a Protracted Meeting," *GA*, 57 (May 27, 1915), 506.

B. Douglas Foster, *As Good as the Best: A Sketch of the Life of Theophilus Brown*

Larimore (Nashville, 1984); Douglas Foster, *Will the Cycle be Unbroken?* (Abilene, 1994), 147–159; F. D. Srygley, *Smiles and Tears, or Larimore and His Boys* (Nashville, 1889); D. L., "Criticism of Larimore," *GA*, 48 (April 13, 1906), 233; J. W. Jackson, "They Couldn't Stand It," *FF*, 7 (January 29, 1891), 5–6; F. D. Srygley, "From the Papers," *GA*, 32 (February 19, 1890), 113; J. M. Powell, "Theophilus Brown Larimore, Gospel Preacher," M.A. thesis, Harding Graduate School of Religion, 1960; Douglas Foster, "The Struggle for Unity during the Period of Division of the Restoration Movement: 1875–1900," Ph.D. dissertation, Vanderbilt University, 1987; Silena Holman, "T. B. Larimore" in John T. Brown, ed., *Churches of Christ* (Louisville, 1904), 475–476.

LEMERT, MARINDA R. (4 March 1811, OH–29 September 1891, Seattle, WA). *Career*: Religious writer.

Marinda R. Lemert was one of the strongest writers of the late nineteenth century who advocated a more prominent role for women in the church. Shortly after her first submission to the *American Christian Review*, she drew "the fire of the knights of the quill," including J. A. Meng of Missouri, J. T. Showalter of Virginia, and Daniel Sommer of Indiana, all of whose responses were dogmatic and warlike. There were others, however, including well-known preachers like Nathan J. Mitchell, who were won by her good-spirited and forceful arguments. A. Burns of Ohio called her analysis of 1 Corinthians 11 "undoubtedly invulnerable." If not, Burns said, "1 Corinthians 11 and 14 are hopelessly in antagonism." Following the death of her husband in 1852, Lemert devoted most of her time to church work and to writing. The good spirit manifested in her writings excelled that of most of her opponents and brought numerous commendations, including commendations from John F. Rowe, editor of the *American Christian Review* and later of the *Christian Leader*. R. B. Neal, field editor of the *Gospel Advocate*, summarized the feeling of many: "This aged handmaiden of the Lord has won my highest regard by her pen work. . . . She is indeed and in truth without a peer among the sisters of this Restoration as a Polemic." Evangelism was always the chief interest of Lemert's life and writing, but she was also critical of the lack of support for missions among society opponents. She raised the ire of editor John F. Rowe of the *American Christian Review*, when she called them "anti-missionary." The *Review* rejected her charges, then denied her space to respond. Lemert resorted to the columns of the *Christian Standard* with a "protest." A few months before her death, seemingly reconciled with editor John F. Rowe, Lemert submitted her last article for the *Christian Leader*, a new paper started by Rowe after he was forced out as editor of the *Review*. She moved to Seattle, Washington, a few months before her death when offered a place of rest by a friend.

Bibliography

A. "Experience and Observation," *ACR*, 22 (May 27, 1879), 169; "A Word by M. R. Lemert," *CL*, 5 (February 17, 1891), 6; "Hebron Items," *ACR*, 28 (April 8, 1885),

113; "Rights of Women," *ACR*, 22 (August 12, 1879), 257; "Women in the Church," *ACR*, 22 (August 19, 1879), 265; "A Few Words of Explanation to the Readers of the 'Review,' " *ACR*, 22 (September 16, 1879), 297; "Review of 'Strictures,' " *ACR*, 22 (September 23, 1879), 309; her response to Daniel Sommer: "Women," *ACR*, 22 (November 4, 1879), 353; a series of twelve articles entitled, "To the Sisterhood," *ACR*, 23 (February–August, 1880); "Universal Equality of the Sexes in Christ," *CS*, 23 (June 16, 1888), 374.

B. R. B. Neal, "Worker Chips," *GA*, 30 (April 4, 1888), 2; R. H. Moss, "Lemert," *CS*, 26 (October 24, 1891), 903; Edward T. Stevens, "A Memorial," *CL*, 5 (November 10, 1891), 6; E. T. Stevens, "Kansas Echoes," *CL*, 5 (June 2, 1891), 5.

LEMMONS, REUEL GORDON (8 July 1912, Pocahontas, AR–25 January 1989, Austin, TX). *Education*: B.A., Abilene Christian College, 1935. *Career*: Minister, Tipton, OK; Cleburne and Austin, TX; editor, *Firm Foundation*, 1955–83; editor, *Image Magazine*, 1985–89; editor, *Action*, 1984–1989.

After preaching for his home church in Tipton, Oklahoma, for seven years and for the influential Central Church of Christ in Cleburne, Texas, Reuel Gordon Lemmons became editor of the *Firm Foundation*, Austin, Texas, and served in that capacity from 1955 to 1983. His weekly editorials in the *Firm Foundation* became probably the most widely read single column among the Churches of Christ for most of those years. He also edited *Action*, a periodical published in the interest of worldwide Bible study, and for five years, 1985–1989, he edited *Image Magazine*. In 1969 Abilene Christian University recognized Lemmons as an outstanding alumnus and in 1974 awarded him an honorary doctorate. He also served on the board of trustees of both Abilene Christian University and Pepperdine University. A minister of the Church of Christ for fifty-three years, Lemmons preached on every continent and in seventy-nine countries. He also preached over a powerful African radio station that reached an estimated 1,800,000 people every week for eight years. One of his principle interests was the expansion of Churches of Christ in Nigeria, South Africa, and Latin America. In 1962 his missionary interest prompted him to establish in 1962 the Pan American Lectures, designed to encourage mission outreach in Latin America, a program he directed for twenty years. In 1976 he started a similar lectureship in Europe. Throughout his editorial career Lemmons sought to be a voice of moderation. He routinely warned against sectarianism on the right and liberalism on the left.

Bibliography

A. *Abundant Living* (Delight, AR, 1950); *The King and His Kingdom* (Abilene, TX, 1968); coeditor, *New Smith's Bible Dictionary* (Garden City, NJ, 1966); "The Seed of Sectarianism," *FF*, 76 (March 3, 1959), 130; editorials, *FF*, 75 (February 11, 1958), 82, and *FF*, 76 (March 3, 1959), 130; periodicals: *FF*, 1955–1983; *Image*, 1985–1989; *Action*, 1984–1989.

B. *Image* (March 1989); *Action* (March 1989); *ACU Today* (1st Qr 1989); *CC* (February

1989); Edwin F. White, *From the Banks of Hubbell Creek: The Spiritual Legacy of Reuel Lemmons* (Glendale, AZ, 2000).

LIPSCOMB, DAVID (21 January 1831, TN–11 November 1917, Nashville, TN). *Education*: Franklin College, 1848. *Career*: Teacher and cofounder, Nashville Bible School; minister; writer; editor, *Gospel Advocate*, 1866–1917.

Through his editing of the *Gospel Advocate* from 1866 through 1917, and through his work with the Nashville Bible School, which he helped establish in 1891, David Lipscomb wielded the greatest influence on the Churches of Christ from 1866 through much of the twentieth century. Tolbert Fanning, Lipscomb's mentor, saw the potential in Lipscomb and carefully tutored him for future leadership. After 1866 Fanning trusted Lipscomb to edit the *Advocate*, the journal Fanning had founded in 1855. Following the Civil War, officials of the Kentucky State Missionary Society notified Lipscomb and Fanning that if they could not support society work, the *Advocate* could expect their persistent opposition to its circulation, a threat faithfully carried out. In 1892 liberal forces attempted to gain control of the *Advocate* by purchasing controlling interest. Failing in these efforts, Lipscomb's progressive opponents surrounded the *Advocate* with rival publications in several states. The *Christian-Evangelist* announced that the *Gospel Advocate* was "slowly marching into the jaws of death." Yet the *Advocate* has continued as the only surviving pre–Civil War restoration periodical.

Lipscomb's teaching contained what to him was "the seed truth, from which all other truth in the universe, spiritual or material, springs." He explained the central idea of his theology: "There is one Lord God, the Creator and Ruler of the universe, . . . that he gives laws to, and regulates all the forces of, the universe." Somewhere Lipscomb picked up an apocalyptic theology of history. The apocalyptic worldviews of Lipscomb and Barton W. Stone were strikingly similar and were at least in part the result of Tolbert Fanning's early connection with the Stone movement and his subsequent influence on Lipscomb. Lipscomb's viewpoint was no romanticized or speculative effort to dogmatize the apocalyptic vision into dispensational premillennialism. Like Tolbert Fanning, he refused to speculate on eschatology. Lipscomb believed that the world became the realm of Satan's rule through human governments. Restoration to Lipscomb consisted in man's return to his primitive allegiance to God. Christians must therefore limit their activities to those institutions authorized by God. All other institutions belong to the world and were opposed to God. His apocalyptic vision also prompted Lipscomb to embrace a pacifist posture toward military service. Not surprisingly, then, Lipscomb called the missionary society "treason" and those who fostered human societies "rebels." Lipscomb argued that "God will reign and rule, and root out and destroy, until he hath put down all rule and authority and power, and his will is done on earth as it is in heaven."

Lipscomb had one objective: to be right. J. M. Barnes said, "David Lipscomb never counts the cost of an article when he pens it. There is only one question—is it right?" Lipscomb wrote that he "cared not what Lexington, or Cincinnati, or Bethany or all combined think" and admitted that he was "greatly lacking in reverence for men and their opinions, whether great or small. If this be a defect it is a great one—and it was born in our very blood and bones—and we fear wholly incurable. So pity us, but bear with us in our weakness." Lipscomb's concern to please God alone prompted his rejection of sectarianism. "If a man is baptized to get into the Baptist church or the church of Christ without reference to obeying Christ," he wrote, "it is no baptism." For this reason he was willing to accept into the Churches of Christ Baptists who had been immersed in order to obey God. His position on this question brought him into a long and bitter conflict with Austin McGary, editor of Texas' *Firm Foundation*.

Bibliography

A. "Babylon," *GA*, 23 (June 2, 1881), 340; "A Monstrous Dogma," *GA* (November 24, 1881), 740f; "Thirty Years Work," *GA*, 38 (January 2, 1896), 4–5; *Christian Unity: How Promoted, How Destroyed* (Nashville, 1890); *Civil Government* (Nashville, 1889; reprint, 1913); *Commentary on the Acts of the Apostles* (Nashville, 1896); *Commentary on the New Testament Epistles*, ed. by J. W. Shepherd (Nashville, 1933–58); *Queries and Answers*, ed. by J. W. Shepherd (Cincinnati, 1918); *Questions Answered, by Lipscomb and Sewell*, ed. by M. C. Kurfees (Nashville, 1921); *Salvation from Sin*, ed. by J. W. Shepherd (Nashville, 1913).

B. Price Billingsley, "David Lipscomb and His New Book," *GA*, 55 (April 3, 1913), 315; Earl I. West, *The Life and Times of David Lipscomb* (Henderson, TN, 1954); Tom Holland, "David Lipscomb: An Example of Ethical Power in Preaching," M.A. thesis, Abilene Christian University, 1964; Robert Hooper, *Crying in the Wilderness: A Biography of David Lipscomb* (Nashville, 1979).

LYNN, BENJAMIN (1750, PA–1814, near Huntsville, AL). *Career*: Frontier scout and preacher.

Benjamin Lynn was a pioneer preacher in the movement led by Barton W. Stone. Prior to that, however, Benjamin and his brother William were contemporaries with Daniel Boone, serving as explorers, hunters, and scouts for Lewis and Clark until 1780, when Benjamin became a frontier minister, one of the earliest Baptist ministers in Kentucky and a leader of the Separate Baptists. Under the leadership of three preachers—John Larue, John Garrard, and Benjamin Lynn—Separate Baptists from Winchester, Virginia, passed through the wilderness and came down the Ohio River in 1781, then landed at a site called Beargrass at the mouth of the Salt River. They settled on a knoll where they made a station or fort. On that knoll Benjamin Lynn preached the first sermon ever uttered in this wilderness region, and here, No Linn Creek became the location of the first church—a Separate Baptist church—in 1782. The congregation was composed of thirteen members and met at Phillips' Fort about a quarter mile from the knoll. When the Separates and Regular Baptists united in

Kentucky in 1803, Lynn became associated with the Stone movement. From 1790 until about 1803, Lynn lived in Green County, Kentucky, where he was active as a minister in the Green River country and where he performed numerous marriages, established churches, and actively participated in the Green River Baptist Association. Lynn joined Lewis Byram in ordaining Samuel Boyd at the Christian Church on Little Barren River in July 1809. Lynn's daughter married Marshall D'Spain, and they became the parents of Benjamin Lynn D'Spain, early Alabama, Tennessee, and Texas preacher. A daughter, Hettie D'Spain, married Joseph Addison Clark, who founded Add-Ran College, Thorp Spring, Texas, in 1873. Lynn's biographer briefly describes his last years when he lived in Madison County, Alabama. Here Lynn "organized a Christian Church near Huntsville, and it was in the churchyard there that he was buried in December, 1814, in the sixty-fifth year of his age. His wife had died in the preceding May."

Bibliography

B. G. W. and Helen P. Beattie, "Pioneers Linns of Kentucky, pt. 2—Benjamin Linn—Hunter, Explorer, Preacher," *Filson Club History Quarterly*, 20 (1946), 156; reprinted in *Genealogies of Kentucky Families* (Baltimore, 1981), 694–718.

M

McBRIDE, THOMAS CRAWFORD (25 July 1777, VA–29 April 1857, Yamhill Co., OR). *Career*: Frontier preacher.

Thomas McBride, a Tennessee contemporary of John Mulkey, united with the Mulkeys and with Barton W. Stone in 1810. McBride left the Baptist Church, since he rejected the practice of closed communion. Of those who agreed with McBride, Abner Hill and Corder Stone began preaching under the tutelage of McBride and the Mulkeys in Tennessee. Hill continued a long ministry in Alabama and Texas from 1836 to 1873. He described this seed time in the Cumberland as "a great revival and in-gathering" when many preachers "arose among us, namely, Jos. McBride, Isaac McBride, Andrew McBride, brothers to Thos. McBride, the old preacher." T. M. Allen looked upon Thomas McBride as the Barton Stone of Missouri. Allen wrote that in "Howard County there are 7 churches of Christ—some of them were planted, gathered, & fed by Bro. McBride—others have reformed from the Baptist ranks." T. P. Haley wrote that during his childhood, no name was more familiar in the churches of Missouri than that of Thomas McBride." Haley added that he "must have been a man of rare powers to impress himself as he did upon all the preachers and churches in an early day."

Bibliography

A. "Extract of a Letter," *ACR*, 10 (April 30, 1867), 139.

B. *C-E*, 5 (November 1854), 429; Abner Hill, "An Autobiography of Abner Hill, Pioneer Preacher of Tennessee, Alabama, and Texas" (c. 1861), typescript housed in Center for Restoration Studies, Abilene Christian University, 15–16; T. M. Allen to John A. Gano, Two Mile Prairie, Boon Co., Mo. (February 8, 1837); *AT*, 9 (April 5, 1877), 213; T. P. Haley, *Historical and Biographical Sketches of the Early Churches and Pioneer Preachers of the Christian Church in Missouri* (Kansas City, 1888), p. 145; "Obituary Notices," *MH*, 4th ser., 7 (October 1857), 599–

600; Jerry Rushford, *Christians on the Oregon Trail* (Joplin, 1998), pp. 86–87, 239–240.

McCALEB, JOHN MOODY (25 September 1861, Hickman Co., TN–7 November 1953, Los Angeles, CA). *Education*: College of the Bible, 1888–91. *Career*: Minister; missionary to Japan, 1892–1941.

John Moody McCaleb was the first career missionary among Churches of Christ, serving in Japan from March 1892 to 1941. During this time his name became synonymous with missions among the Churches of Christ. In fact, the mission literature in this tradition during much of this period consisted almost solely of McCaleb's writings. One of his greatest contributions was to encourage other workers to go to Japan, both men and women. The work of some of those people endured, especially that of Sarah Andrews. McCaleb's work also provided an impetus for missions in Africa, India, and China, especially following World War I. McCaleb's work was moderately successful when measured by the tangible results that survived World War II.

Bibliography

A. *Christ, the Light of the World* (Nashville, 1911); *From Idols to God; or, My Religious Experience* (Cincinnati, 1907); *Health and Happiness* (Austin, 1942); *Once Traveled Roads* (Nashville, 1934); *On the Trail of the Missionaries* (Nashville, 1930).

B. Gary Turner, "Pioneer to Japan: A Biography of J. M. McCaleb," M.A. thesis, Abilene Christian University, 1972.

McGARVEY, JOHN WILLIAM (1 March 1829, Hopkinsville, KY–6 October 1911, Lexington, KY). *Education*: B.A., Bethany College, 1850. *Career*: Scholar, preacher, writer.

John William McGarvey distinguished himself as an outstanding biblical scholar—and clearly the best biblical scholar in the Stone-Lipscomb tradition—in the late nineteenth century: Even the *Times* of London acclaimed him as "in all probability, . . . the ripest Bible scholar on earth." A voice of conservatism, McGarvey devoted his career to Christian evidences and to combating what he viewed as destructive biblical criticism. Because of these efforts members of Churches of Christ revered him, even though his position on missionary societies placed him in that wing of the Stone-Campbell movement that would soon be known exclusively as Disciples of Christ. In addition, he authored a column on biblical criticism that appeared in the *Christian Standard*, a progressive journal that had been launched to counteract the influence of the conservative Church of Christ editor Benjamin Franklin and his *American Christian Review*. McGarvey and David Lipscomb were friends but disagreed on several topics, mostly on the validity of missionary societies and Bible colleges. Lipscomb invited McGarvey to write for the *Gospel Advocate*, but the Kentucky preacher never did so. Still, Lipscomb acknowledged that McGarvey was "seldom wrong." McGarvey considered *The Authorship of the Book of Deuteronomy*, a vindication of the Mosaic authorship of the Pentateuch, as his most important work. From 1865 through 1911, he taught biblical studies at the College of the Bible in Lexington, Kentucky, and served as that institution's president from 1895 through 1911.

Bibliography

A. *The Authorship of the Book of Deuteronomy* (Cincinnati, 1902); *Evidences of Christianity*, 2 vols. (Louisville, 1886–1891); *Lands of the Bible* (Cincinnati, 1880[?]); *The Autobiography of J. W. McGarvey* (Lexington, 1960); *The Fourfold Gospel* (Cincinnati, 1914); coauthor with Philip Y. Pendleton, *Thessalonians, Corinthians, Galatians and Romans* (Cincinnati, 1916).

B. W. C. Morro, *Brother McGarvey* (St. Louis, 1940); Dwight E. Stevenson, *Lexington Theological Seminary, 1865–1965* (St. Louis, 1964), pp. 11–36.

McGARY, AUSTIN (6 February 1846, Huntsville, TX–15 June 1928, Houston, TX). *Education*: A school operated by three Sweeney brothers, Huntsville, TX; McKenzie Institute, Clarksville, TX. *Career*: Preacher; frontier lawman; editor, *Firm Foundation*, 1884–1903.

After moving to Austin, Texas, in 1883, Austin McGary established the *Firm Foundation* in September 1884 in order "to oppose everything in the work and worship of the church, for which there was not a command or an apostolic example or a necessary scriptural inference." McGary wrote mostly on controversial issues with a wit and style seldom equaled in Churches of Christ, and his influence spread quickly among preachers in that tradition, especially in Texas. His "hobby" became the rebaptism issue originally fostered by an old preacher named William McIntire of Dallas County, Texas, who had divided churches in Illinois before he came to Texas. McGary contended that someone who wished to join Churches of Christ but had been immersed in some other tradition (e.g., Baptists) would have to be reimmersed for the proper reason, that is, for the forgiveness of sins. This issue drove a wedge between McGary, editor of the *Firm Foundation* in Texas, and David Lipscomb, editor of the *Gospel Advocate* in Tennessee. When more progressive congregations of Churches of Christ received converts from other churches merely by giving them the right hand of fellowship, McGary condemned this practice as nothing more than "shaking them in." Thomas R. Burnett, editor of the *Christian Messenger* and an equally brilliant writer, was McGary's chief Texas opponent. The clashes between these two racy editors provided readers with some of the wittiest and sharpest exchanges produced in the periodical literature of the Churches of Christ. Austin McGary's father, Isaac McGary, fought at San Jacinto and guarded the captured Mexican General Santa Anna. McGary spent his boyhood in Huntsville, Texas, and received an early education under three preachers of the Church of Christ: Benton, Thomas, and Basil Sweeney. He also attended McKenzie Institute, a Methodist school at Clarksville, Texas. McGary served in the "Huntsville Grays," a unit of the Confederate army, with Sam Houston, Jr. Twice elected sheriff of Madison County, he resigned in his second term to become a conveying agent for the state penitentiary. In two years of conveying condemned prisoners and desperadoes he never lost a man. McGary became a member of the Church of Christ in 188l. After relinquishing control of the *Firm Foundation* in 1903, he moved to California and then to Oregon before returning to Texas. He died on June 15, 1928, in Houston at the age of eighty-two. In *The Lone Star Preacher* John W. Thomason created a fictitious character named Praxiteles Swan supposedly based on tales Thompson had heard about Austin McGary.

Bibliography

A. Periodical: *FF*, 1884–1903.

B. West, Earl Irvin, *The Search for the Ancient Order*, vol. 2 (Indianapolis, 1950), pp. 397–408; Lane Cubstead, "The Firm Foundation, 1884–1957: The History of a Pioneer Religious Journal and Its Editors," M. Journ. thesis, University of Texas at Austin, 1957, pp. 23–48; *FF*, 5 (September 5, 1889), 4.

McKINNEY, COLLIN (17 April 1766, NJ–9 September 1861, Anna, TX). *Career*: Statesman, colonist, Christian patriarch for Texas Churches of Christ.

Collin McKinney, a leader among Kentucky Separate Baptists until the early 1820s, united with the Christian movement led by Barton W. Stone sometime before 1824. But he also distinguished himself as a significant civic leader in Texas, where he settled in 1824 at Pecan Point, north of the present city of Texarkana. McKinney lived under eight governments and participated in forming the last two, the Republic of Texas and the State of Texas. He was the oldest signer of the Texas "Declaration of Independence" and a member of the Constitutional Convention of the Republic of Texas in 1836. He served several terms in the Senate of the Republic and then in the Texas state Senate after statehood in 1845. In addition, McKinney made eleven trips to Kentucky and Tennessee to bring colonists to North Texas, and many families migrated there under his leadership. Many of these were members of the Stone movement and looked to Collin McKinney as a civic and Christian patriarch. Before arriving in Texas, McKinney had held membership in the Hurricane Creek Separate Baptist church in Lincoln County, Kentucky, until 1817 and had been selected as a delegate many times to the South Kentucky Association of Separate Baptists. From 1817 until 1824 he managed the estate of George Campbell of Tennessee while Campbell served as ambassador to Russia. His union with the Stone movement in 1824 may be the result of the influence of Amy Moore, his first wife, whose family and relatives were early members of Churches of Christ in Maury and Marshall Counties in Tennessee. In Texas, besides serving the church in his first home at Pecan Point, he was later an elder in churches at Hickman's Prairie on Red River (established in 1842) and at old Mantua in Collin County in 1846. McKinney was probably the best-known member of the Stone movement in

Texas from the time he settled in Texas until his death. His tombstone in the Van Alstyne, Texas, Cemetery reads: "He was one of natures noble men, an ardent patriot and a true Christian." His close friend and fellow Christian, an early Kentucky and Texas preacher, Benjamin F. Hall, is buried nearby on the McKinney plot.

Bibliography

B. Clara McKinney Reddell, "McKinney Clan," typescript copy; Clara McKinney Reddell, "History: McKinney and Collin County," two-page printed document (McKinney, TX, 1986).

McMILLAN, EDWARD WASHINGTON (27 September 1889, New Baden, TX–15 February 1991, Dallas, TX). *Education*: Gunter Bible College, 1911–17; Austin College; B.A., Baylor University, 1920; M.A., Baylor University, 1921; and coursework for doctorate, Southwestern Baptist Theological Seminary. *Career*: Minister, Waco, TX, 1919–21; Cleburne, TX, 1921–28; College Church of Christ, Abilene, TX, 1928–34; Central Church of Christ, Nashville, 1935–41; Union Avenue Church of Christ, Memphis, 1941–47; Northside Church of Christ, Santa Ana, CA, 1958–61 and 1963–64; professor, Department of Bible, Abilene Christian University, 1928–35, chair of department, 1929–35; founding president, Ibaraki Christian College, Japan, 1948–52; president, Southern Bible Institute (later Southwestern Christian College), Terrell, TX, 1950–53; editor, the *Christian Leader*, 1939–40; author of numerous books and articles.

A minister, educator, author, and editor for more than eighty years, Edward Washington McMillan was born in New Baden, Texas, on September 27, 1889. He was baptized in 1903 and preached his first sermon at Ballinger, Texas, in 1910. Nurtured in the non–Sunday school wing of Churches of Christ, he began his formal education for ministry in 1911 at Gunter Bible College. When he appeared on the Abilene Christian University Lectureship program in 1989, he was in his ninety-ninth year and had spoken on that program in each of seven decades.

A promising baseball pitcher, McMillan left school after the fifth grade and did not return until he was twenty-one. He completed high school at Gunter Bible College, then attended Austin College in Sherman, Texas, before earning his B.A. and M.A. degrees from Baylor University in 1920 and 1921, respectively. Later he completed coursework for a doctorate at Southwestern Baptist Theological Seminary in Fort Worth. Early in his career McMillan ministered to congregations of Churches of Christ in Waco, Cleburne, and Fort Worth, Texas. From 1928 to 1934 he served as minister of the College Church of Christ in Abilene, Texas, and from 1929 to 1935 he chaired the Bible Department at Abilene Christian College. In 1935 he moved to Nashville, Tennessee, where he served as minister of the Central Church of Christ. McMillan's predecessor in that church, Dr. Hall Calhoun, had begun and McMillan continued daily radio broadcasts that made their voices familiar throughout Middle Tennessee. While ministering to that congregation, McMillan also served as editor of the newly refurbished *Christian Leader*, a publication designed to bring healing to a national church beset with journalistic strife. In 1941 McMillan moved to Memphis and the pulpit of the Union Avenue Church of Christ, where he served until 1947. Following World War II he helped to found Ibaraki Christian College in Japan and served as its founding president from 1948 through 1952. From 1950 through 1953, he also served as president of Southern Christian Institute (later Southwestern Christian College), a school for African American students in Terrell, Texas. In 1953 McMillan moved to southern California, where he served first the Whittier Church of Christ and later the Northside Church of Christ in Santa Ana. In addition to carrying out his local work, McMillan engaged in evangelistic efforts in nearly every state in the union and Japan, China, Korea, and India. He served on the faculties of Abilene Christian College, Lubbock Christian College, Christian College of the Southwest, and Columbia Christian College; near the close of his life, he served as minister-in-residence at the Christian Care Center in Mesquite, Texas.

McMillan authored hundreds of articles for religious publications along with several books, including *Class Notes on Sacred History* (2 vols.), 1932; *The Church and the Adult*, 1937; *Worldliness in the Church*, 1951; and *The Minister's Spiritual Life*, 1958. He received honorary doctorates from Harding University in 1947 and Abilene Christian University in 1964. In 1983 Pepperdine University honored him as Distinguished Preacher of the Century. In 1913 he married Elizabeth Baxter, who died in 1922. In 1925 he married Pauline Riddle Owen, who passed away in 1979.

Bibliography

A. *Class Notes on Sacred History*, 2 vols. (Joplin, MO, 1932); *The Church and the Adult* (Nashville, TN, 1938; revised, 1955); *Worldliness of the Church* (n.p., 1951); *The Minister's Spiritual Life* (Austin, TX, 1959); *McMillan-Strong Debate on Instrumental Music in the Worship of God* (Austin, TX, n.d.).

B. William S. Banowsky, *The Mirror of a Movement* (Dallas, 1965); Richard T. Hughes, *Reviving the Ancient Faith* (Grand Rapids, 1996), pp. 194–210.

MATTHEWS, JAMES EVANS (19 March 1799, KY–30 June 1867, DeSoto Co., MS). *Career*: Minister, congressman, Mississippi state treasurer.

A second-generation adherent to the Christian movement led by Barton W. Stone, James Evans Matthews baptized Tolbert Fanning in Alabama in 1826, following a sermon by Benjamin Franklin Hall. Hall's sermon was one of the first in which he preached his newly discovered teaching on baptism for the remission of sins. Afterward, at Hall's prompting, Matthews prepared an article on that subject, which was published in Stone's *Christian Messenger* in 1829. This article led to considerable controversy in subsequent volumes of the *Mes-*

senger, continuing until Stone's death in 1844. Already in January 1828 Stone had published his own exposition of the meaning and purpose of baptism in the Great Commission and the Book of Acts, but little response followed. Matthews was one of the most prominent preachers in the Stone movement in Alabama, and he later became prominent as a preacher in Mississippi as well. In 1839 Matthews moved to Mississippi, where he served as a congressman and as state auditor. His brother, Joseph William Matthews (1807–1862), also a preacher, was governor of Mississippi from 1848 to 1850.

Bibliography

A. "The Gospel Plan of Saving Sinners" (series of three articles) *CM*, 4 (1829).
B. W. C. Rogers, *Recollections of Men of Faith* (St. Louis, 1889), pp. 132–134.

MATTHEWS, MANSIL WALTER (29 December 1806, Cumberland Co., KY–13 April 1891, Paradise, TX). *Career*: Frontier preacher, doctor, lawyer.

Mansil Matthews was a frontier preacher, doctor, and lawyer whose preaching efforts were important to the growth of the Christian movement led by Barton W. Stone in Tennessee, southern Kentucky, and northern Alabama from 1823 to 1835. Late in 1835 the Matthews family, along with other families from Tennessee and Alabama, made up a wagon train guided by David Crockett and started for the Republic of Texas. Matthews held elected offices in the Republic of Texas in the first (1836) and the seventh (1842) congresses. He resigned the first seat to become president of the Board of Land Commissioners of Red River County and also to engage in law practice. His nomadic life began during the 1850s and continued for more than twenty years. He spent summers in North Texas and winters in the Austin area. Matthew's movements can be traced all along the Texas frontier from Cooke, Wise, Parker, Tarrant, and Johnson Counties as far south as Burnet County, with family and large herds "following the grass." In the early years in Texas, Matthews had large landholdings, but he lost almost everything and died impoverished. All things considered, this family with their extended relations had probably more significant, widespread influence on the early history of the Churches of Christ in Texas than any other family. The very noteworthy number of preachers in the Matthews and related families included Joseph W. Matthews and James Evans Matthews, both of Mississippi; and in Texas, John Clinton Matthews, Barton Warren Matthews, Samuel Matthews Crisp, John M. Crisp, Sr., W. C. McKinney, and Abner Hill.

Bibliography

A. "From Thornton," *Christian Messenger* (Bonham, TX), 14 (September 12 and December 5, 1888).
B. Matthews Papers, Texas Christian University Library, Fort Worth, TX; T. F., "Western Texas Report," *GA*, 6 (December 1860), 373; *Wise County Messenger*, 1885–1891.

MATTOX, IRENE YOUNG (31 December 1881, Seymour, TX–20 June 1970, Lubbock, TX). *Education*: One or two summers in college in Denton, TX, and one summer with Jane Addams at Hull House in Chicago, 1904. *Career*: Public school teacher and principal, civic activist.

In 1927 A. R. Holton, a preacher in Norman, Oklahoma, invited Irene Young Mattox to address a large group of Christian women on the topic "A Christian Woman's Responsibility." Her presentation was revolutionary for several reasons. First, Churches of Christ had taught for many years that women were to "be silent" in the church. The Mattox speech was a first, since no one could remember when a woman had made a public presentation in a church context. Second, in her speech Mattox granted that women were not to preach or oversee a congregation, but she nonetheless insisted that women must prepare to teach and exercise their God-given talents. Her presentation provided an example for the larger body of Churches of Christ, and soon women were addressing women's groups in a variety of church settings. She herself pioneered in the teaching of women's Bible classes, taught a large, weekly class for many years at the 10th and Francis Church of Christ in Oklahoma City, and was the first female teacher on the lectureship program of Abilene Christian College.

The presentation Mattox made in 1927 likely would not have been so influential had it not been for the stature she had already achieved. The oldest of thirteen children born to Fountain Livingston and Mattie Higgins Young—two people well respected in Churches of Christ, especially in Texas—Mattox became a schoolteacher in Greenville, Texas, at age seventeen. In 1904, at age twenty-two, she married Judge Perry Mattox, a young farmer and cotton gin operator who preached for small, struggling churches. Perry Mattox was a deeply spiritual man who later in life advocated the premillennial theories of R. H. Boll. The Mattoxes lived successively in Grand Falls and Bishop, Texas, and in Bristow, Oklahoma. In each of these communities they established in their home a congregation of the Church of Christ. Finally they moved to Oklahoma City, where they lived for fifty years and where they established another congregation that grew into the influential 12th and Drexel Church of Christ. In Oklahoma City Mattox served as a public school teacher and principal. A woman dedicated to civic and charitable causes, she organized and headed the county welfare department during the depression; organized and served as president of Oklahoma City's Big Sisters, an organization that provided assistance to young women in trouble; and founded and served as president of the Oklahoma Parent-Teacher Association. A member of the Daughters of the American Revolution and the Women's Christian Temperance Union, she also served as president of the Federated Bible Club and played an active role in state and county political elections. A strong advocate of Christian higher education, Mattox helped establish three women's organizations that raised support for Christian colleges: Stepping Stones at Oklahoma Christian College, Associated Women of Pepperdine, and Lubbock Christian College Associates. When

Irene Mattox died in 1970, a lead story in the *Christian Chronicle*, a newspaper serving Churches of Christ, called her "Outstanding Woman of the Century." Irene and Perry Mattox had seven children. One of those children, Helen, married M. Norvel Young. Helen and M. Norvel Young were arguably the "first family" in Churches of Christ for the second half of the twentieth century. Another child, F. W. Mattox, served as president of Lubbock Christian College.

Bibliography

B. "Irene Young Mattox, 'Outstanding Woman of Century,' Is Dead at 88," *CC*, 27 (July 6, 1970), 1, 6; Mary Eleanor Williams, "A 20th Century Mother," *CWom*, 36 (May 1968), 4–7; Helen (Mattox) Young interview with Richard Hughes, 1992, typescript copy in possession of Richard Hughes; Bill Henegar and Jerry Rushford, *Forever Young: The Life and Times of M. Norvel Young & Helen M. Young* (Nashville, 1999), pp. 45–65.

MILLER, LUKE (16 March 1904, Limestone Co., AL–1 February 1962). *Career*: Minister.

Luke Miller was an outstanding black evangelist and minister for Churches of Christ in Florida, Georgia, and Texas from the 1920s into the 1960s. Following a thirteen-year ministry in Port Arthur, Texas, he began full-time evangelistic work in 1947. In thirty-five years he baptized over 10,000 people and established over 100 congregations of Churches of Christ.

Bibliography

A. *Miller's Sermons* (Austin, TX, 1940); *A Review of the Jesus Only Doctrine* (Austin, 1959).

B. *POT*, vol. 2 (Nashville, 1952), 293; W. D. Sweet, "At Rest: Miller," *GA*, 104 (March 22, 1962), 190.

MILLIGAN, ROBERT (25 July 1814, Ireland–20 March 1875, Lexington, KY). *Education*: B. A., Washington College, Washington, PA, 1840; M.A., Washington College, 1843. *Career*: Professor, Washington College, University of Indiana, Bethany College, University of Kentucky, and College of the Bible; president, College of the Bible, 1866–75.

Churches of Christ have for many years viewed Robert Milligan as a champion of conservatism because of his representative works: *The Scheme of Redemption*, a systematic theology, and *Reason and Revelation*, a discourse on the empirical method applied to the New Testament. Through the mid-twentieth century, young preachers used Milligan's works and T. W. Brents' *Gospel Plan of Salvation* probably more than any books besides the Bible. Cled E. Wallace said that as a boy preacher, "I cut my teeth on these two books." So did many others. *Reason and Revelation* follows the inductive method that Thomas Campbell first presented in his "Declaration and Address" of 1809. In addition to commands and approved precedents, Milligan concluded, propositions fairly inferred from scriptural premises may be biblically correct but should not become terms of fellowship. Milligan taught at Bethany College, Washington College (PA), the University of Indiana, the University of Kentucky, and the College of the Bible, where he also served as president from 1866 to 1875.

Bibliography

A. *An Exposition and Defense of the Scheme of Redemption* (Cincinnati, c. 1868–1869); *The Great Commission of Jesus Christ to His Twelve Apostles* (Lexington, KY, 1873); *Reason and Revelation* (Cincinnati, 1868); *Epistle to the Hebrews* (Des Moines, 1875); *A Guide to Bible Study* (Cleveland, 1897); *Analysis of the New Testament* (Cincinnati, 1874); *A Brief Treatise on Prayer* (Cincinnati, 1867[?]). B. K. Shaw, "Mississippi," *AT*, 10 (May 3, 1878), 5.

MITCHELL, NATHAN J. (2 March 1808, Washington Co., PA–1886, Howard, PA). *Career*: Itinerant minister.

Nathan J. Mitchell was the most significant nineteenth-century minister in the Stone-Campbell tradition in the Bald Eagle Valley region of Pennsylvania, where he established and built up numerous congregations, the most noted at Howard, Pennsylvania. Mitchell's writings appeared extensively in the *American Christian Review*. He vigorously defended a proactive role for women in the worship of these congregations. "No uninspired man's *ipse dixit* can convince me that women shall be silent on the ennobling theme of human redemption from the guilt, power, dominion and punishment of sin," he wrote. "Let the sisters speak, let them pray, let them sing, let them exhort; and God grant that I may often hear them." During the controversy over the role of women in the 1870s and 1880s, he agreed with Marinda R. Lemert's controversial articles in the *American Christian Review* (1879), which affirmed that women could speak without usurping the authority of man. Mitchell's view likely reflected his early experience with the Stone movement when women and girls experienced the jerks and other exercises, shouted, and exhorted.

Bibliography

A. *Life and Travels of a Pioneer Preacher of the 'Ancient' Gospel* (Cincinnati, 1877); Nathan J. Mitchell, *ACR*, 22 (July 8, 1879), 217; (July 15, 1879), 225; (October 14, 1879), 329.

B. "Obituaries," *ACR*, 30 (January 8, 1887), 15; Thomas H. Olbricht, "Historic Howard," *North Atlantic Christian*, 5 (August 1963), 224–225, 237; Thomas H. Olbricht, "Nathan J. Mitchell: Nineteenth Century Preacher," *North American Christian*, 7 (December 1964), 72–74.

MOORE, EPHRAIM D. L. (1782, NC–15 Oct 1859, Red River Co., TX). *Career*: Pioneer preacher.

Ephraim D. Moore was an important, early link between Barton W. Stone and the growth of the Christian movement in Tennessee, Alabama, and Texas.

In 1805 he moved from his native North Carolina to East Tennessee, where by age twenty-five (1807) he was preaching for the Post Oak Springs church near Rockwood. Benjamin F. Hall wrote of Moore in those years, "I thought him one of the most eloquent and powerful preachers I ever heard." During the 1920s Moore moved to northern Alabama, where he became a leading preacher there as well. Northern Alabama, in fact, became an important area for the expanding Stone movement. With leaders like Moore and James Matthews, the number of churches increased steadily. Carroll Kendrick, who began preaching in northern Alabama in the 1820s, said that from 1825 to 1850 at least fifty preachers developed in this northwestern region. Moore's influence there can perhaps best be seen in the number of young men he inspired to be preachers. Tolbert Fanning called Moore his "father in the gospel." In addition to Fanning, the entire list of early Alabama preachers looked to Moore and James E. Matthews as leaders. The movements of Moore are obscure between 1831, when he left Alabama, and 1837, when he arrived in Texas. Moore repeated in Texas the success he had achieved in Alabama. His forceful preaching helped to build churches and increase the corps of preachers there over a twenty-year period until his death in 1859.

Bibliography

B. Harry Christopher Wagner, "History of the Disciples of Christ in Upper East Tennessee," M.A. thesis, University of Tennessee, 1943; Robert C. Horn, *A Brief History of the First Christian Church, McKinney*, a pamphlet in the Matthews Papers, Texas Christian University Library; B. F. Hall, "Obituary," *GA*, 7 (January 1860), 31; Isaac Malkey [Mulkey], "Religious Intelligence," *CM*, 8 (September 1834), 282.

MOSER, KENNY CARL (23 January 1893, Johnson City, TX–17 February 1976, Lubbock, TX). *Education*: Thorp Spring Christian College. *Career*: Minister; author; teacher, Lubbock Christian University, 1964–72.

Kenny Carl Moser pioneered the doctrine of justification by grace through faith among Churches of Christ. In 1932, when Churches of Christ were under the influence of a profoundly legalistic theology, Moser quietly published a little book entitled *The Way of Salvation*. This book argued that justification before God resulted not from obedience to a plan or from works of the law but, rather, from the grace of God, which human beings receive through faith. As revolutionary as it was for Churches of Christ at that time, that book generated very little controversy, possibly because many church leaders read gospel papers more than they read books. In 1934, however, Moser articulated these same ideas in an article published in the gospel paper the *Firm Foundation*. A storm of controversy ensued. Undaunted, Moser continued to promote what he understood as the genuine gospel of Christ and in this way helped move Churches of Christ from legalism to a more evangelical theology. His *Gist of Romans*, published in 1957, was frequently used as a text in biblical studies courses in colleges and universities related to Churches of Christ and helped shape a whole generation of church leaders in the 1960s, 1970s, and 1980s. The author of six books, Moser preached for fifty years for Churches of Christ in Texas and Oklahoma, including seven years (1940–1947) in Oklahoma City.

Bibliography

A. "Thoughts on Romans—Introduction," *FF*, 47 (December 23, 1930), 5; *The Way of Salvation* (Nashville, 1932); *Christ versus the Plan* (Searcy, AR, 1952); *The Gist of Romans* (Delight, AR, 1957); *The Acts* (Austin, 1961); *Attributes of God* (Austin, 1963).

B. John T. Hinds, "Justification of Abraham," *FF*, 41 (June 24, 1924), 1; cf. ibid., May 20, 1; Bill Swetmon, "K. C. Moser," *FF*, 93 (March 23, 1976), 190; John Mark Hicks, "K. C. Moser and Churches of Christ: A Theological Perspective," *RQ*, 37 (4th Qr 1995), 193–211.

MULKEY, JOHN (14 January 1772, SC–13 December 1844, Monroe Co., KY). *Career*: Reformer, pioneer preacher.

John Mulkey was the most significant preacher to convert from the Separate Baptists of Kentucky to the Christian movement led by Barton W. Stone. He did so in 1809. His defection led more than half the preachers in the Stockton Valley Baptist Association to follow suit, thereby augmenting the Stone movement with a veritable wave of former Separate Baptists. Some of those who followed Mulkey into the Christian movement included Thomas McBride, Corder Stone, Abner Hill, William and Robert Randolph, Martin Trapp, Sr., Martin Trapp, Jr., Nicholas Gillentine, Jesse L. Sewell, Elisha G. Sewell, Isaac Sewell, Caleb Wit, Cornelius Deweese, and Roderick Rawlins. By almost any measure Mulkey had been the leading Baptist preacher in southern Kentucky during the first decade of the nineteenth century. In October 1809 charges against Mulkey were established and debated by the Separate Baptists. In November Mulkey proposed that the disputes be dropped and that tolerance and peace prevail. This proposal, however, was "utterly refused." By 1810 Mulkey had already accepted the Stone platform of Christian union and had brought about eighty members with him from the ranks of the Separate Baptists. Dr. W. D. Jourdan became acquainted with John Mulkey in 1820 when living in Monroe, Tennessee, and Jourdan's report helps explain why Mulkey was such an influential figure. "But few men within my hearing," Jourdan wrote, "had a better voice for speaking than John Mulkey. He traveled and preached more, and accomplished more, than almost any man among us." A large number of the preachers influenced by Mulkey eventually moved to other states, thereby expanding the scope of the Stone movement. Lewis Byram, David Stewart, and Samuel Boyd moved to Indiana; Benjamin Lynn, Marshall DeSpain, James Matthews, and Mansil Matthews moved to Alabama; Thomas McBride moved to Missouri; Philip Mulkey moved to Illinois, but John Mulkey stayed in the Cumberland. Stone invited Mulkey to Cane Ridge in 1817 for a communion service typical of such services in the earliest period of the revivals near the turn of the century. John Rogers of Carlisle, Kentucky, remembered Mulkey's visit. He was "quite an orator," Rogers reported. "He had a splendid voice, and sang, and prayed, most admirably."

Bibliography

A. *A Circular Letter Addressed to the Christian Churches in the Western Country*, Glasgow, 1821, quoted in full in E. Clayton Gooden, *A Fork in the Road* (Tucson, 1972), 199–211.

B. John Rogers, *Recollections of Men of Faith* (St. Louis, 1889), p. 186; C. P. Cawthorn and N. L. Warnell, *Pioneer Baptist Church Records of South-Central Kentucky and the Upper Cumberland of Tennessee, 1799–1899* (n.p., 1985); Philip Mulkey Hunt, ed., *The Mulkeys of America* (Portland, OR, 1982), p. 88; Isaac T. Reneau, "Obituary—John Mulkey," *MH*, 3d ser., 2 (August 1845), 380; W. D. Jourdan, "Jourdan to Robertson," *ACR*, 22 (April 1, 1879), 105.

MULKEY, JOHN NEWTON (11 February 1806, Tompkinsville, KY–26 September 1882, Glasgow, KY). *Career*: Pioneer preacher.

John Newton Mulkey, son of the famous John Mulkey who led scores of Separate Baptists into the Christian movement led by Barton W. Stone, became probably the leading evangelist for the Christian movement in southern Kentucky. He later moved to Illinois, where he preached for several years near Mulkeytown, a community established by members of the Mulkey family from southern Kentucky. In his later years he returned to Glasgow, Kentucky, and continued to preach until his death. His body was taken to the historic Old Mulkey Meeting House near Tomkinsville, Kentucky, and laid to rest near the place of his birth and earliest religious experiences. John Newton was three years old when his father "departed in peace" from the Baptists and became the most successful evangelist in the Christian movement in southern Kentucky. Equally successful, the son baptized perhaps 10,000 individuals in the course of his ministry.

Bibliography

B. J. D. Floyd, "The Labors of the Pioneers," *GA*, 36 (June 7, 1894), 353; Philip Mulkey Hunt, ed., *The Mulkeys of America* (Portland, OR, 1982), p. 88; Isaac N. Jones, "The Reformation in Tennessee," included in J. W. Grant, "A Sketch of the Reformation in Tennessee" (c. 1897), typescript in Center for Restoration Studies, Abilene Christian University, p. 54.

MULKEY, PHILIP (3 or 6 April 1775, Fair Forest, SC–26 January 1844, Franklin Co., IL). *Career*: Pioneer preacher.

A brother of John Mulkey, Philip Mulkey labored with John at Mill Creek Church (Old Mulkey) before moving to Jackson County, Tennessee, where he began "an arm" of Mill Creek Church of Brimstone Creek. Philip Mulkey was active in the Stockton Valley Baptist Association until 1809, when the entire membership of Brimstone Baptist Church, like the majority of the Mill Creek Baptist church, left the fellowship of the Separate Baptists. Brimstone grew into a large and influential Church of Christ during the nineteenth century. In fact, Jackson County, Tennessee, where Brimstone Baptist Church was located, has had for many years the largest percentage of members of Churches of Christ relative to the overall population of any county in the United States other than Clay County, which was once a part of Jackson County. Philip later moved to Illinois, where he continued his preaching career.

Bibliography

B. L.A.H., "Obituary—Elder Philip Mulkey," *MH*, 3d ser., 1 (May 1844), 239; Philip Mulkey Hunt, ed., *The Mulkeys of America* (Portland, OR, 1982), p. 415; C. P. Cawthorn and N. L. Warnell, *Pioneer Baptist Church Records of South-Central Kentucky and the Upper Cumberland of Tennessee: 1799–1899* (n.p., 1985), pp. 502–505; W. D. Jourdan, "Jourdan to Robertson," *ACR*, 22 (April 1, 1879), 105.

N

NANCE, CLEMENT (1756, VA–1828, IN). *Education*: Unknown. *Career:* Frontier preacher, farmer, hymn writer.

Clement Nance was a native of southern Virginia, where Mary Stone, the mother of Barton Warren Stone, moved with her children after her husband, John, had died in Maryland. Though considerably older than Stone, Nance knew Stone at that time. At the age of nineteen, Nance joined the Methodist Church and began preaching in 1783, but he later concluded that the Methodist episcopacy was unscriptural and oppressive. Nance did not separate from Methodism with the O'Kelly preachers in 1792, though he did so eight years later in 1800. In 1803 the Nance family migrated to the Green River country of central Kentucky, where they united with the Stone movement in 1804. A voluminous hymn writer, Nance wrote one of the earliest hymns for the Stone movement:

> Come my Christian friends and brethren,
> Bound for Canaan's happy land,
> Come unite and walk together,
> Christ our leader gives command.
> Lay aside your party spirit,
> Wound your Christian friends no more,
> All the name of Christ inherit,
> Zion's peace again restore.

Bibliography

A. "Religious Intelligence," *HGL*, 5 (September 1812), 423; Rice Haggard, ed., *A Selection of Christian Hymns* (Lexington, 1818), hymn 323.

B. George W. Nance, *The Nance Memorial: A History of the Nance Family* (Bloomington, IL, 1904).

NICHOL, CHARLES READY (26 March 1876, Readyville, TN–7 July 1961, Clifton, TX). *Education*: Southwestern Kentucky College; Nashville Bible School, 1892; B.S., Central Texas College; LL.D., Abilene Christian University, 1940. *Career*: Debater; author; evangelist; president, Thorp Spring Christian College, 1916–18; teacher, Harding College, Pepperdine College, 1944–45.

Charles Ready Nichol was one of the great debaters in Churches of Christ from 1898 through the first half of the twentieth century. He held his first religious debate at age twenty-two with Dr. J. A. Payne, a Primitive Baptist. By age twenty-eight Nichol had engaged in sixty such discussions with representatives of almost every denomination in the South. His close friend Charles H. Roberson said that when a need to represent the Church of Christ arose, people often responded, "Call Nick." Nichol was also a successful full-time evangelist who baptized over 5,000 people during the first twenty years of his ministry. Nichol served as president of Thorp Spring Christian College in Thorp Spring, Texas, from 1916 to 1918, and he preached for churches in Corsicana, Denton, and Clifton, Texas, and Seminole, Oklahoma. In 1920 Nichol and R. L. Whiteside published four volumes for use in Sunday schools and Bible classes that eventually served Churches of Christ as a basic theological textbook. The volumes were entitled *Sound Doctrine*. Nichol published some twenty additional books along with frequent articles in periodicals. He also served as front page editor of the *Firm Foundation*.

Bibliography

A. *God's Woman* (Clifton, TX, 1938); *Nichol's Pocket Bible Encyclopedia* (Cincinnati, 1926); *Nichol-Bradley Debate* (Clifton, TX, 1907); *Sound Doctrine*, 4 vols. (Clifton, TX, 1920); *The Possibility of Apostasy* (Clifton, TX, 1951).

B. Maude J. Underwood, *C. R. Nichol, Preacher of Righteousness* (Clifton, TX, 1952).

NICHOLS, GUS (12 January 1892, Walker Co., AL–16 November 1975, Jasper, AL). *Education*: Alabama Christian College, Berry, AL. *Career*: Minister, lecturer, radio preacher.

Gus Nichols preached for more than half a century, devoting forty-three of those years (1932–1975) to a single congregation—the Sixth Avenue Church of Christ in Jasper, Alabama. Nichols was the first person in his family to become a member of the Church of Christ and a preacher as well, but before his death preachers in the Nichols family totaled seventeen. Three of the Nichols sons became full-time ministers. As a staff writer for the *Gospel Advocate*, Gus Nichols was widely read throughout the Church of Christ. In addition, his sermons were published weekly in the Jasper, Alabama, newspaper, the *Mountain Eagle*, beginning in 1947. His sermons later appeared in three volumes. Nichols was known nationally through his gospel meetings, debates, radio preaching, and writing.

Bibliography

A. *Nichols-Weaver Debate* (Nashville, 1943); *Sermons* (Jasper, AL, 1948); *Speaking the Truth in Love* (Chattanooga, 1956).
B. *POT*, vol. 2 (Nashville, 1952), 316–317.

NICHOLS, JAMES WALTER (24 November 1927, Abilene, TX–12 June 1973, Los Angeles, CA). *Education:* B.A., Abilene Christian College, 1947; graduate work at University of Iowa. *Career*: Minister, Church of Christ, Cedar Rapids, IA, 1947–51; cofounder, "Herald of Truth" radio and television ministry, 1952; radio evangelist, "Herald of Truth," 1952–54; editor, *Christian Chronicle*, 1955–57; executive vice president, Fidelity Enterprises, Inc., 1957–66; president, Fidelity Enterprises, Inc., 1966–69.

While attending the University of Iowa and preaching for the Church of Christ in Cedar Rapids, Iowa, 1947–1951, James Walter Nichols began a radio ministry supported by fifteen churches and broadcast over eight stations in five states. Nichols and James D. Willeford, a preacher of the Church of Christ in Madison, Wisconsin, soon conceived the idea of launching a national radio program supported by the Churches of Christ. By 1952 the "Herald of Truth" was on the air on eighty-five stations nationwide, sponsored by the Highland Street Church of Christ in Abilene, Texas. Nichols served from 1952 through 1954 as the program's first speaker. To raise initial support for the "Herald of Truth," Nichols traveled 21,000 miles in five southern states and raised $250,000 in only three months. The program had increased to 500 radio stations and 150 television stations by 1972. Nichols also established a publishing and production company that not only produced the "Herald of Truth" programs but which also published three religious periodicals, *Teenage Christian, Christian Woman*, and *Christian Chronicle*, which he edited from 1955 to 1957.

Bibliography

A. *The Churches of Christ Salute You* (Abilene, 1953).
B. *POT*, vol. 4 (Nashville, 1970), 233; "James Walter Nichols Dies," *CC*, 30 (June 19, 1973), 1.

NORTH, IRA LUTTS (31 August 1922, Ethridge, TN–15 January 1984, Lawrenceburg, TN). *Education*: B.A., Abilene Christian University; M.A., University of Illinois; Ph.D., Louisiana State University. *Career*: Minister, writer, radio and television preacher.

Ira Lutts North was nationally known for his weekly "Amazing Grace" Bible class, a television program broadcast from the Madison, Tennessee, Church of Christ. A colorful and inspirational preacher, North served this congregation as its pulpit preacher for almost thirty years. Under his leadership this congregation grew to become the largest congregation of Churches of Christ in the world with a membership of roughly 5,500 at the time of his death in 1984. Dr. North also served on the David Lipscomb College faculty for several years. His great-grandfather, Ira North, Sr., and his grandfather, Ira North, Jr., were both preachers. His father, O. L. North, was for many years an elder of the church in Lawrenceburg, Tennessee. North regularly spoke on lectureship programs sponsored by colleges and universities related to Churches of Christ.

Bibliography

A. *You Can March for the Master* (Nashville, 1959); coeditor, *At Work for the Master* (Nashville, 1963).

B. Obituary, *CC*, 41 (February 1984), 1.

O

OFFICER, ROBERT WALLACE (18 August 1845, Murray Co., GA–23 August 1930, Turkey, TX). *Career*: Minister; missionary to Native Americans in OK, 1890–1904.

R. W. Officer conducted a successful mission outreach to Native Americans in Oklahoma, especially during the last decade of the nineteenth century. Churches among Native Americans numbered seventy-five before the end of the century. Officer was supported by congregations at Paris, Texas, and then at Atoka, Indian Territory, and David Lipscomb regarded his work as a model of scriptural congregational cooperation and an alternative to the missionary society. Officer first preached in Alabama and Tennessee until the 1880s, when he moved to Texas and preached at Gainesville and Paris. When he saw the opportunities in the Indian Territory across the Red River, he persuaded his friend, Elder W. Askew, also a Choctaw Indian, to begin preaching there. Officer and his wife furnished one-half of Askew's support while B. F. Overton, chief of the Chickasaw Nation, paid the other half until Askew's death. When he was unable to find a replacement for Askew, Officer resigned his "city evangelist" position with the Paris, Texas, church and went to the Indian Territory, determined to remain for the long term. Charges that Officer was unsound theologically eventually undermined his work in the Indian Territory. Some held that he preached the Millennial Dawn theories promoted especially by A. S. Bradley and W. L. Gibbs, who edited *Word and Work* in Abilene, Texas, from 1895 to 1907. He was labeled "unsound" as early as 1902, though he denied the charge and defended his views. In any event, midway through the first decade of the twentieth century, Officer left the Indian Territory and began preaching in West Texas, New Mexico, and occasionally Colorado. After many years of writing mission reports and doctrinal articles published in almost every Church of Christ–related periodical, Officer suddenly ceased to write; only a few references to him can be found for the last twenty-five years of his life. Officer died in Turkey, Texas, in 1930.

Bibliography

A. "Heresy Trial" in F. D. Srygley, *Biographies and Sermons* (Nashville, 1898), pp. 321–337.

B. Lawrence W. Scott, ed., *Texas Pulpit of the Church of Christ* (St. Louis, 1888), pp. 384, 309; Michael D. Slate, "R. W. Officer: An Example of Frontier Individualism," *RQ*, 22 (3d Qr. 1979), 144–159.

O'KELLY, JAMES (1738, Ireland–1826, Chatham Co., NC). *Career*: Reformer, frontier preacher, writer.

James O'Kelly is perhaps best known for leading a revolt of Methodist circuit riders in 1792 against what they perceived as the autocratic rule of Bishop Francis Asbury. O'Kelly and his followers soon established the "Republican Methodists," a name they quickly abandoned for the simple name of "Christian." O'Kelly made significant contributions to the early emphasis on religious liberty, individualism, and congregationalism that characterized the early Christian movement and that has always characterized Churches of Christ. Inscribed on the seldom-visited monument that marks his burial site in Chatham County, North Carolina, are these words: "The Southern Champion of Christian Freedom." The old abandoned cemetery is on O'Kelly's farm, one mile west of the O'Kelly Chapel near Durham, North Carolina. Although O'Kelly's emphasis on religious freedom and the Christian name contributed directly to the origin and subsequent development of the Churches of Christ, he rejected the one doctrinal formulation that eventually defined this fellowship: baptism by immersion. He felt so strongly about this matter that he boycotted a meeting led by William Guirey, Elias Smith, and other immersionists in Virginia in 1810.

Bibliography

A. *The Author's Apology for Protesting against the Methodist Episcopal Government* (Richmond, 1798); *A Vindication of the Author's Apology* (Raleigh, 1801).

B. William Guirey, *The History of Episcopacy* (Raleigh, 1799); Wilbur E. MacClenney, *The Life of the Rev. James O'Kelly* (Raleigh, NC, 1910).

OLIPHANT, DAVID (1821, St. Andrews, Scotland–17 March 1885, London, Ontario). *Education*: Bethany College, 1841 or 1842. *Career*: Editor, minister.

David Oliphant graduated from Alexander Campbell's Bethany College and became one of the most prominent restoration leaders in Canada. Having inherited the Scotch Baptist principles of his parents, Oliphant is especially remembered for his early opposition to the missionary society, established in Cincinnati in 1849. Oliphant's arguments against the society changed the views of Benjamin Franklin while Franklin was still secretary of the society. Their written discussion in the 1858 volume of the *American Christian Review*, edited by Franklin, was a pivotal event, since the *Review* soon became the most influential periodical in the movement. In addition, an article by Oliphant was the earliest statement against the society published in the *Gospel Advocate*. From 1845 until approximately 1865, Oliphant edited and published five periodicals, totaling twenty-seven volumes, under the titles *Witness of Truth, Christian Mirror, Christian Banner, Banner of the Faith*, and *Message of Good Will to Men*.

Bibliography

A. Periodicals: *Witness of Truth* (1845–1850); *Christian Mirror* (1851); *Christian Banner* (1852–1858); *Banner of the Faith* (1859–1863); and *Message of Good Will to Men* (1845–1865 [?]).

B. Eugene C. Perry, "The Life and Works of David Oliphant, Jr.," unpublished paper, Abilene Christian University, 1963, copy in Center for Restoration Studies, Abilene Christian University.

OLIVE, ABEL, SR. (20 July 1765, Johnston Co., NC–22 August 1822, Trigg Co., KY). *Career*: Pioneer preacher.

According to W. E. MacClenny, James O'Kelly's biographer, "Rev. Abel Olive, of North Carolina, was a contemporary of Rev. James O'Kelly. He organized Catawba Springs church in 1803, and moved West in 1807, and continued to preach among the Christians." In addition to the reference by MacClenny, the only other notice on Abel Olive appears in Evan William Humphreys' *Memoirs of Deceased Christian Ministers*, on which MacClenny apparently depended. Humphreys wrote, "Abel Olive was a native of North Carolina, living in Wake County. He moved to the West in 1807, and died there before 1826. He was a contemporary of James O'Kelly and the dissenters from the Methodists in 1793." The Catawba Springs church to which MacClenny refers is now known as Pleasant Hill and still meets near Cary, North Carolina. MacClenny cited the Catawba Springs church as an example of some congregations that began in North Carolina under circumstances different from James O'Kelly's Republican Methodists and became known as Christian Baptists, having separated from the Baptists over the Baptist practice of closed communion. It is possible that some Christian Baptist churches were originally with O'Kelly, but they deserted him about 1810 because of his rejection of baptism by immersion. MacClenny does inform us that in "the early history of this (Catawba Springs) church, we find that some of the Christian churches in North Carolina, preceding the year 1831, practiced baptism by immersion only, and rejected infant baptism." So prejudiced were these churches against "sectarian literature" that for several years they refused even to have their minutes printed. Abel Olive had moved to Tennessee before 1810 and was therefore not involved in the controversy over baptism that divided the Christian movement in Virginia and North Carolina. Most of the churches in the West (Kentucky and Tennessee), resulting from a merger of the Stone and O'Kelly people in that region, accepted immersion as early as 1807, when a number of Stone's fellow preachers, most notably Reuben Dooley and David Purviance, were immersed in Stoner Creek just outside Paris, Kentucky. Stone was immersed a little later. Land records indicate that Abel Olive moved to Trigg County, Kentucky, in 1802, although one record says 1807. Family records establish the date and place of his residence on the Cumberland River in Kentucky north of the Tennessee line at a place that became known as Olive's Landing. After Abel's death two of his sons, Uel Olive and James Olive, were instrumental in establishing two early congregations of the Christian movement. Uel Olive's home in Graves County, Kentucky, was the site of the early meetings of the Knob Creek Church of Christ, the oldest Church of Christ in western Kentucky. James migrated to Illinois and established the Silver Creek Church in his home near Stanton, Illinois, shortly after arriving there in 1829.

Bibliography

B. W. E. MacClenny, *The Life of Rev. James O'Kelly* (reprint, Indianapolis, 1950), pp. 131, 149–150; Evan William Humphreys, *Memoirs of Deceased Christian Ministers* (Dayton, OH, 1880), p. 261; William Guirey, *History of Episcopacy* (Raleigh, NC, 1799), p. 381; Joseph Thomas, *The Travels and Gospel Labors of Joseph Thomas* (Winchester, VA, 1812), p. 81; "Proceeding of a Conference in Kentucky, and Address to Elder Badger," *CH*, 9 (June 1826?), 56; J. J. Kathcart, "Obituaries," *Chr*, 18 (June 2, 1881), 7; *C-E*, 71 (August 30, 1934), 1139; *James Olive Family* (Fort Worth, TX, 1965), pp. 187–191.

P

PACK, FRANK (27 March 1916, Memphis, TN–9 December 1998, Upland, CA). *Education*: B.A., University of Chattanooga; M.A., Vanderbilt University, 1939; Ph.D., University of Southern California, 1948. *Career*: Preacher; professor of biblical studies, David Lipscomb College, 1940–44; Pepperdine University, 1945–49 and 1964–86; and Abilene Christian College, 1949–63.

Frank Pack spent sixty years as a preacher in Churches of Christ and over forty years as a distinguished professor of biblical studies in three colleges related to Churches of Christ: David Lipscomb College (1940–1944), Abilene Christian College (1949–1963), and Pepperdine University (1945–1949 and 1964–1986). With his doctorate in textual criticism of the New Testament, Pack was one of the most distinguished biblical scholars among Churches of Christ. Pepperdine University recognized him as Distinguished Professor of Religion in 1978. He authored nine books and more than 300 periodical articles. At his retirement, twenty-five of his former students prepared a volume of sermons in his honor: *We Preach Christ Crucified.* Later his former colleagues at Pepperdine University honored him with a *festschrift* entitled *Johannine Studies.*

Bibliography

A. *Sermons of Frank Pack* (Abilene, 1963); coauthor, *Preaching to Modern Man* (Abilene, TX, 1969).

B. Jerry Rushford, "Committed to New Testament Christianity: A Profile of Frank Pack" in *We Preach Christ Crucified* (Malibu, 1986), pp. ix–xxiv; R. L. Roberts and Steven Martin, "Frank Pack: A Bibliography," ibid., 157–168; James E. Priest, ed., *Johannine Studies: Essays in Honor of Frank Pack* (Malibu, CA, 1989).

PALMER, FRANCIS ROSE (30 August 1789, SC–22 October 1873, Liberty, MO). *Career*: Pioneer preacher in TN, KY, MO.

Francis Palmer was among the "New Light" preachers who helped establish Barton W. Stone's Christian movement in Tennessee as early as 1812, long before Alexander Campbell's influence was first felt in that state. Palmer and his brother, Henry, first preached in Tennessee near Murfreesboro in a neighborhood where Daniel Travis and Barton W. Stone were also preaching. The Palmer brothers later preached in Sumner County, (Southwest) Tennessee, before Francis moved to Missouri in 1836. Along with other noted preachers, including Allen Wright, Moses E. Lard, and J. J. Wyatt, Palmer helped make Missouri the leading state in the Stone-Campbell movement with more churches than any other state by 1900. Palmer eventually became a close friend of Alexander Campbell, whose biographer, Robert Richardson, thought he helped unite the Stone and Campbell movements.

Bibliography

B. T. M. Allen, "Correspondence," *ACR*, 10 (July 10, 1867), 111; Robert Richardson, *Memoirs of Alexander Campbell*, vol. 2 (Cincinnati, 1898), p. 385; T. P. Haley, *Historical and Biographical Sketches of the Early Churches and Pioneer Preachers of the Christian Church in Missouri* (Kansas City, 1888), pp. 541–544; W. C. Rogers, "Elder F. R. Palmer," *AT*, 5 (December 11, 1873), 6.

PALMER, HENRY DULANY (1792, SC–September 1861, Eureka, IL). *Career*: Frontier preacher.

Ordained to preach by Barton W. Stone in 1809, Henry Palmer, along with his brother, Francis, was one of the early Tennessee preachers mentored by Stone. Following the pattern of many adherents to the Stone movement in those early years, in 1815 Henry Palmer took his slaves to Illinois, where he freed them and gave them portions of his estate. Along with these former slaves, Palmer settled on Allison [Ellison] Prairie, Edward County, Illinois, and established a church at Carlisle, Sullivan County, in 1818. He was active as an evangelist in Indiana and Illinois until his death at Half Moon, Illinois, where he lived from 1835 until his death in 1861.

Bibliography

A. "From an Old Pioneer," *CA*, 8 (April 29, 1852), 66.
B. Robert Richardson, *Memoirs of Alexander Campbell*, vol. 2 (Cincinnati, 1898), pp. 385–386.

PEPPERDINE, GEORGE (20 June 1886, Mound Valley, KS–31 July 1962, Los Angeles, CA). *Education*: Parsons Business College, 1905. *Career*: Founder, Western Auto Stores; founder and benefactor of Pepperdine University.

George Pepperdine founded George Pepperdine College in September 1937 with a $2 million gift plus a $1 million endowment. Reflecting his heritage in the wing of Churches of Christ led by Daniel Sommer, Pepperdine did not want a college as an arm of the church. He envisioned instead "a good private educational institution with a Christian environment." Above all, he said, the college "should not try to dominate or meddle in the affairs of the church or ask the churches for money." He wanted the college "to do its best to strengthen and deepen the faith of young people." Pepperdine felt that what the world needed most was Christian businessmen. Pepperdine began what eventually became the chain of Western Auto Supply stores in March 1909 with 500 one-cent stamps used to mail a list of auto supplies available for good prices via mail orders. From the first order of $1.90 he made a profit of 20 cents. From this small beginning the chain grew until Pepperdine had more than 200 stores in the western states. George and Helen Pepperdine moved to California in 1916, and George retired from Western Auto Supply Company in 1939. His benevolence extended to churches, preachers, missionaries, child-care facilities, camps, and the Boy Scouts.

Bibliography

A. "George Pepperdine College," *GG*, 3 (April 24, 1952), 1, 9–11; *Faith Is My Fortune* (Los Angeles, 1962).

B. Bill Youngs, *Faith Was His Fortune* (Malibu, CA, 1976).

POLLY, NATHAN H. O. (1820, KY–2 November 1902, Rockwall, TX). *Education*: Walter Scott. *Career*: Pioneer preacher.

Nathan H. O. Polly, whose ministry in Texas began in 1848 and lasted for more than fifty years, established many North Texas congregations and strengthened many of the churches in the Dallas area. He was the first judge of Montague County, Texas, where he started a frontier church. Rockwall, Texas, became his permanent home from which he preached and established many churches in surrounding counties. In 1892 Polly stated that he had traveled and preached in North Texas for forty-three years but had never received enough support to keep him in decent clothes. Polly died in 1902 at eighty-two years of age, having preached for a total of sixty-four years. In the course of his career, he baptized some 3,000 people. Polly was a link to the pioneers of the Stone-Campbell tradition, having received his education from Walter Scott as a younger man.

Bibliography

A. "From Bro. Polly," *FF*, 5 (May 2, 1889), 3.

B. A. P. Hardin, obituary, *FF*, 18 (November 25, 1902), 6.

PURVIANCE, DAVID (14 November 1766, Iredell Co., NC–19 August 1847, Preble Co., OH). *Education*: Trained in the classics by James Hall of NC. *Career*: State legislator in KY and OH, elder and frontier preacher in Churches of Christ in KY (Cane Ridge) and OH.

David Purviance was an associate of Barton W. Stone whose influence was felt in southern Kentucky and Tennessee during the formative years of Stone's movement. David moved with his father, John Purviance, from Iredell County, North Carolina, to the frontier in Middle Tennessee (Sumner County) in 1790, but the death of David's brother, John, caused the family to move to Kentucky, where they became active in the Cane Ridge church. In 1802 the parents returned to Tennessee. David Purviance continued his association with Barton Stone, but his father rejected the Stone reform in favor of the Cumberland Presbyterians. David moved from Cane Ridge to Preble County, Ohio, in summer 1807 and organized there the New Paris church, the oldest Christian church in that area. The Shiloh church grew out of the New Paris church, and Purviance preached for both congregations. New Paris divided in 1839 between the "Old Christians" (Stoneites) and the "Reformers" (Campbellites). Barton Stone visited New Paris in June 1843 on his last visit to Cane Ridge and Kentucky. Several of the pioneers of the Stone movement were present to hear Stone preach, including David Purviance, John Adams, and Nathan Worley, all between seventy and eighty years old.

Bibliography

B. Levi Purviance, *The Life of David Purviance* (Dayton, 1848).

R

RAINS, ANNIE (1825, TN?–November 1912, Thornton, TX). *Career*: Texas pioneer, Christian housewife, and mother who devoted her life to the care of orphans.

Little is known of Annie Rains except what is written about her in an obituary published after her death. Her life is best told by one brief line: "She cared for and reared more than thirty orphan children." Possibly none of the women in the Church of Christ on the Texas frontier cared for as many orphans as did she. At the same time, she typified many frontier Christian women who discharged similar roles in their households. Annie Rains believed the Bible "literally," including the part that defines pure and undefiled religion before God and the world as visiting the orphans and widows in their affliction and keeping oneself unspotted from the world. Even during her lifetime Annie Rains was little known outside of the small Texas community of Bald Prairie in Robertson County, where she, her husband, Elijah Rains, and her son, Joshua Rains, were faithful members of the Church of Christ established there in 1847. She is buried at Thornton, Texas, where Joshua lived at the time of her death. Elijah Rains and Joshua are buried in the churchyard at Bald Prairie. Joshua Rains, the Church of Christ, and the Bald Prairie community were the subjects of a novel by Jewel Gibson, *Joshua Beene and God* (1946), and a movie based on the book in which Burl Ives played the role of Joshua.

Bibliography

B. Mollie Cannon, "Rains," *GA*, 55 (June 26, 1913), 621; Jewel Gibson, *Joshua Beene and God* (New York, 1946).

RANDOLPH, ROBERT (11 January 1789–2 January 1866, Freestone Co., TX). *Career*: Frontier preacher, TN.

Robert Randolph was an important preacher in Middle Tennessee who did much to further the Christian movement led by Barton W. Stone in the early nineteenth century. Isaac N. Jones, a contemporary of Randolph, has left us with a rare description of his preaching. "Not being very pugnacious and possessing large benevolence and veneration, he was especially adapted to the work of building up churches and keeping them in trim. After the Mulkeys left Tennessee he was heard to lament his loneliness in building up, exclaiming: 'Rees [Jones] is a host in himself; he can do the fighting, but I have no one to help build up.' While his sermons were plain and didactic, when occasion demanded it he could most thoroughly arouse an audience by exhortation. But he was peculiar. In strong excitement he became, as spiritualists would say, in rapport. Then seizing the front edge of the hand-board with hands about two feet apart, and gradually raising his voice to a pitch that may be called 'stentorian,' and with no gesticulation save that of raising his rigid body on his toes and then dropping on his heels at emphatic points, for fifteen minutes he would pour forth a torrent of scripture [and] swept everything before him. When done he dropped into his seat exhausted, and limp as a withered leaf." Numerous members of the Randolph family became preachers who helped spread the Christian movement in Tennessee, Alabama, Missouri, and Texas. A 1847–1848 directory of restoration churches in America and Great Britain listed four Randolph preachers in Tennessee. Robert Randolph and John Mee are listed as preacher and elder for a congregation in Charleston, Macon County, Tennessee. Two other Randolph elders (preachers) listed with no first names appear in Bradley County, Tennessee. Another Elder Randolph (Elihu?) preached for the New Hermon church in Bedford County, Tennessee. Elisha Randolph died in September 1856. Jeremiah Randolph, of Alabama, was a prominent second-generation preacher who carried on the Randolph family preaching tradition in Alabama. It is likely that the Randolph family entered the Stone movement in part, at least, because of the influence of the Mulkey family. We do know, at least, that Robert Randolph's father, William, had been a Baptist preacher along with Jonathan Mulkey in the Holston Baptist Association of East Tennessee in 1800.

Bibliography

B. O. W. Taylor, *Early Tennessee Baptists* (Nashville, 1957), 141; *The Christian Register*, Ohio, 1848, reprinted in *GA*, 92 (August 3, 1950), 490; J. R. Hooten, no title, *GA*, 8 (September 4, 1866), 570; C. R. Nichol, *Gospel Preachers Who Blazed the Trail* (Austin, 1962); I. N. Jones, "Obituaries—Slaughter," *GA* (August 19, 1891), 523; Isaac N. Jones, "The Reformation in Tennessee" included in J. W. Grant, "Sketch of the Reformation in Tennessee" (1897), typescript in Center for Restoration Studies, Abilene Christian University, 55–57.

RAWLINS, RODERICK (11 March 1776, Guilford Co., NC–27 April 1848, Lancaster, TX). *Career*: Pioneer preacher in Dallas Co., TX.

Roderick Rawlins and his family were the earliest settlers (September 1844) on Ten Mile Creek in the southern part of Dallas County, Texas. There they established a pioneer congregation of Churches of Christ in a region where Churches of Christ would eventually have considerable strength. The Rawlins established that church in July 1846 with fifteen charter members. Rawlins began his career as a Baptist preacher in East Tennessee. When his wife died in 1805, he moved to southern Kentucky, where he was closely associated with John Mulkey. He then moved to Indiana, and then to Illinois in 1821. In Illinois he left the Baptists and associated himself with the Churches of Christ. In fall 1844 he moved to the frontier of Dallas County, Texas, along with a group of thirty-five relatives he led there from Illinois. The words inscribed on the old wooden marker that marks Rawlins' grave are still readable: "The early pioneer and first settler on the waters of this beautiful stream."

Bibliography

B. Vivian Richardson, "The Man Texas Forgot," *Dallas Morning News*, January 21, 1934; W. Rawlins, "Correspondence," *C-E*, 5 (July 1854), 275.

RENEAU, ISAAC TIPTON (9 December 1805, Clinton Co., KY–9 August 1885, near Albany, KY). *Education*: Training by Dr. W. D. Jourdan. *Career*: Frontier preacher, teacher.

Between 1850 and 1885 Isaac Tipton Reneau was the leading preacher among Churches of Christ in southern Kentucky and Middle Tennessee, where he ministered to numerous churches and educated many young people. Like so many other pioneers in the Stone movement, Reneau had deep roots in the Separate Baptist tradition. His grandfather, William Reno (Reneau, originally Reneault), was clerk of the Sinking Creek Baptist Church in Washington County, Tennessee, in 1785. According to David Bennedict, Jonathan Mulkey, William Reno, and other ministers from the Separate Baptist church at Sandy Creek, North Carolina, immigrated to Tennessee and established several of the earliest Separate Baptist churches in the region that became East Tennessee. Reneau and Mulkey descendants moved farther west and became leading preachers in the Upper Cumberland region of Tennessee and Kentucky. In 1834 while a student of medicine under Dr. W. D. Jourdan in Tennessee, Reneau visited Kentucky and heard "Raccoon" John Smith preach in a grove of trees near the Clear Fork church building. Prior to this experience Reneau had been a "seeker or mourner" for eleven years and had given up all hope of ever "getting religion." Smith, however, convinced Isaac that he must be "immersed for the remission of sins." He was baptized by Dr. W. D. Jourdan after returning to Tennessee. Reneau first preached on May 15, 1835, and became an untiring mountain preacher in southern Kentucky and Middle Tennessee, where he preached an average of one sermon per day for forty years. He also established a reputation as an English and Greek scholar who shared his knowledge with numerous young people. For almost twenty-five years Reneau was "supported" by the Kentucky Missionary Society. Reneau's experience with society support furnished critics like David Lipscomb with an example of money from churches going mostly for administrative costs. J. W. McGarvey, secretary of the Kentucky Missionary Society, wrote in 1866, "We expect this to be the great year of our Society's history" and urged the mountain preacher to prevail on the churches to send more money. Seven months later, in April 1867, McGarvey wrote that a hard winter had made support for evangelists impossible unless churches where they preached sent more money. On September 10, 1868, McGarvey reported to Reneau that the society treasury ended the year in debt "with nothing to distribute among the Evangelists." Reneau's final preaching journey was in winter 1885, when he was seventy-nine years of age. He delivered his final sermon at Albany, Kentucky, near his home when he was barely able to stand. In his last days he frequently said that he had never preached a word of doctrine that he wished to take back. His son, John Wycliffe Reneau, became a preacher in the same region where his father had worked for many years.

Bibliography

A. *A Discourse . . . on the Claim of the Baptist Churches to Descend from John the Baptist* (Bowling Green, KY, 1859); Reneau Papers, Lexington Theological Seminary, Lexington, KY; Reneau Papers, University of West Virginia, Morgantown, WV.

B. Richard John McLean, "Go Tell It on the Mountain: The Life and Times of Isaac Tipton Reneau," unpublished B.D. thesis, Lexington Theological Seminary, 1960; H. Leo Boles, *Biographical Sketches of Gospel Preachers* (Nashville, 1932), pp. 115–119.

ROBERSON, CHARLES HEBER (28 February 1879, Robersonville, NC–30 March 1953, Abilene, TX). *Education*: B.S., Georgia Robertson College, 1901; M.A., Georgia Robertson Christian College, 1902; M.A., Texas Christian University, 1919. *Career*: Teacher, Abilene Christian University, 1906–08, 1932–51; Clebarro College, 1910–17; Thorp Spring Christian College, 1917–18; director, University of Texas Bible Chair, 1919–28; president, Texas Christian College, 1928–31.

Charles Heber Roberson is the father of the scholarly movement among Churches of Christ in the twentieth century. He and a close friend, A. B. Barret, worked closely together at four different institutions, first as original faculty members at Childers Classical Institute (now Abilene Christian University) founded by Barret in 1906; then at Southwestern Christian College, Denton, Texas, in 1908, again with Barret as president. In 1910, they cofounded Clebarro College in Cleburne, Texas. Roberson remained there through 1917. In 1918, they and G.H.P. Showalter established the Bible Chair at the University of Texas which Roberson directed from 1919 to 1928. In 1929 Roberson became president of Texas Christian College, formerly Thorp Spring Christian College, which moved to Terrell, Texas, for a brief time but was forced to close during the financially depressed 1930s. Roberson returned to Abilene Christian College in 1932 and taught Bible and biblical languages there for the next twenty years. More than anyone he was responsible for the strong undergraduate curriculum in biblical literature and languages at Abilene Christian University.

Bibliography

A. *What Jesus Taught* (Austin, 1930); coauthor, *The Bible versus Modernism* (Nashville, 1935); *Studies in the Revelation* (Tyler, TX, 1957).

B. Jim Mankin, "Charles Heber Roberson: Extraordinary Teacher and Greek Scholar," *RQ*, 36 (1st Qr 1994), 25–32; David Edwin Harrell, Jr., *The Churches of Christ in the 20th Century: Homer Hailey's Personal Journey of Faith* (Tuscaloosa, 2000), pp. 255–260.

ROBERTS, J W (28 August 1918, Henderson Co., TN–15 April 1973, Abilene, TX). *Education*: Freed-Hardeman College; B.A., Abilene Christian College, 1943; M.A., Wichita University; Ph.D., University of Texas, 1955. *Career*: Minister; professor of Bible and Greek, Abilene Christian University, 1946–73; director of graduate studies in Bible, Abilene Christian University, 1965–73.

J W Roberts taught Bible and Greek at Abilene Christian University for more than twenty-five years, joining the faculty in 1946. He authored several commentaries on New Testament books and more than 350 articles, most of them in popular religious periodicals. As a staff writer for the *Firm Foundation*, he addressed a variety of problems and issues disturbing Churches of Christ. He paid particular attention to the questions of instrumental music in worship and the adequacy of various biblical translations. He especially loved teaching and sought to acquaint his students with the biblical languages and the best scholarly tools for biblical study. He also encouraged missions as a deacon at the University Church of Christ in Abilene, Texas. A founder and editor of the scholarly journal the *Restoration Quarterly*, he devoted his career to encouraging scholarship among Churches of Christ. His letter files literally bulged with requests for help with hermeneutical problems faced by church leaders, preachers, and Bible class teachers.

Bibliography

A. *A Commentary on the Epistle of James* (Austin, 1963); *The Letters of John* (Austin, 1968); *The Revelation to John (The Apocalypse)* (Austin, 1974); "The Use of Conditional Sentences in the Greek New Testament As Compared with Homeric, Classical and Hellenistic Uses," Ph.D. dissertation, University of Texas at Austin, 1955; *RQ*, 17 (1st Qr 1974), entire issue.

B. "Professor J. W. Roberts, 1918–1973," *RQ*, 17 (1st Qr 1974), pp. 1–2.

ROGERS, JOHN (6 December 1800, Clark Co., KY–4 January 1867, Dover, KY). *Education*: Unknown. *Career*: Frontier preacher, author.

John Rogers, who spent most of his adult career as the preacher for the Church of Christ in Carlisle, Kentucky, was an important link between the religious movements led by Barton W. Stone and Alexander Campbell. In 1818 Barton W. Stone baptized Rogers and ordained him two years later. Rogers' ordination certificate read,

> The elders of the Christian Church assembled at Minerva, April 10, 1820, have unanimously ordained our brother, John Rogers, to the ministry of the Gospel, according to the will of God, our Savior, by the commendation of the Christian Church at Georgetown, in which he has lived and labored for some time past.
>
> Signed by the order of the Elders.
>
> Barton W. Stone, E.C.C.

The initials "E.C.C." meant "Elder of the Church of Christ." In spite of his close association with Stone, Rogers responded favorably to the preaching of Alexander Campbell when he heard Campbell speak in Kentucky in 1823. Rogers found especially impressive Campbell's rejection of the "mourner's bench" tradition. According to this legacy of American frontier Calvinism, the convert wept and mourned for his or her sins, sometimes for years, before obtaining evidence that one was indeed among the chosen and therefore forgiven and saved. Campbell taught that the sinner submitted to immersion for the forgiveness of sins and, as Rogers put it, in that very moment, one was "pardoned, & knew it, & rejoiced in it. Here," he said, "was nothing doubtful, mystical or difficult, no mourning and seeking salvation, for years, or months, or weeks, or even days." Campbell's articles in the *Christian Baptist* emphasizing the purity and simplicity of the apostolic order especially delighted Rogers. Upon reading an article entitled "Purity of Speech," Rogers reported that he "was in raptures." In his later years he served as a powerful advocate for the Campbellian understanding of Scripture and for what he called the "simple, divine arrangement of the elements of the gospel." In 1832, after the "Christians" (followers of Barton W. Stone) and "Reformers" (followers of Alexander Campbell) formally united at a meeting in Lexington, Kentucky, the delegates to that meeting selected John Rogers and John Smith to ride together, bearing news to all the churches of both persuasions that the two movements were now formally one.

Bibliography

A. "Life and Times of John Rogers" in John Rogers Books, 1800–1859, Southern Historical Collection, Manuscripts Department, University of North Carolina at Chapel Hill; Roscoe M. Pierson and Richard L. Harrison, Jr., eds., "The Life and Times of John Rogers, 1800–1867, of Carlisle, Kentucky," *Lexington Theological Quarterly*, 19 (January–April 1984); "Letter of John Rogers," *CM*, 14 (August 1844), 106–107; "Letters to Elder Walter Scott," *ACR*, 2 (February 25, 1859), 31; *The Biography of Elder J. T. Johnson*, 2d ed. (Cincinnati, 1861); *Discourse on Dancing* (Cincinnati, 1846 [?]); *Review of the "Report of T. V. Presbytery on the Validity of the Baptism Administered in the Reform or Campbellite Body"*

(Cincinnati, 1859); "Recollections" in W. C. Rogers, *Recollections of Men of Faith* (St. Louis, 1889).

B. John T. Brown, *Churches of Christ* (Louisville, 1904), pp. 450–451.

ROGERS, SAMUEL (6 November 1789, Charlotte Co., VA–23 June 1877, Cynthiana, KY). *Career*: Pioneer preacher of OH, IN, IL, MO, and KY.

Under the preaching of Barton W. Stone and Reuben Dooley, Samuel Rogers was immersed into Christ in 1812 and became an effective evangelist for the Stone movement. In 1825 Rogers heard Alexander Campbell preach for the first time and became at that point a devoted advocate of Campbell's understanding of the Christian gospel. Later in life he wrote that Campbell's rational approach to Scripture had delivered him from the subjective speculation that he felt had characterized the Stone tradition. In this way Rogers became an important link between the Stone and Campbell movements, though in truth, his later allegiance to Campbell overshadowed his earlier allegiance to Stone. In light of the pacifist stance that characterized so many in the Stone movement, it is interesting to note that shortly after his baptism in 1812, Rogers enlisted as a soldier to fight in the War of 1812. He preached throughout the Midwest, especially in Ohio, Indiana, Illinois, Missouri, and Kentucky, and added some 7,000 converts to the Stone-Campbell movement. His converts included several men who later became notable preachers in the Stone-Campbell movement in their own right, especially Benjamin Franklin, Elijah Goodwin, and Winthrop Hopson.

Bibliography

A. John I. Rogers, ed., *Autobiography of Elder Samuel Rogers* (Cincinnati, 1880).

B. John T. Brown, ed., *Churches of Christ* (Louisville, 1904), pp. 447–449; Leroy Garrett, *The Stone-Campbell Movement: The Story of the American Restoration Movement* (rev. ed., Joplin, MO, 1994), pp. 200–206.

S

SALLEE, ABRAHAM S. (2 December 1803–14 August 1884, Moss, TN). *Career*: Frontier preacher.

A second-generation preacher for Churches of Christ for almost fifty years, Abraham S. Sallee was instrumental in building churches in the Cumberland region, including Jackson County and Clay County, Tennessee, and Cumberland County, Kentucky—counties where Churches of Christ have historically claimed over 50 percent of the church-going population. Sallee was a principle reason for the strength of Churches of Christ in these areas. In Spring 1841, Sallee and Samuel Dewhitt debated two Mormon missionaries in Smith County, Tennessee. That debate was published in *Crihfield's Christian Family Library* in July and August, 1842.

Bibliography

A. Written debate on Mormonism, *CFL* (July 18, 1842), 211; (July 25, 1842), 217–219; (August 1, 1842), 228–229; (August 15, 1842), 236–238.

B. Obituary, *AT*, 8 (August 17, 1876), 524; Richard T. Hughes, "Two Restoration Traditions: Mormons and Churches of Christ in the Nineteenth Century," *JMH*, 19 (Spring 1993), 46–47.

SCOTT, WALTER A. (31 October 1796, Moffat, Scotland–23 April 1861, Mays Lick, KY). *Education*: University of Edinburgh. *Career*: Teacher, evangelist, editor.

Clearly one of the four most significant leaders in the founding years of Churches of Christ—the others being Alexander and Thomas Campbell and Barton Stone—Walter Scott made numerous lasting contributions to this tradition. Enamored with John Locke, on the one hand, and Scottish Common Sense Realism, on the other, Scott contributed greatly to the rationalism that would characterize Churches of Christ for two centuries. Scott also devised the five-finger "plan of salvation" that became a staple of orthodoxy among Churches of Christ in a slightly altered from. Based on the success he achieved as a missionary from the Mahoning Baptist Association to the Western Reserve in 1827–1828, Scott claimed that he had restored "the ancient gospel." His success there also convinced Thomas and Alexander Campbell that the movement they led was not doomed to regional status. From 1832 to 1835 and again from 1838 to 1842, he edited an influential gospel paper that he called *The Evangelist*. He also authored three significant books, one with the title *The Gospel Restored*. Scott was sometimes a most eloquent preacher, but his tendency toward moodiness and depression often undermined his effectiveness. A native Scot, he aligned himself with a radically restorationist sect in Pittsburgh shortly after arriving in America in 1818. His commitment to the restoration principle never wavered. He and Alexander Campbell were the closest friends, and Scott often thought of himself as Campbell's "Melanchthon."

Bibliography

A. *A Discourse on the Holy Spirit* (Bethany, WV, 1831); *The Gospel Restored* (Cincinnati, 1836); *The Messiahship or Great Demonstration* (Cincinnati, 1860); *The Union of Christians on Christian Principles* (Cincinnati, 1852); Periodicals: *The Evangelist*, 1832–1835; 1838–1842; *Protestant Unionist*, 1844–1848; *The Christian Age and Protestant Unionist*, 1849–1850.

B. John W. Neth, *Walter Scott Speaks* (Milligan College, TN, 1967); Dwight E. Stevenson, *Walter Scott: The Voice of the Golden Oracle* (St. Louis, 1946); Mark Toulouse, ed., *Walter Scott: Nineteenth-Century Evangelist* (St. Louis, 1999).

SECREST, JOHN (c.1795–?). *Career*: Frontier evangelist.

A Stoneite preacher in Ohio, John Secrest was responsible for helping Alexander Campbell understand the practical import of a doctrine that would become central to Churches of Christ—immersion for forgiveness of sins. Secrest visited the Mahoning Baptist Association meeting in September 1827 and talked to Campbell about the success a number of traveling "Christian" preachers had experienced in East and Southeast Ohio, even though their message had been immersion for the remission of sins. Campbell's interest was immediate; he reported in the *Christian Baptist*, "Elder John Secrest told me at the meeting of the Mahoning association, Ohio, on the 27th ult. that he had immersed three hundred persons within the last three months. I asked him, *Into what* did he immerse them? He replied, he immersed them into the faith of Christ, for the remission of their sins." For the first time Campbell saw the practical application of the argument on the relation of baptism to remission that he had developed in his debate with W. L. McCalla (1823) merely to win the argument against infant sprinkling. Campbell continued to monitor Secrest's work with great interest. After a visit in November, Campbell wrote that John Secrest had proclaimed "the gospel and Christian immersion in its primitive simplicity and import." Campbell knew of no other person who had "fairly and fully tested" the practice as Secrest had, and Campbell began to see Secrest as a model for primitive evangelism and Bible baptism. During the year 1827 Secrest had immersed about 700 converts. He reported, "Great excitement is among the people; many are inquiring what shall we do? We tell them to reform and be immersed in the name of Jesus Christ, for the remission of sins, and you shall receive the gift of the Holy Spirit; and then to continue steadfast in the Apostle's doctrine and fellowship, and breaking of bread or the Lord's supper, and prayers. And when they obey, we can truly say, from all appearances, the promise is fulfilled, and like the Eunuch, they go on their way rejoicing." Secrest's views on conferences also are important in understanding the Stone movement and its merger with the Campbell movement. Secrest was one of the first in the Stone movement to reject a call by some Christian Connection preachers for national conferences. "Away with conferences and church records, they are a patch of Babylon—they are so destitute of precept and example in scripture, that it would be impossible to establish such things where I preach." Although John Secrest died in disfavor after some unfortunate experiences, his early work had a profound influence on Alexander Campbell and subsequently on the united movements of Campbell and Barton W. Stone.

Bibliography

A. "Extract of a Letter from Elder John Secrest," *CM*, 2 (July 1828), 214–215.

B. "A Year's Labor," *CB*, 5 (February 5, 1828), 173; "An Extract from the Christian Baptist," *CM*, 2 (November 1827), 22–24; *CH*, 10 (May 1827), 35; John Rogers, "The Life and Times of John Rogers," in John Rogers Books, 1800–1859, Book I, p. 163, in Southern Historical Collection, Manuscripts Department, University of North Carolina at Chapel Hill.

SEWELL, DAISY ELIZABETH (19 June 1876–17 May 1944, San Antonio, TX). *Education*: Carlton College, Bonham, TX; Ward-Belmont Seminary; David Lipscomb College; John Longman Art School, New York City. *Career*: Teacher; author; dean of women, Abilene Christian College, 1912–24.

Daisy McQuigg Sewell was widely recognized as the most influential female teacher and writer among the Churches of Christ during the first half of the twentieth century. She served Abilene Christian College as dean of women from 1912 to 1924, the same years her husband served as president of the college. During that period she was so heavily involved in the life of the school that many viewed her as "the mother" of Abilene Christian College. Shortly after they completed their service at the college, the Sewells moved to San Antonio, Texas; there Jesse P. Sewell embarked on a lengthy ministry for the Grove Avenue Church of Christ, where he served from 1927 until Daisy's death in 1944. During that period Daisy extended her reputation as a Christian writer. She is perhaps best known for her books on Christian womanhood (*Ideal Womanhood*, 1927) and the Christian home (*The Home as God Would Have It*, 1937).

Bibliography

A. *Ideal Womanhood* (Austin, 1927); *The Home as God Would Have It* (Austin, 1937).
B. *FF*, 61 (June 6, 1944), 2–3; "In Memory," *CWom*, 12 (July 1944), 21.

SEWELL, JESSE LOUDERMAN (25 May 1818, Overton Co., TN–29 June 1890, Viola, TN). *Career*: Minister.

Jesse Louderman Sewell was widely regarded as one of the most influential preachers among Churches of Christ in Tennessee during the mid-to late nineteenth century. Sewell belonged to a family of preachers widely respected for their oratorical powers. Three of his brothers—Isaac, Caleb W., and Elisha G.—and four of his sons—Joseph, William A. (the father of Jesse P.), L. Rice, and Caleb W.—all served Churches of Christ in the preaching capacity. In addition, Jesse L. Sewell recruited more than twenty additional men to the ministry. Yet, most were agreed that none was as effective as Sewell himself. David Lipscomb observed that "the hold . . . upon the people of Middle Tennessee" by the Christian movement was "due under God to Jesse Sewell, more than any one man." Lipscomb thought that Sewell was a better preacher, all things considered, than any he had heard, including Alexander Campbell. Originally a Baptist preacher, Sewell was converted to the Christian movement by John Newton Mulkey. Shortly after his conversion, the Wolf River Baptist Church charged Sewell with heresy and excluded him from its fellowship. Two of Jesse's brothers, Isaac and Caleb, forthwith requested that their names be taken off the church roll as well. After their mother, Annie, was excluded, their father, Stephen—a deacon—stood up in the congregation and declared that he also was withdrawing because of the manner in which his family had been treated by the church. In this way, the entire Sewell family abandoned the Baptists and committed itself to the Christian movement.

Bibliography

A. *GA*, 23 (December 29, 1881), 813.
B. David Lipscomb, *The Life and Sermons of Jesse L. Sewell* (Nashville, 1891); Granville Lipscomb, "Reminiscences of Jesse L. Sewell," *GA* (November 12 and 19, 1903), 730, 739, 803; H. Leo Boles, *Biographical Sketches of Gospel Preachers* (Nashville, 1932), pp. 179–185.

SEWELL, JESSE PARKER (21 January 1876, Viola, TN-4 July 1969, Abilene, TX). *Education*: Viola Normal College, 1892; Nashville Bible School, 1893–94. *Career*: Minister; president, Abilene Christian College, 1912–24.

A grandson of the noted Tennessee preacher of the mid-nineteenth century, Jesse Louderman Sewell, Jesse Parker Sewell distinguished himself as a noted Texas preacher and educator during the first half of the twentieth century. A product of the Nashville Bible School, where he attended for two years, 1893 and 1894, Sewell preached his first sermon in 1895 at age nineteen. He later moved to Texas, where he built congregations of the Churches of Christ in Sherman, Dallas (the Pearl and Bryan congregation, now Highland Oaks), and San Angelo. He was also an associate editor for the *Gospel Advocate and Christian Leader*. An avid worker for the prohibition cause, Sewell developed a reputation as the strongest anti-saloon worker in Texas. Perhaps his most notable contribution to the work of Churches of Christ in Texas was his service to fledgling Abilene Christian College, established in 1906. Sewell took the presidential reins of that institution in 1912 and continued in that position until 1924. During his tenure Abilene Christian became first a two-year college and then a four-year college. Accordingly, Sewell was known as the "father of Abilene Christian College." From 1927 through 1944, Sewell served as the pulpit minister for the Grove Avenue Church of Christ in San Antonio, Texas. In the late 1930s and early 1940s Sewell, Clinton Davidson, and E. W. McMillan engineered the drive to derail the negative journalism fostered by Foy E. Wallace, Jr., and to create among Churches of Christ a more constructive journalistic style.

Bibliography

A. *The Church and the Ideal Educational Situation* (Austin, 1931); *In the Beginning, God* (Abilene, TX, 1966).

B. James F. Jones, "The Educational Contributions of Jesse Parker Sewell," Ed.D. dissertation, Oklahoma State University, 1961.

SHANNON, JAMES (22 April 1799, Ireland–1859, Canton, MO). *Education*: B.A., M.A., Royal University of Belfast, Ireland; LL.D., University of Missouri; D.D., University of Georgia. *Career*: Rector of a Presbyterian academy, Sunbury, GA, 1820s; professor of ancient languages, University of Georgia, 1830–35; president of the following colleges and universities: College of Louisiana, Baton Rouge, 1835–40; Bacon College, Harrodsburg, KY, 1840–50; University of Missouri, Columbia, MO, 1850–56; Christian University, Canton, MO, 1856–59.

A leading figure in higher education in the South during the 1830s, 1840s, and 1850s, James Shannon rivaled Alexander Campbell in intellect, educational background, and persuasive powers. Yet, Shannon worked at cross-purposes with Campbell on one fundamental issue: slavery. In fact, Shannon quickly became one of the leading voices in the South supporting slavery and opposing abolition. He argued that slavery was sanctioned "by the light of Nature, the Constitution of the United States, and the clear teaching of the Bible." A contemporary, W. C. Rogers, recalled that he had heard no one who "could array as many and as strong, plausible arguments from the Scriptures, in favor of this position, as could he." After receiving his education at the Royal University of Belfast in Ireland, Shannon immigrated to the United States in the 1820s and soon developed a reputation as a noted educator in the South. After teaching ancient languages at the University of Georgia from 1830 to 1835, Shannon served successively as president of the College of Louisiana (1835–1840), Bacon College (1840–1850), the University of Missouri (1850–1856), and Christian University in Canton, Missouri (1856–1859). His presidency of Bacon College was particularly important in the history of Churches of Christ, since Bacon College was the first institution of higher learning in the Stone-Campbell tradition. Founded in 1836 and based on the philosophy of Common Sense Rationalism, Bacon College attracted Walter Scott, one of the founders of the Stone-Campbell movement, to serve as its first president. Shannon's inaugural address as president of Bacon College, delivered on November 13, 1840, was hailed as a significant statement of philosophy of higher education in the Stone-Campbell movement and was published in Alexander Campbell's *Millennial Harbinger*. Shannon's presidency of the University of Missouri was also important, since that position provided him with a political platform for his pro-slavery views, a platform that he leveraged to the hilt. With public opinion inflamed by the Kansas-Nebraska Act of 1854, Shannon gave one inflammatory speech after another across the state of Missouri. By 1856 pressure from moderate voices forced Shannon to resign.

Bibliography

A. "Inaugural Address," *MH*, new ser., 5 (March 1841), 126–132, and new ser., 5 (April 1841), 149–156; "Address to the People of the United States, Together with the Proceedings and Resolutions of the Pro-slavery Convention of Missouri, Held at Lexington, July, 1855" (St. Louis, 1855).

B. Thomas Preston Haley, *Historical and Biographical Sketches of Early Churches and Pioneer Preachers of the Christian Church in Missouri* (Kansas City, 1888), pp. 456–459; W. C. Rogers, *Recollections of Men of Faith* (St. Louis, 1889), pp. 15–18; George L. Peters, "James Shannon—Christian Educator," typed biographical sketch in James Shannon Collection, Disciples of Christ Historical Society.

SHAW, KNOWLES (1835, Lebanon, OH-7 June 1878, near McKinney, TX). *Career*: Singer, songwriter, evangelist.

Known as the "singing evangelist," Knowles Shaw distinguished himself as the most successful evangelist among Stone-Campbell churches in the Mississippi Valley for some twenty years prior to his untimely death at age forty-three in 1878. Eccentric in the pulpit, Shaw interspersed preaching with singing. David Lipscomb thought his eccentricities would have made anyone else appear ridiculous, but Lipscomb contended that since Shaw's work was "heartily for the Lord" and natural for Shaw, "his labor is right." C. M. Wilmeth, editor of the *Christian Preacher*, heard Shaw preach in Dallas and later wrote, "He reasons like Paul; is as bold as Peter; and as tender as John. . . . He sings with the energy of Sankey and plays with the action of Blind Tom. He can support the character, in the same scene, of clergyman and clown, actor and ape, nightingale and parrot." Strong both physically and mentally, Shaw worked incessantly. During one thirteen-year period, there were only two weeks when he failed to hold a gospel meeting.

Bibliography

A. "Tennessee," *AT*, 9 (January 11, 1878), 10.

B. "Knowles Shaw," editorial, *AT*, 10 (June 14, 1878), 8; "Death on the Rail—a Horrible Accident at McKinney," *AT*, 10 (June 21, 1878), 6; William Baxter, *Life of Knowles Shaw* (Cincinnati, 1879); C. M. Wilmeth, editorial, *CPr*, quoted in William Baxter, 152.

SHELBURNE, G. B., JR. (15 January 1913, Runnels Co. [near Hatchel], TX—9 January 2000, Pasadena, TX). *Education*: B.A., Abilene Christian College, 1935. *Career*: Founder and director, a preacher-training school first known as Kerrville Bible Training Work, Kerrville, TX, 1946–53; then in Amarillo, TX; and finally as the South Houston Bible Institute, Houston, TX, 1975–80; preacher, Kerrville, Amarillo, and Houston, TX; founding editor, *Gospel Tiding*, 1936–56.

For almost half a century—from the 1950s through the 1990s—G. B. Shelburne, Jr., was the leading representative of the non–Sunday school wing of Churches of Christ in Texas and the West. He earned his B.A. in 1935 from Abilene Christian College, where he graduated as valedictorian of his class. Shortly after graduation he undertook his full-time preaching ministry. He established congregations in San Angelo, Texas, and Corpus Christi, Texas, and in the course of his life preached all over the United States and abroad, helping to establish a successful mission work at Namikango Mission in Malawi. He devoted long years to preaching assignments in Kerrville, Amarillo, and Houston, Texas. In 1946 he went to Kerrville, where he organized a preacher-training school he called the Kerrville Bible Training Work. In 1953 he moved that school to Amarillo; and in 1975 he moved the school to Houston, where it became known as the South Houston Bible Institute. From 1936 to 1956, he served as the founding editor of *Gospel Tidings*, a publication that served the non–Sunday school wing of Churches of Christ. Shelburne was known especially for his irenic spirit in a time when Churches of Christ were badly divided over the propriety of Sunday schools among other issues.

Bibliography

A. *A Providential Journey: 58 Years of Preaching* (Englewood, CO, 1991); "The Spread of the Gospel in Poland and Adjoining Countries" in *The Harvest Field*, comp. by Howard L. Schug and Jesse P. Sewell (Athens, AL, 1947); various articles in *Gospel Tidings*, 1936–1956.

B. Leroy Garrett, *The Stone-Campbell Movement*, rev. ed. (Joplin, MO, 1994), p. 437; Thomas Langford, "Foreword" to G. B. Shelburne, *A Providential Journey: 58 Years of Preaching* (Englewood, CO, 1991), pp. v-viii.

SHEPHERD, JAMES WALTON (18 August 1861, Irvine, KY–27 July 1948, Detroit, MI). *Education*: College of the Bible, 1884. *Career*: Minister, author.

James Walter Shepherd exerted a significant influence among Churches of Christ through his preaching but especially through two books that he authored. James A. Harding described Shepherd's *Handbook on Baptism*, first published in 1894, as "by far the fullest, the best arranged, and most valuable collection of learned testimonies on the action, subjects, and design of baptism ever published in a single volume." Shepherd also wrote an influential work that reflected the historiographic perspective of Churches of Christ, *The Church, the Falling Away, and the Restoration*, first published in 1929. In his capacity as office editor of the *Gospel Advocate*, Shepherd also edited commentaries on various books of the New Testament by David Lipscomb; edited *Queries and Answers* and *Salvation from Sin*, also by David Lipscomb; and edited Robert Henry Boll's *Truth and Grace*. Shepherd studied at the College of the Bible in Lexington, Kentucky, under J. W. McGarvey, who influenced the young preacher to undertake mission work to New Zealand and Australia. Shepherd undertook that work from 1888 through 1891. While there he established congregations of Churches of Christ, worked with existing congregations, and wrote for the *Christian Pioneer*, an Australian periodical. Shepherd did much of the research on his *Handbook on Baptism* in libraries in New Zealand and Australia. It is possible that his pioneering mission work in Australia and New Zealand inspired the preeminent missionary among Churches of Christ in the late nineteenth and early twentieth centuries, J. M. McCaleb, to undertake mission efforts in Japan.

Bibliography

A. *Handbook on Baptism* (Nashville, 1894; 2d ed., 1912); *The Church, the Falling Away, and the Restoration* (Cincinnati, 1929).

B. "J. W. Shepherd Passes," *GA*, 90 (August 5, 1948), 748.

SHOWALTER, GEORGE HENRY PRYOR (15 October 1870, Snowville, VA–17 October 1954, Austin, TX). Education: B.A. and M.A., Milligan College, Johnson City, TN. *Career*: Preacher teacher; president, Lockney Christian College, 1897–1907; co-founder, Bible; chair, University of Texas, 1918; editor, *Firm Foundation*, 1908–54.

By virtue of the fact that he edited one of the most influential publications among Churches of Christ, the *Firm Foundation*, George Henry Pryor Showalter was without question one of the most powerful figures in Churches of Christ for most of the first half of the twentieth century. In that capacity Showalter served as one of the few "editor-bishops" who defined orthodox faith and practice in this tradition. As the son of John T. Showalter, who for many years wrote for the *American Christian Review* and other periodicals related to the Stone-Campbell tradition, George Showalter in some ways inherited his interest in

Christian journalism. Prior to his editorial responsibilities with the *Firm Foundation*, Showalter served from 1897 to 1907 as president of Lockney Christian College in the small town of Lockney on the West Texas plains. In 1918, with Charles Heber Roberson and A. B Barret, Showalter helped establish the Bible chair at the University of Texas. Showalter was many things to the Churches of Christ: editor, evangelist, publisher, teacher, college president, elder, and preacher. After his death in 1954, those who looked to him for leadership in the church praised him for many things, but especially for his balance. According to M. Norvel Young, he was "outstanding in his balance, his moderation, his holding to the truth without compromise and yet refusing to be driven to extreme." Cecil N. Wright praised the editorials written "in his prime" as "in my judgement, unexcelled." L. R. Wilson, president of Oklahoma Christian College, praised Showalter's generous style of leadership. "He would much prefer to err on the side of leniency and kindness than severity and harshness," Wilson wrote. And Arthur R. Holton pointed to his role as an unofficial bishop in Churches of Christ: "We shall miss him when we look for someone to say the word that will be final when our brethren have disagreements and when controversial issues arise." Most agreed that the Churches of Christ had lost their "balance-wheel." Showalter was a strong supporter of Christian education and benevolent efforts and served on the board of directors of Belle Haven Orphans' Home at Luling, Texas.

Bibliography

A. *Travel Talks* (Austin, 1938); *Showalter-Clark Discussion on the Lord's Day Bible School Involving a Consideration of the Class System and Women Teachers* (Austin, 1940); editorials, *FF*, 1907–1954.

B. *FF*, 71 (November 23, 1954): memorial issue in honor of G.H.P. Showalter.

SHOWALTER, WINIFRED WATTS (1885, Rogers, AR–9 April 1956, Strafford, MO). *Career*: Editor, writer.

Winifred Watts Showalter was the founding editor of *Christian Woman*, the oldest women's publication of its kind in the United States. While she was married to Marshall Spencer Mason, an itinerant preacher, she established a millinery business in Springdale, Arkansas, to support the family and allow her husband to devote full time to traveling and preaching for small congregations in northern Arkansas and adjacent areas of Missouri. During that period she began Bible classes for both women and children at a time when such classes were seldom conducted in congregations of Churches of Christ. Her life changed, however, when her husband was shot and killed by a man apparently with a vendetta against the Church of Christ and its preachers. Mason had written for the publication *Christian Worker* prior to his death, and the editor, Homer E. Moore, invited Winifred Mason to start a column in the *Worker*. Her column, "The Home Department," began in March 1931. In June 1933 Winifred Mason married Homer E. Moore and the couple moved to Wichita, Kansas, where she began the *Christian Woman* in October 1933. She edited that publication for the next twenty-two years. Upon the death of Homer Moore, Winifred was married again in 1945, this time to G.H.P. Showalter, editor of the *Firm Foundation*, and moved to Austin, Texas.

Bibliography

A. Various articles, *CWom*, 1–22 (1933–1954).

B. Alma McNeese, "Winifred Showalter: A Woman before Her Time," *CWom*, 47 (November/December 1985), 40–41, 64.

SMITH, FLETCHER WALTON (12 March 1858, Lincoln Co., TN–11 November 1930, Franklin, TN). *Career*: Minister, writer.

Fletcher Walton Smith was one of the most successful evangelists in Middle Tennessee from roughly 1880 until his death in 1930. He also conducted numerous gospel meetings for congregations of Churches of Christ throughout the United States and Canada. Many of those meetings resulted in more than 100 additions to the church and a few won more than 150. He began his preaching career as a farmer-preacher soon after his conversion at Pulaski, Tennessee, during a meeting held by J. C. McQuiddy and W. H. Dickson in 1881. For some forty years Smith contributed clear and concise articles to the *Gospel Advocate* on a weekly basis. He held a clear conception of the meaning of the nondenominational nature of the church and contended that the church of Christ consisted of *all* children of God—a position sometimes misunderstood and even opposed by members of Churches of Christ who held a sectarian spirit. In 1903 Smith began a ministry with the Church of Christ in Franklin, Tennessee, that lasted until his death in 1930.

Bibliography

A. Various articles in *GA*, 1890–1930.

B. H. Leo Boles, *Biographical Sketches of Gospel Preachers* (Nashville, 1932), pp. 443–447; F. B. Srygley, "The Passing of F. W. Smith," *GA*, 72 (November 27, 1930), 1140; Hall L. Calhoun, "An Appreciation," *GA*, 72 (November 27, 1930), 1141.

SMITH, JOHN (15 October 1784, Sullivan Co., TN–28 February 1868, Mexico, MO). *Career*: Pioneer preacher.

When Philip S. Fall was asked who had done most to promote primitive Christianity in Kentucky besides Alexander Campbell and Barton Stone, he replied without a moment's hesitation, "Undoubtedly, John Smith." "Raccoon" John Smith both strengthened and shaped the Churches of Christ, especially in his native Stockton Valley in southern Kentucky. In that region Smith converted outstanding Baptist ministers like John D. Steele, Jonathan H. Young, and John Calvin Smith, and he inspired other young men, including Isaac T. Reneau of

Albany, Kentucky who fulfilled a ministry of fifty years in the Upper Cumberland region. In that same area two of Smith's grandsons, William L. Smith and Henry J. Boles, served as preachers in the Stone-Campbell movement. Boles was the father of H. Leo Boles, a well-known leader in Churches of Christ in Tennessee in the early twentieth century.

W. C. Rogers authored many articles on outstanding personalities in the Stone-Campbell tradition but regarded John Smith as "the greatest and mightiest natural man I have ever known." James Mason, an elder at the Grassy Lick church in Kentucky, thought John Smith was "a host within himself." Isaac Reneau first heard Smith preach at the September 1820 meeting of the Stockton Valley Baptist Association. He later wrote, "We were all spell-bound to our seats, listening in death-like stillness and silence to the gushing forth, as from a fountain, of the unrestrained torrent of his all-conquering eloguence." One of the preachers remarked afterward that he did not believe that there was a man in America who would attempt to follow John Smith with a discourse.

Smith was ordained in the Tates' Creek Baptist Association, a Calvinistic organization that accepted the Philadelphia Confession of Faith. The tragic death of two of his children in a fire that consumed the Smith home while he was away preaching prompted Smith to reassess and finally to reject the doctrine of predestination. During this time of doubt, Smith began subscribing to Alexander Campbell's *Christian Baptist*. In 1826 Smith abandoned the Baptists and became a leading preacher in the Christian movement led by Alexander Campbell and Barton W. Stone. In 1832 Smith played a pivotal role in the process by which the Stone and Campbell movements formally united. At a meeting held in Lexington, Kentucky, over the New Year's Day weekend, 1831–1832, Smith represented Campbell's "Disciples" in conversation with Barton Stone's "Christians." Once the decision was made to move forward with the union, Smith, again representing the Campbell forces, and John Rogers, representing the Stone forces, were commissioned to travel from congregation to congregation to herald the news of the union that created the Stone-Campbell movement.

Bibliography

A. "Address to the Disciples," in John Augustus Williams, *Life of Elder John Smith* (Cincinnati, 1870); F. L. Rowe, ed., *Pioneer Sermons and Addresses* (Cincinnati, 1925), pp. 183–192; "The Transfiguration of Christ," *CP*, 8 (April 2, 1868), 113–118; "Farewell Sermon," *CP*, 8 (April 23, 1868), 161–165.

B. A sketch by Isaac T. Reneau in the Reneau Papers, University of West Virginia, 7–8; John Augustus Williams, *Life of Elder John Smith* (Cincinnati, 1870); J. Kendrick Reid, "A Glance through the Field," *AT*, 10 (June 21, 1878), 10–11; Louis Cochran, *Raccoon John Smith* (New York, 1963 [an historical novel]); Everett Donaldson, *Raccoon John Smith: Frontiersman and Reformer* (Mt. Sterling, KY, 1991), and Everett Donaldson, *The Legacy of Raccoon John Smith* (Mt. Sterling, KY, 1995).

SMITH, NATHAN WILLIAMSON (4 September 1813, Rockingham Co., NC–10 August 1899, Acworth, GA). *Career*: Minister.

Nathan Smith was an evangelist for a congregation in Clarke County, Georgia, aligned with the Republican Christian Church or Republican Church of Christ, a coalition of congregations originally connected to the movements led by James O'Kelly in Virginia and Barton W. Stone in Kentucky. By 1832 when Smith was immersed by Elder A. Dupree, this church had come increasingly under the influence of Stone, and its members were known as "New Lights" or "Stone-ites." In the year that Smith was immersed, the movement led by Barton Stone and the movement led by Alexander Campbell joined forces. Most of the members in Georgia accepted the merger, though a small minority of "old side" members sought to rid the Clark County churches of "the Reformers-Campbellites," as they called them. As a result, division came to these churches in 1842. For a while after the union of the Stone and Campbell forces, these churches saw no increase. Thacker V. Griffin from Tennessee preached among them in 1833 without visible results. From 1842 after the division to 1845, however, the Republican church more than doubled its membership. In 1844 it launched an evangelistic effort by putting Nathan Smith "in the field." The field included Georgia, Alabama, and South Carolina. Smith described the results. "I immersed a great many persons and organized several congregations, that were built up from very small beginnings to large and respectable churches." Dr. Daniel Hook and an S. C. Dunning joined Smith in these evangelistic endeavors. Smith also played a prominent role in the post-Civil War benevolent work conducted by Churches of Christ in the South. Smith wrote to David Lipscomb, editor of Nashville's *Gospel Advocate*, about the devastation his area had suffered during the war. When Lipscomb publicized the need in Georgia, Churches of Christ contributed over $100,000 in relief during the next few years. Concurrent with relief by the Tennessee churches, church growth in Middle Tennessee for the decade 1866 to 1875 was unparalleled. Their work was so impressive that Henry Ward Beecher's *Christian Union* gave national attention to the benevolent work of the Churches of Christ of Middle Tennessee.

Bibliography

A. No title, *CFL* (1842), 278; "An Old Preacher's Experience," nos. 1–6, *CS*, 14 (May 3–June 7, 1879), 142, 150, 158, 166, 174, 182.

SOMMER, DANIEL (11 January 1850, St. Mary Co., MD–19 February 1940, Indianapolis, IN). *Education*: Bethany College. *Career*: Minister, editor, writer.

Daniel Sommer stood for the "old paths" defined by his Indiana forebear, Benjamin Franklin, and came to be known especially for his hard-nosed and legalistic opposition to church-related colleges. He especially attacked the Nashville Bible School, established by James A. Harding and David Lipscomb in 1891. "Bible Readings," a series of intense study periods held in various locations, replaced the college classroom among the churches most influenced by

Sommer. Late in life Sommer made a lengthy trip to the South and visited David Lipscomb College, Freed-Hardeman College, and Abilene Christian College to see firsthand the type of work that he had long opposed. What he found differed from what he had attacked and led to a subsequent conciliatory attitude.

In 1883 Sommer began a periodical that he named *The Octograph*, a title suggested by the number of men who wrote the New Testament. Following the death of Benjamin Franklin, Sommer purchased the *American Christian Review* that Franklin had edited but changed its title to *Octographic Review*. Sommer eventually reverted, however, to the original name, *American Christian Review*. Sommer opposed virtually every innovation that might have altered the "ancient order" defined by Alexander Campbell in the *Christian Baptist*. Sommer's style was particularly caustic. Following an exchange with Sommer on the role of women in the church, Mrs. M. R. Lemert called his style of writing "wrathy." Sommer alienated many, including David Lipscomb, who refused to read his articles after Sommer reneged on his agreement to publish one of Lipscomb's. The lasting influence of Daniel Sommer seems practically nil at the dawn of the twenty-first century.

Bibliography

A. *Hector Among the Doctors, or, A Search for the True Church: A Volume of Thoughts for Thinkers* (Indianapolis, 1896).

B. Matthew C. Morrison, "Daniel Sommer's Seventy Years of Religious Controversy," Ph.D. dissertation, Indiana University, 1972; Matthew C. Morrison, *Like a Lion: Daniel Sommer's Seventy Years of Preaching* (Murfreesboro, TN, 1975); William Wallace, *Daniel Sommer, 1850–1940: A Biography* (Lufkin, TX, 1969); Stephen Wolfgang, "A Life of Humble Fear: The Biography of Daniel Sommer, 1850–1940," M.A. thesis, Butler University, 1975.

SPAIN, ROBERT CARL (23 October 1917, Chattanooga, TN–21 December 1990, Abilene, TX). *Education*: David Lipscomb College, 1936; and B.A., Abilene Christian University, 1938; M.A. and B.D., Southern Methodist University, 1947; Th.D., Southwestern Baptist Theological Seminary, 1963. *Career*: Professor, Harding College, 1946–47; founder and director, Church of Christ Bible Chair at Texas Tech University, 1947–51; minister, Central Church of Christ, Houston, and Graham Street and Hillcrest Churches of Christ, Abilene, TX; professor of Bible, Abilene Christian University, 1954–84.

Carl Spain served for many years as a preacher and a Bible professor at Abilene Christian University in Abilene, Texas. Then, six years after the U.S. Supreme Court handed down its *Brown v. Board of Education* decision, Spain took a step that would bring him lasting fame among Churches of Christ. In 1960, six years after that decision had been rendered, colleges related to Churches of Christ had still not taken steps to enforce racial integration. At the Abilene Christian College Bible Lectureship in 1960, therefore, Spain launched a blistering attack on racism and segregation in colleges and universities related to Churches of Christ. He called the speech "Modern Challenges to Christian Morals." William S. Banowsky, in his study of the ACU Lectures, called it "the most spectacular speech ever delivered" at the Abilene forum if measured by the audience reaction and the shock wave it generated in the churches and in the press. Abilene Christian College responded by officially admitting blacks to graduate school in 1961 and to undergraduate work in 1962.

Bibliography

A. *Bible Lectures*, Abilene Christian University (Abilene, 1960); *The Letters of Paul to Timothy and Titus* (Austin, TX, 1970).

SRYGLEY, FLETCHER D. (22 December 1856, Rock Creek, AL–2 August 1900, Donelson, TN). *Education*: Mars Hill Academy. *Career*: Preacher; author; associate editor, *Old Path Guide*, 1881–84; front page editor, *Gospel Advocate*, 1889–1900.

In a lifespan of only forty-three years, stretching from 1856 to 1900, Fletcher Douglas Srygley distinguished himself for his witty, incisive editorial writing in a variety of publications that served Churches of Christ. He served as associate editor of the *Old Path Guide* from 1881 to 1884, and front page editor of the *Gospel Advocate* from 1889 to 1900. In addition, he published several books that were favorites among members of Churches of Christ for generations. When Srygley was only fourteen years old, the famed T. B. Larimore visited his mountain village of Rock Creek, Alabama, to preach for the tiny congregation where Srygley and his family worshipped. Srygley admired Larimore from that day forward, and the two men eventually became close friends. In fact, no man did more to shape the course of Srygley's career than did T. B. Larimore. Srygley attended school at Larimore's Mars Hill Academy near Florence, Alabama. In addition, Larimore baptized Srygley in 1873 and married Srygley and his bride, Ella Parkhill, in 1878. In 1889 Srygley published *Smiles and Tears, or, Larimore and His Boys*, a book that recounted both the life of Larimore as well as the lives of some of Larimore's students at his Mars Hill school. In 1900, knowing his life was short, Srygley rushed to compile his second book on Larimore, *Letters and Sermons of T. B. Larimore*. But Srygley had other interests as well. With his characteristic wit he defended the concept of nondenominational Christianity, a theme central to the identity of Churches of Christ, in his book *The New Testament Church*, a compilation of editorials he had published in the *Gospel Advocate* from 1889 to 1900. In 1881 Srygley and David Lipscomb had a serious disagreement over the question of the missionary society, a hot political issue among Churches of Christ in the waning years of the nineteenth century. Lipscomb opposed these extracongregational organizations, but Srygley could find nothing in them to condemn. In the aftermath of their disagreement, Srygley abandoned Lipscomb and the *Gospel Advocate* and accepted a post as associate editor of F. G. Allen's *Old Path Guide*, a prosociety paper published in Louisville, Kentucky. By 1889 Srygley and Lipscomb had reconciled, though they continued to disagree over the question of the missionary society. In spite of that disagreement, Lipscomb appointed Srygley as front page editor of the *Advocate*, a position he held from 1889 until his premature death in 1900.

Bibliography

A. "From the Papers," *GA*, 32 (April 23, 1890), 24–25; "From the Papers," *GA* (April 9, 1890), 225; *Smiles and Tears, or, Larimore and His Boys* (Nashville, 1889); *Biographies and Sermons* (Nashville, 1898); *Letters and Sermons of T. B. Larimore* (Nashville, 1900); *The New Testament Church* (Nashville, 1910); *Seventy Years in Dixie* (Nashville, 1914); *What Is the New Testament Church?* (Nashville, 1954).

B. Earl I. West, *Search for the Ancient Order*, vol. 2 (Indianapolis, 1950), pp. 320–331; H. Leo Boles, *Biographical Sketches of Gospel Preachers* (Nashville, 1932), pp. 426–429.

STEELE, JOHN D. (16 February 1793–1876, KY). *Career*: Pioneer preacher, religious reformer.

John D. Steele, originally a Baptist preacher who came under the influence of "Raccoon" John Smith, became a noted preacher for Churches of Christ in the Green River and Cumberland River sections of southern Kentucky during the middle years of the nineteenth century. Steele typified many of the frontier preachers of the Stone-Campbell movement in his passionate defense of cultural and biblical primitivism. He found in the writings of Isaac Errett, editor of the progressive *Christian Standard* based in Cincinnati, evidence for the corruption of both church and civilization. After Cincinnati's Central Christian Church built its $140,000 building with its forty-eight-foot Catherine wheel and its expensive organ, Steel wrote to a fellow primitivist, Jacob Creath, Jr., "Is it expedient to build such fine houses . . . in cities and elsewhere? Brother Creath, when I look at all these things in our ranks, I say to myself, give me caves and dens of the earth to worship God in, rather then to conform to the world in this way." Steele warned that when "we give up the Bible alone in connection with the independence of the churches we are (to use a common saying) *gone*." Steele held up the virtues of frontier preachers: "There was earnestness *then*, there was love *then*, there was honesty *then*, there was humility then, there was plainness and simplicity then." He wondered out loud, "Where have many of these christian virtues fled?"

Bibliography

A. Jacob Creath, Jr., "A Copy of a Letter from a Pioneer Preacher in Kentucky," *GA*, 14 (November 28, 1872), 1119–1120.

B. John Augustus Williams, *The Life of Elder John Smith* (Cincinnati, 1870), pp. 322–327.

STONE, BARTON WARREN (22 December 1772, Port Tobacco, MD–9 November 1844, Hannibal, MO). *Education*: David Caldwell's Academy. *Career*: Reformer; evangelist; teacher; editor, *Christian Messenger*, 1826–44.

Along with Alexander Campbell, Barton W. Stone was one of the two primary leaders of the Christian movement of the early nineteenth century, a movement whose congregations were known as Churches of Christ, Christian Churches, and Disciples of Christ. If Alexander Campbell brought to Churches of Christ a spirit of rationalism rooted in the eighteenth-century Enlightenment, Stone brought to Churches of Christ a deep personal piety rooted in the revivals of the eighteenth and early nineteenth centuries. In 1790 Stone studied under David Caldwell, whose North Carolina "log college" still bore the influence of the Great Awakening. One of Caldwell's students, William Hodge, converted Stone in a revival in 1791. When Stone received his license as a Presbyterian minister, another revival preacher, Henry Patillo, addressed the candidates. Patillo had been a student of Samuel Davies, whose revival work perpetuated the influence of the Great Awakening in the South. Little wonder that Stone's own preaching in his Presbyterian congregation at Cane Ridge, Kentucky, helped trigger the famed Cane Ridge Revival of 1801.

Stone's work not only differed substantively from that of Alexander Campbell, but to the extent that Stone and Campbell stood in agreement, Stone's work predated that of Campbell in a variety of ways. Long before the name of Alexander Campbell was even known in the Stoneite heartland of southern Kentucky, Middle Tennessee, and northern Alabama, some 200 preachers and dozens of congregations had followed the leadership of Barton W. Stone to become Christians only, with no ties of any kind to any historic denomination. In many instances Stone and his associates had established those congregations. Participants in the Stone movement called themselves "Christians," and congregations sometimes used the designation "Christian church," but most often they employed the title "Churches of Christ," the term most in agreement with Stone's commitment never to "be the member of any church, which is not called the Church of Christ, and who[se members] are not called Christians." Even though Alexander Campbell embraced the designation "Disciples," Stone denounced that term. Long before Alexander Campbell suggested that instrumental music in worship was like "a cowbell in a concert," Stone had labeled that practice "the extreme of folly." Stone's coined rule of "neither inviting nor debarring" pious folk from the Lord's table has continued as a general practice among Churches of Christ for many years. Stone extended fellowship to the "pious unimmersed" since he hoped to win those he considered virtually Christians or pious in character but ignorant of their full duty. At the same time Stone embraced the doctrine of believer's baptism for the remission of sins, a distinctive feature of Churches of Christ since the inception of the movement. On this point priority once again belongs to Stone rather than to Campbell, since Stone argued this view in January 1827, a full year before Campbell began to take this doctrine seriously.

Several commitments marked the ministry and career of Barton W. Stone. First, Stone and his followers devoted themselves to maintaining Christian freedom. This commitment was so pronounced that for the first twenty-two years of the Stone movement (i.e., 1801–1823), the Stoneites refused to develop any theological, structural or liturgical tradition whatsoever for fear that these traditions might preclude the freedom of the individual believer. Second, Stone and his followers committed themselves to a vision of primitive Christianity that side-stepped the historical developments of the Christian faith. Third, Stone emerged as a powerful advocate for the union of all Christians. In fact, it was Stone, not Alexander Campbell, who provided the major impetus for the tangible union of the Stone and Campbell movements at a meeting in Lexington, Kentucky, on New Year's Day weekend, 1831–1832. Fourth, Stone embraced an apocalyptic perspective, that is, a commitment to lead his life *as if* the final rule of the kingdom of God were fully present in the here and now. That commitment translated itself into his refusal to vote, to participate in political activity, or to involve himself in military affairs. Indeed, Stone promoted among Churches of Christ a rigorous pacifism, grounded squarely in his apocalyptic orientation. And fifth, Stone's revival piety sustained a gentleness of spirit that precluded, for example, debates and religious arguments. This position stood in stark contrast to Alexander Campbell, who once commented that a week of debating was worth a year of preaching.

In 1823 Alexander Campbell visited Kentucky for the first time, and his systematic exposition of the form and structure of the primitive church, along with his rhetorical presentation of immersion for the forgiveness of sins, began to exert a significant influence on the Stoneites in that region. As time passed, the rationalism of Campbell slowly triumphed over the revival piety of Stone, just as Campbell's this-worldly progressivism slowly eroded the apocalyptic perspective Stone had fostered in the hearts of many of his followers.

Bibliography

A. *The Biography of Eld. Barton Warren Stone*, ed. by John Rogers (Cincinnati, 1847); periodical: *CM*, 1826–1836, 1840–1845.

B. Newell Williams, *Barton Stone: A Spiritual Biography* (St. Louis, 2000); Charles C. Ware, *Barton Warren Stone: Pathfinder of Christian Union* (St. Louis, 1932); W. G. West, *Barton Warren Stone: Early American Advocate of Christian Unity* (Nashville, 1954); Colby D. Hall, *The "New Light Christians": Initiators of the Nineteenth-Century Reformation* (Fort Worth, 1959); Anthony L. Dunnavant, *Cane Ridge in Context* (Nashville, 1992); Paul K. Conkin, *Cane Ridge: America's Pentecost* (Madison, WI, 1990).

T

TANT, JEFFERSON DAVIS (28 June 1861, Pauling Co., GA–1 June 1941, Los Fresnos, TX). *Career*: Preacher, debater.

Perhaps more than any other preacher in Churches of Christ from the 1880s through the 1930s, Jefferson Davis Tant symbolized the discomfort the old-time, pioneer preachers felt with the shift among Churches of Christ from rural sect to urban denomination. Because he so effectively symbolized opposition to this change, he also emerged as a prominent spokesperson for preachers who, like him, resisted this transition. From 1880 until 1941—precisely the years of Tant's ministry—the rural population of Texas decreased from 91.8 percent to almost 50 percent, and the urban churches that emerged in that milieu grew less and less distinctive. As early as 1907, therefore, Tant began to criticize denominational trends among Churches of Christ, and in 1909 he began to conclude his frequent articles with his famous warning, "We are drifting." By "drifting," Tant meant that Churches of Christ were becoming like the denominations. A few others sounded the same refrain, but none did so with the consistency and sharpness of Tant, who seldom wrote without criticism and often wrote with severity. Cled Wallace called Tant "a cantankerous old maverick," and Tant generally acknowledged the truth in this claim. Tant routinely criticized professionalism among preachers and the colleges that helped create a professional ministry. Indeed, he often complained that some of the very churches he had established would not let him preach, since they only wanted younger, college-bred pulpiteers. A product of the Texas frontier, Tant lacked refinement and regularly employed crude expressions in his preaching. For example, he criticized the "pure-hearted preachers" from Tennessee who took offense when Tant "said 'bull' in the pulpit." Tant also criticized expensive church buildings that fostered institutional maintenance rather than evangelism and outreach. As an itinerant evangelist, himself, Tant served as a "full-time," located preacher only once in his life, and that was for eighteen months—in 1935 and 1936—in Brownsville, Texas. Aside from those two years, Tant spent his career holding gospel meetings in one town after another, mainly in the South, but sometimes in other states as well. In 1911 he held gospel meetings in twenty states, baptized over 3,000 individuals, and had 100 public debates. During the first four years of his preaching career, 1881–1885, Tant received no money for his preaching, and in the fifth year received only $9.75. For many years his travel expenses exceeded his support from the churches. Tant often accused the churches of stinginess and pointed to their failure to support itinerant evangelists like him, especially when preaching in destitute places.

Even while he criticized denominational trends, Tant consistently emerged as an outspoken supporter of orphans' homes that were funded by members of Churches of Christ. He worked on behalf of homes ranging from the Belle Haven Home in Luling, Texas, to the Tennessee Orphan Home in Columbia, Tennessee, to the Sunny Glen Orphan Home in San Juan, Texas. Even while he supported homes like these, Tant believed it would be far better if every congregation of Churches of Christ could serve as an orphans' home to three or four orphans, thereby eliminating the need for extracongregational institutions. The irony lies in the fact that J. D. Tant's son, Fanning Yater Tant, became a leader in the anti-institutional movement among Churches of Christ during the 1950s, a movement that generally opposed congregational support for institutions like orphans' homes.

Bibliography

A. "Coming Back Home," *FF*, 51 (May 15, 1934), 5; "Where Will It All End?" *FF*, 55 (January 25, 1938), 7; "To the Brotherhood," *FF*, 55 (February 8, 1938), 5; "Reaching Out," *GA*, 77 (October 10, 1935), 974; "Church News," *GA*, 50 (September 10, 1908), 589; "Planning for Next Year," *GA*, 70 (December 28, 1929), 1242–1243; *The Gospel X-ray* (Austin, 1933).

B. Harriet Helm Nichol, *Preachers of Texas and Oklahoma* (Clifton, TX, 1911); Fanning Yater Tant, "The Overflow," *GG*, 5 (October 22, 1953), 380; Fanning Yater Tant, *J. D. Tant: Texas Preacher* (Lufkin, TX, 1958); Nannie Yater Tant, *Nannie Yater Tant—Reminiscences of a Pioneer Preacher's Wife* (Indianapolis, 1990).

TANT, NANNIE GREEN YATER (13 February 1872, Partsville, TN–23 September 1961, San Angelo, TX). *Education*: Carr-Burnette College, Sherman, TX. *Career*: Volunteer on behalf of support for orphans' homes; preacher's wife.

Because Nannie Yater Tant was so passionately devoted to the care of orphans, she and her husband, J. D. Tant, worked tirelessly for the support of orphans' homes funded by members of Churches of Christ. In this way Nannie Yater Tant helped elevate the vision of Churches of Christ regarding their obligation to orphan children. In 1928, as field representative for the Tennessee Orphan Home in Columbia, Tennessee, J. D. Tant wrote 1,000 letters begging churches for support. Yet, he indicated that Nannie was the driving force behind this work. In 1930 Nannie Tant traveled for the Tennessee Orphan Home and raised several thousand dollars by urging women individually and in groups (she never talked to groups of men) to set aside "a-penny-a-day." She traveled over most of Tennessee, northern Mississippi, and Alabama with short trips into Kentucky until some "very able brethren" claimed that her work was unscriptural. Rather than become involved in controversy, she ceased her appeals. When the Tants lived in the Rio Grande Valley in Texas, they raised $25,000 for the Sunny Glen Orphan Home in San Juan, Texas, "so we could care for one hundred children." Nannie's parents, William and Fannie Mills Yater, moved to Texas in 1878. After high school Nannie taught school for two years and attended Carr-Burnette College in Sherman under O. A. Carr.

Bibliography

A. *Nannie Yater Tant—Reminiscences of a Pioneer Preacher's Wife* (Indianapolis, 1990).

B. J. D. Tant, "The Crisis Has Come," *GA*, 72 (April 3, 1930), 334.

THOMAS, JOSEPH (1791, VA–9 April 1835, Johnsonburg, NJ). *Career*: Frontier preacher, writer, poet, hymn writer.

In addition to the fact that he was perhaps the most colorful figure in the Christian movement in its earliest years, Joseph Thomas was significant in three respects. First, his autobiography provides the fullest account of the scope and nature of the movement led by Barton W. Stone in Kentucky and Tennessee prior to 1812. Second, Thomas may well have been the only preacher who sustained relations with all the major leaders of the Christian movement in the South—Elias Smith, James O'Kelly, Rice Haggard, William Guirey, and Barton W. Stone—during the first decade of the nineteenth century. During that period Alexander Campbell was still unknown, since he did not immigrate to the United States until 1809. Third, Thomas became a powerful spokesperson for the great themes of the Christian movement: primitive Christianity, religious freedom, and the union of Christians.

James O'Kelly baptized Thomas by pouring in 1807. In that very same year, when Thomas was only sixteen years old, he set out to preach. Soon Thomas heard of the "Christians in the West"—the "Christian" movement led by Barton W. Stone. Anxious to learn about these people and their teachings, Thomas began a journey in June 1810 that took him some 7,000 miles and that required a year and a half to complete. Upon his return to the mountains of Virginia, at the ripe old age of twenty-two, he wrote his autobiography, *The Travels and Gospel Labors of Joseph Thomas, Minister of the Gospel and Elder in the Christian Church*. This is the document that provides invaluable information on the Stone movement for those years. In 1817, Thomas revised his autobiography under the title *The Life of the Pilgrim Joseph Thomas*. The word "pilgrim" refers to Thomas's attempt to conform his preaching to the apostolic style. In 1815 he rid himself of his preaching clothes and his horse, donned a white robe and sandals, and went preaching on foot throughout the Blue Ridge Mountains for most of the rest of his life. He quickly earned the nickname "the white pilgrim." Thomas moved to western Ohio in the 1820s and spent his last years as an active preacher among the Christian Connexion churches, but he never accepted the union between the movements led by Barton Stone and Alexander Campbell.

Bibliography

A. "Religious Intelligence," *HGL* (June 21, 1811), 294; *The Travels and Gospel Labors of Joseph Thomas* (Winchester, VA, 1812); *The Life of the Pilgrim Joseph Thomas* (Winchester, VA, 1817); *Poems, Religious, Moral and Satirical, by Joseph Thomas, the Pilgrim: To Which Is Prefixed a Compend of the Life, Travels and Gospel Labors of the Author* (Lebanon, OH, 1829; reprint 1861).

B. "Elder Joseph Thomas," *CPal*, 4 (May 1, 1835), 9–10; Richard T. Hughes, " 'Christians' in the Early South: The Perspective of Joseph Thomas, 'The White Pilgrim,' " *Disc*, 46 (Fall 1986), 33–43.

THORNBERRY, JAMES L. (1814, Dry Run, Scott Co., KY–1886, IL). *Education*: Transylvania University. *Career*: Lawyer, itinerant frontier preacher.

Deeply inspired by Barton W. Stone, James L. Thornberry was a second-generation preacher in the movement led by Stone and typified the commitments that characterized the Stone tradition. More than that, Thornberry revealed the extent to which the apocalyptic values of Barton Stone could be amalgamated with the lower-class values of the southern frontier. Stone baptized Thornberry in 1833 near the brick meeting house on Dry Run in Kentucky, where Thornberry's forefathers had settled. Stone said to him on that occasion, "God bless you, my son. I pray God you may be a blessing to yourself, your family, and the world." Years later Thornberry confessed, "That prayer follows me. I see the tears of that good man in memory." Indeed, Barton W. Stone was his model.

Thornberry became a lawyer after studying at Transylvania University, but largely because of Stone's influence he abandoned a law career to spend his life as an itinerant preacher. After a long struggle Thornberry consented to preach his first sermon in fall of 1846. Like Barton Stone, Thornberry rejected the prevalent values of the world, even when those values were common in the church. He warned against the creation of "big preachers." He encouraged young preachers to "go out among the poor, and jealous preachers will not trouble you there." Throughout his career, he took his own advice. For fifty years he was by his own description "a homeless wanderer . . . poor in earthly goods, and all this because I believe God put me in the ministry." His fellow preachers knew him as the man with "headquarters in the saddle." He also warned against fine houses of worship, organs, and college trained preachers who sported their fashionable apparel. Committed to the nondenominational ideal that characterized the southern Christians, Thornberry urged, "Just say we are Christians and belong to the Christian church, that is a church composed of Christians without prefix or affix. Preachers should be called simply 'Christian preachers.' " By 1850 Thornberry had lost faith in Alexander Campbell. That year he attended a meeting of preachers in Lexington, Kentucky. He reported that he heard Campbell say, "It was not enough, to hand a man the New Testament and say, That is my creed. We would have to explain a little. Also that the name Christian would not do now; if we say we are the Christian church, we are saying others are not; and that we must now have an educated ministry, who could pronounce the language properly. . . . I was vexed."

Bibliography

A. "James, Chap. 3, Verse 10," *CRe*, 2d ser., 6 (August–November, 1855); "Bro. Thornberry's Adieu," *CRe*, 2d ser., 6 (December 1855), 364; "Fifty Years Ago," *AC*, 6 (September 1884), 20–21; "Are We a Sect or a Denomination?" *AT*, 5 (February 1874), 3; "A Friendly Letter to the Kentucky Brethren," *AT*, 10 (April 5, 1878), 3.

B. "Farm and Household," *GA*, 20 (December 5, 1878), 764.

TRAVIS, DANIEL, SR. (d. 25 July 1826, Gallatin, TN). *Career*: Frontier preacher.

When preachers from the earliest years of the Stone movement compiled lists of their contemporaries, the name of Daniel Travis almost always appeared first. According to Isaac Jones, who wrote an early history of the Stone movement in Tennessee, "Travis was an old man when he went into the Reformation." We also know that Travis died before Stone began his journal, the *Christian Messenger*. His age may help account for the high regard in which he was held, but his contemporaries also revered him for his character and his talent as a preacher. Jones reported that Travis "was described to me as a bold reasoner, a fluent talker, and a warm exhorter. He cared more for practical morality than for theoretic theology." In an obituary published in the *Christian Messenger*, Stone observed of Travis, "He was beloved, even by those who differed from him in opinion. None questioned his honesty, piety, or great talents, unwavering faith of that gospel, which he had preached to others." Accordingly, when Dr. W. D. Jourdan published in 1882 a list of forty-two Tennessee ministers from a memorandum written during the winter of 1824–1825, the name of Daniel Travis heads the list. The list begins: "Tennessee—Daniel Travis, John Mulky, Philip Mulky, John Bowman." Another list refers to a "First Group" called "a grand army": "Daniel Travis, [Randle, or B. F.?] Hall, [James E.] Matthews, [Nix] Murphee, and Corder Stone." Dr. Jourdan's "Certificate of Ordination" dated March 9, 1825, was signed first by "Daniel Travers" [sic]. Travis preached primarily in Rutherford, Cannon, and Warren Counties in Tennessee. He influenced several young men to become preachers, including W. D. Jourdan and Andrew P. Davis. The date on Travis' tombstone—August 25, 1827—is incorrect. Travis died away from home while on a preaching tour on July 25, 1826.

Bibliography

B. "Obituary," *CM*, 1 (November 25, 1826), 22–23; W. D. Jourdan, "Extract of a Letter," *GL*, 3 (October 1827), 248; Isaac Newton Jones, "The Reformation in Tennessee" in J. W. Grant, "A Sketch of the Reformation in Tennessee" (c. 1897), typescript in Center for Restoration Studies, Abilene Christian University, pp. 40–41.

TROTT, JAMES J. (4 November 1800, NC–10 December 1868, near Gallatin, TN). *Education:* Unknown. *Career*: Missionary to Cherokee Indians, preacher.

James J. Trott spent much of his life as a missionary to the Cherokee Indians, first in North Carolina and later in Arkansas and Oklahoma. The cooperative work by Tennessee Churches of Christ that sponsored this later work may have been the earliest cooperative effort by Churches of Christ on behalf of missions outside the borders of the United States. Trott began his career as a Methodist circuit rider in Georgia in 1823. From 1826 through 1832, Trott worked among the Cherokees in Georgia under Methodist auspices. When the government required that all persons in the Cherokee Nation (including residents) take an oath of allegiance to the state, Trott and two Presbyterian preachers—all Native Americans—refused and were sent to a Georgia prison in chains. Concurrent with his incarceration Trott's wife, "a pious Cherokee," passed away, leaving behind two children. Methodist leaders, on the whole, made no effort to support Trott or to assist him with attorneys. It should come as no surprise, therefore, that Trott was open to exploring the teachings of other churches. While in prison he acquired and read some of the writings of Alexander Campbell. He was deeply impressed by Campbell's plea for primitive Christianity and for the Scripture as the sole authority for the Christian church. Once out of prison he returned to Tennessee and there was immersed by a popular Baptist preacher, Payton Smith. Because of his immersion, the director of the Methodist mission to the Cherokees refused to give Trott an additional appointment. Trott therefore withdrew from the Methodist Church and became a member of the Church of Christ. From 1837 to 1859, Trott and Tolbert Fanning traveled together and preached throughout Middle Tennessee. In 1857 the congregation that met at Franklin College in Nashville selected Trott as a missionary to the Cherokee Indians in Arkansas. He also preached in the Cherokee Nation on Grand River near the present location of Vinita, Oklahoma. That work, however, was cut short by the outbreak of the Civil War in 1861. Robbed and mistreated, Trott was forced to go to Kansas, where he "labored, in poverty and perils" until 1865, when he returned to Arkansas. In 1867 Trott grew ill and in 1868 returned to Tennessee, hoping the journey would help restore his health. In Nashville, however, his illness intensified and, despite the attention of Dr. W. H. Wharton, he died of pneumonia on December 10, 1868.

Bibliography

A. "To the Editor of the Millennial Harbinger," *MH*, 3 (February 6, 1832), 85; letter from James J. Trott to Alexander Campbell, *MH*, 3 (August 6, 1832), 389–390; "Visit to Grand Prairie, Cherokee Nation," *GA*, 5 (1860), 379.

B. *CMag*, 1 (1848), 60, 93; L. C. Chisholm, "Spiritual Life," *FF*, 19 (January 13, 1903), 1; Tolbert Fanning, "James J. Trott: Messenger of the Church of Christ at Franklin College, Tenn., to the Cherokee Nation," *GA*, 11 (March 25, 1869), 271–273; William G. McLoughlin, *Cherokees and Missionaries, 1789–1839* (New Haven, 1984), pp. 175, 262, 291, 295, 296, 314, 326–327, 332, 342.

TUGGLE, ANNIE C. (1890, near Germantown, TN–1976, CA). *Education*: Lane Junior College, LeMoyne Normal Institute, Silver Point Christian Institute, Walden College, Fisk University, A&I State College in Nashville. *Career*: Teacher, author.

Through her work as a teacher and an author, Annie Tuggle emerged as an important influence among African American Churches of Christ in the twentieth century. At age seventeen she became a Christian and then converted friends and other members of her family, who formed the nucleus of a new congregation of Churches of Christ near Memphis. Armed with a ninth-grade education from Lane Junior College in Jackson, Tennessee, and a teacher's certificate from LeMoyne Normal Institute of Memphis, she served as an elementary teacher and later as an administrator for three schools. In 1913 she attended the first Christian school for blacks, the Silver Point Christian Institute in Silver Point, Tennessee, founded by G. P. Bowser, one of the two most influential figures among African American congregations in the early twentieth century. When she complained that the school's physical facilities were inadequate, Bowser commissioned her to serve as a field agent, raising funds for the school. In 1920 she enrolled in Walden College, where she completed her high school education in 1923. In 1924 she enrolled as a freshman in Fisk University in Nashville, but she dropped out when she realized that required chapel services at Fisk would preclude her participation in Sunday worship with the Church of Christ. In the early 1940s Tuggle once again raised funds for a school established by G. P. Bowser, this time for the Bowser Christian Institute of Fort Smith, Arkansas, forerunner of Southwestern Christian College in Terrell, Texas. From 1942 to 1944, Tuggle taught at the Nashville Christian Institute, a school for black youth operated by African American members of Churches of Christ in Nashville. In 1943 Tuggle developed arthritis, a malady for which her doctor prescribed sunshine and hot baths. Her chosen remedy was the cotton patch. Picking cotton in the hot sun brought healing, and Annie was able to plunge into a vigorous life in Detroit, Michigan, in 1944. During her twenty years in Detroit, she served the church, sold insurance, operated a restaurant, established a Christian school for small children, and wrote her first book. Following a brief sojourn back home in Memphis, Tuggle did missionary work in Jamaica, the

Bahamas, and Haiti. After reaching eighty years of age, she moved to California, where she worshipped with an integrated church at Perris. While in California she wrote her autobiography—*Another World Wonder*—which, in effect, serves as a reliable history of African American congregations of Churches of Christ in the twentieth century.

Bibliography

A. *Our Ministers and Song Leaders of the Church of Christ* (Detroit, n.d.); *Another World Wonder* (Los Angeles, 1973).

B. Michael Casey, "Annie C. Tuggle: Historian and Educator for the Black Churches of Christ," *Leaven*, 3 (1995), 47–48.

W

WALLACE, FOY E., JR. (30 September 1896, Wise Co., TX–18 December 1979, Hereford, TX). *Education*: Southwestern Christian College, Thorp Spring Christian College. *Career*: Minister; debater; editor, *Gospel Advocate*, 1930–34; *Gospel Guardian*, 1935–36; *Bible Banner*, 1938–49; *Torch*, 1950–52.

Foy E. Wallace, Jr., was without question the single most powerful preacher among Churches of Christ in the 1930s and 1940s. Wallace attempted to identify "by name, rank, and number" those preachers who were "soft" on premillennialism, encouraged others to do the same, and in that way helped promote the climate of paranoia that gripped Churches of Christ during that period.

Probably no preacher in this fellowship drew as much praise and criticism as did Foy E. Wallace. The praise began when churches in Texas recognized that "little Foy" was a wonder preacher. The criticism initially stemmed from his arrogant and public rebukes of young mothers whose children disturbed his long sermons. One of his ardent young admirers, James W. Adams, candidly pointed out that Wallace "was utterly intolerant of a point of view different from his own. Any person who ever engaged in a personal confrontation with him found this out."

Ancestors of the Wallace family were among the earliest participants in the "Christian" movement led by Barton W. Stone in Tennessee and Alabama in the early nineteenth century. Apparently Jonathan Wallis, an early preacher in Tennessee and Alabama, was the earliest minister in this family of ministers. From Alabama, members of this family migrated to Wise County, Texas, where Foy E. Wallace, Sr., the father of the subject of this sketch, was born in 1871.

Foy E. Wallace, Jr., became prominent while serving as editor of the *Gospel Advocate* between 1930 and 1934. In 1935 he established the *Gospel Guardian*, a paper he used as a weapon to eradicate the premillennial sentiment from the ranks of Churches of Christ. In 1938 he launched a third paper, the *Bible Banner*, which continued the war against premillennial sympathizers. Wallace edited the *Bible Banner* through 1949. For all those years, he trained his guns especially on Robert H. Boll, whom he regarded as the chief architect of the premillennial sentiment in this communion. But Wallace also attacked any preacher who refused to line up in the crusade against Boll and his sympathizers.

By the late 1940s the premillennial issue was essentially dead among Churches of Christ. In its place emerged the question of whether local congregations could cooperate financially for the support of foreign and domestic missions, orphans' homes, and colleges. The fact that this question even emerged reflected the passionate commitment of Churches of Christ to a radically congregational polity. Foy Wallace essentially left this battle to younger men, but he did lead a short-lived attack on cooperative endeavors in the pages of the *Bible Banner*, shortly before its demise, and in the *Torch*, which he edited from 1950 to 1952. Though Wallace refused to take the long-term lead in the battle against cooperative structures, the men who led that attack generally looked to Wallace as their mentor.

The third crusade that Wallace led was directed against pacifism in Churches of Christ. Pacifism had emerged in this communion as a natural corollary of the nineteenth-century apocalyptic perspective, best articulated by Barton Stone and later by David Lipscomb. Interestingly, even Wallace had at one time been a champion of nonresistance. But Japan's attack on Pearl Harbor triggered Wallace's conversion, and by spring 1942 Wallace was lambasting pacifists in Churches of Christ as "men with a dwarfed conscience" and "freak specimen[s] of humanity." Since the apocalyptic perspective among nineteenth-century Churches of Christ helped to spawn the pacifist sentiment, it seems clear that Wallace used his attack on pacifism as an additional way to undermine premillennialism.

Fourth and finally, during the last fifteen years of his life, Wallace "exposed" the new translations of Scripture—those "perversions," as he chose to call them. In *A Review of the New Versions* (1973) he demonstrated his own lack of knowledge either of textual criticism or of the Greek text; he misquoted scholars with opposite views in order to bolster his own position, and essentially elevated the "Authorized Version" above the Greek New Testament. Still, his views were popular with many ministers and in a large number of local congregations of Churches of Christ.

During the course of his career, Wallace held numerous debates. Those forensic encounters included discussions with Charles M. Neal, premillennialist of Winchester, Kentucky (1933); J. Frank Norris, Fundamental Baptist of Fort Worth, Texas (1934); E. F. Webber, millennialist of Oklahoma City (1937); and John Matthews of Los Angeles on Anglo-Israelism (1944). Wallace also had encounters with a number of Disciples of Christ over instrumental music and missionary societies. After the famous Fort Worth debate, J. Frank Norris, a nationally known fundamentalist, said that he would never debate him again, a sentiment that seems to have been common among all of Wallace's opponents.

Bibliography

A. *The Certified Gospel* (Port Arthur, TX, 1937); *The Christian and the Government* (Nashville, 1969); *God's Prophetic Word* (Houston, 1946); *Bulwarks of the Faith* (Oklahoma City, 1951); *The Gospel for Today* (Nashville, 1967); *The Mission and Medium of the Holy Spirit* (n.p., 1967); *A Review of the New Versions* (Fort Worth, 1973); *Neal-Wallace Discussion on the Thousand Years Reign of Christ* (Nashville, 1933).

B. John T. Lewis, *The Christian and the Government* (Birmingham, AL, 1945); James W. Adams, "Foy E. Wallace, Jr.: Militant Warrior" in *They Being Dead yet Speak* (Florida College Annual Lectures for 1981; Temple Terrace, FL, 1981), 171–186; Robert E. Hooper, *A Distinct People: A History of the Churches of Christ in the 20th Century* (West Monroe, LA, 1993); David E. Harrell, Jr., *The Churches of Christ in the 20th Century: Homer Hailey's Personal Journey of Faith* (Tuscaloosa, 2000).

WARLICK, JOSEPH SALE (1 November 1866, near St. Louis, MO–2 January 1941, Dallas, TX). *Career*: Minister, editor, debater.

Joseph Sale Warlick established himself as one of the most powerful religious debaters in the state of Texas, and his claim to lasting fame rides mainly on his astounding forensic record. Warlick possessed a phenomenal memory that was almost always superior to that of his opponents. On most occasions his forensic opponent would bring stacks of books to the discussion while Warlick brought only a Bible. In many debates the Bible lay on the podium unopened, since Warlick could quote almost any passage under consideration. Once, when engaging J. Carroll Stark on the topic of instrumental music, Warlick was thoroughly familiar with Stark's arguments and procedures. Warlick made his speech, went outside to play with the children, and then returned to answer every argument his opponent had made. Warlick began preaching at age nineteen in his home community of Cash Creek near Seymour, Baylor County, Texas. For many years he preached for the Pearl and Bryan Church of Christ in Dallas, now the Highland Oaks Church of Christ. He published the *Gospel Review* from 1903 to 1904 and the *Gospel Guide* from 1905 to 1929.

Bibliography

A. *A Debate between J. Carroll Stark and Joe S. Warlick* (Nashville, 1910); periodicals: *Gospel Review*, 1903–1904; *Gospel Guide*, 1905–1929.

B. Harriet Helm Nichol, *Preachers of Texas and Oklahoma* (Clifton, TX, 1911).

WATKINS, BENJAMIN UTTER (1811, Springfield, OH–April 1892, Cameron, MO). *Education*: Self-educated and taught by Walter Scott. *Career*: Minister, debater, writer.

Benjamin U. Watkins was an important advocate of the apocalyptic perspective articulated by Barton W. Stone, even though he spent most of his career in the North, not in the South. He became a member of the Church of Christ in Carthage, Ohio, where he lived for a time with Walter Scott. In many ways Scott became his teacher, although Barton W. Stone also exerted a strong influence on the young man. In his youth Watkins lost his vision for four years, but he regained sight in one eye and decided to educate himself for greater usefulness. Recognition of his scholarship led to an invitation to work on the American Bible Union translation of the New Testament (an immersionist version promoted by Baptists and Disciples). Because the American Bible Union had snubbed Alexander Campbell's translation of *Acts*, however, Watkins refused the invitation. During the 1850s Watkins was associated with *The Christian Luminary* and conducted a "School of the Prophets" in his own hired house in Ohio. After moving to Main Prairie, Minnesota, in 1861, he became widely known for his speaking and debating. In fact, members of Churches of Christ regularly called on him to represent them in the forensic arena. Watkins learned of David Lipscomb soon after Lipscomb became editor of the *Gospel Advocate* in Nashville. Watkins wrote approvingly of the editor's articles on world powers and human governments. "I am more than pleased with the Advocate, I am delighted. Thank God, that we have such a radical advocate for primitive Christianity." David Lipscomb acknowledged his debt to Watkins for some of his own views on civil government, views that Lipscomb first expressed in 1866. Watkins testified to his own commitment to this perspective when he wrote to Tolbert Fanning, "I am thankful that you have the moral courage to advocate the true view of human governments. For more than thirty years have I been advocating the same sentiments, and have been treated with neglect on account of such advocacy, and even thought to be almost insane." The *Advocate* had few such ardent supporters in the North in the years following the Civil War. As he grew older, Watkins suffered recurring trouble with poor sight that limited his activity. He moved in the 1880s to Cameron, Missouri, where he died in April 1892.

Bibliography

A. Series on "Universalism Philosophy," nos. 1–6, *Ev* (1841 and 1842); "Correspondence," *GA*, 11 (August 5, 1869), 737; "Items, Personals, Etc.," *GA*, 18 (July 20, 1876), 697; "Human Governments" in David Lipscomb, *Civil Government* (Nashville, 1889), pp. 153–155. For a bibliography of his later and more scholarly writings, see index to *C-E*.

B. Thomas Preston Haley, *Historical and Biographical Sketches . . . of the Christian Church in Missouri* (Kansas City, 1888), p. 353; Henry K. Shaw, *Buckeye Disciples: A History of Disciples of Christ in Ohio* (St. Louis, 1952), p. 91.

WHITE, LLOYD SMITH (11 April 1867, Jackson Co., TN–28 February 1949, Fort Worth, TX). *Education*: Ogden College, Bowling Green, KY. *Career*: Minister, writer, debater.

Historian Earl West called Lloyd Smith White "the pioneer among churches of Christ in the work of the local minister." This judgment is significant, since preachers in Churches of Christ prior to White's era generally thought of themselves as itinerant evangelists, not as located ministers who received a salary from the congregation that employed them. Indeed, many in Churches of Christ viewed such work in which White engaged as aping "the denominations" and their "pastor system." White grew up in the Bagdad Church of Christ in Jackson County, Tennessee. He attended Ogden College in Bowling Green, Kentucky, where he became a close friend of one of his classmates, Cordell Hull, who would later serve as secretary of state under Franklin D. Roosevelt. In 1893 White plunged into the kind of evangelistic preaching and debating that characterized so many preachers of Churches of Christ in the nineteenth century. That work, however, was followed by seven years of fruitful ministry at the Gallatin, Tennessee, Church of Christ. Because his ministry in Gallatin was so successful, the Pearl and Bryan congregation in Dallas, the oldest congregation in that city, invited White to become its permanent minister. He accepted that position in 1906 and remained there until 1917. During his tenure there White engaged in a written debate with James A. Harding on the merits of the located, salaried minister. That debate graphically revealed the tension between the traditional primitivism and the growing spirit of modernization that bedeviled Churches of Christ in the early years of the twentieth century. Later White enjoyed similar success with the Houston Street congregation in Sherman, Texas, where he held several great meetings during the years 1909–1911. Congregations in Waxahachie, Wichita Falls, and Fort Worth also profited from the work of L. S. White. In addition to his work with local congregations, White brought thousands into the Churches of Christ through his gospel meetings and his debates. He held his most notable debate with Jehovah's Witness Charles Taze Russell in Cincinnati in 1907.

Bibliography

A. *Radio Sermons* (Austin, TX, 1930); *Sermons on Revelation* (Cincinnati, 1917); *Russell-White Debate* (Cincinnati, 1908).

B. Earl West, "L. S. White," *RQ*, 20 (3d Qr 1977), 151–155; Burton Coffman, "L. S. White," *GA*, 91 (May 26, 1949), 333; Batsell Baxter, "L. S. White," *GA*, 91 (June 2, 1949), 349f.

WHITESIDE, ROBERTSON LAFAYETTE (27 December 1869, Hickman Co., TN–5 January 1951, Denton, TX). *Education*: West Tennessee Christian College, 1890; Nashville Bible School, 1893. *Career*: Minister; writer; president, Abilene Christian College, 1910–12.

His admirers referred to Robertson Lafayette Whiteside as the "David Lipscomb of Texas" because of his writing and his reputation as a thinker. Indeed, in 1920 Whiteside and C. R. Nichol coauthored four volumes entitled simply *Sound Doctrine*. Intended for use in adult Bible classes, these volumes served as a systematic theology for Churches of Christ for many years. Because of his skill as a writer, the *Gospel Advocate* secured Whiteside from 1937 to 1944 as author of its *Annual Lesson Commentary*, a study guide for adult Bible classes. Whiteside also published regularly in both the *Gospel Advocate*, published in Nashville, Tennessee, and the *Firm Foundation*, published in Austin, Texas. A popular preacher in Corsicana and Denton, Texas, Whiteside also served as the third president of Abilene Christian College from 1910 to 1912.

Bibliography

A. *A New Commentary on Paul's Letter to the Saints at Rome* (Denton, TX, 1945); *Doctrinal Discourses* (Denton, TX, 1955); *Kingdom of Promise and Prophecy* (Denton, TX, 1956); *Reflections* (Denton, TX, 1965); *Sound Doctrine: A Series of Bible Studies for Sunday School Classes, Prayer Meetings, Private Study, College Classes, Etc.*, 4 vols., coauthored with C. R. Nichol (Clifton, TX, 1920).

B. Harriet Helm Nichol, *Gospel Preachers of Texas and Oklahoma* (Clifton, TX, 1911).

WILMETH, COLLIN McKINNEY (2 January 1848, McKinney, TX–12 October 1898, Bryan City, Mexico). *Education*: University of Kentucky. *Career*: Preacher; journalist; debater; missionary; and president, Nazareth University.

Collin McKinney Wilmeth was the leading preacher and debater among Churches of Christ in Texas from 1875 until his death in 1898. The son of Joseph B. Wilmeth, a preacher in Texas and Arkansas, Mack—as he was called—attended Muse Academy at McKinney, Texas, near his home; he then graduated from the College of the Bible at Lexington, Kentucky. With his older brother, James R. Wilmeth, a Bethany College graduate, Mack published the *Texas Christian Monthly* at McKinney for two years, 1875–1876. This publication later merged with the *Iron Preacher* of Waco and was renamed the *Christian Preacher*. Wilmeth also founded Nazareth University in Dallas, although he later moved both his school and his paper to Corinth, Arkansas. Wilmeth through his publications and T. R. Burnett through his *Christian Messenger* were probably the most influential journalists among Churches of Christ in Texas for the last quarter of the century. Early in life both Mack and his brother, James R., had a desire to work in Mexico as missionaries. James R. preached briefly in Mexico in the 1870s. Mack began preparation for work in Mexico several years before his actual departure in 1898. He taught his children Spanish and recruited a large colony of church members who did, in fact, accompany him to Mexico. This was the first of several colonization efforts in Mexico by Churches of Christ. This mission to Bryan City near Tampico, Mexico, ended abruptly, however, when Wilmeth died from malaria and too much physical exertion shortly after his arrival there.

Bibliography

A. *TCM*, 1875–1876; *CP*, 1877–1883.

B. Nicholas Kassebaum, "He Built for Eternity: C. M. Wilmeth, an Early Texas

Preacher," M.A. thesis, Abilene Christian University, 1967; Wilmeth, Mary Emerson interview, January 24, 1966, typescript housed in Center for Restoration Studies, Abilene Christian University, 48–49; Robert C. Horne, *Annals of Elder Horn* (New York, 1930).

WILSON, LAWRENCE RAY (23 December 1896, Cord, AR–31 May 1968, Dallas, TX). *Education*: Freed-Hardeman College, Union University, Birmingham-Southern College. *Career*: Preacher; teacher, University of Tennessee, 1929–34; president, Florida College, 1946–49, and Central Christian College (now Oklahoma Christian University), 1949–54; editor, *Voice of Freedom*, 1956–68.

Lawrence Ray Wilson was prominent in Churches of Christ, serving them as a local preacher, a college president (twice), and editor of the *Voice of Freedom*, a publication designed to warn Christians of the dangers allegedly posed to the United States by Catholicism, on the one hand, and communism, on the other. Baptized in 1916, Wilson began preaching the following year in Arkansas. Upon his graduation from Birmingham-Southern College, the Church of Christ in Knoxville, Tennessee, invited him as its local minister. During the five years that he served in that capacity (1929–1934), he also taught religious education at the University of Tennessee. Following his tenure in Knoxville, Wilson served several well-known congregations in Tulsa, Oklahoma (1936–1939), San Antonio, Texas (1939–1946), Amarillo, Texas (1954–1955), and Cleburne, Texas (1955–1956). Wilson was the founding president of two colleges related to Churches of Christ: Florida College (1946–1949) and Central Christian College, now Oklahoma Christian University of Science and Arts (1949–1954). In 1956 he was appointed editor of the *Voice of Freedom*, a position he held until his death in 1968.

Bibliography

A. *The Triumphant Jesus* (Bartlesville, OK, 1952); *The New Testament Church* (Austin, TX, 1953); *Congregational Development* (Nashville, 1959); "What I Would Not, That I Do," *GA*, 91 (June 2, 1949), 339–340; periodical: *Voice of Freedom*, 1956–1968.

WOMACK, S. W. (d. 13 July 1920, Nashville, TN). *Career*: Minister.

S. W. Womack was one of the most influential African American preachers among Churches of Christ from roughly 1900 until 1920, the year of his death. Womack was baptized in 1866 when the lines dividing Churches of Christ from Disciples of Christ were not as apparent as they would become by 1900. Early in the twentieth century Womack met another African American preacher, Alexander Campbell, who had left the Christian Church in 1900 and had become an evangelist for the Churches of Christ. Campbell exerted a strong influence on Womack, who soon followed suit. Together Womack and Campbell established the Jackson Street Church of Christ in Nashville, a congregation that flourished for over forty years. G. P. Bowser, another African American preacher, who left the Methodists in 1897 for the Churches of Christ, aligned himself with Campbell and Womack, and these three men—Womack, Campbell, and Bowser—provided dynamic leadership for African American Churches of Christ well into the twentieth century. Womack's influence perpetuated itself in other ways as well: two of his daughters married the two greatest figures among African American Churches of Christ in the twentieth century—G. P. Bowser and Marshall Keeble. Womack, in fact, won Keeble out of the Disciples of Christ. Keeble quickly distinguished himself as the most effective evangelist among Churches of Christ in the twentieth century, black or white. Some have suggested that Womack was to the black churches what David Lipscomb was to the white churches. The fact is that Womack enjoyed a close association with David Lipscomb and others of the *Gospel Advocate* staff. When Womack died in 1920, a notice of his death in the *Advocate* described him as "one of the most useful and highly esteemed preachers" among Churches of Christ and a man of "irreproachable character."

Bibliography

A. "Attitude of the Races," *GA*, 57 (December 30, 1915), 1326; "Among the Colored Folks," *GA*, 62 (May 27, 1920), 532.

B. M. Keeble, "A Great Man Gone," *GA*, 62 (July 29, 1920), 744.

Y

YOUNG, FOUNTAIN LIVINGSTON (29 November 1855, Concordia Parish, LA–5 August 1933, Dallas, TX). *Education*: B.A., Add-Ran College, 1881; Texas Christian University. *Career*: Preacher, Paris, Denton, Amarillo, and elsewhere in TX.

A cultured and educated preacher and, in fact, the first preacher among Texas Churches of Christ to earn a B.A. degree (Add-Ran College, 1881), Fount Livingston Young exerted enormous influence on Churches of Christ in that state between 1885 and his death in 1933. During the period of the instrumental music controversy that divided Churches of Christ in Texas during the late nineteenth and early twentieth centuries, Young's was a voice urging fidelity to the a capella tradition. For example, the Texas debater, Joe S. Warlick recalled an "annual meeting" at Thorp Spring, Texas, when "the brethren were taking sides over instrumental music." The progressives claimed that "all intelligent, educated people, who loved music, and culture, were for the instrument, and all ignorant and uneducated were the ones against it." When the cultured and much-admired Fount Young arrived at the meeting and took his stand against the instrument, many of the preachers who had wavered now followed his leadership. No wonder that one of the preachers wrote of Young: "He is the pilot for much of Texas." At the same time Young was a staunch advocate of the love and grace of God at a time when Churches of Christ suffered under the weight of considerable legalism and sectarianism.

Not only was Young educated and cultured, but his pedigree in the Stone-Campbell movement was impeccable. Several of his uncles, graduates of Alexander Campbell's Bethany College, prompted in Fount Young his lifelong love of learning. One uncle, Thomas Campbell, was president of two Christian colleges, one in Missouri and one in Oregon, and married the niece of Alexander Campbell. A cousin, Prince Campbell, became president of the University of

Oregon. Harry Hamilton, a well-known East Texas preacher, baptized Young, and Addison Clark, founder of Add-Ran College, presided at Young's marriage to Mattie May Higgins on December 2, 1880.

Young's parents moved from Louisiana to Trinity County, Texas, when Young was five years old, and he grew up working with his brothers on the family farm. Following his graduation from Add-Ran College in 1881, he taught school at Seymour and Whitt, Texas, hoping to become a lawyer. During a revival, however, he began to give serious consideration to preaching and finally made the decision to enter the ministry. He spent his career preaching for congregations of Churches of Christ in Texas, most notably at Paris, Denton, and Amarillo, and holding evangelistic meetings.

Bibliography

B. H. F. Williams, "Field Findings," *GA*, 45 (December 26, 1905), 832; John W. Harris, "Texas Work," *OR*, 38 (September 24, 1895), 6; *FF*, September 13, 1933, issue was a "Memorial to F. L. Young;" Irene Young Mattox, "F. L. Young," *20thCC* (January 1959), 31–33.

YOUNG, MATT NORVEL (5 October 1915, Nashville, TN–18 February 1998, Malibu, CA). *Education*: A.A., David Lipscomb College, 1934; B.A., Abilene Christian College, 1936; Ph.D., George Peabody College, 1943; additional study at Vanderbilt University, Columbia University, and the University of Southern California. *Career*: Preacher, York Boulevard Church of Christ, Los Angeles, 1938; Van Nuys (CA) Church of Christ, 1939–40; Granny White Church of Christ, Nashville, TN, 1941–44; Broadway Church of Christ, Lubbock, TX, 1944–57; president, Pepperdine University, 1957–71, chancellor, 1971–85, and chancellor emeritus, 1985–98; cofounder and editor, *20th Century Christian* and *Power for Today*; member, board of directors, Union Rescue Mission, 1990–98.

From the 1950s through the 1990s, the influence of M. Norvel Young over Churches of Christ is incalculable. In 1938 Young became a faculty member at George Pepperdine College in Los Angeles, a position he held for three years. While there he met his future wife, Helen Mattox, who would become as influential among Churches of Christ as would Young himself. During that time Young also preached for the York Boulevard and the Van Nuys congregations of Churches of Christ in the Los Angeles area. In 1941 he returned to his hometown of Nashville, Tennessee, where he earned his Ph.D. in history from George Peabody College. During his years of graduate study, he preached for the Belmont Church of Christ and the Granny White Church of Christ in Nashville.

In 1944, during World War II, Young moved to Lubbock, Texas, where he began his ministry with the Broadway Church of Christ, a ministry that would last until 1957. During those years Young came to the forefront of Churches of

Christ. Under his leadership the Broadway congregation grew into a sizable and influential congregation. Young also led that church in the construction of an imposing new building that became a model for church construction among Churches of Christ. Through his book *The Church Is Building* Young helped motivate many congregations to follow the lead of the Broadway church and become more visionary in their construction plans and building site locations. While at Broadway Young also spearheaded a postwar mission thrust, especially to Germany, raising a then-staggering $500,000 for humanitarian aid for that nation. For ten years he also edited a bulletin, *Germany for Christ*. Under his guidance the Broadway congregation became a leader in foreign mission work among Churches of Christ. During the Broadway years Young also helped establish Lubbock Christian College, the Children's Home of Lubbock, and a Bible chair at Texas Tech University. In 1957 Young accepted the presidency of George Pepperdine College in Los Angeles. Under his guidance Pepperdine reversed its downward-spiraling fiscal fortunes, and in 1972, under the leadership of Young and William S. Banowsky, Pepperdine developed a new campus in Malibu, California, where the institution has continued to flourish. Young's interest in Christian journalism led him to cofound the *20th Century Christian* in 1937 and a devotional peridiodical, *Power for Today*, in 1950. He edited both publications during the 1950s and 1960s.

Bibliography

A. *History of Colleges Established and Controlled by Members of the Churches of Christ* (Kansas City, 1949); *Sermon Digests by Representative Evangelists*, ed. by Young, Raymond Kelcy, and Weldon Bennett (Murfreesboro, TN, 1951); *Preachers of Today: A Book of Brief Biographical Sketches and Pictures of Living Gospel Preachers*, 5 vols., ed. by Young and Batsell Barrett Baxter (Nashville, 1952); *The Church Is Building*, coauthored with James Marvin Powell (Nashville, 1956); *Great Preachers of Today* (Abilene, TX, 1960–1966); *New Testament Churches of Today: A Book of Brief Sketches and Pictures of Twentieth-Century Churches of Christ*, ed. by Young and Batsell Barrett Baxter (Nashville, 1960–1968); *Poison Stress Is a Killer*, in collaboration with John J. Dreher (Malibu, CA, 1978); *Pepperdine University: A Place, a People, a Purpose* (New York, 1982); *Living Lights, Shining Stars: Ten Secrets to Becoming the Light of the World*, with Mary Hollingsworth (West Monroe, LA, 1997).

B. Bill Henegar and Jerry Rushford, *Forever Young: The Life and Times of M. Norvel Young and Helen M. Young* (Nashville, 1999).

CHRONOLOGY

1801	Barton W. Stone participates in Cane Ridge Revival, Cane Ridge, Kentucky.
1802	Barton W. Stone and four other dissenters organize the Springfield Presbytery.
1804	Barton W. Stone and five other dissenters issue "The Last Will and Testament of the Springfield Presbytery."
1807	Thomas Campbell arrives in Southwest Pennsylvania from Northern Ireland.
1809	*Declaration and Address* issued by the Christian Association of Washington (PA).
1809	Alexander Campbell arrives in Southwest Pennsylvania from Northern Ireland.
1823	Alexander Campbell begins publication of the *Christian Baptist.*
1823	Alexander Campbell debates William L. McCalla at Maysville, Kentucky, and for the first time makes the acquaintance of Barton W. Stone.
1826	Barton W. Stone begins publication of the *Christian Messenger.*
1829	Walter Scott reports to the Mahoning Baptist Association his surprising number of conversions on the Western Reserve and claims he has restored the "ancient gospel."
1830	Alexander Campbell begins publication of the *Millennial Harbinger.*
1832	Some of the followers of Campbell and Stone unite in Lexington, Kentucky.
1832	Walter Scott begins publication of *The Evangelist.*

1837	Alexander Campbell responds to a querist from Lunenburg, Virginia, and affirms his ecumenical posture.
1840	Alexander Campbell establishes Bethany College.
1844	Death of Barton W. Stone.
1849	American Christian Missionary Society established in Cincinnati, Ohio. Alexander Campbell elected president.
1855	Tolbert Fanning begins publication of the *Gospel Advocate*.
1856	Benjamin Franklin begins publication of the *American Christian Review*.
1856	Tolbert Fanning and Robert Richardson engage in a heated editorial exchange over the role of Lockean philosophy in the Campbell movement.
1866	Death of Alexander Campbell.
1866	Tolbert Fanning and David Lipscomb resurrect the *Gospel Advocate* following the Civil War.
1874	T. W. Brents publishes *The Gospel Plan of Salvation*.
1884	Austin McGary begins publication of the *Firm Foundation* in Austin, Texas.
1891	David Lipscomb and James A. Harding establish the Nashville Bible School.
1897	Marshall Keeble begins a preaching career that continues for seventy-two years.
1902	George Phillip Bowser begins the *Christian Echo*.
1906	Abilene Christian University established in Abilene, Texas.
1907	David Lipscomb recommends that the federal census of 1906 list Churches of Christ separately from the Disciples of Christ.
1907	George Phillip Bowser begins the school that becomes Silver Point Christian Institute.
1915	R. H. Boll forced off staff of the *Gospel Advocate* and becomes editor of *Word and Work* in Louisville, Kentucky.
1915–45	Mainstream leaders seek to drive premillennial sentiment out of Churches of Christ.
1922	N. B. Hardeman holds first "Hardeman Tabernacle Meeting," Nashville.
1923	N. B. Hardeman holds second "Hardeman Tabernacle Meeting," Nashville.

1928	N. B. Hardeman holds third "Hardeman Tabernacle Meeting," Nashville.
1932	K. C. Moser publishes *The Way of Salvation.*
1934	Harding College opens its doors in Searcy, Arkansas.
1935	Foy E. Wallace, Jr., begins publication of the *Gospel Guardian.*
1936	G. C. Brewer publishes *Communism and Its Four Horsemen.*
1937	George Pepperdine College established in Los Angeles.
1938	Foy E. Wallace, Jr., begins publication of the *Bible Banner.*
1938	N. B. Hardeman holds fourth "Hardeman Tabernacle Meeting," Nashville.
1938	M. Norvel Young, James D. Bales, George DeHoff, and Woodrow Whitten begin publication of *20th Century Christian.*
1939	The new *Christian Leader* appears, edited by E. W. McMillan.
1940	The new *Christian Leader* collapses.
1941	Nashville Christian Institute begins in Nashville.
1942	N. B. Hardeman holds the fifth and final "Hardeman Tabernacle Meeting," Nashville.
1943	Olan Hicks begins publication of *Christian Chronicle.*
1944	First graduate program in Bible and religion established among Churches of Christ at George Pepperdine College, Los Angeles.
1949	Roy Cogdill resurrects the *Gospel Guardian* to serve the cause of the anti-institutional movement among Churches of Christ.
1950	Supporters of anti-institutional movement scorn mainstream opposition to "rock-throwing" incident in Italy.
1950	Under leadership of minister M. Norvel Young, Broadway Church of Christ, Lubbock, Texas, builds the largest sanctuary among Churches of Christ for that time.
1952	Churches of Christ inaugurate "Herald of Truth" national radio broadcast.
1953	*Voice of Freedom* begins publication.
1954	"Herald of Truth" expands from radio to a national television format.
1954	G. C. Goodpasture, editor of the *Gospel Advocate*, "quarantines" anti-institutional movement.
1955	Reuel Lemmons assumes editorship of Texas's *Firm Foundation.*

1956	M. Norvel Young and James Marvin Powell publish *The Church Is Building.*
1957	Carl Ketcherside turns *Mission Messenger* in ecumenical directions.
1957	*Restoration Quarterly* begins publication.
1959	Leroy Garrett begins publication of *Restoration Review.*
1960	In a lectureship speech at Abilene Christian College, Carl Spain rebukes the college and the larger Church of Christ for their racism.
1961	Abilene Christian College affirms racial integration for its graduate programs.
1966	Dwain Evans' Abilene Christian College address triggers controversy over Holy Spirit.
1967	Jim Bevis and Rex Vermillion named codirectors of Campus Evangelism.
1967	Chuck Lucas begins work with the Crossroads Church of Christ, Gainesville, Florida, and gives birth to the "Crossroads Movement."
1967	The doors of Nashville Christian Institute close for good.
1967	*Mission* begins publication.
1967	*First Century Christian* begins publication.
1969	*Integrity* begins publication.
1969	*Spiritual Sword* begins publication.
1969	Pat Boone's charismatic experience renews controversy over Holy Spirit.
1979	Kip McKean begins work with the Church of Christ in Lexington, Massachusetts, laying the foundation for the Boston Church of Christ, later the International Churches of Christ.
1985	*Image* begins publication.
1992	*Wineskins* begins publication.

BIBLIOGRAPHIC ESSAY

The following essay is intended as a guide to further research in the history of Churches of Christ and is by no means an exhaustive bibliography of those sources. Before discussing traditional print materials, this essay should note Professor Hans Rollmann's website (*http://www.mun.ca/rels/restmov/*), which offers a veritable wealth of texts, indexes, photographs, and analyses that cover virtually every phase of the history of the Stone-Campbell tradition.

GENERAL HISTORIES

Most early histories of the Stone-Campbell movement were written by members of the Disciples of Christ and from a distinctly Disciples of Christ perspective. Benjamin Tyler authored *A History of the Disciples of Christ* (New York: Christian Literature Co., 1894), a volume that appeared in the American Church History Series published under the auspices of the American Society of Church History. Errett Gates produced two books of enduring value: *The Early Relation and Separation of Baptists and Disciples* (Chicago: Christian Century Co., 1904) and *The Disciples of Christ* (New York: Baker and Taylor Co., 1905). James H. Garrison produced a centennial history of the Disciples in *The Story of a Century* (St. Louis: Christian Publishing Co., 1909), and that same year William T. Moore released *A Comprehensive History of the Disciples of Christ* (New York: Revell, 1909). A sociological exploration of the history of this movement appears in Oliver Read Whitley, *Trumpet Call of Reformation* (St. Louis: Bethany Press, 1959).

In many ways William E. Garrison emerged as the definitive historian of the movement to come from the ranks of the Disciples of Christ in the early twentieth century. Two books in particular merit mention: *Religion Follows the Frontier: A History of the Disciples of Christ* (New York: Harper & Row, 1931) and *An American Religious Movement: A Brief History of the Disciples of Christ* (St. Louis: Christian Board of Publication, 1945). Then, in 1948, Garrison collaborated with Alfred T. DeGroot to produce what for many years served as the standard history of the movement: *The Disciples of Christ: A History* (St. Louis: Christian Board of Publication, 1948). Half a century later William E. Tucker and Lester G. McAllister produced a volume that superceded Garrison and

DeGroot: *Journey in Faith: A History of the Christian Church (Disciples of Christ)* (St. Louis: Bethany Press, 1975). More recently, Mark Toulouse has written an analysis of the Disciples' theological heritage in *Joined in Discipleship: The Shaping of Contemporary Disciples Identity* (St. Louis: Chalice Press, 1997).

The earliest histories of the movement written by members of Churches of Christ were, by and large, uncritical. In 1884 John F. Rowe published a history that sought to demonstrate the extent of apostasy in Christian history, the variety of efforts to restore the ancient church, and the success of the restoration movement led by Alexander Campbell: *A History of Reformatory Movements: Resulting in a Restoration of the Apostolic Church* (Cincinnati: G. W. Rice, 1884). Over the next seventy-five years members of Churches of Christ produced several other apologetically oriented historical studies: George Adam Klingman, *Church History for Busy People* (Cincinnati: F. L. Rowe, 1909); J. W. Shepherd, *The Church, the Falling Away, and the Restoration* (Cincinnati: F. L. Rowe, 1929); Eli Monroe Borden, *Church History, Showing the Origin of the Church of Christ and Its History from the Days of the Apostles to Our Time* (Austin: Firm Foundation, 1939); John Dee Cox, *A Concise Account of Church History* (Murfreesboro, TN: DeHoff Publications, 1951); and F. W. Mattox, *The Eternal Kingdom: A History of the Church of Christ* (Delight, AR: Gospel Light, 1961).

Between 1950 and 1987 Earl Irvin West produced the first comprehensive history of Churches of Christ: *The Search for the Ancient Order*. This project appeared in four separate volumes published by the Gospel Advocate Company (vol. 1, 1964) and Religious Book Service (vol. 2, 1950; vol. 3, 1979; and vol. 4, 1987). A second comprehensive history of Churches of Christ appeared several years later in Richard T. Hughes, *Reviving the Ancient Faith: The Story of Churches of Christ in America* (Grand Rapids: Eerdmans, 1996). In 1966 David Edwin Harrell, Jr., produced a two-volume social history of this tradition in the nineteenth century and the first genuinely critical book-length study of the Stone-Campbell movement written by a member of the Churches of Christ. The two volumes are *Quest for a Christian America: The Disciples of Christ and American Society to 1866* (Nashville: Disciples of Christ Historical Society, 1966) and *The Social Sources of Division in the Disciples of Christ, 1865–1900* (Atlanta and Athens, GA: Publishing Systems, 1973). A summary of Harrell's social-origins thesis is "The Sectional Origins of the Churches of Christ," *Journal of Southern History* 30 (August 1964): 261–277. Robert Hooper has written a comprehensive history of Churches of Christ in the twentieth century: *A Distinct People: A History of the Churches of Christ in the Twentieth Century* (West Monroe, LA: Howard Publishing, 1993). The most recent history of Churches of Christ in the twentieth century is David Edwin Harrell, Jr.'s *The Churches of Christ in the 20th Century: Homer Hailey's Personal Journey of Faith* (Tuscaloosa: University of Alabama Press, 2000). Stephen D. Eckstein has written an important regional history: *History of the Churches of Christ in Texas: 1824–1950* (Austin: Firm Foundation, 1963).

Several volumes offer a comprehensive history of the entire Stone-Campbell tradition, embracing the stories of Churches of Christ, Disciples of Christ, and Christian Churches/Churches of Christ. These include James DeForest Murch, *Christians Only: A History of the Restoration Movement* (Cincinnati: Standard Publishing, 1962); Henry E. Webb, *In Search of Christian Unity: A History of the Restoration Movement* (Cincinnati: Standard Publishing, 1990); James B. North, *Union in Truth: An Interpretive History of the Restoration Movement* (Cincinnati: Standard Publishing, 1994); and Leroy Garrett, *The*

Stone-Campbell Movement: The Story of the American Restoration Movement, rev. ed. (Joplin, MO: College Press, 1994).

Mention should be made here of several specialized histories that are nonetheless comprehensive in terms of their chronology. Ronny F. Wade has written the only history of the nonclass, one-cup Churches of Christ: *The Sun Will Shine Again, Someday: A History of the Non-Class, One Cup Churches of Christ* (Springfield, MO: Yesterday's Treasures, 1986). In an important Ph.D. dissertation Myer Phillips has explored the history of one of the most important themes in Churches of Christ—their exclusivism: "Historical Study of the Attitudes of the Churches of Christ toward Other Denominations" (Ph.D. diss., Baylor University, 1983). In a book that is now badly dated but that nonetheless deserves mention here, M. Norvel Young tracked the history of higher education in this tradition in *A History of Colleges Established and Controlled by Members of the Church of Christ* (Kansas City: Old Paths Book Club, 1949). And Leonard Allen called attention to voices that represent positions once held among Churches of Christ but are now largely forgotten in his *Distant Voices: Discovering a Forgotten Past for a Changing Church* (Abilene, TX: ACU Press, 1993).

Finally, a book waiting to be written is a history of African American Churches of Christ. Little has been written on this tradition to date. Among the books that must be consulted by anyone wishing to take this story farther are the following: J. E. Choate, *Roll, Jordan, Roll: A Biography of Marshall Keeble* (Nashville: Gospel Advocate, 1974); Willie Cato, *His Hand and Heart: The Wit and Wisdom of Marshall Keeble* (Winona, MS: J. C. Choate Publications, 1990); B. C. Goodpasture, ed., *Biography and Sermons of Marshall Keeble, Evangelist* (Nashville: Gospel Advocate Co., 1936); Vernon Boyd, *Undying Dedication: The Story of G. P. Bowser* (Nashville: Gospel Advocate Co., 1985); and Annie C. Tuggle, *Another World Wonder* (n.p.: n.p., n.d.).

ORIGINS OF CHURCHES OF CHRIST IN AMERICA

Clearly, we know more about the earliest years of Churches of Christ in the United States than about any other period.

Alexander and Thomas Campbell

More has been written about Alexander Campbell than perhaps any other figure in the history of this tradition. Two biographies exist, though both are badly dated: Robert Richardson, *Memoirs of Alexander Campbell*, 2 vols. (Nashville: Gospel Advocate Co., 1956; first published in 1897), and Benjamin Lyon Smith, *Alexander Campbell* (St. Louis: Bethany Press, 1930).

A wealth of primary literature came from the pen of Alexander Campbell and can be found especially in the *Christian Baptist* (1823–1830) and the *Millennial Harbinger* (1830–1870), periodicals that Campbell edited. A comprehensive bibliography of Campbell's writings, compiled by the former curator of the Disciples of Christ Historical Society, Claude Spencer, appears in Samuel Morris Eames, *The Philosophy of Alexander Campbell* (Bethany, WV: Bethany College, 1966).

A number of specialized studies on Campbell's life and thought appeared in the twentieth century. Among the works that explore Campbell's theological understandings are these: Winfred Ernest Garrison, *Alexander Campbell's Theology: Its Sources and*

Historical Setting (St. Louis: Christian Publishing Co., 1900); Samuel Morris Eames, *The Philosophy of Alexander Campbell* (Bethany, WV: Bethany College, 1966); Robert Frederick West, *Alexander Campbell and Natural Religion* (New Haven: Yale University Press, 1948); and William J. Richardson, *The Role of Grace in the Thought of Alexander Campbell* (Los Angeles: Westwood Christian Foundation, 1991). Two books explore Campbell's concept of the church: D. Ray Lindley, *Apostle of Freedom* (St. Louis: Bethany Press, 1957); and Eva Jean Wrather, *Creative Freedom in Action* (St. Louis: Bethany Press, 1968).

A number of studies examine the relation Campbell sustained to the social order: Harold Lunger, *The Political Ethics of Alexander Campbell* (St. Louis: Bethany Press, 1954); Robert O. Fife, "Alexander Campbell and the Christian Church in the Slavery Controversy" (Ph.D. diss., Indiana University, 1960); Robert Tibbs Maxey, *Alexander Campbell and the Peculiar Institution* (primarily a sourcebook) (El Paso: Spanish American Evangelism, 1986); Richard T. Hughes, "From Primitive Church to Civil Religion: The Millennial Odyssey of Alexander Campbell," *Journal of the American Academy of Religion* 64 (March 1976): 87–103; and Mont Whitson, "Campbell's Post-Protestantism and Civil Religion," *West Virginia History* 37 (January 1976): 109–121.

Three important collections of essays on aspects of Campbell's life and thought have appeared since 1960: Perry E. Gresham, comp., *The Sage of Bethany: A Pioneer in Broadcloth* (St. Louis: Bethany Press, 1960); *Lectures in Honor of the Alexander Campbell Bicentennial, 1788–1988* (Nashville: Disciples of Christ Historical Society, 1988); and *Restoration Quarterly* 30 (2d & 3d Qrs 1988). Bill J. Humble examines the five important debates of Campbell in *Campbell and Controversy* (Rosemead, CA: Old Paths Book Club, 1952). Finally, two Campbell source books deserve mention: Royal Humbert, *Compend of Alexander Campbell's Theology* (St. Louis: Bethany Press, 1961); and Lester G. McAllister, ed., *An Alexander Campbell Reader* (St. Louis: CBP Press, 1988). Loretta Long has written the definitive biography of Campbell's second wife, Selina: *A Fellow Soldier in the Cause of Reformation: The Life of Selina Campbell* (Tuscaloosa: University of Alabama Press, 2000).

Scholars have done far less research on Thomas Campbell, Alexander's father, than they have on Alexander. Still, there are some notable publications. Alexander, himself assembled the first book on his father: *Memoirs of Elder Thomas Campbell, Together with a Brief Memoir of Mrs. Jane Campbell* (Cincinnati: H.S. Bosworth, 1861). Two twentieth-century biographies have appeared: William H. Hanna, *Thomas Campbell: Seceder and Christian Union Advocate* (Cincinnati, 1935); and Lester G. McAllister, *Thomas Campbell: Man of the Book* (St. Louis: Bethany Press, 1954). More recently, Hiram J. Lester has written a number of articles that shed fresh light on Thomas Campbell, especially his Irish backgrounds: "An Irish Precursor for Thomas Campbell's Declaration and Address," *Encounter* (Summer 1989): 247–267; "The Disciple Birthday—a Disciple Passover," *Discipliana* 44 (Winter 1984); 51–54; and "Alexander Campbell's Early Baptism in Ecumenicity and Sectarianism," *Restoration Quarterly* 30 (2d & 3d Qrs 1988); 85–101. Like Lester, David M. Thompson has also explored the Irish background to Campbell in "The Irish Background to Thomas Campbell's *Declaration and Address,*" *Discipliana* 46 (Summer 1986): 23–27. A critical analysis of Campbell's *Declaration and Address* appeared in Thomas H. Olbricht and Hans Rollmann (eds.), *The Quest for Christian Unity, Peace, and Purity in Thomas Campbell's Declaration and Address* (Lanham, MD: Scarecrow Press, 2000).

Barton W. Stone

Literature exploring the life and thought of Barton W. Stone is far more sparse than literature on Alexander Campbell. Among other items, primary literature includes the *Christian Messenger* that Stone edited from 1826 until his death in 1844; Stone and James M. Mathes, *Works of Elder B. W. Stone to Which Is Added a Few Discourses and Sermons* (Cincinnati, 1859); and *The Biography of Eld. Barton Warren Stone* (1847) in *The Cane Ridge Reader*, ed. Hoke S. Dickinson (n.p.: n.p., 1972). A valuable, early description of the Stone movement in the first decade of the nineteenth century is Robert Marshall and John Thompson, *A Brief Historical Account of Sundry Things in the Doctrines and State of the Christian, or as It Is Commonly Called, the Newlight Church* (Cincinnati, 1811). But the best extant description of the Stone movement during its earliest years are the two autobiographies of Joseph Thomas, the "White Pilgrim": *The Travels and Gospel Labors of Joseph Thomas* (Winchester, VA, 1812) and *The Life of the Pilgrim Joseph Thomas* (Winchester, VA, 1817). On Thomas see Richard T. Hughes, "Joseph Thomas, the White Pilgrim, and the 'Christians in the West,' " *Discipliana* 46 (Winter 1986).

Two early biographies of Stone present him as an apostle of Christian union: Charles Crossfield Ware, *Barton Warren Stone: Pathfinder of Christian Union* (St. Louis: Bethany Press, 1932); and William Garrett West, *Barton Warren Stone: Early American Advocate of Christian Union* (Nashville: Disciples of Christ Historical Society, 1954). The most recent life of Stone is Newell Williams' *Barton Stone: A Spiritual Biography* (St. Louis: Chalice Press, 2000).

Since the Cane Ridge Revival was such an important event in Stone's life, two recent books on that revival must be noted. Anthony Dunnavant, ed., *Cane Ridge in Context: Perspectives on Barton W. Stone and the Revival* (Nashville: Disciples of Christ Historical Society, 1992), is a collection of essays by leading Stone scholars. Paul Conkin has provided the best historical analysis of the Cane Ridge Revival in *Cane Ridge: America's Pentecost* (Madison: University of Wisconsin Press, 1990).

Walter Scott

In addition to Thomas and Alexander Campbell and Barton W. Stone, historians often count Walter Scott as one of the four leading founders of the Stone-Campbell movement. Important primary material from Scott's pen includes *A Discourse on the Holy Spirit* (Bethany, WV, 1831), *The Gospel Restored* (Cincinnati, 1836), *The Messiahship or Great Demonstration* (Cincinnati, 1860), *The Union of Christians on Christian Principles* (Cincinnati, 1852), and the following periodicals which Scott edited: *The Evangelist*, 1832–1835 and 1838–1842; *The Protestant Unionist*, 1844–1848; and *The Christian Age and Protestant Unionist*, 1849–1850. Three biographies of Scott have appeared over the course of the twentieth century: William Baxter, *Life of Elder Walter Scott* (St. Louis: Bethany Press, 1926); Dwight E. Stevenson, *Walter Scott: Voice of the Golden Oracle* (St. Louis: Christian Board of Publication, 1946); and William A. Gerrard, "Walter Scott: Frontier Disciples Evangelist," Ph.D. diss., Emory University, 1982. More recently, a number of scholars have assessed Scott's contributions from a variety of perspectives in Mark G. Toulouse, ed., *Walter Scott: A Nineteenth-Century Evangelical* (St. Louis:Chalice Press, 1999).

American Origins of Churches of Christ

Since 1964 three important scholarly articles on the American origins of Churches of Christ have appeared in scholarly journals: David Edwin Harrell, Jr., "The Sectional Origins of the Churches of Christ," *Journal of Southern History* 30 (August 1964): 261–277; Nathan O. Hatch, "The Christian Movement and the Demand for a Theology of the People," *Journal of American History* 67 (December 1980): 545–567; and Richard T. Hughes, "The Apocalpytic Origins of Churches of Christ and the Triumph of Modernism," *Religion and American Culture: A Journal of Interpretation*, 2 (Summer 1992): 181–214. These three articles can be found in a single volume: *American Origins of Churches of Christ* (Abilene, TX: ACU Press, 2000). Hatch expands on his article in *The Democratization of American Christianity* (New Haven: Yale University Press, 1989); Harrell expands on his article in *Quest for a Christian America* and in *The Social Sources of Division in the Disciples of Christ, 1865–1900* (see discussion above); Hughes expands on his article in *Reviving the Ancient Faith: The Story of Churches of Christ in America* (see discussion above). Finally, Richard M. Tristano has written an important history of the founding years of this tradition: *The Origins of the Restoration Movement: An Intellectual History* (Atlanta: Glenmary Research Center, 1988).

CHURCHES OF CHRIST: BALANCE OF THE NINETEENTH CENTURY

Once we move beyond the time of the founding period, literature dealing with Churches of Christ becomes infinitely more sparse. Several biographies deal with first- and second-generation leaders: Alvin Ray Jennings, *Thomas M. Allen: Pioneer Preacher of Kentucky and Missouri* (Fort Worth, TX: Star Bible and Tract Corporation, 1977); Earl Irvin West, *Elder Ben Franklin: Eye of the Storm* (Indianapolis: Religious Book Service, 1983); and James R. Wilburn, *The Hazard of the Die: Tolbert Fanning and the Restoration Movement* (Austin: R. B. Sweet, 1969). On Fanning's Franklin College, see James E. Scobey, ed., *Franklin College and Its Influences* (Nashville: McQuiddy Printing Co., 1906).

Two biographies explore the life and thought of David Lipscomb: Earl Irvin West, *The Life and Times of David Lipscomb* (Henderson, TN: Religious Book Service, 1954); and Robert Hooper, *Crying in the Wilderness: A Biography of David Lipscomb* (Nashville, David Lipscomb College, 1979). On Lipscomb's editorial power see Richard T. Hughes, "The Editor Bishop: David Lipscomb and the *Gospel Advocate*" in James M. Seale, comp., *The Power of the Press: The Forrest F. Reed Lectures for 1986* (Nashville: Disciples of Christ Historical Society, 1986). On Lipscomb's attitude toward wealth and poverty see Anthony L. Dunnavant, "David Lipscomb and the 'Preferential Option for the Poor' among Post-Bellum Churches of Christ" in Dunnavant, ed., *Poverty and Ecclesiology: Nineteenth-Century Evangelicals in the Light of Liberation Theology* (Collegeville, MN: Liturgical Press, 1992).

Lloyd Cline Sears has written the definitive biography of James A. Harding: *The Eyes of Jehovah: The Life and Faith of James Alexander Harding* (Nashville: Gospel Advocate Co., 1970). Two works deal with Daniel Sommer: Mathew C. Morrison, *Like a Lion: Daniel Sommer's Seventy Years of Preaching* (Murfreesboro, TN: Dehoff Publications, 1975); and William Wallace, comp., *Daniel Sommer, 1850–1940: A Biography* (n.p.: n.p., 1969).

Several works have explored the impact of slavery and the Civil War on Churches of Christ. Of first importance in this regard is David Edwin Harrell's "The Sectional Origins of the Churches of Christ," *Journal of Southern History* 30 (August 1964): 261–277. However, the most complete and systematic chronology of the important war-related events that helped precipitate the division between Churches of Christ and Disciples of Christ is Bill J. Humble, "The Influence of the Civil War," *Restoration Quarterly* 8 (4th Qr 1965): 233–247. Also notable is Henry E. Webb, "Sectional Conflict and Schism within the Disciples of Christ Following the Civil War" in *Essays on New Testament Christianity* (Cincinnati: Standard Publishing Co., 1978). Finally, Robert O. Fife has produced the definitive examination of the relation of the Stone-Campbell tradition to the institution of slavery: *Teeth on Edge* (Grand Rapids: Baker Book House, 1971).

Two other important works dealing with nineteenth-century Churches of Christ are Jerry Rushford, *Christians on the Oregon Trail: Churches of Christ and Christians Churches in Early Oregon, 1842–1882* (Joplin, MO: College Press, 1997); and Fred A. Bailey, "The Status of Women in the Disciples of Christ Movement, 1865–1900" (Ph.D. diss., University of Tennessee, 1979).

CHURCHES OF CHRIST: EARLY TWENTIETH CENTURY

William Woodson has written a notable regional history that covers the first half of the twentieth century: *Standing for Their Faith: A History of Churches of Christ in Tennessee, 1900–1950* (Henderson, TN: J & W Publications, 1979). Several works explore the life and thought of significant figures in the early twentieth century. Lloyd Cline Sears has produced the biography of J. N. Armstrong: *For Freedom: The Biography of John Nelson Armstrong* (Austin: Sweet Publishing Co., 1969). The work of R. H. Boll has sparked recent interest among scholars, resulting in Thomas G. Bradshaw, *R. H. Boll: Controversy and Accomplishment among Churches of Christ* (Louisville: Word and Work Publishers, 1998); and Hans Rollmann, "Our Steadfastness and Perseverance Depends on Perpetual Expectation of Our Lord: The Development of Robert Henry Boll's Premillennialism (1895–1915)," *Discipliana* 59 (Winter 1999): 113–126. Adron Doran and J. E. Choate have written *The Christian Scholar: A Biography of Hall Laurie Calhoun* (Nashville: Gospel Advocate Co., 1985); also two recent biographies have appeared on George S. Benson: John C. Stevens, *Before Any Were Willing: The Story of George S. Benson* (n.p.: n.p., 1991); and L. Edward Hicks, *"Sometimes in the Wrong, but Never in Doubt": George S. Benson and the Education of the New Religious Right* (Knoxville: University of Tennessee Press, 1995). Mary Nelle Hardeman Powers' book on N.B. Hardeman remains the only biography of this important leader: *N.B.H.: A Biography of Nicholas Brodie Hardeman* (Nashville: Gospel Advocate Co., 1964).

The collapse of the pacifist sentiment among Churches of Christ is surely one of the most important developments in this tradition in the early twentieth century. Michael W. Casey has documented this story in a variety of articles: "From Patriotism to Pacifism: The Emergence of Civil Religion in the Churches of Christ in World War One," *Mennonite Quarterly Review* 66 (July 1992): 376–390; "Pacifism and Non-violence: The Prophetic Voice of the African-American Churches of Christ," *Discipliana* 59 (Summer 1999): 35–49; "The Closing of Cordell Christian College: A Microcosm of American Intolerance during World War I," *Chronicles of Oklahoma* 76 (Spring 1998): 20–37; "Churches of Christ and World War II Civilian Public Service: A Pacifist Remnant" in Theron Schlabach and Richard Hughes, eds., *Proclaim Peace: Christian Pacifism from*

Unexpected Quarters (Urbana: University of Illinois Press, 1997); "Warriors against War: The Pacifists of the Churches of Christ in World War Two," *Restoration Quarterly* 35 (3d Qr 1993): 159–174; "New Information on Conscientious Objectors of World War I and the Churches of Christ," *Restoration Quarterly* 34 (2nd Qr 1992): 83–96; and Casey and Michael Jordan, "Government Surveillance of the Churches of Christ in World War I: An Episode of Free Speech Suppression," *Free Speech Yearbook* 34 (1996): 102–111.

CHURCHES OF CHRIST: LATE TWENTIETH CENTURY

Among the most important developments in Churches of Christ in the late twentieth century was the debate over hermeneutics. Michael W. Casey has chronicled the development of the hermeneutic tradition in this fellowship in his book *The Battle over Hermeneutics in the Stone-Campbell Movement, 1800–1870* (Lewiston, NY: Edwin Mellen, 1998). Thomas H. Olbricht has explored the hermeneutic tradition in twentieth-century Churches of Christ in an autobiography, *Hearing God's Voice: My Life with Scripture in the Churches of Christ* (Abilene, TX: ACU Press, 1996). The content of preaching generated considerable interest among scholars in the waning years of the twentieth century. Michael W. Casey explored the history of preaching in this tradition in his *Saddlebags, City Streets, & Cyberspace: A History of Preaching in the Churches of Christ* (Abilene, TX: ACU Press, 1995). Bill Love offered an historical critique of preaching among Churches of Christ in his book *The Core Gospel: On Restoring the Crux of the Matter* (Abilene, TX: ACU Press, 1992). William S. Banowsky tracked the history of ideas among twentieth-century Churches of Christ by exploring the history of the Abilene Christian University lectureship: *Mirror of a Movement* (Dallas: Christian Publishing, 1965). Finally, a good collection of essays on mostly twentieth-century preachers in this tradition is Melvin Curry, ed., *They Being Dead yet Speak: Florida College Annual Lectures, 1981* (Temple Terrace, FL: Florida College Bookstore, 1981).

CHRISTIAN PRIMITIVISM: CHURCHES OF CHRIST IN COMPARATIVE PERSPECTIVE

Churches of Christ are one of many Christian primitivist movements both in the United States and in the larger flow of Christian history. Accordingly, several works have emerged in recent years that examine Churches of Christ in relation to other restorationist traditions both in Europe and in America, and even in relation to the restorationist sentiment that characterized the nation itself in the early nineteenth century. Some of those works include Richard T. Hughes and C. Leonard Allen, *Illusions of Innocence: Protestant Primitivism in America, 1630–1875* (Chicago: University of Chicago Press, 1988); Richard T. Hughes, ed., *The American Quest for the Primitive Church* (Urbana: University of Illinois Press, 1988); Richard T. Hughes, ed., *The Primitive Church in the Modern World* (Urbana: University of Illinois Press, 1995); Richard T. Hughes, "A Comparison of the Restitution Motifs of the Campbells (1809–1830) and the Anabaptists (1524–1560)," *Mennonite Quarterly Review* (October 1971): 312–330; Richard T. Hughes, "Two Restoration Traditions: Mormons and Churches of Christ in the Nineteenth Century," *Journal of Mormon History* 19 (Spring 1993): 34–51; and Richard T. Hughes, "Recovering First Times: the Logic of Primitivism in American Life" in Rowland A. Sherrill, ed., *Religion and the Life of the Nation: American Recoveries* (Urbana: University of Illinois Press, 1990).

Two articles by Hughes explore Churches of Christ in relation to American evangelicalism: "Are Restorationists Evangelicals?" in Donald Dayton and Robert Johnston, eds., *The Variety of American Evangelicalism* (Knoxville: University of Tennessee Press, 1991); and "Why Restorationists Don't Fit the Evangelical Mold; Why Churches of Christ Increasingly Do," in Douglas Jacobsen and William Trollinger, eds., *Re-forming the Center: American Protestantism, 1900 to the Present* (Grand Rapids, MI: Eerdmans, 1998). For typologies of restorationist movements, including Churches of Christ, see Samuel S. Hill, Jr., "A Typology of American Restitutionism: From Frontier Revivalism and Mormonism to the Jesus Movement," *Journal of the American Academy of Religion* 64 (March 1976): 65–76; and Richard T. Hughes, "Christian Primitivism as Perfectionism: From Anabaptists to Pentecostals" in Stanley M. Burgess, ed., *Reaching Beyond: Chapters in the History of Perfectionism* (Peabody, MA: Hendrickson, 1986). Two books explore the historical roots of Churches of Christ. Lynn McMillon examines the influence of Scottish Independency on Churches of Christ in *Restoration Roots* (Dallas: Gospel Teachers Publications, 1983), and Leonard Allen and Richard Hughes explore a variety of roots of Churches of Christ that reach as far back as the Renaissance and the Reformation: *Discovering Our Roots: The Ancestry of Churches of Christ* (Abilene, TX: ACU Press, 1988).

INDEX

Page numbers for main entries in the Biographical Dictionary section are set in **boldfaced** type.

Abilene Christian College, 106, 111, 135, 138, 139–40, 144
Acuff, J. E., 135
Adams, John, **163–64**
Allen, Jimmy: and message of grace, 153; and racial justice, 137
Allen, Thomas Miller, 33, **164–65**
American Christian Missionary Society, 25
American Christian Review, 47–51, 216
Andrews, Sarah Shepherd, **165–66**
Apocalyptic worldview, 6–7, 61–62; and Boll, R. H., 10, 83–85; collapse of, 9; and Fanning, Tolbert, 76–77; and Harding, James A., 82–83; and Lipscomb, David, 78–81; and Stone, Barton, 6–7, 69–73
Armstrong, John Nelson, 86, 91–92, 104–5, 122, **166**
Ash, Joseph, **166–67**
Axe on the Root, 143

Baconianism: and Campbell, Alexander, 21; and Fanning, Tolbert, 43–45; and Lard, Moses, 53; and Lipscomb, David, 77; and Scott, Walter, 26–27
Bales, J. D.: and racial issues, 131; and *20th Century Christian*, 104
Barker, Squire Leander, **168–69**
Barret, Allen Booker, **169–70**
Barrett, Thomas R., **170**
Baxter, Batsell, **170–71**
Baxter, Batsell Barrett, **171–72**; and "Herald of Truth," 114; and *Voice of Freedom*, 125
Belknap, Ona, **172**
Bell, Robert Clark, 82, 91, 102, **172–73**
Benson, George Stuart, 101, **173**; and anti-Communism, 122–23
Bering Drive Church of Christ, Houston, Texas, 159 n.11
Bernard, Elizabeth, **174**
Berry, Joseph, **174**
Bethany College, 25
Bible Banner, 90
Bible Talk, 139
Billingsley, Nancy Mulkey, **175**
Billingsley, Price, **175–76**
Bills, Daniel Gersham, **176**
Bledsoe, Jesse, **176–77**
Blue, Joe Hubert, **177–78**
Boles, Henry Leo, **178**
Boll, Robert Henry, 82–89, **178–80**; and apocalyptic worldview, 83–85; and change in perspective, 88–89; and dispensational premillennialism, 84; and

grace, 85–86; premillennial leader in Churches of Christ, 10; *Word and Work*, 10
Boston Church of Christ, Boston, Massachusetts, 145
Bowman, John, **180**
Bowser, George Phillip, 133–34, **181**
Boyd, Samuel, **181–82**
Brents, Thomas Wesley, **182–83**
Brewer, Grover Cleveland, **183–84**; and anti-Catholicism, 126; and anti-Communism, 123–25; and anti-institutional movement; and European missions, 107–9; and grace, 85–86; and sermon at Broadway Church of Christ, 117; and the new *Christian Leader*, 101; and *Voice of Freedom*, 125
Brightwell, W. E., 106
Broadway Church of Christ, Lubbock, Texas, 117; sponsoring congregation for European missions, 107–8
Brookline Church of Christ, Brookline, Massachusetts, 159 n.11
Burch, Walter: and *Mission* magazine, 141; and racial justice, 137
Burnet, David Staats, 48–49
Burnett, Thomas R., **184–85**
Burton, A. M., 134, 135
Busby, Horace Wooten, **185**
Byram, Lewis, **186**

Cahaba Valley Church of Christ, Birmingham, Alabama, 159 n.11
Calhoun, Hall Laurie, **187–88**
Camp, Franklin, 142
Campbell, Alexander, **188–89**; *Christian Baptist*, 16; *Christian System*, 28; civil religion in thought of, 24–25; and debating, 75; ecumenism in thought of, 18–19, 36; and Fanning, Tolbert, 46; grace and legalism in thought of, 18; and his growing dominance over Churches of Christ, 9; *Millennial Harbinger*, 16; and postmillennial ideal, 6, 19–20; and Protestantism, 23–24; restoration vision of, 19–20; and scientific understanding of biblical text, 21–22; sectarianism in thought of, 16–17; and slavery, 127; and social ethics, 128; and Stone, Barton W., 73–76; and union with Stoneites, 75–76
Campbell, Alexander Cleveland, **189–90**
Campbell, Selina Huntington Bakewell, **190–91**
Campbell, Thomas, 7, 27–28, **191–93**
Cane Ridge Revival, 63–64
Carnes, William Davis, **193–94**
Cassius, Amos Lincoln, **194–95**
Cassius, S. R., **195**
Catholicism: and Campbell, Alexander, 22–23; and 20th-century Churches of Christ, 125–27
Central Christian Church, Cincinnati, Ohio, 49–50
Central Church of Christ, Nashville, Tennessee, 101–2
Chalk, John Allen, 137
Chambers, Stanford, 85
Chism, Jehu Willborn, **196**
Christian Baptist, 16
Christian Chronicle, 155
Christian Echo, 133–34
Christian Leader, new, 100–104
Christian Woman, 296
Christian Woman's Board of Missions, 156
Church buildings, 115–17
Church of Christ in Chapel Hill, North Carolina, 159 n.11
Churches of Christ: and division from Disciples of Christ, 3; and membership data and growth rates, 4, 151; and non-denominational self-understanding, 5
Clark, Joseph Addison, **196–97**
Clark, Nimrod Lafayette, **197–98**
Clarke, Jennie Everton, **198**
Coffman, Burton, 116–17
Cogdill, Roy, 107, 111, 112, **198–99**
Colleges: funding for, 111–13; opposition to, 110–11
Communism, 122–25
Contending for the Faith, 143
Cordell Christian College, 91
Cox, James Franklin, 101, **199–200**

Creath, Jacob, Jr., 34, **200–201**
Creath, Jacob, Sr., **201–2**
Crescent Hill Church of Christ, Brownwood, Texas, 108
Crihfield, Arthur, 31–32, 66, **202–3**
Crossroads Movement, 145
Curlee, Calvin, **203**
Cypert, Lillie, **204**

David Lipscomb College, 106
Davidson, Clinton V., 100–104, **205–6**
Davis, Andrew Pickens, **206**
Dayspring Church of Christ, Edmond, Oklahoma, 159 n.11
DeFee, William, **206–7**
DeHoff, George, 104
DeWhitt, Samuel, **207**
Disciples of Christ, 3
Division between Churches of Christ and Disciples of Christ, 3; reasons for, 8
Dixon, H. A., 125
Dooley, Reuben, **207–8**
Dorris, C. E., 134
Dudrey, Russ, 155
Dunn, Louise Elizabeth, **208–9**
Durst, John S., **209**

Elam, Edwin Alexander, 129, **210**
Elmore, Alfred, **211**
Evans, Dwain: and *Mission* magazine, 141; and racial justice, 137
Evans, Jack, 136
Ewing, Hettie Lee, **211**

Fall, Philip Slater, **212–13**
Fanning, Charlotte Fall, **213–14**
Fanning, Tolbert, 41–47, **214–15**; and Baconianism, 43–45; and Campbell, Alexander, 33, 34, 42; *Christian Review*, 41; *Gospel Advocate*, 41; and Lipscomb, David, 76–77; and Locke, John, 43–45; and missionary societies, 54–55; and Richardson, Robert, 43–46; *Religious Historian*, 41; and the "true church," 42–43
Ferguson, Everett: and *Mission* magazine, 141; and theological education, 140
Firm Foundation, 90, 104
First Century Christian, 142
Forshey, Harold, 140
Franklin, Benjamin, 47–51, **215–16**; and Alexander Campbell's *Christian Baptist*, 47–48; and an educated ministry, 51; and instrumental music, 56–57; and Lipscomb, David, 80; and missionary societies, 55–56; and a plain gospel, 48–51; and slavery, 127–28
Freed, Arvy Glenn, **216–17**
Freed-Hardeman College, 106
Fundamentalism: and Boll, R. H., 88–89; and Churches of Christ, 124–25

Gano, John Allen, **218–19**
Gano, Richard Montgomery, **219–20**
Garrett, Leroy, 138–39
Gatewood, Otis, 108, **220–21**
General Christian Missionary Society, 156
Giles, Samuel Boliver, **221**
Gillentine, John, **221**
Goodpasture, Benton Cordell, **222**; and anti-Catholicism, 126; and "quarantine" of anti-institutional movement, 112–13; and *Voice of Freedom*, 125
Gospel Advocate, 41, 76, 89, 101
Gospel Guardian, 89, 107
Gray, Fred, 136
Griffin, Thacker Vivian, **222–23**
Guirey, William, **223**
Gurganus, George, 137

Haden, Joel Harris, **224–25**
Haggard, David, **225**
Haggard, Rice, 64–65, **225–27**
Hairston, Andrew, 137
Hall, Benjamin Franklin, 66, 71, **227–28**
Hall, S. H., 101
Hardeman, Nicholas Brodie, **229–30**; and anti-institutional issue, 111–12; and racial issues, 131–32; and "Tabernacle Meetings," 102
Harding College, 91–92, 106; and anti-Communism of George S. Benson, 122–23
Harding, James Alexander, 82–83, **229**
Harding, Johnson, **230**
Harper College, 91, 122, 139

Harper, Ernest Rosenthal, 92, 93, **231**
Harrell, Pat, 140
Harris, S. E., 129
Haymes, Don, and *Mission* magazine, 141
Hays, Katie, 159 n.11
Hearn, Roy, 142
Henry, John, **231–32**
"Herald of Truth," 11; and anti-institutional movement, 113–15; and racial prejudice, 137
Hermeneutic "crisis," 154
Higher Education, 139–40
Highland Church of Christ, Abilene, Texas, 11, 113–14
Hill, Abner, **232**
Hinds, John T., 101
Hogan, Richard Nathaniel, 133–35, 136, **233–34**
Holman, Silena Moore, **234**
Holt, G. P., 136, 138
Holton, Arthur Reeves, **235**
Holy Spirit: and Crihfield, Arthur, 66; and Hall, B. F., 66; and Stone, Barton W., 66
Hooten, John H., **235–36**
Howard, Bob, 143
Howard, John R., 29–31, **236**
Howard, V. E., and anti-Catholicism, 126
Hughs, James, **236–37**

Ijams, Elvin H., 101, **238–39**
Image magazine, 154
Institution building, dispute over, 11–12, 105–17
Instrumental music, 56–57
Integrity, 141
International Church of Christ, Boston, Massachusetts, 145–46

Jeter, Jeremiah, 18, 32, 52
Jones, David, 137
Jones, John, Jr., **240–41**
Jones, Sandy E., **241**
Jourdan, William D., **241–42**

Keeble, Marshall, 131–32, 136, **243**
Kendrick, Carroll, **244**
Kennedy, Levi, 133
Ketcherside, William Carl, 138–39, **245**
King, Martin Luther, Jr., 130–31
Klingman, George Adam, **245–46**
Kurfees, Marshall Clement, 88, **246–47**

Lard, Moses Easterly, 52–54, **248–49**; and Baconianism, 53
Lard's Quarterly, 52
Larimore, Theophilus Brown, **249–50**
Last Will and Testament of the Springfield Presbytery, 63–64
Lawton, Eugene, 137
Lemert, Marinda R., **250–51**
Lemmons, Reuel Gordon, **251–52**; and anti-Catholicism, 126; and *Firm Foundation*, 126; and ideological divide, 138; and *Image* magazine, 154; and racial issues, 130–31
Lewis, Jack, 140
Lewis, LeMoine G., 140
Lipscomb, David, 76–82, **252–53**; and apocalyptic worldview, 78–81; and Baconianism, 77; and Campbell, Alexander, 34–35; and cholera epidemic, 80; *Civil Government*, 78, 93; and division from Disciples of Christ, 3; and Fanning, Tolbert, 76–77; genius of, 81–82; *Gospel Advocate*, 76; and politics, 80–81; and the poor, 81; and premillennialism, 79–80; and separation from the world, 80–81; and slavery, 129–30; and women's role in the church, 156–57
Lucas, Charles H., 145
Lunenburg letter, 25, 36
Lynn, Benjamin, **253–54**

McBride, Thomas Crawford, **255–56**
McCaleb, John Moody, **256**
McCalla, W. L., 7, 67, 75, 82
McCorkle, Samuel S., 20
McGarvey, John William, **256–57**
McGary, Austin, 90, **257–58**
McGaughey, Don, 140
McKean, Kip, 145–46
McKinney, Collin, **258–59**

McMillan, Edward Washington, 100–104, **259–60**
McNemar, Richard, 63
McQuiddy, J. C., 84, 87–88, 101
Mahoning Baptist Association, 28
Malherbe, Abraham: and *Mission* magazine, 141; and theological education, 140
Malibu Church of Christ, Malibu, California, 159 n.11
Mathes, James M., 73
Matthews, James Evans, **260–61**
Matthews, Mansil Walter, **261**
Mattox, Irene Young, **262–63**
Millennial Harbinger, 16
Miller, Luke, **263**
Milligan, Robert, **263–64**
Mission magazine, 141–42
Mission Messenger, 139
Mission work: mission activity in 20th century, 108; quarrel over "sponsoring congregation" concept, 107–9
Missionary societies, 54–56
Mitchell, Nathan J., **264**
Money, Royce, 138
Moore, Ephraim D. L., **264–65**
Moore, W. T., 49–50, 115
Moser, Kenny Carl, 86, **265–66**
Mulkey, John, **266–67**
Mulkey, John Newton, **267**
Mulkey, Philip, **267–68**

Nance, Clement, **269**
Nashville Bible School, 82, 106
Nashville Christian Institute, 135–36
Nichol, Charles Ready, 85, **270**
Nichols, Gus, **270–71**
Nichols, James Walter, 113, **271**
1960s, defining decade for Churches of Christ, 12–13, 121–50
North, Ira Lutts, 137, **271–72**

Officer, Robert Wallace, **273–74**
O'Kelly, James, **274**
Olbricht, Thomas H.: and hermeneutic "crisis," 154–55; and *Mission* magazine, 141; and theological education, 140
Oliphant, David, **274–75**
Olive, Abel, Sr., **275–76**
Orphans' homes, opposition to, 112

Pack, Frank, 141, **277**
Palmer, Francis Rose, **277–78**
Palmer, Henry Dulany, **278**
Pepperdine College, 106, 139
Pepperdine, George, **278–79**
Pettus, Karl, 130
Pinkerton, L. L., 56
Plan of salvation, 27–28
Polly, Nathan H. O., **279**
Postmillennial ideal, Campbell, Alexander, 6, 19–20
Potter Bible College, 91
Powell, James Marvin, 116, 125
Premillennial ideal: Boll, R. H., 10, 84; Lipscomb, David, 79–80; Stone, Barton W., 6–7, 72–73
Pulley, Micki, 159 n.11
Pullias, Athens Clay, 104, 135
Purcell, John Baptist, 24
Purviance, David, **279–80**

Race relations workshops, 137
Racial turmoil, 13, 127–38
Rains, Annie, **281**
Randolph, Robert, **281–82**
Randolph, Robert M., 143
Rawlins, Roderick, **282–83**
Reneau, Isaac Tipton, **283–84**
Restoration Quarterly, 140
Restoration Review, 139
Rhodes, B. F., 91
Rice, Ira Y., 143
Richardson, Robert, 34, 35; dispute with Tolbert Fanning, 44–46
Roberson, Charles Heber, **284–85**
Roberts, J W, **285**; and *Mission* magazine, 141; and theological education, 140
Rogers, John, 68, 71, **285–87**
Rogers, Samuel, **287**
Rotenberry, Paul, 140

Sallee, Abraham S., **288**
Sanders, J. P., 104
Schools of preaching, 144–45

Schrader Lane Church of Christ, Nashville, Tennessee, 137
Scott, Walter A., 26–29, **288–89**
Secrest, John, **289–90**
Separate Baptists, 64
Sewell, Daisy Elizabeth, **290–91**
Sewell, Jesse Louderman, **291**
Sewell, Jesse Parker, 100–104, **291–92**
Shannon, James, **292–93**
Shaw, Knowles, **293–94**
Shelburne, G. B., Jr., **294**
Shelly, Rubel, 142–43
Shepherd, James Walton, **295**
Sherrod, Paul, 108
Showalter, George Henry Pryor, 103, **295–96**
Showalter, Winifred Watts, **296–97**
Silver Point Christian Institute, 134
Simpson Street Church of Christ, Atlanta, Georgia, 137
Smith, Derwood, 143
Smith, Fletcher Walton, **297**
Smith, John, **297–98**
Smith, Nathan Williamson, **298–99**
Sommer, Daniel, 110–11, **299–300**
Sound Doctrine, 85
Southwestern Christian College, 133
Spain, Robert Carl, **300–301**; and *Mission* magazine, 141; and speech on racism, 135
Spiritual Sword, 142
Srygley, Fletcher D., 85, 124, **301–2**
Steele, John D., **302**
Steward, G. E., 133
Stone, Barton W., 62–76, **303–4**; and apocalyptic worldview, 6–7, 69–73; and baptism, 67–68; and Campbell, Alexander, 73–76; and Christian freedom, 65–66; and debating, 75; and Haggard, Rice, 64–65; and the Holy Spirit, 66–67; and non-denominational Christianity, 65–69; and politics, 72–73; premillennial ideal, 6–7, 72–73; and revivalism, 62–64; and Separate Baptists, 64; and separation from the world, 70–72; and slavery, 128–29; and union with Campbell forces, 75–76

Tant, Fanning Yater, 107, 109
Tant, Jefferson Davis, **305–6**
Tant, Nannie Green Yater, **306–7**
Thomas, John, 32–33
Thomas, Joseph, **307–8**
Thornberry, James L., 33–34, **308–9**
Tiner, Hugh, 104
Travis, Daniel, Sr., **309–10**
Trott, James J., **310–11**
Tuggle, Annie C., **311–12**
Turner, Rex, 130
20th Century Christian, 104–5, 137–38

Union Avenue Church of Christ, Memphis, Tennessee, 108

Vietnam War, 13
Voice of Freedom, 125

Wallace, Cled, 92, 109, 112–13
Wallace, Foy E., Jr., 89–93, 99–104, 123, **313–15**; and Hardeman, N. B., 112; and Harding College, 91–92; and Lipscomb, David, 92–93; and racial issues, 131–32
Wallace, Foy E., Sr., 90
Ward, Roy Bowen: and *Mission* magazine, 141; and theological education, 140
Warlick, Joseph Sale, **315**
Warren, Thomas B., 142–43
Watkins, Benjamin Utter, **315–16**
Welch, Alonzo, 125
Wells, Roosevelt, 137
West, W. B., 139
West Islip Church of Christ, West Islip, New York, 159 n.11
White, Howard A., 132
White, Lloyd Smith, **316–17**
Whiteside, Robertson Lafayette, 85, **317–18**
Whitten, Woodrow, 104
Willeford, James D., 113
Wilmeth, Collin McKinney, **318–19**
Wilson, Lawrence Ray, **319**
Winrow, Dewayne, 132
Winston, J. S., 133

Womack, S. W., **319–20**
Women's role in Churches of Christ, 156–57
Woods, Guy N., and critique of *Mission* magazine, 141–42
Word and Work, 84
World War I, 10, 86–88
World War II, 11, 106
Worship renewal, 155–57
Wright, Cecil N., 109–10

Young, Fountain Livingston, **321–22**
Young, Matt Norvel, **322–23**; and church buildings, 116–17; and European missions, 108; and *20th Century Christian*, 104

About the Authors

RICHARD T. HUGHES is Distinguished Professor of Religion at Pepperdine University. He has published many books, including *Models for Christian Higher Education*, *Proclaim Peace*, *Reviving the Ancient Faith*, *The Primitive Church in the Modern World*, and *The American Quest for the Primitive Church*, among other titles. His numerous articles have appeared in various scholarly journals.

R. L. ROBERTS was the Archivist in the Center for Restoration Studies at Abilene Christian University.